**Sixth Edition**

Book **6**

# The Humanistic Tradition

Modernism, Postmodernism, and the Global Perspective

W9-BWR-790

S 11849507
S 10787326
S 11119598

**Sixth Edition**

# The Humanistic Tradition

## Modernism, Postmodernism, and the Global Perspective

**Book 6**

**Gloria K. Fiero**

Connect
Learn
Succeed™

Boston   Burr Ridge, IL   Dubuque, IA   New York   San Francisco   St. Louis
Bangkok   Bogotá   Caracas   Kuala Lumpur   Lisbon   London   Madrid   Mexico City
Milan   Montreal   New Delhi   Santiago   Seoul   Singapore   Sydney   Taipei   Toronto

THE HUMANISTIC TRADITION, BOOK 6
MODERNISM, POSTMODERNISM, AND THE GLOBAL PERSPECTIVE

Published by McGraw-Hill, an imprint of The McGraw-Hill Companies, Inc.,
1221 Avenue of the Americas, New York, NY, 10020.

Copyright © 2011, 2006, 2002, 1998, 1995, 1992. All rights reserved. No part of this publication may be reproduced or distributed in any form or by any means, or stored in a database or retrieval system, without the prior consent of The McGraw-Hill Companies, Inc., including, but not limited to, in any network or other electronic storage or transmission, or broadcast for distance learning.

This book is printed on acid-free paper.

6 7 8 9 0 / 0

Library of Congress Cataloging-in-Publication Data

Fiero, Gloria K.
    The humanistic tradition / Gloria K. Fiero.– 6th ed.
        p. cm.
    Includes bibliographical references and index.
    ISBN-13: 978-0-07-352397-2 (bk. 1 : alk. paper)
    ISBN-10: 0-07-352397-6 (bk. 1 : alk. paper)
        1. Civilization, Western–History–Textbooks.
        2. Humanism–History–Textbooks.
        I. Title.

    CB245.F47 2009
    909'.09821–dc22

                                                              2009027018

Permissions Acknowledgments appear on page 174, and on this page by reference.

Publisher: *Chris Freitag*
Director of Development: *Rhona Robbin*
Associate Sponsoring Editor: *Betty Chen*
Editorial Coordinator: *Sarah Remington*
Marketing Manager: *Pamela Cooper*
Managing Editor: *David Staloch*
Senior Production Supervisor: *Tandra Jorgensen*
Typeface: *10/12 Goudy*
Printer: *Phoenix Offset, Hong Kong*

http://www.mhhe.com

 This book was designed and produced by
Laurence King Publishing Ltd., London
www.laurenceking.com

Commissioning Editor: *Kara Hattersley-Smith*
Senior Editor: *Melissa Danny*
Production Controller: *Simon Walsh*
Picture Researcher: *Emma Brown*
Designer: *Robin Farrow*

*Front cover*
Noriko Yamaguchi, *Keitai Girl*, 2003.
© Noriko Yamaguchi, courtesy MEM, Inc.

*Back cover*
Niki de Saint Phalle, *Black Venus*, 1965–1967. Painted polyester, 9 ft. 2 in. x 35 in. x 24 in. Whitney Museum of American Art, New York. Gift of the Howard and Jean Lipman Foundation, Inc. Photograph © 2000 Whitney Museum of American Art. Photography by Sandak, Inc/A Division of Macmillan Publishing.
© 2009 Niki Charitable Foundation/ADAGP/DACS 2010.

*Frontispiece*
Romare Bearden, *Empress of the Blues*, 1974, detail. Acrylic and pencil on paper and printed paper on paperboard, 3 ft. 10 in. x 4 ft. 2 in. Smithsonian American Art Museum, Washington, D.C., 1996.71. © Smithsonian American Art Museum/Art Resource, New York/Scala, Florence.

# Series Contents

# Book 6 Contents

# Preface

Each generation leaves a creative legacy, the sum of its ideas and achievements. This legacy represents the response to our effort to ensure our individual and collective survival, our need to establish ways of living in harmony with others, and our desire to understand our place in the universe. Meeting the challenges of *survival, communality,* and *self-knowledge,* we have created and transmitted the tools of science and technology, social and political institutions, religious and philosophic systems, and various forms of personal expression—the totality of which we call *culture.* Handed down from generation to generation, this legacy constitutes the humanistic tradition, the study of which is called *humanities.*

*The Humanistic Tradition* originated more than two decades ago out of a desire to bring a global perspective to my humanities courses. My fellow humanities teachers and I recognized that a western-only perspective was no longer adequate to understanding the cultural foundations of our global world, yet none of the existing texts addressed our needs. At the time, the challenge was daunting—covering the history of western poetry and prose, art, music, and dance was already an ambitious undertaking for a survey course; how could we broaden the scope to include Asia, Africa, and the Americas without over-packing the course? What evolved was a thematic approach to humanities, not as a collection of disciplines, but as a discipline in itself. This thematic approach considers the interrelatedness of various forms of expression as they work to create, define, and reflect the unique culture of a given time and place. It offers a conceptual framework for students to begin a study of the humanistic tradition that will serve them throughout their lives. I am gratified that others have found this approach to be highly workable for their courses, so much so that *The Humanistic Tradition* has become a widely adopted book for the humanities course.

*The Humanistic Tradition* pioneered a flexible six-book format in recognition of the varying chronological range of humanities courses. Each slim volume was also convenient for students to bring to classes, the library, and other study areas. The sixth edition continues to be available in this six-book format, as well as in a two-volume set for the most common two-term course configuration.

## The Sixth Edition of *The Humanistic Tradition*

While the sixth edition of *The Humanistic Tradition* contains a number of new topics, images, and selections, it remains true to my original goal of offering a manageable and memorable introduction to global cultures. At the same time, I have worked to develop new features that are specifically designed to help students master the material and critically engage with the text's primary source readings, art

reproductions, and music recordings. The integration of literary, visual, and aural primary sources is a hallmark of the text, and every effort has been made to provide the most engaging translations, the clearest color images, and the liveliest recorded performances, as well as the most representative selections for every period. The book and companion supplements are designed to offer all of the resources a student and teacher will need for the course.

### New Features that Promote Critical Thinking

New to the sixth edition are special features that emphasize connections between time periods, styles, and cultures, and specific issues of universal significance. These have been added to encourage critical thinking and classroom discussion.

- **Exploring Issues** focuses on controversial ideas and current debates, such as the battle over the ownership of antiquities, the role of the non-canonical Christian gospels, the use of optical devices in Renaissance art, the dating of African wood sculptures, and creationism versus evolution.
- **Making Connections** brings attention to contrasts and continuities between past and present ideas, values, and styles. Examples include feudalism East and West, Classical antiquities as models for Renaissance artists, and African culture as inspiration for African-American artists.

### New Features that Facilitate Learning and Understanding

The sixth edition provides chapter introductions and summaries that enhance the student's grasp of the materials, and a number of features designed to make the materials more accessible to students:

- **Looking Ahead** offers a brief, preliminary overview that introduces students to the main theme of the chapter.
- **Looking Back** closes each chapter with summary study points that encourage students to review key ideas.
- **Iconographic "keys"** to the meaning of images have been inset alongside selected artworks.
- **Extended captions** to illustrations throughout the text provide additional information about artworks and artists.
- **Chronology boxes** in individual chapters place the arts and ideas in historical background.
- **Before We Begin** precedes the Introduction with a useful guide to understanding and studying humanities.

### Organizational Improvements and Updated Content

The sixth edition responds to teachers' requests that the coverage of Mesopotamia precede Egypt and other ancient African cultures in the opening chapters. The global coverage has been refined with revised coverage of the early Americas, new content on archeological discoveries in ancient Peru, a segment on the role of the West in the Islamic Middle East, and a discussion of China's global ascendance. Chapters 36 through 38 have been updated and reorganized: Ethnicity and ethnic identity have been moved to chapter 38 (Globalism and the Contemporary World), which brings emphasis to recent developments in digital technology, environmentalism, and global terrorism. Other revisions throughout the text also respond to teacher feedback; for example, a description of the *bel canto* style in music has been added; Jan van Eyck's paintings appear in both chapters 17 and 19 (in different contexts); and T. S. Eliot's works are discussed in both chapters 32 and 35.

Among the notable writers added to the sixth edition are William Blake, Jorge Luis Borges, Seamus Heaney, and John Ashbury. New additions to the art program include works by Benozzo Gozzoli, Buckminster Fuller, Kara Walker, Jeff Wall, Damien Hirst, El Anatsui, and Norman Foster.

## Beyond *The Humanistic Tradition*

### Connect Humanities

*Connect Humanities* is a learning and assessment tool designed and developed to improve students' performance by making the learning process more efficient and more focused through the use of engaging, assignable content, which is text-specific and mapped to learning objectives, and integrated tools. Using this platform, instructors can deliver assignments easily online, and save time through an intuitive and easy to use interface and through modifiable pre-built assignments.

Connect provides instructors with the Image Bank, a way to easily browse and search for images and to download them for use in class presentations.

Visit mcgrawhillconnect.com

### Traditions: Humanities Readings through the Ages

*Traditions* is a new database conceived as both a stand-alone product as well as a companion source to McGraw-Hill's humanities titles. The collection is broad in nature, containing both western and non-western readings from ancient and contemporary eras, hand-picked from such disciplines as literature, philosophy, and science. The flexibility of Primis Online's database allows the readings to be arranged both chronologically and by author.

Visit www.primisonline.com/traditions

## Music Listening Compact Discs

Two audio compact discs have been designed exclusively for use with *The Humanistic Tradition*. CD One corresponds to the music listening selections discussed in Books 1–3 (Volume I), and CD Two contains the music in Books 4–6 (Volume II). Music logos (right) that appear in the margins of the text refer to the Music Listening Selections found on the audio compact discs. The compact discs can be packaged with any or all of the six books or two-volume versions of the text.

## Online Learning Center

A complete set of web-based resources for *The Humanistic Tradition* can be found at

www.mhhe.com/fierotht6e

Materials for students include an audio pronunciation guide, a timeline, research and writing tools, links to select readings, and suggested readings and Web sites. The instructor side of the Online Learning Center includes discussion and lecture suggestions, music listening guides, key themes and topics, and study questions for student discussion and review and written assignments.

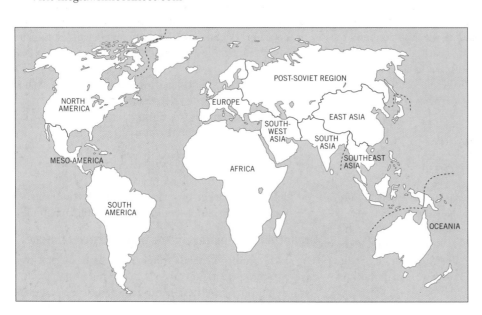

Key map indicating areas shown as white highlights on the locator maps

# Acknowledgments

Personal thanks go to my discerning editor, Betty Chen (McGraw-Hill), and to the editorial and production staff of Laurence King Publishing. As with former editions, my colleague and husband, James H. Dormon, read all parts of the manuscript and made substantive editorial suggestions. This edition is dedicated to him. I am also grateful to Eric C. Shiner (curator and art historian) for his assistance in contemporary Asian art.

In the preparation of the sixth edition, I have benefited from the suggestions and comments generously offered by Donald F. Andrews (Chattanooga State Technical Community College), Samuel Barnett (University of Maryland), Bobbie Bell (Seminole Community College), Marjorie Berman (Red Rocks Community College), Terri Birch (Harper College), Pat Bivin (International Academy of Design and Technology), Casey Blanton (Daytona Beach Community College), Diane Boze (Northeastern State University), Nellie Brannan (Brevard Community College), Diane S. Brown (Valencia Community College, Osceola), Joyce Caldwell Smith (University of Tennessee at Chattanooga), Cynthia Clegg (Pepperdine University), Harry S. Coverston (University of Central Florida), Julie deGraffenried (Baylor University), Ann Dunn (University of North Carolina, Asheville), Renae Edge (Norwalk Community College), Monika Fleming (Edgecombe Community College), A. Flowers (College of Alameda), Rod Freeman (Estrella Mountain College), Arby L. Frost (Roanoke College), Samuel Garren (North Carolina A&T University), Caryl Gibbs (Rose State College), Robin Hardee (Santa Fe College), Melissa T. Hause (Belhaven College), Barbara A. Hergianto (South Florida Community College), Dale Hoover (Edison College), Ron Israel (San Diego Mesa College), Marian Jacobson (Albany College of Pharmacy), Theresa James (South Florida Community College), Judith Jamieson (Providence College), Keith W. Jensen (William Rainey Harper College), Jerry Jerman (University of Oklahoma), Patrick Kiley (Marian College), Donald Koke (Butler County College), Jayson Larremore (Oral Roberts University), Bonnie Loss (Glendale Community College), Diana Lurz (Rogers State University), Eldonna Loraine May (Wayne State University), Barbara J. Mayo (Northeast Lakeview College), Susan McClung (Hillsborough Community College), Trudy McNair (Valencia Community College), Richard Middleton-Kaplan (Harper College), Yvonne J. Milspaw (Harrisburg Area Community College), Maureen Moore (Cosumnes River College), Sean P. Murphy (College of Lake County), Judy Navas (Sonoma State University), Jack L. Nawrocik (St. Philip's College), James Norwood (University of Minnesota), Craig Payne (Indian Hills College), Randall M. Payne (South Florida Community College), Laurel S. Peterson (Norwalk Community College), Richard W. Peyton (Florida Agricultural and Mechanical University), Anne L. Pierce (Hampton University), William H. Porterfield (West Virginia State Community & Technical College), Judith Poxon (Sacramento City College), Robin Poynor (University of Florida), Verbie Lovorn Prevost (University of Tennessee at Chattanooga), Andreas W. Reif (Southern New Hampshire University), Denise M. Rogers (University of Louisiana at Lafayette), Karen Rumbley (Valencia Community College), Maria Rybakova (San Diego State University), John Scolaro (Valencia Community College), Vanessa Sheldon (College of the Desert), Mary Slater (Missouri Valley College), Linda Spain (Linn-Benton Community College), Hartley S. Spatt (SUNY Maritime College), Lisa Stokes (Seminole Community College), Alice Taylor (West Los Angeles College), Andreia Thaxton (Florida Community College at Jacksonville), Randall K. Van Schepen (Roger Williams University), Andrew Vassar (Northeastern State University), John Michael Vohlidka (Gannon University), Laura Wadenpfuhl (New Jersey City College), John R. Webb (Highland Community College), Jason Whitmarsh (Florida State College at Jacksonville), and Linda Woodward (Lone Star Montgomery College).

—Gloria K. Fiero

# BEFORE WE BEGIN

Studying humanities engages us in a dialogue with *primary sources*: works original to the age in which they were produced. Whether literary, visual, or aural, a primary source is a text; the time, place, and circumstances in which it was created constitute the context; and its various underlying meanings provide the subtext. Studying humanities from the perspective of text, context, and subtext helps us understand our cultural legacy and our place in the larger world.

## Text

The *text* of a primary source refers to its medium (that is, what it is made of), its form (its outward shape), and its content (the subject it describes).

**Literature**: Literary form varies according to the manner in which words are arranged. So, *poetry*, which shares rhythmic organization with music and dance, is distinguished from *prose*, which normally lacks regular rhythmic patterns. Poetry, by its freedom from conventional grammar, provides unique opportunities for the expression of intense emotions. Prose usually functions to convey information, to narrate, and to describe.

*Philosophy*, (the search for truth through reasoned analysis), and *history* (the record of the past) make use of prose to analyze and communicate ideas and information.

In literature, as in most forms of expression, content and form are usually interrelated. The subject matter or form of a literary work determines its *genre*. For instance, a long narrative poem recounting the adventures of a hero constitutes an *epic*, while a formal, dignified speech in praise of a person or thing constitutes a *eulogy*.

**The Visual Arts**: The visual arts employ a wide variety of media, ranging from the traditional colored pigments used in painting, to wood, clay, marble, and (more recently) plastic and neon used in sculpture, to a wide variety of digital media, including photography and film. The form or outward shape of a work of art depends on the manner in which the artist manipulates the elements of color, line, texture, and space. Unlike words, these formal elements lack denotative meaning.

The visual arts are dominantly spatial, that is, they operate and are apprehended in space. Artists manipulate form to describe or interpret the visible world (as in the genres of portraiture and landscape), or to create worlds of fantasy and imagination. They may also fabricate texts that are non-representational, that is, without identifiable subject matter.

**Music and Dance**: The medium of music is sound. Like literature, music is durational: it unfolds over the period of time in which it occurs. The major elements of music are melody, rhythm, harmony, and tone color—formal elements that also characterize the oral life of literature.

However, while literary and visual texts are usually descriptive, music is almost always nonrepresentational: it rarely has meaning beyond sound itself. For that reason, music is the most difficult of the arts to describe in words.

Dance, the artform that makes the human body itself the medium of expression, resembles music in that it is temporal and performance-oriented. Like music, dance exploits rhythm as a formal tool, and like painting and sculpture, it unfolds in space as well as in time.

Studying the text, we discover the ways in which the artist manipulates medium and form to achieve a characteristic manner of execution or expression that we call *style*. Comparing the styles of various texts from a single era, we discover that they usually share certain defining features and characteristics. Similarities between, for instance, ancient Greek temples and Greek tragedies, or between Chinese lyric poems and landscape paintings, reveal the unifying moral and aesthetic values of their respective cultures.

## Context

The *context* describes the historical and cultural environment of a text. Understanding the relationship between text and context is one of the principal concerns of any inquiry into the humanistic tradition. To determine the context, we ask: In what time and place did our primary source originate? How did it function within the society in which it was created? Was it primarily decorative, didactic, magical, or propagandistic? Did it serve the religious or political needs of the community? Sometimes our answers to these questions are mere guesses. For instance, the paintings on the walls of Paleolithic caves were probably not "artworks" in the modern sense of the term, but, rather, magical signs associated with religious rituals performed in the interest of communal survival.

Determining the function of the text often serves to clarify the nature of its form, and vice-versa. For instance, in that the Hebrew Bible, the *Song of Roland*, and many other early literary works were spoken or sung, rather than read, such literature tends to feature repetition and rhyme, devices that facilitate memorization and oral delivery.

## Subtext

The *subtext* of a primary source refers to its secondary or implied meanings. The subtext discloses conceptual messages embedded in or implied by the text. The epic poems of the ancient Greeks, for instance, which glorify prowess and physical courage, suggest an exclusively male perception of virtue. The state portraits of the seventeenth-century French king Louis XIV bear the subtext of unassailable and absolute power. In our own time, Andy Warhol's serial adaptations of Coca-Cola bottles offer wry commentary on the commercial mentality of American society. Examining the implicit message of the text helps us determine the values of the age in which it was produced, and offers insights into our own.

# Chapter

# 32

## The Modernist Assault
### ca. 1900–1950

*"What is real is not the external form,
but the essence of things."*
Constantin Brancusi

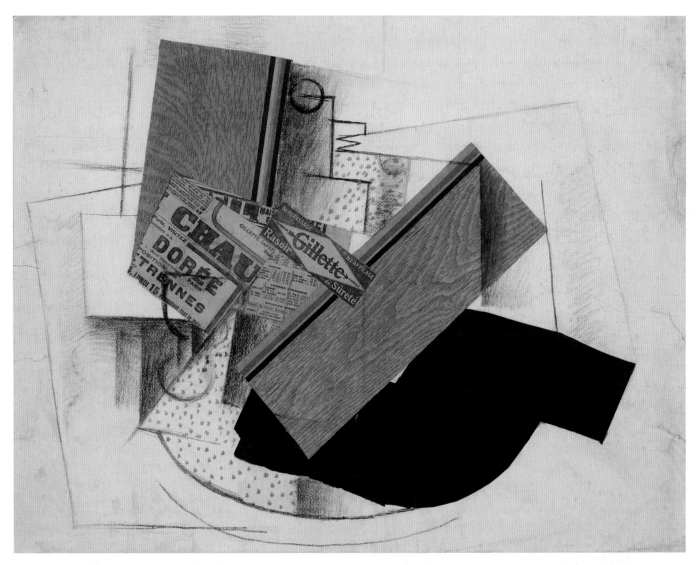

**Figure 32.1 GEORGES BRAQUE**, *Still Life on a Table*, ca. 1914. Collage on paper,
18⅛ × 24¾ in. Trained as a decorator, Braque introduced stenciled letters, sand, and
sawdust into his artworks. His use of newspaper clippings, wallpaper, wine bottle
labels, and wrappers gave his works greater density and challenged viewers to view
everyday objects from different perspectives—conceptual and perceptual.

# LOOKING AHEAD

Since the birth of civilization, no age has broken with tradition more radically or more self-consciously than the twentieth century. In its first decades, the spirit and the style of this new direction came to be called "Modernism." Modernism rejected former cultural values and conventions in favor of innovation, experimentation, and (at its most extreme) anarchy, the absolute dissolution of established norms.

The Modernist revolution in the creative arts responded to equally revolutionary changes in science and technology. The transformation in technology began at the end of the nineteenth century with the invention of the telephone (1876), wireless telegraphy (1891), and the internal combustion engine (1897), which made possible the first gasoline-powered automobiles. In France and the United States, the mass production of automobiles was underway by 1900. Among the swelling populations of modern cities, the pace of living became faster than ever before. By 1903, the airplane joined the string of enterprises that ushered in an era of rapid travel and communication—a "shrinking" of the planet that would produce the "global village" of the late twentieth century. Advances in scientific theory proved equally significant: atomic physics, which provided a new understanding of the physical universe, was as momentous for the twentieth century as metallurgy was for the fourth millennium B.C.E. But while the latter contributed to the birth of civilization, the former, which ushered in the nuclear age, threatened its survival.

The Modern Era—roughly the first half of the twentieth century—is considered thematically in the next three chapters. The first, chapter 32, deals with the Modernist assault on tradition in the arts. Chapter 33 examines the shaping influence of the great Austrian psychiatrist Sigmund Freud, whose writings had a shattering effect on every form of cultural expression. Chapter 34 considers the brutal impact of Totalitarianism and the two world wars that put the potentially liberating tools of the new science and technology to horrifically destructive ends.

## The New Physics

At the turn of the twentieth century, atomic physicists advanced a model of the universe that challenged the one Isaac Newton had provided two centuries earlier. Newton's universe operated according to smoothly functioning laws that generally corresponded with the world of sense perception. Modern physicists found, however, that at the physical extremes of nature—the microcosmic (the very small or very fast) realm of atomic particles and the macrocosmic world of heavy astronomical bodies—the laws of Newton's *Principia* did not apply. A more comprehensive model of the universe began to emerge after 1880 when two American physicists, Albert Michelson and Edward Morley, determined that the speed of light is a universal constant. In 1897, the English physicist, Joseph J. Thompson (1846–1940) identified the electron, the elementary subatomic particle whose interaction between atoms is the main cause of chemical bonding. Three years later, the German physicist Max Planck (1858–1947) suggested that light waves sometimes behaved as *quanta*, that is, as separate and discontinuous bundles of energy.

Alongside this and other groundbreaking work in *quantum physics* (as the field came to be called), yet another German physicist, Albert Einstein (1879–1955), made public his *special theory of relativity* (1905), a radically new approach to the new concepts of time, space, motion, and light. While Newton had held that objects preserved properties such as mass and length whether at rest or in motion, Einstein theorized that as an object's speed approached the speed of light, its mass increased and its length contracted; no object could move faster than light, and light did not require any medium to carry it. In essence, Einstein's theory held that all measurable motion is relative to some other object, and that no universal coordinates, and no hypothetical ether, exist.

Building on Einstein's theories, Werner Heisenberg (1901–1976) theorized that since the very act of measuring subatomic phenomena altered them, the position and the velocity of a subatomic particle could not be measured simultaneously with absolute accuracy. Heisenberg's *principle of uncertainty* (1927)—the more precisely the position of a particle is determined, the less precisely its momentum can be known—replaced the absolute and rationalist model of the universe with one whose exact mechanisms at the subatomic level are indeterminate.

Quantum physics gave humankind greater insight into the workings of the universe, but it also made the operation of that universe more remote from the average person's understanding. The basic components of nature—subatomic particles—were inaccessible to both the human eye and the camera, hence beyond the realm of the senses. Nevertheless, the practical implications of the new physics were immense: radar technology, computers, and consumer electronics were only three of its numerous long-range consequences. Atomic fission, the splitting of atomic particles (begun only after 1920), and the atomic bomb itself (first tested in 1945) confirmed the validity of Einstein's famous formula, $E=mc^2$, which shows that mass and energy are different manifestations of the same thing; and therefore (in his words), "a very small amount of mass [matter] can be converted into a very large amount of energy." The new physics paved the way for the atomic age. It also radically altered the way in which human beings understood the physical world.

# Early Twentieth-Century Poetry

Modern poets had little use for the self-indulgent sentiments of the nineteenth-century romantics and the idealism of the Symbolists. They found in nature neither ecstasy nor redemption. If nature was indeed both random and relative, the job of these poets might be to find a new language for conveying its unique character, one that captured the disjunctive eccentricities of an indifferent cosmos. At the least, they would produce a style that was as conceptual and abstract as that of modern physics.

## The Imagists

The leaders in the search for a more concentrated style of expression were a group of poets who called themselves *Imagists*. For the imagist, the writer was like a sculptor, whose technique required that he carve away all extraneous matter in a process of **abstraction** that aimed to arrive at an intrinsic or essential form. Verbal compression, formal precision, and economy of expression were the goals of the Imagists. Renouncing traditional verse forms, fixed meter, and rhythm, their style of free verse became notorious for its abrupt and discontinuous juxtaposition of images. Essentially an English-language literary movement, Imagism attracted a number of talented American women, including Amy Lowell (1874–1925) and Hilda Doolittle (1886–1961), who signed her poems simply "H.D."

Imagism's most influential poet was the American expatriate Ezra Pound (1885–1972). By the age of twenty-three, Pound had abandoned his study of language and literature at American universities for a career in writing that led him to Europe, where he wandered from England to France and Italy. A poet, critic, and translator, Pound was thoroughly familiar with the literature of his contemporaries. But he cast his net wide: he studied the prose and poetry of ancient Greece and Rome, China and Japan, medieval France and Renaissance Italy—often reading the work of literature in its original language. As a student of East Asian calligraphy, he drew inspiration from the sparseness

and subtlety of Chinese characters. He was particularly fascinated by the fact that the Chinese poetic line, which presented images without grammar or syntax, operated in the same intuitive manner that nature worked upon the human mind. It was this vitality that Pound wished to bring to poetry.

In Chinese and Japanese verse—especially in the Japanese poetic genre known as **haiku** (see chapter 21)—Pound found the key to his search for concentrated expression. Two of his most famous *haiku*-like poems are found in the collection called *Personae*. He claimed that it took him a year and a half to write the first of these poems, cutting down the verse from thirty lines to two.

## READING 32.1 From Pound's *Personae* (1926)

**"In a Station of the Metro"**
The apparition of these faces in the crowd;
Petals on a wet, black bough.

**"The Bath Tub"**
As a bathtub lined with white porcelain,
When the hot water gives out or goes tepid,
So is the slow cooling of our chivalrous passion,
O my much praised but-not-altogether-satisfactory lady.

**Q** In what ways are these poems abstract?

**Q** What effects are created by the juxtaposition of the key images?

Pound imitated the *haiku*-style succession of images to evoke subtle, metaphoric relationships between things. He conceived what he called the "rhythmical arrangement of words" to produce an emotional "shape."

In the *Imagist Manifesto* (1913) and in various interviews, Pound outlined the cardinal points of the Imagist doctrine: poets should use "absolutely no word that does not contribute to the presentation"; they should employ free verse rhythms "in sequence of the musical phrase." Ultimately, Pound summoned his contemporaries to cast aside traditional modes of Western verse-making and "make it new"—a dictum allegedly scrawled on the bathtub of an ancient Chinese emperor. "Day by day," wrote Pound, "make it new/cut underbrush/pile the logs/keep it growing." The injunction to "make it new" became the rallying cry of Modernism.

The Imagist search for an abstract language of expression stood at the beginning of the Modernist revolution in poetry. It also opened the door to a more concealed and elusive style of poetry, one that drew freely on the cornucopia of world literature and history. The poems that Pound wrote after 1920, particularly the *Cantos* (the unfinished opus on which Pound labored for fifty-five years), are filled with foreign language phrases, obscene jokes, and arcane literary and historical allusions juxtaposed without connective tissue. These poems contrast sharply with the terse precision and eloquent purity of Pound's early Imagist efforts.

## T. S. Eliot

No English-speaking poet advanced the Modernist agenda more powerfully than the American-born writer T. S. (Thomas Stearns) Eliot (1888–1965). Meeting Pound in 1914, Eliot joined him in the effort to rid modern poetry of romantic sentiment. He held that poetry must seek the verbal formula or "objective correlative" (as he called it) that gives precise shape to feeling. Eliot's style soon became notable for its inventive rhythms, irregular cadences, and startling images, many of which draw on personal reminiscences and obscure literary resources.

Educated at Harvard University in philosophy and the classics, Eliot was studying at Oxford when World War I broke out. He remained in England after the war, becoming a British citizen in 1927 and converting to the Anglican faith in the same year. His intellectual grasp of modern philosophy, world religions, anthropology, and the classical literature of Asia and the West made him the most erudite literary figure of his time.

Begun in 1910, Eliot's poem, "The Love Song of J. Alfred Prufrock" (reproduced here in full), captures the waning idealism that pervaded the years leading up to World War I. The "love song" is actually the dramatic monologue of a timid, middle-aged man who has little faith in himself or his capacity for effective action. Prufrock's cynicism anticipated the disillusion and the sense of impotence that marked the postwar generation (discussed in greater detail in chapter 34).

---

**READING 32.2** Eliot's "The Love Song of J. Alfred Prufrock" (1915)

*S'io credesse che mia risposta fosse*
*A persona che mai tornasse al mondo,*
*Questa fiamma staria senza piu scosse.*
*Ma perciocche giammai di questo fondo*
*Non torno vivo alcun s'i'odo il vero,*
*Senza tema d'infamia ti rispondo.*[1]

Let us go then, you and I,                                                1
When the evening is spread out against the sky
Like a patient etherised upon a table;
Let us go, through certain half-deserted streets,
The muttering retreats                                                    5
Of restless nights in one-night cheap hotels
And sawdust restaurants with oyster-shells:
Streets that follow like a tedious argument
Of insidious intent
To lead you to an overwhelming question . . .                             10
Oh, do not ask, "What is it?"
Let us go and make our visit.

In the room the women come and go
Talking of Michelangelo.

The yellow fog that rubs its back upon the window-panes,                  15
The yellow smoke that rubs its muzzle on the window-panes
Licked its tongue into the corners of the evening,
Lingered upon the pools that stand in drains,
Let fall upon its back the soot that falls from chimneys,
Slipped by the terrace, made a sudden leap,                               20
And seeing that it was a soft October night,
Curled once about the house, and fell asleep.

And indeed there will be time
For the yellow smoke that slides along the street,
Rubbing its back upon the window-panes;                                   25
There will be time, there will be time
To prepare a face to meet the faces that you meet;
There will be time to murder and create,
And time for all the works and days of hands[2]
That lift and drop a question on your plate;                              30
Time for you and time for me,
And time yet for a hundred indecisions,
And for a hundred visions and revisions,
Before the taking of a toast and tea.

In the room the women come and go                                         35
Talking of Michelangelo.

And indeed there will be time
To wonder, "Do I dare?" and, "Do I dare?"
Time to turn back and descend the stair,
With a bald spot in the middle of my hair—                               40
(They will say: "How his hair is growing thin!")
My morning coat, my collar mounting firmly to the chin,
My necktie rich and modest, but asserted by a simple pin—
(They will say: "But how his arms and legs are thin!")
Do I dare                                                                 45
Disturb the universe?
In a minute there is time
For decisions and revisions which a minute will reverse.

For I have known them all already, known them all—
Have known the evenings, mornings, afternoons,                           50
I have measured out my life with coffee spoons;
I know the voices dying with a dying fall
Beneath the music from a farther room.
So how should I presume?

And I have known the eyes already, known them all—                       55
The eyes that fix you in a formulated phrase,
And when I am formulated, sprawling on a pin,
When I am pinned and wriggling on the wall,
Then how should I begin
To spit out all the butt-ends of my days and ways?                       60
And how should I presume?

---

[1] Lines from Dante's "Inferno," Canto 27, 61–66, spoken by Guido da Montefeltro, who was condemned to Hell for the sin of false counseling. In explaining his punishment to Dante, Guido is still apprehensive of the judgment of society.

[2] An ironic allusion to the poem "Works and Days" by the eighth-century B.C.E. poet Hesiod, which celebrates the virtues of hard labor on the land.

And I have known the arms already, known them all—
Arms that are braceleted and white and bare
(But in the lamplight, downed with light brown hair!)
Is it perfume from a dress                                65
That makes me so digress?
Arms that lie along a table, or wrap about a shawl.
    And should I then presume?
    And how should I begin?

                    . . . . .

    Shall I say, I have gone at dusk through narrow streets     70
And watched the smoke that rises from the pipes
Of lonely men in shirt-sleeves, leaning out of windows? . . .

    I should have been a pair of ragged claws
Scuttling across the floors of silent seas.

                    . . . . .

    And the afternoon, the evening, sleeps so peacefully!       75
Smoothed by long fingers,
Asleep . . . tired . . . or it malingers,
Stretched on the floor, here beside you and me.
Should I, after tea and cakes and ices,
Have the strength to force the moment to its crisis?           80
But though I have wept and fasted, wept and prayed,
Though I have seen my head (grown slightly bald)
    brought in upon a platter,
I am no prophet—and here's no great matter;³
I have seen the moment of my greatness flicker,
And I have seen the eternal Footman hold my coat, and
    snicker,                                                   85
And in short, I was afraid.

    And would it have been worth it, after all,
After the cups, the marmalade, the tea,
Among the porcelain, among some talk of you and me,
Would it have been worth while,                                90
To have bitten off the matter with a smile,
To have squeezed the universe into a ball⁴
To roll it toward some overwhelming question,
To say: "I am Lazarus, come from the dead,⁵
Come back to tell you all, I shall tell you all"—             95
If one, settling a pillow by her head,
    Should say: "That is not what I meant at all,
    That is not it, at all."

    And would it have been worth it, after all,
Would it have been worth while,                               100
After the sunsets and the dooryards and the sprinkled streets,
After the novels, after the teacups, after the skirts that
    trail along the floor—

And this, and so much more?—
It is impossible to say just what I mean!
But as if a magic lantern threw the nerves in patterns on
    a screen:                                                 105
Would it have been worth while
If one, settling a pillow or throwing off a shawl,
And turning towards the window, should say:
    "That is not it at all,
    That is not what I meant, at all."                        110

                    . . . . .

    No! I am not Prince Hamlet, nor was meant to be;
Am an attendant lord, one that will do
To swell a progress, start a scene or two,
Advise the prince; no doubt, an easy tool,⁶
Deferential, glad to be of use,                               115
Politic, cautious, and meticulous;
Full of high sentence, but a bit obtuse;
At times, indeed, almost ridiculous—
Almost, at times, the Fool.

    I grow old . . . I grow old . . .                         120
I shall wear the bottoms of my trousers rolled.⁷

    Shall I part my hair behind? Do I dare to eat a peach?
I shall wear white flannel trousers, and walk upon the beach.
I have heard the mermaids singing, each to each.
I do not think that they will sing to me.                     125
I have seen them riding seaward on the waves
Combing the white hair of the waves blown back
When the wind blows the water white and black.

We have lingered in the chambers of the sea
By sea-girls wreathed with seaweed red and brown              130
Till human voices wake us, and we drown.

**Q** How would you describe the
personality of Eliot's Prufrock?

**Q** What do each of the literary allusions
add to our understanding of the poem?

The tone of Eliot's poem is established by way of powerfully compressed (and gloomy) images: "one-night cheap hotels," "sawdust restaurants," "soot that falls from chimneys," "narrow streets," and "lonely men in shirt-sleeves." Eliot's literary vignettes, and allusions to biblical prophets and to the heroes of history and art (Hamlet and Michelangelo) work as foils to Prufrock's bankrupt idealism, underlining his self-conscious retreat from action, and his loss of faith in the conventional sources of wisdom. The voices of inspiration, concludes Prufrock, are submerged by all-too-human voices, including his own. Prufrock's moral inertia made him an archetype of the condition of spiritual loss associated with Modernism.

³ A reference to John the Baptist, who was beheaded by Herod (Matthew 14: 3–11). Prufrock perceives himself as victim but as neither saint nor martyr.
⁴ A reference to the line "Let us roll all our strength and all our sweetness up into one ball," from the poem "To his Coy Mistress," by the seventeenth-century English poet Andrew Marvell, in which Marvell presses his lover to "seize the day."
⁵ According to the Gospel of John (11: 1–44), Jesus raised Lazarus from the grave.

⁶ A reference to Polonius, the king's adviser in Shakespeare's *Hamlet*, as well as to Guido da Montefeltro—both of them false counselors.
⁷ In Eliot's time, rolled or cuffed trousers were considered fashionable.

## Frost and Lyric Poetry

Robert Frost (1874–1963), the best known and one of the most popular of American poets, offered an alternative to the abstract style of the Modernists. While Frost rejected the romantic sentimentality of much nineteenth-century verse, he embraced the older tradition of Western lyric poetry. He wrote in metered verse and jokingly compared the Modernist use of free verse to playing tennis without a net. Frost avoided dense allusions and learned references. In plain speech he expressed deep affection for the natural landscape and an abiding sympathy with the frailties of the human condition. He described American rural life as uncertain and enigmatic—at times, notably dark. "My poems," explained Frost, "are all set to trip the reader head foremost into the boundless." Frost's "The Road Not Taken" is written in the rugged and direct language that became the hallmark of his mature style. The poem exalts a profound individualism as well as a sparseness of expression in line with the Modernist injunction to "make it new."

### READING 32.3 Frost's "The Road Not Taken" (1916)

| | |
|---|---:|
| Two roads diverged in a yellow wood, | 1 |
| And sorry I could not travel both | |
| And be one traveler, long I stood | |
| And looked down one as far as I could | |
| To where it bent in the undergrowth; | 5 |
| | |
| Then took the other, as just as fair, | |
| And having perhaps the better claim, | |
| Because it was grassy and wanted wear, | |
| Though as for that the passing there | |
| Had worn them really about the same, | 10 |
| | |
| And both that morning equally lay | |
| In leaves no step had trodden black. | |
| Oh, I kept the first for another day! | |
| Yet knowing how way leads on to way, | |
| I doubted if I should ever come back. | 15 |
| | |
| I shall be telling this with a sigh | |
| Somewhere ages and ages hence: | |
| Two roads diverged in a wood, and I— | |
| I took the one less traveled by, | |
| And that has made all the difference. | 20 |

**Q** Why might Frost's choice of roads have made "all the difference"?

**Q** How does the poem illustrate Frost's fondness for direct language?

# Early Twentieth-Century Art

As with Modernist poetry, the art of the early twentieth century came to challenge all that preceded it. Liberated by the camera from the necessity of imitating nature, **avant-garde** artists questioned the value of art as a faithful recreation of the visible world. They pioneered an authentic, "stripped down" style that, much like imagist poetry, *evoked* rather than *described* experience. They pursued the intrinsic qualities and essential meanings of their subject matter to arrive at a concentrated emotional experience. The language of pure form did not, however, rob modern art of its humanistic dimension; rather, it provided artists with a means by which to move beyond traditional ways of representing the visual world. Abstraction—one of the central tenets of Modernism—promised to purify nature so as to come closer to its true reality.

Early modern artists probed the tools and techniques of formal expression more fully than any artists since the Renaissance. Deliberately blurring the boundaries between painting and sculpture, they attached three-dimensional objects to two-dimensional surfaces, thereby violating traditional categories of style and format. Like the Imagists, they found inspiration in non-Western cultures in which art shared the power of ritual. Innovation, abstraction, and experimentation became the hallmarks of the Modernist revolt against convention and tradition.

## Picasso and the Birth of Cubism

The giant of twentieth-century art was the Spanish-born Pablo Picasso (1881–1973). During his ninety-two-year life, Picasso worked in almost every major art style of the century, some of which he himself inaugurated. He produced thousands of paintings, drawings, sculptures, and prints—a body of work that in its size, inventiveness, and influence is nothing short of phenomenal. As a child, he showed an extraordinary gift for drawing, and by the age of twenty his precise and lyrical line style rivaled that of Raphael and Ingres. In 1903, the young painter left his native Spain to settle in Paris. There, in the bustling capital of the Western art world, he came under the influence of Impressionist and Postimpressionist painting, taking as his subjects café life, beggars, prostitutes, and circus folk. Much like the imagists, Picasso worked to refine form and color in the direction of concentrated expression, reducing the colors of his palette first to various shades of blue and then, after 1904, to tones of rose.

By 1906, the artist began to abandon traditional Western modes of pictorial representation. Adopting the credo that art must be subversive—that it must defy all that is conventional, literal, and trite—he initiated a bold new style. Picasso's foremost assault on tradition was *Les Demoiselles d'Avignon*, a large painting of five nude women—the prostitutes of a Barcelona bordello (Figure **32.2**). The subject matter of the work embraced the long, respectable tradition of the female nude group in a landscape setting (see Figure 32.3). However, *Les Demoiselles* violated every shred of tradition, making even Manet's *Olympia* (see Figure 30.19) look comfortably old-fashioned.

The manner in which Picasso "made new" a traditional subject in Western art is worth examining: in the early sketches for the painting, originally called *The Philosophical Brothel*, Picasso included two male figures, one of whom resembled the artist himself. However, in the summer of 1907, Picasso fell deeply under the spell of African art on

**Figure 32.2 PABLO PICASSO**, *Les Demoiselles d'Avignon*, Paris, 1907. Oil on canvas, 8 ft. × 7 ft. 8 in.

display at the Musée d'Ethnographie du Trocadéro in Paris. Reworking the canvas, he transformed the five prostitutes into a group of fierce iconic images. For what he would later call his "first exorcism picture," he seems to have taken apart and reassembled the figures as if to test the physics of disjunction and discontinuity. At least three of the figures are rendered not from a single vantage point but from multiple viewpoints, as if one's eye could travel freely in time and space. The body of the crouching female on the far right is seen from the back, while her face, savagely striated like the scarified surface of an African sculpture, is seen from the front. The noses of the two central females appear in profile, while their eyes are frontal—a convention Picasso may have borrowed from ancient Egyptian frescoes. The relationship between the figures and the shallow space they occupy is equally disjunctive, a condition compounded by brutally fractured planes of color—brick reds and vivid blues—that resemble shards of glass. Picasso stripped the female of all sensuous appeal. In one disquiet-ing stroke, he banished the alluring female nude from the domain of Western art.

*Les Demoiselles* was the precursor of an audacious new style known as *Cubism*, a bold and distinctive formal language that came to challenge the principles of Renaissance painting as dramatically as Einstein's theory of relativity had challenged Newtonian physics. In the Cubist canvas, the recognizable world of the senses disappears beneath a scaffold of semitransparent planes and short, angular lines; ordinary objects are made to look as if they have exploded and been reassembled somewhat arbitrarily in geometric bits and pieces that rest on the surface of the picture plane (Figure **32.5**).

With *Analytic Cubism*, as the style came to be called, a multiplicity of viewpoints replaced one-point perspective. The Cubist image, conceived as if one were moving around, above, and below the subject and even perceiving it from within, appropriates the fourth dimension—time itself. Abrupt shifts in direction and an ambiguous spatial field call up the uncertainties of the new physics. As Picasso and

# MAKING CONNECTIONS

Figure 32.3 PAUL CÉZANNE, *The Large Bathers*, 1906. Oil on canvas, 6 ft. 10⅞ in. × 8 ft. 2¾ in.

Figure 32.4 Kota reliquary figure, from Gabon. Wood covered with strips of copper and brass, 30¾ in.

Picasso's pre-Cubist style was shaped by two major forces: Cézanne's paintings, which had been the focus of two large Paris exhibitions; and the arts of Africa, Iberia, and Oceania, examples of which were appearing regularly in Paris galleries and museums (see chapters 18 and 31). In Cézanne's canvases, with their flattened planes and arbitrary colors (Figure **32.3**), Picasso recognized a rigorous new language of form that seemed to define nature's underlying structure. And in African and Oceanic sculpture he discovered the power of art as the palpable embodiment of potent supernatural forces.

Scholars continue to debate exactly which works of tribal art Picasso encountered on his visits to the Ethnographic Museum in Paris. The artist would also have been familiar with African imports sold by Paris art dealers in the early twentieth century. These were purchased by artists (including Picasso himself) and collectors, such as Picasso's expatriate American friends, Gertrude Stein and her brother. It is indisputable that Picasso knew the copper-clad Kota statues that functioned originally as African guardian figures (Figure **32.4**). Installed above a container holding the bones of an ancestor, such reliquary icons were not representations of the deceased, but power-objects that protected the deceased from evil. Of the tribal masks and sculptures with which he was familiar, Picasso later explained: "For me, [they] were not just sculptures; they were magical objects . . . intercessors against unknown, threatening

spirits." The union of expressive abstraction and dynamic distortion clearly characterizes both the Kota image and the treatment of the two figures on the right in *Les Demoiselles d'Avignon* (Figure **32.2A**).

Figure 32.2A PABLO PICASSO, *Les Demoiselles d'Avignon*, Paris, 1907. Oil on canvas, 8 ft. × 7 ft. 8 in.

**Figure 32.5 PABLO PICASSO**, *Man with a Violin*, 1911. Oil on canvas, 3 ft. 3½ in. × 29⅝ in. A comparison of this painting with *Les Demoiselles d'Avignon* shows how far toward abstraction Picasso had moved in less than four years. Knit by a lively arrangement of flat shaded planes, monochromatic in color, figure and ground are almost indistinguishable.

his French colleague Georges Braque (1882–1963) collaborated in a search for an ever more pared down language of form, their compositions became increasingly abstract and colors became cool and controlled: Cubism came to offer a new formal language, one wholly unconcerned with narrative content. Years later, Picasso defended the viability of this new language: "The fact that for a long time Cubism has not been understood . . . means nothing. I do not read English, an English book is a blank book to me. This does not mean that the English language does not exist."

Around 1912, a second phase of Cubism, namely *Synthetic Cubism*, emerged, when Braque first included three pieces of wallpaper in a still-life composition. Picasso and Braque, who thought of themselves as space pioneers (much like the Wright brothers), pasted mundane objects such as wine labels, playing cards, and scraps of newspaper onto the surface of the canvas—a technique known as **collage** (from the French *coller*, "to paste"). The result was a kind of art that was neither a painting nor a sculpture, but both at the same time. The two artists filled their canvases with puns, hidden messages, and subtle references to contemporary events; but the prevailing strategy in all of these artworks was to test the notion of art as illusion.

In Braque's *Still Life on a Table* (see Figure 32.1), strips of imitation wood graining, a razor blade wrapper, and newspaper clippings serve the double function of "presenting" and "representing." Words and images wrenched out of context here play off one another like some cryptographic billboard. Prophetic of twentieth-century art in general, Braque would proclaim, "The subject is not the object of the painting, but a new unity, the lyricism that results from method."

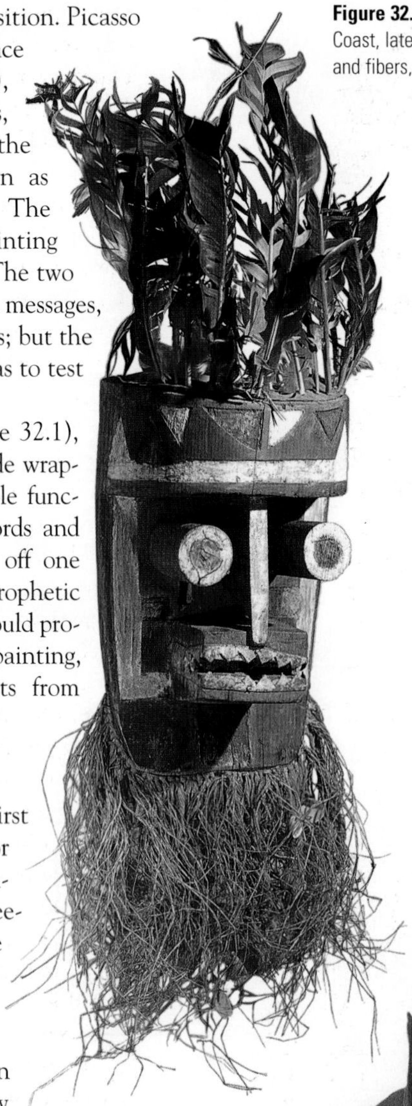

## Assemblage

In these same years, Picasso created the first **assemblages**—artworks that were built up, or pieced together, from miscellaneous or commonplace materials. Like the collage, the three-dimensional assemblage depended on the inventive combination of found objects and materials. As such, it constituted a radical alternative to traditional techniques of carving in stone, metal casting, and modeling in clay or plaster. The art of assemblage clearly drew inspiration from African and Oceanic traditions of combining natural materials (such as cowrie beads and raffia) for masks and costumes; it also took heed of the expressive simplifications that typify power objects, reliquaries, and other tribal artforms (Figure **32.6**). Picasso's *Guitar* of 1912–1913 achieves its powerful effect by means of fragmented planes, deliberate spatial inversions (note the projecting soundhole), and the wedding of sheet-metal and wire (Figure **32.7**).

Within a decade, Western sculptors were employing the strategies of Synthetic Cubism in ways that reflected abstract models of time and space. The Russian-born cubist Alexander Archipenko (1887–1964), for instance, fashioned the female form so that an area of negative space actually constitutes the head (Figure **32.8**).

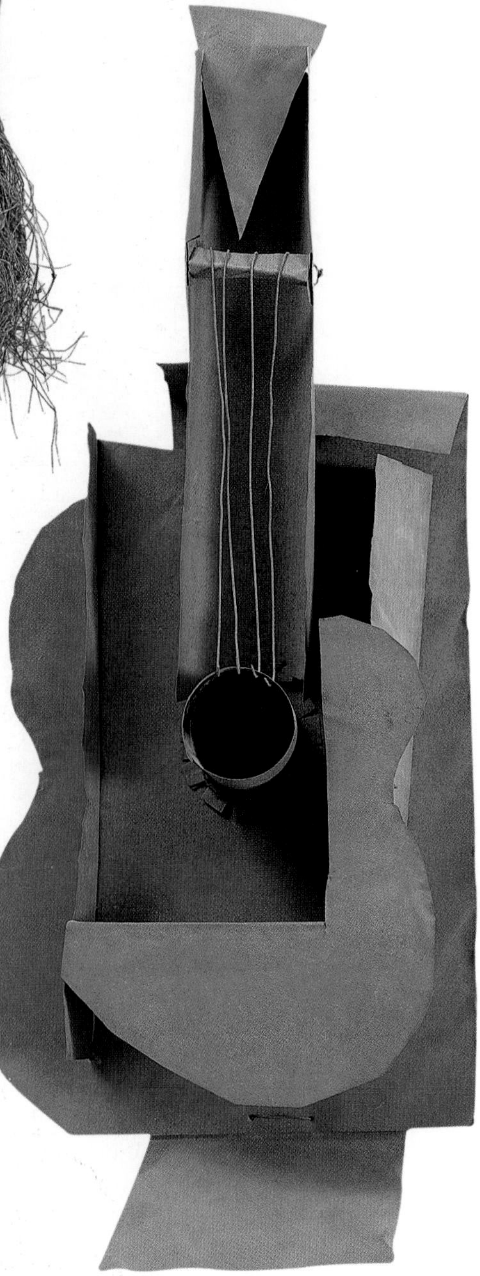

## Futurism

Intrigued by the dynamism of modern technology, the avant-garde movement known as *Futurism* emerged in Italy. Originally a literary movement, it soon came to embrace all of the arts, including architecture and film. Its founder, the poet and iconoclast Filippo Tommaso Marinetti (1876–1944), issued a series of manifestoes

**Figure 32.6** Ceremonial mask, from Wobé or Grebo, Ivory Coast, late nineteenth century. Painted wood, feathers, and fibers, height 11 in.

**Figure 32.7 PABLO PICASSO**, *Guitar*, 1912–1913. Construction of sheet metal and wire, 30½ × 13¾ × 7⅞ in.

**Figure 32.8 ALEXANDER ARCHIPENKO**,
*Woman Combing Her Hair,* 1915.
Bronze, 13¾ × 3¼ × 3⅛ in.
(including base).

attacking literary formalism, museum art, and academic culture. He called for a style that linked contemporary expression to industry, technology, and urban life. Marinetti, who held that "war was the only healthgiver of the world," demanded an art of "burning violence" that would free Italy from its "fetid gangrene of professors, archeologists, antiquarians, and rhetoricians." "We declare," he wrote in his *Futurist Manifesto* of 1909, "that there can be no modern painting except from the starting point of an absolutely modern sensation. ... A roaring motorcar is more beautiful than the winged *Victory of Samothrace*" (the famous Hellenistic sculpture illustrated as Figure 5.32). "The gesture that we would reproduce on canvas shall no longer be a fixed moment in universal dynamism. It shall simply be the dynamic sensation itself."

The futuristic alternative to static academicism was produced by Umberto Boccioni (1882–1916). His near life-sized bronze sculpture captures the sensation of motion as it pushes forward like a automated robot (Figure **32.9**). The striding figure, which consists of an aggressive series of dynamic, jagged lines, is clearly human in form, despite Boccioni's assertion (in his 1912 *Technical Manifesto of Futurist Sculpture*) that artists should "abolish . . . the traditionally exalted place of subject matter."

The Futurists were enthralled by the speed and dynamism of automobiles, trains, and airplanes, and by such new forms of technology as the machine gun and the electric light. In the painting *Street Light* (Figure **32.10**), the Italian Futurist Giacomo Balla (1871–1958) paid homage to the electric Brunt Arc lamps that were installed in the streets of Rome during the first decade of the century. Balla wittily claimed that this painting, in which electric light outshines moonlight, hailed the demise of romantic art in the West.

Futurists were also inspired by the time-lapse photography of Eadweard Muybridge (see Figure 31.9), the magical properties of X-rays (not in wide use until 1910), and by pioneer efforts in the new industry of motion pictures, in which "multiple profiles" gave the appearance of movement in time and space. These modern phenomena shaped the early career of the French artist Marcel Duchamp (1887–1968). When Duchamp's *Nude Descending a Staircase, No. 2* (Figure **32.11**) was exhibited

## Science and Technology

| | |
|---|---|
| **1901** | the first international radio broadcast is made by Guglielmo Marconi (Italian) |
| **1903** | Orville and Wilbur Wright (American) make the first successful airplane flight |
| **1927** | the first motion picture with synchronized sound (*The Jazz Singer*) is released |
| **1927** | Werner Heisenberg (German) announces his "uncertainty principle" |

at the International Exhibition of Modern Art (known as the Armory Show) in New York City, one critic mockingly called it "an explosion in a shingle factory." Yet, from the time of its first showing in 1913, the painting (and much of the art in the Armory exhibition) had a formative influence on the rise of American Modernism. Futurism did not last beyond the end of World War I, but its impact was felt in both the United States and Russia, where Futurist efforts

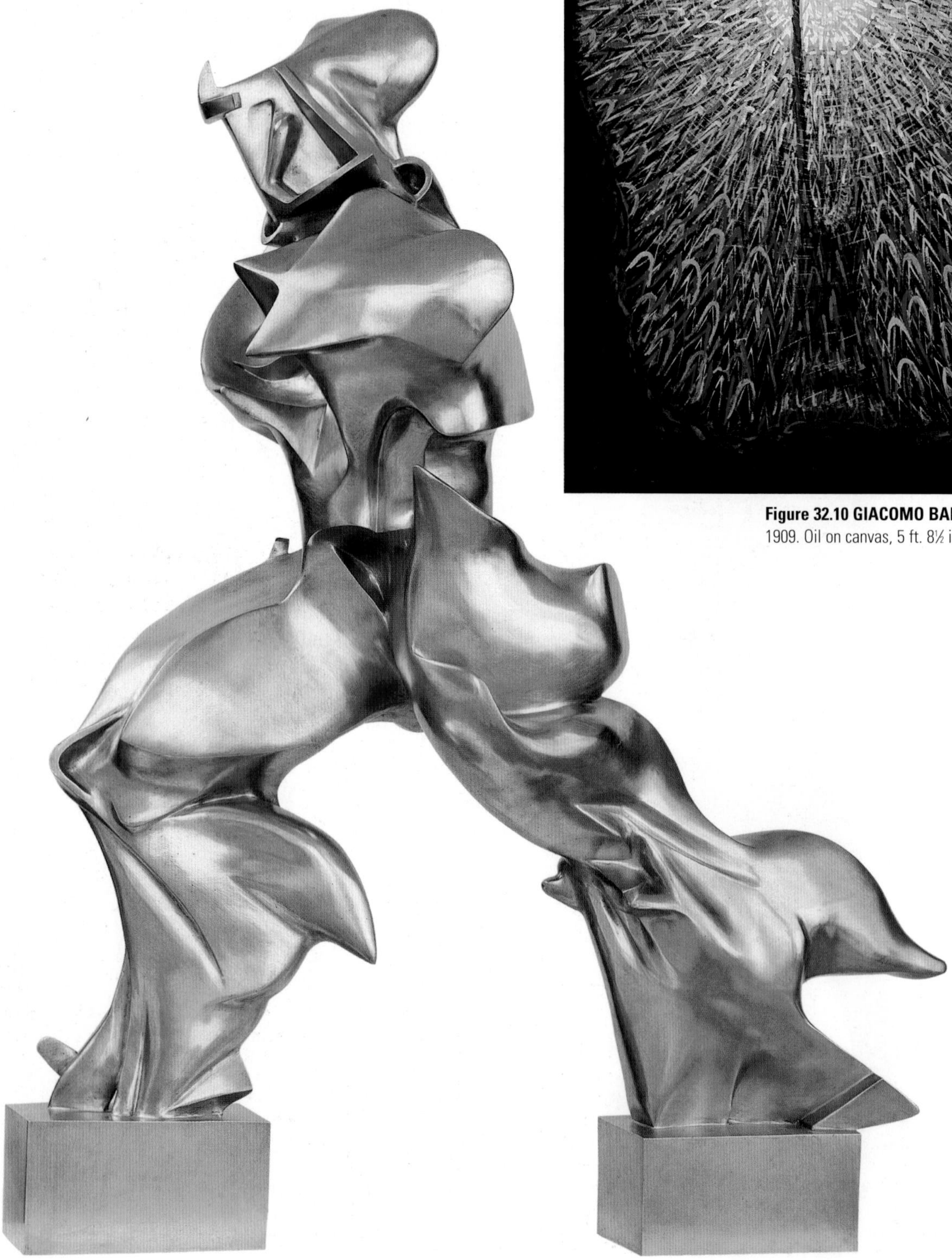

**Figure 32.9 UMBERTO BOCCIONI**, *Unique Forms of Continuity in Space*, 1913. Bronze (cast 1931), 3 ft. 7⅞ in. × 34⅛ in. × 15¾ in.

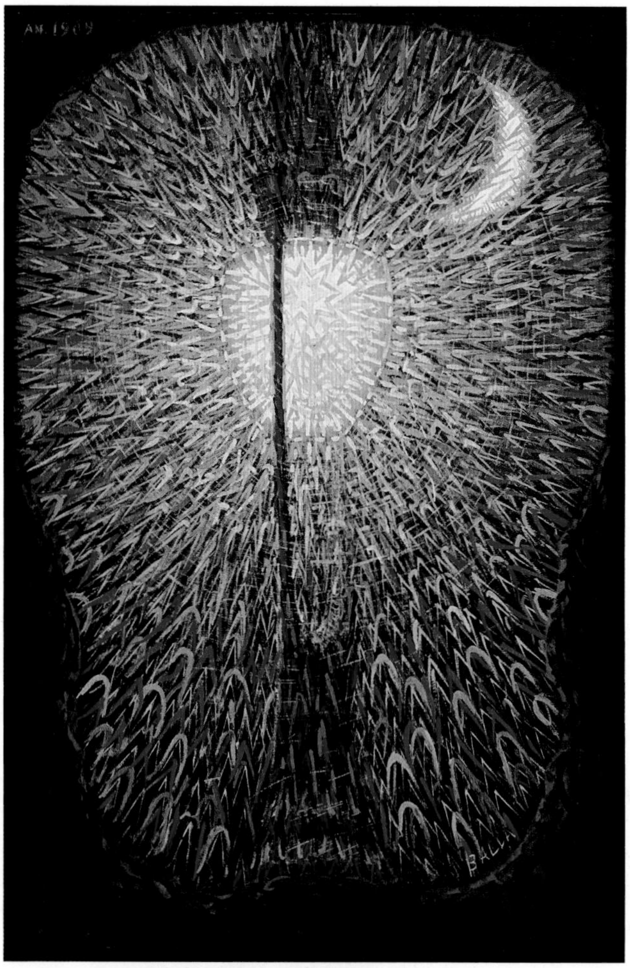

**Figure 32.10 GIACOMO BALLA**, *Street Light*, 1909. Oil on canvas, 5 ft. 8½ in. × 3 ft. 8⅛ in.

to capture the sense of form in motion would coincide with the first developments in the technology of cinematography (see "The Birth of Motion Pictures").

## Matisse and Fauvism

While Cubists and Futurists were principally concerned with matters of space and motion, other Modernists, led by the French artist Henri Matisse (1869–1954), made *color* the principal feature of their canvases. This group, branded as "Fauves" (from the French *fauve*, "wild beast") by a critic who saw their work at a 1905 exhibition in Paris, employed flat, bright colors in the arbitrary manner of van Gogh and Gauguin. But whereas the latter had used color to evoke a mood or a symbolic image, the younger artists

**Figure 32.11 MARCEL DUCHAMP**, *Nude Descending a Staircase, No. 2*, 1912. Oil on canvas, 4 ft. 10 in. × 35 in. Movement is suggested by the successive superimposition of figures, a technique that mimics the motion of a stroboscope, a device invented in 1832.

## The Birth of Motion Pictures

It is no coincidence that the art of motion pictures was born at a time when artists and scientists were obsessed with matters of space and time. Indeed, as an artform that captures rapidly changing experience, cinema is the quintessentially modern medium. The earliest public film presentations took place in Europe and the United States in the mid-1890s: in 1895, Thomas Edison (1867–1931) was the first American to project moving images on a screen. In France the brothers Auguste and Louis Lumière (1862–1954; 1864–1948) perfected the process by which cellulose film ran smoothly in a commercial projector. They pioneered the first cinematic projection in an auditorium equipped with seats and piano accompaniment. These first experiments delighted audiences with moving pictures of everyday subjects.

It was not until 1902, however, that film was used to create a reality all its own: in that year the French filmmaker Georges Méliès (1861–1938) completed a fourteen-minute theatrical sequence called *A Trip to the Moon*, an engaging fantasy based on a Jules Verne novel. One year later, the American director Edwin S. Porter (1869–1941) produced the twelve-minute silent film *The Great Train Robbery*, which treated the myth of American frontier life in its story of a sensational holdup, followed by the pursuit and capture of the bandits. These pioneer narrative films established the idiom for two of the most popular genres in cinematic history: the science fiction film and the "western."

Between 1908 and 1912, Hollywood became the center of American cinema. D. W. Griffith (1875–1948), the leading director of his time, made major innovations in cinematic technique. He introduced the use of multiple cameras and camera angles, as well as such new techniques as close-ups, fade-outs, and flashbacks, which, when joined together in an edited sequence, greatly expanded the potential of film narrative. Griffith's three-hour-long silent film, *The Birth of a Nation* (1915), was an epic account of the American Civil War and the Reconstruction Era that followed in the South. Unfortunately, despite the film's technical excellence, its negative portrayal of African-Americans contributed to stereotyping them as violent and ignorant savages.

Until the late 1920s, all movies were silent—filmmakers used captions to designate the spoken word wherever appropriate and live musical accompaniment was often provided in the theater. Well before the era of the "talkies," cinematographers began to use the camera not simply as a disinterested observer, but as a medium for conveying the emotional states of the characters. In the absence of sound, they were forced to develop the affective structure of the film by essentially visual means. According to some film critics, the aesthetics of film as a medium were compromised when sound was added. Nevertheless, by 1925 it was apparent that film was destined to become one of the major artforms of the Modern Era.

were concerned with color only as it served pictorial structure; their style featured bold spontaneity and the direct and instinctive application of pigment. Critics who called these artists "wild beasts" were in fact responding to the use of color in ways that seemed both crude and savage. They attacked the new style as "color madness" and "the sport of a child." For Matisse, however, color was the font of pure and sensuous pleasure. In his portrait of Madame Matisse (which he subtitled *The Green Line*), broad flat swaths of paint give definition to a visage that is bisected vertically by an acid-green stripe (Figure **32.12**).

Matisse brought daring to Cézanne's flat color patches, using them to simplify form that achieved the visual impact of the tribal artworks he collected. At the same time, he invested the canvas with a thrilling color radiance, that, like smell (as Matisse himself observed), subtly but intensely suffuses the senses. In contrast with Picasso, who held that art was a weapon with which to jar the senses, Matisse sought "an art of balance, of purity and serenity, devoid of troubling or depressing subject matter . . . something like a good armchair in which to rest from physical fatigue."

Matisse was among the first to articulate the Modernist scorn for representational art: "Exactitude is not truth," he insisted. In *Notes of a Painter*, published in 1908, he described colors and shapes as the equivalents of feelings rather than the counterparts of forms in nature. Gradually, as he came to be influenced by Islamic miniatures and Russian icons, his style moved in the direction of linear simplicity and color sensuousness. A quintessential example of his facility for color abstraction is *Dance I* (Figure **32.13**). In its lyrical arabesques and unmodeled fields of color, the painting calls to mind the figural grace of ancient Greek vase paintings. At the same time, it captures the exhilaration of the primordial round—the traditional dance of almost all Mediterranean cultures.

**Figure 32.12 HENRI MATISSE**,
*Madame Matisse (The Green Line)*,
1905. Oil on canvas, 16 × 12¾ in.

**Figure 32.13 HENRI MATISSE**, *Dance 1*, 1909. Oil on canvas, 8 ft. 6½ in. × 12 ft. 9½ in. Matisse painted a second version of *The Dance* for the home of his patron, the Russian art collector Sergei Shchukin. It is now in Saint Petersburg's Hermitage Museum.

## Brancusi and Abstraction

Although Cubists, Futurists, and Fauves pursued their individual directions, they all shared the credo of abstract art: the artist must evoke the essential and intrinsic qualities of the subject rather than describe its physical properties. In early modern sculpture, the guardian of this credo was Constantin Brancusi (1876–1957). Born in Romania and trained in Bucharest, Vienna, and Munich, Brancusi came to Paris in 1904. There, after a brief stay in Rodin's studio, he fell under the spell of ancient fertility figures and the sculpture of Africa and Polynesia. Inspired by these objects, whose spiritual power lay in their visual immediacy and their truth to materials, Brancusi proceeded to create an art of radically simple, organic forms. While he began by closely observing the living object—whether human or animal—he progressively eliminated all naturalistic details until he arrived at a form that captured the essence of the subject. Like his good friend Ezra Pound, Brancusi achieved a concentrated expression in forms so elemental that they seem to speak a universal language.

A case in point is *Bird in Space* (Figure **32.14**), of which Brancusi made more than thirty versions in various sizes and materials. The sculpture is of no particular species of feathered creature, but it captures perfectly the concept of "birdness." It is, as Brancusi explained, "the essence of flight." "What is real," he insisted, "is not the external form, but the essence of things." The elegant form, curved like a feather, unites birdlike qualities of grace and poise with the dynamic sense of soaring levitation characteristic of mechanical flying machines, such as rockets and airplanes. Indeed, when Brancusi's bronze *Bird* first arrived in America, United States customs officials mistook it for a piece of industrial machinery.

## Abstraction and Photography

Photography enthusiastically embraced the Modernist aesthetic. The American photographer Edward Weston (1886–1953) was among the pioneers of photographic abstraction. His close-up photograph of two nautilus shells evokes the twin ideas of flower (a magnolia blossom, according to Weston himself) and female (Figure **32.15**). Weston took photography beyond the realm of the representational: he used the camera not simply to record the natural world, but to explore new avenues of visual experience.

**Figure 32.14 CONSTANTIN BRANCUSI**, *Bird in Space*, 1928. Polished bronze, height 4 ft. 6 in.

**Figure 32.15 EDWARD WESTON**, *Two Shells*, 1927. Photograph. Print by Cole Weston.

## Nonobjective Art

Between 1909 and 1914, three artists working independently of one another in different parts of Europe moved to purge art of all recognizable subject matter. The Russians Wassily Kandinsky (1866–1944) and Kasimir Malevich (1878–1935) and the Dutchman Piet Mondrian (1872–1944), pioneers of **Nonobjective Art**, had all come into contact with the principal art movements of the early twentieth century: Cubism, Futurism, and Fauvism. They acknowledged the Postimpressionist premise that a painting was, first and foremost, a flat surface covered with colors assembled in a particular order. But their quest for subjectless form had a unique goal: that of achieving an art whose purity would offer a spiritual remedy for the soullessness of modern life.

***Kandinsky*** Kandinsky, whose career in art only began at the age of forty, was deeply influenced by the Fauves, the Symbolists (see chapter 31), and by Russian folk art. While he filled his early paintings with vibrant hues, he observed with some dismay that the subject matter in his canvases tended to "dissolve" into his colors. One evening, upon returning to his studio in Munich, Kandinsky experienced a "revelation" that led him to abandon pictorial subject matter. The incident is described in his *Reminiscences* of 1913:

> I saw an indescribably beautiful picture drenched with an inner glowing. At first I hesitated, then I rushed toward this mysterious picture, of which I saw nothing but forms and colors, and whose content was incomprehensible. Immediately I found the key to the puzzle: it was a picture I had painted, leaning against the wall, standing on its side. . . . Now I knew for certain that the [pictorial] object harmed my paintings.

From this point on, Kandinsky began to assemble colors, lines, and shapes without regard to recognizable objects (Figure **32.16**). He called his nonrepresentational paintings "improvisations" or "abstract compositions" and numbered them in series. In his treatise *Concerning the Spiritual in Art* (1910), he argued that form and color generate meaning without reference to the natural world. "Color can exercise enormous influence upon the body," wrote Kandinsky; it functions to influence mood. Such insights anticipated modern research in chromotherapy, that is, the use of colors and colored light to affect body states. According to Kandinsky, painting was a spiritually liberating force akin to music—he himself was an amateur cellist and friend of many avantgarde composers. "Painting," he proclaimed, "is a thundering collision of different worlds, intended to create a new world."

**Malevich** Kandinsky's Russian contemporary Kasimir Malevich arrived at nonrepresentational art not by way of Fauvism but through the influence of Analytic Cubism, which asserted the value of line over color. Seeking to "free art from the burden of the object" and to rediscover "pure feeling in creative art," Malevich created an austere style limited to the strict geometry of the square, the circle, and the rectangle (Figure **32.17**). Malevich called these shapes "suprematist elements" and his style *Suprematism*. "To the suprematist," wrote Malevich, "the visual phenomena of the objective world are, in themselves, meaningless; the significant thing is feeling . . . quite apart from the environment in which it is called forth." By restricting his art to the arrangement of ideal geometric shapes on the two-dimensional picture plane, Malevich replaced the world of appearance with a language of form as abstract and exacting as that of modern physics.

**Figure 32.16 WASSILY KANDINSKY**, *Panel for Edwin Campbell No. 1*, 1914. Oil on canvas, 5 ft. 4 in. × 3 ft. ¼ in. Kandinsky was among the first of the Modernists to confess indebtness to atomic theory. He urged young artists to study the new physics.

**Figure 32.17 KASIMIR MALEVICH**, *Suprematist Composition: White on White*, 1918. Oil on canvas, 31¼ × 31¼ in.

**Figure 32.18 PIET MONDRIAN**, *Tree,* 1912. Oil on canvas, 29¼ × 43⅞ in. In this early study of a tree, the transition from a realistic depiction to an abstraction is evident. Mondrian finally stripped away all representational associations to arrive at his signature grid patterns. © 2009 Mondrian/Holtzman Trust c/o HCR International Warrenton, Virginia, USA.

***Mondrian*** The early works of the third pioneer of Nonobjective Art, Piet Mondrian, reveal this Dutch artist's inclination to discover geometric order in the landscape of his native country (Figure **32.18**). By 1910, however, he began to strip his canvases of references to recognizable subject matter. Eventually, he limited his visual vocabulary to "pure" forms: rectangles laid out on a grid of horizontal and vertical lines, the three primary colors (red, yellow, and blue), and three values—white, gray, and black (Figure **32.19**). The paring-down process achieved a compositional balance of geometric elements, an "equivalence of opposites" similar to the dynamic equilibrium of an algebraic equation.

Although Mondrian would eventually emigrate to America, the movement he helped to create would continue to flourish. Taking its name from a magazine founded in 1917, it was called simply *De Stijl* ("the Style"). Its Dutch adherents were devoted to the evolution of pure, abstract art: "a direct expression of the universal." Despite differences of opinion among its members—Mondrian resigned in 1925 in opposition to a colleague's use of diagonals—De Stijl was to have worldwide impact, especially in the areas of architecture and furniture design (Figure **32.20**).

The disappearance of the object in early twentieth-century art is often mistakenly associated with the dehumanization of modern life. However, one of the great ironies of the birth of Nonobjective Art is its indebtedness to the mystical and transcendental philosophies that were current in the early Modern Era. One of the most influential of these was

**Figure 32.19 PIET MONDRIAN,**
*Composition with Large Red Plane, Yellow, Black, Gray, and Blue,* 1921. Oil on canvas, 23⅜ × 23⅜ in. © 2009 Mondrian/Holtzman Trust c/o HCR International Warrenton, Virginia, USA.

*theosophy,* a blend of Eastern and Western religions that emphasizes communion with nature by purely spiritual means. Mondrian, a member of the Dutch Theosophical Society, equated spiritual progress with geometric clarity. In his view, the law of equivalence reflected "the true content of reality." "Not only science," wrote Mondrian, "but art also, shows us that reality, at first incomprehensible, gradually reveals itself by the mutual relations that are inherent in things. Pure science and pure art, disinterested and free, can lead the advance in the recognition of the laws which are based on these relationships." The commitment to pure abstraction as the language of spirituality—a commitment central to the careers of Kandinsky, Malevich, and Mondrian—reflects the utopian humanism of those Modernists who perceived their art as a wellspring of social harmony and order.

## Russian Constructivism

While utopian Modernism swept across Europe, one of the most utilitarian of the movements for "pure art" flourished in prerevolutionary Russia. *Constructivism,* which had its roots in both Futurism and the purist teachings of Malevich, advocated the application of geometric abstraction to all forms of social enterprise. Russian Constructivists, who called themselves

**Figure 32.20 GERRIT RIETVELD,** *Red Blue Chair,* 1923. Painted wood, 34⅛ × 26 × 33 in; seat height 13 in.

"artist–engineers," worked to improve the everyday lives of the masses by applying the new abstraction to the industrial arts, theater, film, typography, textile design, and architecture. Liubov Popova (1889–1924), one of the many talented female advocates of this movement, designed stage sets and costumes for the Russian theater (Figure **32.21**), thus putting into practice the Constructivist motto "Art into production." Like other Modernists, the Constructivists worked to break down the barriers between fine and applied art, but unlike any other modern art movement, Constructivism received official state sanction. Following the Russian Revolution, however, the Soviet Union would bring about its demise, almost obliterating Russia's most innovative contribution to twentieth-century Modernism (see chapter 34).

## Early Twentieth-Century Architecture

The revolution in visual abstraction found monumental expression in architecture. Early modern architects made energetic use of two new materials—structural steel and **ferroconcrete**—in combination with **cantilever** construction.

The cantilever, a horizontal beam supported at only one end and projecting well beyond the point of support, had first appeared in the timber buildings of China (see chapter 14); but the manufacture of the structural steel cantilever ushered in a style whose austere simplicity had no precedents. That style was inaugurated by Frank Lloyd Wright (1869–1959), the leading figure in the history of early modern architecture.

### The Architecture of Wright

Frank Lloyd Wright, the first American architect of world significance, was the foremost student of the Chicago architect Louis Sullivan (see chapter 30). Wright's style combined the new technology of steel and glass with the aesthetic principles of Asian architecture. Wright visited Japan when he was in his thirties and was impressed by the grace and purity of Japanese art. He especially admired the respect for natural materials and the sensitivity to the relationship between setting and structure that characterized traditional Japanese architecture (see chapter 14). In his earliest domestic commissions, Wright embraced the East Asian principle of horizontality, by which the building might hug the earth. He imitated the low, steeply pitched

**Figure 32.21 LIUBOV POPOVA**, set design for Fernand Crommelynk, *Le Cocu magnifique*, State Institute of Theatrical Art, Moscow, 1922. Gouache on paper, 19½ × 27 in.

**Figure 32.22 FRANK LLOYD WRIGHT**, Robie House, Chicago, Illinois, 1909. Brick, glass, natural rock.

roofs of Japanese pavilions and temples. From Japanese interiors, where walls often consist of movable screens, Wright borrowed the idea of interconnecting interior and exterior space. He used the structural steel frame and the cantilever to create large areas of uninterrupted space. In every one of Wright's designs, the exterior of the structure reflects the major divisions of its interior space. Wright refined this formula in a series of innovative homes in the American Midwest, pioneering the so-called "Prairie School" of architecture that lasted from roughly 1900 until World War I.

The classic creation of Wright's early career was the Robie House in Chicago, completed in 1909 (Figure **32.22**). The three-story house marks the first use of welded steel beams in residential construction. Making the fireplace the center of the architectural plan, Wright crossed the long main axis of the house with counteraxes of low cantilevered roofs that push out into space over terraces

and verandas. He subordinated decorative details to the overall design, allowing his materials—brick, glass, and natural rock—to assume major roles in establishing the unique character of the structure. As Wright insisted, "To use any material wrongly is to abuse the integrity of the whole design." The result was a style consisting of crisp, interlocking planes, contrasting textures, and interpenetrating solids and voids—a domestic architecture that was as abstract and dynamic as an Analytic Cubist painting. Wright's use of the cantilever and his integration of landscape and house reached new imaginative heights in Fallingwater, the residence he designed in 1936 for the American businessman Edgar J. Kaufmann at Bear Run, Pennsylvania (Figure **32.23**). Embracing a natural waterfall, the ferroconcrete and stone structure seems to grow organically out of the natural wooded setting, yet dominates that setting by its pristine equilibrium.

**Figure 32.23 FRANK LLOYD WRIGHT**, Fallingwater, Kaufmann House, Bear Run, Pennsylvania, 1936–1939. Reinforced concrete, stone, masonry, steel-framed doors and windows, enclosed area 5800 sq. ft. Wright rejected the machinelike qualities of International Style architecture. At Fallingwater, he made use of the local stone, integrating the cascading waters and local stream into the design.

## The Bauhaus and the International Style

Wright's synthesis of art and technology anticipated the establishment of the *Bauhaus*, Modernism's most influential school of architecture and applied art. Founded in 1919 by the German architect and visionary Walter Gropius (1883–1969), the Bauhaus pioneered an instructional program that united the technology of the Machine Age with the purest principles of functional design. Throughout its brief history (1919–1933), and despite its frequent relocation (from Weimar to Dessau, and finally Berlin), the Bauhaus advocated a close relationship between the function of an object and its formal design, whether in furniture, lighting fixtures, typography, photography, industrial products, or architecture.

Bauhaus instructors had little regard for traditional academic styles; they endorsed the new synthetic materials of modern technology, a stark simplicity of design, and the standardization of parts for affordable, mass-produced merchandise, as well as for large-scale housing. Some of Europe's leading artists, including Kandinsky and Mondrian, taught at the Bauhaus. Like Gropius, these artists envisioned a new industrial society liberated by the principle of abstraction. They shared with the Russian Constructivists the utopian belief in the power of the arts to transform society. When the Nazis closed down the school in 1933, many of its finest instructors, such as the photographer László Moholy-Nagy, architect and designer Marcel Breuer, and artist Josef Albers, emigrated to the United States, where they exercised tremendous influence on the development of American architecture and industrial art. (In 1929, a group of wealthy Americans had already established the first international collection of modern art: New York City's Museum of Modern Art.)

Under the direction of Gropius, the Bauhaus launched the *International Style* in architecture, which brought to the marriage of structural steel, ferroconcrete, and sheet glass a formal precision and geometric austerity resembling a Mondrian painting (see Figure 32.19). In the four-story glass building Gropius designed to serve as the Bauhaus craft shops in Dessau, unadorned curtain walls of glass (which meet uninterrupted at the corners of the structure) were freely suspended on structural steel cantilevers (Figure 32.24). This fusion of functional space and minimal structure produced a purist style that paralleled the abstract trends in poetry, painting, and sculpture discussed earlier in this chapter.

### Le Corbusier

The revolutionary Swiss architect and town planner Charles-Edouard Jeanneret (1887–1965), who called himself Le Corbusier (a pun on the word "raven"), was not directly affiliated with the Bauhaus, but he shared Gropius' fundamental concern for efficiency of design, standardization of building techniques, and the promotion of low-cost housing. In 1923, Le Corbusier wrote the treatise *Towards a New Architecture*, in which he proposed that

**Figure 32.24 WALTER GROPIUS**, workshop wing, Bauhaus Building, Dessau, Germany, 1925–1926. Steel and glass.

**Figure 32.25 LE CORBUSIER**, Villa Savoye, Poissy, France, 1928–1929. Ferroconcrete and glass. The house illustrates the five principles for domestic architecture laid out by Le Corbusier in 1923: 1) elevation above the ground, 2) the flat roof, 3) the open floor plan, 4) exterior curtain walls, and 5) horizontal bands of windows.

modern architectural principles should imitate the efficiency of the machine. "Machines," he predicted, "will lead to a new order both of work and of leisure." Just as form follows function in the design of airplanes, automobiles, and machinery in general, so it must in modern domestic architecture. Le Corbusier was fond of insisting that "the house is a machine for living [in]." With utopian fervor he urged,

> We must create the mass-production spirit.
> The spirit of constructing mass-production houses.
> The spirit of living in mass-production houses.
> The spirit of conceiving mass-production houses.
>
> If we eliminate from our hearts and minds all dead concepts in regard to the house, and look at the question from a critical and objective point of view, we shall arrive at the "House-Machine," the mass-production house, healthy (and morally so too) and beautiful in the same way that the working tools and instruments that accompany our existence are beautiful.

In the Villa Savoye, a residence located outside of Paris at Poissy, Le Corbusier put these revolutionary concepts to work (Figure **32.25**). The residence, now considered a "classic" of the International Style, consists of simple and unadorned masses of ferroconcrete punctured by ribbon windows. It is raised above the ground on *pilotis*, pillars that free the ground area of the site. (More recently, architects have abused the pilotis principle to create parking space for automobiles.) The Villa Savoye features a number of favorite Le Corbusier devices, such as the roof garden, the open floor plan that allows one to close off or open up space according to varying needs, and the free façade that consists of large areas of glass—so-called "curtain walls."

Le Corbusier's genius for fitting form to function led, during the 1930s, to his creation of the first high-rise urban apartment buildings—structures that housed more than a thousand people and consolidated facilities for shopping, recreation, and child care under a single roof (Figure **32.26**). These "vertical cities," as stripped of decorative details as the sculptures of Brancusi, have become hallmarks of urban Modernism.

**Figure 32.26 LE CORBUSIER**, Unité d'Habitation apartment block, Marseilles, France, 1946–1952.

# Early Twentieth-Century Music

The music of the early twentieth century shared the Modernist assault on tradition, and most dramatically so in the areas of tonality and meter. Until the late nineteenth century, most music was tonal; that is, structured on a single key or tonal center. However, by the second decade of the twentieth century, musical compositions might be **polytonal** (having several tonal centers) or **atonal** (without a tonal center). Further, instead of following a single meter, a modern composition might be **polyrhythmic** (having two or more different meters at the same time), or (as with Imagist poems) it might obey no fixed or regular metrical pattern.

Modern composers tended to reject conventional modes of expression, including traditional harmonies and instrumentation. Melody—like recognizable subject matter in painting—became of secondary importance to formal composition. Modernists invented no new forms comparable to the fugue or the sonata; rather, they explored innovative effects based on dissonance, the free use of meter, and the inventive combination of musical instruments, some of which they borrowed from non-Western cultures. They employed unorthodox sources of sound, such as sirens, bullhorns, and doorbells. Some incorporated silence in their compositions, much as Cubist sculptors introduced negative space into mass. The results were as startling to the ear as Cubism was to the eye.

## Schoenberg

The most radical figure in early twentieth-century music was the Austrian composer Arnold Schoenberg (1874–1951). Schoenberg was born in Vienna, the city of Mozart and Beethoven. He learned to play the violin at the age of eight and began composing music in his late teens. Schoenberg's first compositions were conceived in the romantic tradition, but by 1909 he began to develop a new musical language punctuated by dissonant and unfamiliar chords. Instead of organizing tones around a home key (the tonal center) in the time-honored tradition of Western musical composition, he treated all twelve notes of the chromatic scale equally. Schoenberg's atonal works use abrupt changes in rhythm, tone color, and dynamics—features evidenced in his expressionistic song cycle *Pierrot Lunaire* (*Moonstruck Pierrot*; see also chapter 33) and in his *Five Pieces for Orchestra*, Opus 16, both written in 1912. In the former work, which one critic described as "incomprehensible as a Tibetan poem," the instruments produce a succession of individual, contrasting tones that, like the Nonobjective canvases of his good friend Kandinsky, resist harmony and resolution.

During the 1920s, Schoenberg went on to formulate a unifying system for atonal composition based on **serial technique**. His type of *serialism*, called the **"twelve-tone system,"** demanded that the composer use all twelve tones of the chromatic scale either melodically or in chords before any one of the other eleven notes might be repeated. The twelve-tone row might be inverted or played upside down or backwards—there are actually forty-eight possible musical combinations for each tone row. Serialism, like quantum theory or Mondrian's "equivalence of opposites," involved the strategic use of a sparse and elemental language of form. It engaged the composer in a rigidly formulaic (even mathematical) disposition of musical elements. In theory, the serial technique invited creative invention rather than mechanical application. Nevertheless, to the average listener, who could no longer leave the concert hall humming a melody, Schoenberg's atonal compositions seemed forbidding and obscure.

See Music Listening Selections at end of chapter.

## Stravinsky

In 1913, the same year Ezra Pound issued his *Imagist Manifesto* and Malevich and Kandinsky painted their first Nonobjective canvases—a Paris audience witnessed the premiere of the ballet *Le Sacre du printemps* (*The Rite of Spring*). The piece was performed by the Ballets Russes, a company of expatriate Russian dancers led by Sergei Diaghilev (1872–1929), and the music was written by the Russian composer Igor Stravinsky (1882–1971; Figure **32.27**). Shortly after the music began, catcalls, hissing, and booing disrupted the performance, as members of the audience protested the "shocking" sounds that were coming from the orchestra. By the time the police arrived, Stravinsky had disappeared through a backstage window. What offended this otherwise sophisticated audience was Stravinsky's bold combination of throbbing rhythms and dissonant harmonies, which, along with the jarring effects of a new style in choreography, ushered in the birth of modern music.

Stravinsky was one of the most influential figures in the history of twentieth-century music. Like Schoenberg, he began to study music at a young age. His family pressed him to pursue a career in law, but Stravinsky was intent on becoming a composer. At the age of twenty-eight, he left Russia for Paris, where he joined the Ballets Russes. Allied with some of the greatest artists of the time, including Picasso, the writer Jean Cocteau, and the choreographer Vaslav Nijinsky (1888–1950), Stravinsky was instrumental in making the Ballets Russes a leading force in modern dance theater. His influence on American music was equally great, especially after 1939, when he moved permanently to the United States.

Russian folk tales and songs provided inspiration for many of Stravinsky's early compositions, including *The Rite of Spring*. Subtitled *Pictures from Pagan Russia*, this landmark piece was based on an ancient Slavonic ceremony that invoked the birth of spring with the ritual sacrifice of a young girl. The themes of death and resurrection associated with traditional pagan celebrations of seasonal change provided the structure of the suite, which was divided into two parts: "The Fertility of the Earth" and "The Sacrifice." Like Picasso and Gauguin, Stravinsky was captivated by primitivism; he shared the fascination with ancient rituals and tribal culture that had gripped late nineteenth-century Europe (see chapter 31). These subjects were popularized by Sir James Frazer in his widely acclaimed book, *The Golden Bough* (1890), which had been reissued in twelve volumes between 1911 and 1915.

*The Rite of Spring* is a pastoral piece, but its music lacks the calm grace traditionally associated with that genre. Its harsh chordal combinations and jarring shifts of meter set it apart from earlier pastorals, such as Debussy's *Prelude to the Afternoon of a Faun*. While Debussy's tonal shifts are

**Figure 32.27 PABLO PICASSO**, *Igor Stravinsky*, 1920. Drawing. Picasso, a master draftsman, was capable of switching from one style to another with great ease. Even as he executed drawings like this one, he was painting abstract canvases in the Synthetic Cubist style.

as subtle and nuanced as a Monet seascape, Stravinsky's are as abrupt and disjunctive as Picasso's *Demoiselles*, so disjunctive, in fact, that critics questioned whether the composer was capable of writing conventional musical transitions. Although not atonal, portions of the composition are polytonal, while other passages are ambiguous in tonality, especially in the opening sections. If the shifting tonalities and pounding rhythms of the piece were "savage," as critics claimed, so too were its orchestral effects: Stravinsky's unorthodox scoring calls for eighteen woodwind instruments, eighteen brass instruments, and a *quiro* (a Latin American gourd that is scraped with a wooden stick). *The Rite* had an impact on twentieth-century music comparable to that of *Les Demoiselles d'Avignon* on the visual arts. It shattered the syntax of traditional musical language with a force similar to that which this painting had attacked traditional pictorial norms. It rewrote the rules of musical composition as they had been practiced for centuries. No greater assault on tradition could have been imagined at the time.

# The Beginnings of Modern Dance

## Nijinsky

Only a year after his daring performance in Debussy's *Afternoon of a Faun* (see chapter 31), Vaslav Nijinsky aroused even greater controversy with his choreography for *The Rite of Spring*. He took the raw, rhythmic complexity of Stravinsky's score as inspiration for a series of frenzied leaps and wild, wheeling rounds that shocked the audience— and even disturbed Stravinsky. "They paw the ground, they stamp, they stamp, they stamp, and they stamp," complained one French critic. Like *The Rite* itself, such choreography seemed to express what the critics called "the hidden primitive in man." Interestingly enough, some of Nijinsky's body movements—angular, disjunctive, and interrupted by frozen stillness (see Figure 31.2)—were reminiscent of Cubist paintings. Tragically, Nijinsky's career came to an end in 1917, when he became incurably insane. In his ten years as the West's first dance superstar, Nijinsky choreographed only four ballets; and not until 1987 was his most famous ballet, *The Rite of Spring*, revived for the American stage.

## Graham

The innovative character of early modern dance owed much to the pioneer American choreographer Martha Graham (1894–1991). Following Isadora Duncan (see chapter 31) and Nijinsky, Graham rejected the rules and conventions of classical ballet, preferring to explore the expressive power of natural movement. Drawing on the dance traditions of Asia, Africa, and Native America, she sought a direct correspondence between intangible emotions and physical gesture. Much of her choreography, such as that produced for Aaron Copland's 1944 ballet suite, *Appalachian Spring*, was the visual narrative for a specific story (see chapter 34). Just as the Imagists arranged words to convey an emotional "shape" or sensation, so Graham found definitive gestures to express ineffable states of mind. Her dancers were trained to expose the process and techniques of dancing, rather than to conceal displays of physical effort, as was expected in classical dance.

### Balanchine

In contrast with Graham, George Balanchine (1904–1983) developed a dance idiom that was storyless, abstract, and highly structured. Balanchine was a Russian choreographer who spent his early career in Paris with Diaghilev's Ballets Russes. He was deeply influenced by the musical innovations of his friend and compatriot, Igor Stravinsky, with whom he often collaborated—Stravinsky wrote the scores for at least four of his ballets.

Balanchine prized musically driven dance and pure artistic form. Loyal to the 350-year-old idiom of classical ballet, he insisted on rigorous academic dance training and the use of traditional toe-shoes. However, he rejected the dance-drama vocabulary of former centuries, preferring a Modernist energy that emphasized speed and verve. His choreography, according to one critic, "pushed dance into the space age." In 1934, Balanchine was persuaded to come to the United States, where he helped to found the School of American Ballet.

### Dunham

The development of modern dance owes much to the genius of Katharine Dunham (1909–2006). The "Mother of Black Dance," Dunham was both a choreographer and a trained anthropologist. Her doctoral work at the university of Chicago investigated the vast resources of the black heritage, ranging from African-American slave dances to the dance histories of the Caribbean. Her choreography drew on the dance styles of the late nineteenth century, when all-black theatrical companies and minstrel shows toured the United States. Freely improvising on tap-dance styles and on popular American dances such as the high-stepping cakewalk, she would, in her later career (see chapter 36) give serious attention to the dance idioms of native societies in Haiti and Trinidad. In the 1930s, she formed her own company—the first, and for some thirty years, the only black dance company in America.

## LOOKING BACK

### The New Physics

- During the first decades of the twentieth century, quantum physicists provided a new model of the universe. Albert Einstein theorized that matter is a form of energy, and time and space are relative to the position of the observer. Werner Heisenberg concluded that the operations of the universe cannot be measured with absolute certainty.
- Revolutionary changes in science and technology provided the context for the Modernist assault on traditional modes of expression.

### Early Twentieth-Century Poetry

- Modern poets moved away from Romanticism to adopt a conceptual and abstract literary style. The poems of the Imagists demonstrated a reduction of form that overtook naturalism and realistic representation.

- Led by Ezra Pound, the Imagists used free verse in the concentrated style of the Japanese *haiku*. Pound called on writers to "make it new" by eliminating all extraneous expression from their poems.
- T. S. Eliot's *Prufrock* conveys the spiritual condition of the modern urban antihero in erudite free verse. Robert Frost's straightforward, metered lyrics provided an alternative to the Modernist taste for dense literary allusions.

### Early Twentieth-Century Art

- Picasso assaulted tradition with the landmark painting *Les Demoiselles d'Avignon,* which led the way to Cubism. Inspired by the works of Cézanne and by African art, Picasso, Braque, and Brancusi pursued the concentrated reduction of form.
- In Italy Futurists linked artistic expression to the machine technology of speed, electric lighting, and the new phenomenon of moving pictures.

- Matisse led the Fauves in employing flat bright colors for canvases that critics condemned as "color madness."
- With Kandinsky, Malevich, and Mondrian, painting freed itself entirely of recognizable objects. These artists shared a utopian faith in the reforming power of purist, Nonobjective Art.
- A more practical application of Nonobjective abstraction was undertaken by the Russian Constructivists, who applied purist design to functional products, including industrial arts, theater sets, textile design, typography, and architecture.

## Early Twentieth-Century Architecture

- Frank Lloyd Wright invested the techniques of glass and steel technology and the functional principle of the cantilever with the aesthetics of Japanese art to create a modern style of domestic architecture.
- Gropius, founder of the Bauhaus in Germany, established a program of functional design that featured the use of new synthetic materials and the pursuit of geometric austerity in art and architecture. Bauhaus instructors provided the models for modern industrial design.
- Le Corbusier, pioneer of the vertical city, developed the International Style, which proclaimed the credo: form follows function. Insisting that "the house is a machine for living [in]," Le Corbusier introduced some of the classic elements of modern urban architecture, including the open floor plan, the flat roof, and the use of glass "curtain walls."

## Early Twentieth-Century Music

- Arnold Schoenberg and Igor Stravinsky introduced atonality, polytonality, and polyrhythm as formal alternatives to the time-honored Western traditions of pleasing harmonies and uniform meter.

- Schoenberg, who started working in traditional forms, turned to atonality with a serial technique known as the "twelve-tone system," by which the composer makes use of all twelve tones on the chromatic scale before repeating any one of the other tones.
- As a powerful form of disjunctive expression, Stravinsky's *The Rite of Spring* had an effect on musical composition equivalent to that of *Les Demoiselles d'Avignon* on painting.

## The Beginnings of Modern Dance

- The Russian dancer Vaslav Nijinsky followed the call to "make it new" with wild and frenzied choreography that broke with the traditions of academic dance.
- America's Martha Graham, who studied the dance history of other cultures, emphasized expressive natural movement to reflect human emotions in her choreography.
- Working closely with Stravinsky, Balanchine created non-narrative ballets that invested Modernist abstraction with rigorous academic dance training.
- The first black dance company was founded by Katharine Dunham who was strongly influenced by popular American dance styles and by the dance traditions of Haiti and Trinidad.

## Music Listening Selections

**CD Two Selection 17** Schoenberg, *Pierrot Lunaire*, Op. 21, Part 3, No. 15, "Heimweh," 1912.

**CD Two Selection 18** Stravinsky, *The Rite of Spring*, "Sacrificial Dance," 1913, excerpt.

# Glossary

**abstraction** the process by which subject matter is pared down or simplified in order to capture intrinsic or essential qualities; also, any work of art that reflects this process

**assemblage** an artwork composed of three-dimensional objects, either natural or manufactured; the sculptural counterpart of collage

**atonality** in music, the absence of a tonal center or definite key

**avant-garde** (French, "vanguard") those who create or produce styles and ideas ahead

of their time; also, an unconventional movement or style

**cantilever** a projecting beam firmly anchored at one end and unsupported at the other

**collage** (French, *coller*, "to paste") a composition created by pasting materials such as newspaper, wallpaper, photographs, or cloth on a flat surface or canvas

**ferroconcrete** a cement building material reinforced by embedding wire or iron rods; also called "reinforced concrete"

*haiku* a Japanese light verse form consisting of seventeen syllables (three lines of five, seven, and five)

**Nonobjective Art** art that lacks recognizable subject matter; also called "nonrepresentational art"

**polyrhythm** in music, the device of using two or more different rhythms at the same time; also known as "polymeter"

**polytonality** in music, the simultaneous use of multiple tonal centers or keys; for compositions using only

two tonal centers, the word "bitonality" applies

**serial technique** in music, a technique that involves the use of a particular series of notes, rhythms, and other elements that are repeated over and over throughout the piece

**twelve-tone system** a kind of serial music that demands the use of all twelve notes of the chromatic scale (all twelve half-tones in an octave) in a particular order or series; no one note can be used again until all eleven have appeared

# Chapter

# 33

## The Freudian Revolution
### ca. 1900–1950

*"Only children, madmen, and savages truly understand the 'in-between' world of spiritual truth."*
Paul Klee

**Figure 33.1 PAUL KLEE**, *Fish Magic*, 1925. Oil on canvas, mounted on board, 30⅜ × 3 ft. 2½ in. This pictorial fairy tale may have been inspired by Klee's visit to an aquarium in Naples, Italy. Describing his style, Klee wrote, "My aim is to create much spirituality out of little."

# LOOKING AHEAD

No figure in modern Western history has had more influence on our perception of ourselves than Sigmund Freud. This brilliant physician rocked the modern West with writings that opened the subjects of human sexuality and behavior to public discourse and debate. He was the first to map the geography of the *psyche* (mind), making it the object of methodical, scientific research. Freud's theories suggested that the conscious self was only a small part of one's psychical life. He presented a radical model of the human mind that would resonate through the arts of the twentieth century, affecting literature and theater, music and the visual arts, including the new medium of film.

While Freud himself believed as firmly as any Enlightenment *philosophe* in the reforming power of reason, his model of the unconscious challenged the supremacy of reason itself. Copernicus had dislodged human beings from their central place in the cosmos; Darwin had deposed *Homo sapiens* from his privileged status as God's ultimate creation; now Freud, uncovering the mysterious realm of the unconscious, challenged the long-standing belief that reason was the fundamental monitor of human behavior.

# Freud

Sigmund Freud (1856–1939) graduated in medicine from the university of Vienna in 1880. His early work with severely disturbed patients, followed by a period of intensive self-analysis, led him to develop a systematic procedure for treating emotional illnesses. The founder of psychoanalysis, a therapeutic method by which repressed desires are brought to the conscious level to reveal the sources of emotional disturbance, Freud pioneered its principal tools: dream analysis and "free association" (the spontaneous verbalization of thoughts). He favored these techniques over hypnosis, the procedure preferred by notable physicians with whom he had studied.

Freud theorized that instinctual drives, especially the libido, or sex drive, governed human behavior. Guilt from the repression of instinctual urges dominates the unconscious life of human beings and manifests itself in emotional illness. Most psychic disorders, he argued, were the result of sexual traumas stemming from the child's unconscious attachment to the parent of the opposite sex and jealousy of the parent of the same sex, a phenomenon Freud called the Oedipus complex (in reference to the ancient Greek legend in which Oedipus, king of Thebes, unwittingly kills his father and marries his mother). Freud shocked the world with his analysis of infant sexuality and, more generally, with his claim that the psychic lives of human beings were formed by the time they were five years old.

Of all his discoveries, Freud considered his research on dream analysis the most important. In 1900 he published *The Interpretation of Dreams*, in which he defended the significance of dreams in deciphering the unconscious life of the individual. In *Totem and Taboo* (1913), he examined the function of the unconscious in the evolution of the earliest forms of religion and morality. And in "The Sexual Life of Human Beings," a lecture presented to medical students at the university of Vienna in 1916, he examined the psychological roots of sadism, homosexuality, fetishism, and voyeurism—subjects still considered taboo in some social circles. Freud's theories opened the door to the clinical appraisal of previously guarded types of human behavior. By bringing attention to the central place of erotic desire in human life, his writings irrevocably altered popular attitudes toward human sexuality. His work also had a major impact on the treatment of the mentally ill. Until at least the eighteenth century, people generally regarded psychotic behavior as evidence of possession by demonic or evil spirits, and the mentally ill were often locked up like animals. Freud's studies argued that neuroses and psychoses were illnesses that required medical treatment.

## The Tripartite Psyche

In describing the activities of the human mind, Freud proposed a theoretical model, the terms of which (though often oversimplified and misunderstood) have become basic to *psychology* (the study of mind and behavior) and fundamental to our everyday vocabulary. This model pictures the psyche as consisting of three parts: the *id*, the *ego*, and the *superego*. The id, according to Freud, is the seat of human instincts and the source of all physical desires, including nourishment and sexual satisfaction. Seeking fulfillment in accordance with the pleasure principle, the id (and in particular the libido) is the compelling force of the unconscious realm.

Freud described the second part of the psyche, the ego, as the administrator of the id: the ego is the "manager" that attempts to adapt the needs of the id to the real world. Whether by dreams or by **sublimation** (the positive modification and redirection of primal urges), the ego mediates between potentially destructive desires and social necessities. In Freud's view, civilization is the product of the ego's effort to modify the primal urges of the id. The third agent in the psychic life of the human being, the superego, is the moral monitor commonly called the "conscience." The superego monitors human behavior according to principles inculcated by parents, teachers, and other authority figures.

## *Civilization and Its Discontents*

By challenging reason as the governor of human action, Freud questioned the very nature of human morality. He described benevolent action and altruistic conduct as mere masks for self-gratification, and religion as a form of mass delusion. Such views were central to the essay *Civilization and Its Discontents*, in which Freud explored at length the relationship between psychic activity and human society. Enumerating the various ways in which all human beings attempt to escape the "pain and unpleasure" of life, Freud argued that civilization itself was the collective product of sublimated instincts. The greatest impediment to civilization, he claimed, was human aggression, which he defined as "an original, self-subsisting instinctual disposition in man." The following excerpts offer some idea of Freud's incisive analysis of the psychic life of human beings.

## READING 33.1 From Freud's *Civilization and Its Discontents* (1930)

We will . . . turn to the less ambitious question of what men themselves show by their behavior to be the purpose and intention of their lives. What do they demand of life and wish to achieve in it? The answer to this can hardly be in doubt. They strive after happiness; they want to become happy and to remain so. This endeavor has two sides, a positive and a negative aim. It aims, on the one hand, at an absence of pain and unpleasure, and, on the other, at the experiencing of strong feelings of pleasure. In its narrower sense the word "happiness" only relates to the last. In conformity with this **10** dichotomy in his aims, man's activity develops in two directions, according as it seeks to realize—in the main, or even exclusively—the one or the other of these aims.

As we see, what decides the purpose of life is simply the programme of the pleasure principle. This principle dominates the operation of the mental apparatus from the start. There can be no doubt about its efficacy, and yet its programme is at loggerheads with the whole world, with the macrocosm as much as with the microcosm. There is no possibility at all of its being carried through; all the regulations of the universe **20** run counter to it. One feels inclined to say that the intention that man should be "happy" is not included in the plan of "Creation." What we call happiness in the strictest sense comes from the (preferably sudden) satisfaction of needs which have been dammed up to a high degree, and it is from its nature only possible as an episodic phenomenon. When any situation that is desired by the pleasure principle is prolonged, it only produces a feeling of mild contentment. We are so made that we can derive intense enjoyment only from a contrast and very little from a state of things. Thus our **30** possibilities of happiness are already restricted by our constitution. Unhappiness is much less difficult to experience. We are threatened with suffering from three directions: from our own body, which is doomed to decay and dissolution and which cannot even do without pain and anxiety as warning signals; from the external world, which may rage against us with overwhelming and merciless forces of destruction; and finally from our relations to other men. The suffering which comes from this last source is perhaps more painful to us than any other. We tend to regard it as a kind of gratuitous **40** addition, although it cannot be any less fatefully inevitable than the suffering which comes from elsewhere. . . .

An unrestricted satisfaction of every need presents itself as the most enticing method of conducting one's life, but it means putting enjoyment before caution, and soon brings its own punishment. The other methods in which avoidance of

unpleasure is the main purpose, are differentiated according to the source of unpleasure to which their attention is chiefly turned. Some of these methods are extreme and some moderate; some are one-sided and some attack the problem **50** simultaneously at several points. Against the suffering which may come upon one from human relationships the readiest safeguard is voluntary isolation, keeping oneself aloof from other people. The happiness which can be achieved along this path is, as we see, the happiness of quietness. Against the dreaded external world one can only defend oneself by some kind of turning away from it, if one intends to solve the task by oneself. There is, indeed, another and better path: that of becoming a member of the human community, and, with the help of a technique guided by science, going over to the attack **60** against nature and subjecting her to the human will. Then one is working with all for the good of all. But the most interesting methods of averting suffering are those which seek to influence our own organism. In the last analysis, all suffering is nothing else than sensation; it only exists in so far as we feel it, and we only feel it in consequence of certain ways in which our organism is regulated.

The crudest, but also the most effective among these methods of influence is the chemical one—intoxication. I do not think that anyone completely understands its mechanism, **70** but it is a fact that there are foreign substances which, when present in the blood or tissues, directly cause us pleasurable sensations; and they also so alter the conditions governing our sensibility that we become incapable of receiving unpleasurable impulses. The two effects not only occur simultaneously, but seem to be intimately bound up with each other. But there must be substances in the chemistry of our own bodies which have similar effects, for we know at least one pathological state, mania, in which a condition similar to intoxication arises without the administration of any **80** intoxicating drug. Besides this, our normal mental life exhibits oscillations between a comparatively easy liberation of pleasure and a comparatively difficult one, parallel with which there goes a diminished or an increased receptivity to unpleasure. It is greatly to be regretted that this toxic side of mental processes has so far escaped scientific examination. The service rendered by intoxicating media in the struggle for happiness and in keeping misery at a distance is so highly prized as a benefit that individuals and people alike have given them an established place in the economics of their **90** libido.[1] We owe to such media not merely the immediate yield of pleasure, but also a greatly desired degree of independence from the external world. For one knows that, with the help of this "drowner of cares," one can at any time withdraw from the pressure of reality and find refuge in a world of one's own with better conditions of sensibility. As is well known, it is precisely this property of intoxicants which also determines their danger and their injuriousness. They are responsible, in certain circumstances, for the useless waste of a large quota of energy which might have been employed for the **100** improvement of the human lot. . . .

---

[1] The instinctual desires of the id, most specifically, the sexual urge.

Another technique for fending off suffering is the employment of the displacements of libido which our mental apparatus permits of and through which its function gains so much in flexibility. The task here is that of shifting the instinctual aims in such a way that they cannot come up against frustration from the external world. In this, sublimation of the instincts lends its assistance. One gains the most if one can sufficiently heighten the yield of pleasure from the sources of psychical and intellectual work. When that is so, fate can do little against one. A satisfaction of this kind, such as an artist's joy in creating, in giving his phantasies body, or a scientist's in solving problems or discovering truths, has a special quality which we shall certainly one day be able to characterize in metapsychological terms. At present we can only say figuratively that such satisfactions seem "finer and higher." But their intensity is mild as compared with that derived from the sating of crude and primary instinctual impulses; it does not convulse our physical being. And the weak point of this method is that it is not applicable generally: it is accessible to only a few people. It presupposes the possession of special dispositions and gifts which are far from being common to any practical degree. And even to the few who do possess them, this method cannot give complete protection from suffering. It creates no impenetrable armor against the arrows of fortune, and it habitually fails when the source of suffering is a person's own body. . . .

Another procedure operates more energetically and more thoroughly. It regards reality as the sole enemy and as the source of all suffering, with which it is impossible to live, so that one must break off all relations with it if one is to be in any way happy. The hermit turns his back on the world and will have no truck with it. But one can do more than that; one can try to re-create the world, to build up in its stead another world in which its most unbearable features are eliminated and replaced by others that are in conformity with one's own wishes. But whoever, in desperate defiance, sets out upon this path to happiness will as a rule attain nothing. Reality is too strong for him. He becomes a madman, who for the most part finds no one to help him in carrying through his delusion. It is asserted, however, that each one of us behaves in some one respect like a paranoiac, corrects some aspect of the world which is unbearable to him by the construction of a wish and introduces this delusion into reality. A special importance attaches to the case in which this attempt to procure a certainty of happiness and a protection against suffering through a delusional remoulding of reality is made by a considerable number of people in common. The religions of mankind must be classed among the mass-delusions of this kind. No one, needless to say, who shares a delusion ever recognizes it as such. . . .

Religion restricts this play of choice and adaptation, since it imposes equally on everyone its own path to the acquisition of happiness and protection from suffering. Its technique consists in depressing the value of life and distorting the picture of the real world in a delusional manner—which presupposes an intimidation of the intelligence. At this price, by forcibly fixing them in a state of psychical infantilism and by drawing them into a mass-delusion, religion succeeds in sparing many people an individual neurosis. But hardly anything more. . . .

During the last few generations mankind has made an extraordinary advance in the natural sciences and in their technical application and has established his control over nature in a way never before imagined. The single steps of this advance are common knowledge and it is unnecessary to enumerate them. Men are proud of those achievements, and have a right to be. But they seem to have observed that this newly-won power over space and time, this subjugation of the forces of nature, which is the fulfillment of a longing that goes back thousands of years, has not increased the amount of pleasurable satisfaction which they may expect from life and has not made them feel happier. From the recognition of this fact we ought to be content to conclude that power over nature is not the *only* precondition of human happiness, just as it is not the *only* goal of cultural endeavor; we ought not to infer from it that technical progress is without value for the economics of our happiness. One would like to ask: is there, then, no positive gain in pleasure, no unequivocal increase in my feeling of happiness, if I can, as often as I please, hear the voice of a child of mine who is living hundreds of miles away or if I can learn in the shortest possible time after a friend has reached his destination that he has come through the long and difficult voyage unharmed? Does it mean nothing that medicine has succeeded in enormously reducing infant mortality and the danger of infection for women in childbirth and, indeed, in considerably lengthening the average life of a civilized man? And there is a long list that might be added to benefits of this kind which we owe to the much-despised era of scientific and technical advances. But here the voice of pessimistic criticism makes itself heard and warns us that most of these satisfactions follow the model of the "cheap enjoyment" extolled in the anecdote—the enjoyment obtained by putting a bare leg from under the bedclothes on a cold winter night and drawing it in again. If there had been no railway to conquer distances, my child would never have left his native town and I should need no telephone to hear his voice; if travelling across the ocean by ship had not been introduced, my friend would not have embarked on his sea-voyage and I should not need a cable to relieve my anxiety about him. What is the use of reducing infantile mortality when it is precisely that reduction which imposes the greatest restraint on us in the begetting of children, so that, taken all round, we nevertheless rear no more children than in the days before the reign of hygiene, while at the same time we have created difficult conditions for our sexual life in marriage, and have probably worked against the beneficial effects of natural selection? And, finally, what good to us is a long life if it is difficult and barren of joys, and if it is so full of misery that we can only welcome death as a deliverer? . . .

. . . men are not gentle creatures who want to be loved, and who at the most can defend themselves if they are attacked; they are, on the contrary, creatures among whose instinctual endowments is to be reckoned a powerful share of aggressiveness. As a result, their neighbor is for them not only a potential helper or sexual object, but also someone who tempts them to satisfy their aggressiveness on him, to exploit his capacity for work without compensation, to use him sexually without his consent, to seize his possessions, to humiliate him, to cause him pain, to torture and to kill him. . . .

The existence of this inclination to aggression, which we **220** can detect in ourselves and justly assume to be present in others, is the factor which disturbs our relations with our neighbor and which forces civilization into such a high expenditure [of energy]. In consequence of this primary mutual hostility of human beings, civilized society is perpetually threatened with disintegration. The interest of work in common would not hold it together; instinctual passions are stronger than reasonable interests. Civilization has to use its utmost efforts in order to set limits to man's aggressive instincts and to hold the manifestations of them in check by **230** psychical reaction-formations. Hence, therefore, the use of methods intended to incite people into identifications and aim-inhibited relationships of love, hence the restriction upon sexual life, and hence too the [idealist] commandment to love one's neighbor as oneself—a commandment which is really justified by the fact that nothing else runs so strongly counter to the original nature of man. In spite of every effort, these endeavors of civilization have not so far achieved very much. It hopes to prevent the crudest excesses of brutal violence by itself assuming the right to use violence against criminals, but **240** the law is not able to lay hold of the more cautious and refined manifestations of human aggressiveness. The time comes when each one of us has to give up as illusions the expectations which, in his youth, he pinned upon his fellowmen, and when he may learn how much difficulty and pain has been added to his life by their ill-will. . . .

**Q** What, according to Freud, are the three main sources of human suffering? By what means does one fend off suffering?

**Q** What does Freud see as the greatest threat to civilized society?

## Freud's Followers

Freud's immediate followers recognized that they stood in the shadow of an intellectual giant. Although some theorists disagreed with his dogmatic assertion that all neuroses stemmed from the traumas of the id, most took his discoveries as the starting point for their own inquiries into human behavior. For instance, Freud's Viennese associate Alfred Adler (1870–1937), who pioneered the field of individual psychology, worked to explain the ego's efforts to adapt to its environment. Coining the term "inferiority complex," Adler concentrated on analyzing problems related to the ego's failure to achieve its operational goals in everyday life.

Another of Freud's colleagues, the Swiss physician Carl Gustav Jung (1875–1961), found Freud's view of the psyche too narrow and overly deterministic. Jung argued that the personal, unconscious life of the individual rested on a deeper and more universal layer of the human psyche, which he called the **collective unconscious**. According to Jung, the collective unconscious belongs to humankind at large, that is, to the human family. It manifests itself throughout history in the form of dreams, myths, and fairy tales. The **archetypes** (primal patterns) of that realm reflect the deep psychic needs of humankind as a species. They reveal themselves as familiar motifs and characters, such as "the child-god," "the hero," and "the wise old man." Jung's investigations into the cultural history of humankind disclosed similarities between the symbols and myths of different religions and bodies of folklore. These he took to support his theory that the archetypes were the innate, inherited contents of the human mind.

Some of Jung's most convincing observations concerning the life of the collective unconscious appear in his essay "Psychological Aspects of the Mother Archetype" (1938). Here, Jung discusses the manifestations of the female archetype in personal life, as mother, grandmother,

# EXPLORING ISSUES

## Freud versus the Critics

As with most great thinkers, Freud made some questionable judgments, many of which came under attack before the end of the twentieth century. Revisionists questioned his theories on repression, arguing that they were scientifically untestable. Feminists took issue with his analysis of female sexuality (which holds that "penis envy" afflicts women), and his patriarchal perception of womankind as passive, weak, and dependent (see chapter 36). Proponents of biomedical psychiatry and behavioral psychology questioned the effectiveness of psychoanalysis itself. Still in progress is the debate as to whether mental illnesses are *biological* dysfunctions (best treated pharmacologically), *psychological*

dysfunctions related to infant or early childhood trauma (best treated by some form of psychotherapy), or both.

While Freud may be less valued today as an empirical scientist, he remains celebrated as a monumental visionary. His writings anticipated many of the recent developments in neuropsychiatry, the branch of medicine dealing with diseases of the mind and the nervous system. His theories continue to be tested. In the long run, however, Freud's most important contributions may be found to lie in modern intellectual history, specifically, in his thesis that the inner functions of the mind are valid and meaningful elements of the personality, and in his assertion that dreams and fantasies are as vital to human life as reason itself.

stepmother, nurse, or governess; in religion, as the redemptive Mother of God, the Virgin, Holy Wisdom, and the various nature deities of ancient myth and religion; and in the universal symbols associated with fertility and fruitfulness, such as the cornucopia, the garden, the fountain, the cave, the rose, the lotus, the magic circle, and the uterus. The negative aspect of the female archetype, observed Jung, usually manifests itself as the witch in traditional fairy tales and legends.

Jung emphasized the role of the collective unconscious in reflecting the "psychic unity" of all cultures. He treated the personal psyche as part of the larger human family, and, unlike Freud, he insisted on the positive value of religion in satisfying humankind's deepest psychic desires.

## The New Psychology and Literature

The impact of the new psychology was felt throughout Europe. Freud's theories, and particularly his pessimistic view of human nature, intensified the mood of uncertainty produced by the startling revelations of atomic physics and the outbreak of World War I. The Freudian revolution affected all aspects of artistic expression, not the least of which was literature. A great many figures in early twentieth-century fiction were profoundly influenced by Freud; three of the most famous of these are Marcel Proust, Franz Kafka, and James Joyce. In the works of these novelists, the most significant events are those that take place in the psychic life of dreams and memory. The narrative line of the story may be interrupted by unexpected leaps of thought, intrusive recollections, self-reflections, and sudden dead ends. Fantasy may alternate freely with rational thought. The lives of the heroes—or, more exactly, antiheroes—in these stories are often inconsequential, while their concerns, though commonplace or trivial, may be obsessive, bizarre, and charged with passion.

### Proust's Quest for Lost Time

Born in Paris, Marcel Proust (1871–1922) spent his youth troubled by severe attacks of asthma and recurring insecurities over his sexual orientation. Devastated by the death of his mother in 1905, Proust withdrew completely from Parisian society. He retreated into the semidarkness of a cork-lined room, where, shielded from noise, light, and frivolous society, he pursued a life of introspection and literary endeavor. Between 1909 and 1922 Proust produced a sixteen-volume novel entitled *A la recherche du temps perdu* (literally, "In Search of Lost Time," but usually translated as *Remembrance of Things Past*). This lengthy masterpiece provides a reflection of the society of turn-of-the-century France, but its perception of reality is wholly internal. Its central theme is the role of memory in retrieving past experience and in shaping the private life of the individual. Proust's mission was to rediscover a sense of the past by reviving sensory experiences buried deep within his psyche, that is, to bring the unconscious life to the conscious level. "For me," explained Proust, "the novel is . . . psychology in space and time."

In the first volume of *A la recherche du temps perdu*, entitled *Swann's Way*, Proust employs the Freudian technique of "free association" to recapture from the recesses of memory the intense moment of pleasure occasioned by the taste of a piece of cake soaked in tea. The following excerpt illustrates Proust's ability to free experience from the rigid order of mechanical time and to invade the richly textured storehouse of the psyche. It also illustrates the modern notion of the mental process as a "stream of thought," a concept that had appeared as early as 1884 in the writings of the American psychologist William James (1842–1910) and in the works of Henri Bergson (1859–1941), who described reality as a perpetual flux in which past and present are inseparable (see chapter 31).

### READING 33.2 From Proust's *Swann's Way* (1913)

The past is hidden somewhere outside the realm, beyond the       1
reach of intellect, in some material object (in the sensation
which that material object will give us) which we do not
suspect. And as for that object, it depends on chance whether
we come upon it or not before we ourselves must die.

Many years had elapsed during which nothing of Combray,
save what was comprised in the theatre and the drama of my
going to bed there, had any existence for me, when one day in
winter, as I came home, my mother, seeing that I was cold,
offered me some tea, a thing I did not ordinarily take. I       10
declined at first, and then, for no particular reason, changed
my mind. She sent out for one of those short, plump little
cakes called "petites madeleines," which look as though they
had been moulded in the fluted scallop of a pilgrim's shell.
And soon, mechanically, weary after a dull day with the
prospect of a depressing morrow, I raised to my lips a spoonful
of the tea in which I had soaked a morsel of the cake. No
sooner had the warm liquid, and the crumbs with it, touched
my palate than a shudder ran through my whole body, and I
stopped, intent upon the extraordinary changes that were       20
taking place. An exquisite pleasure had invaded my senses,
but individual, detached, with no suggestion of its origin. And
at once the vicissitudes of life had become indifferent to me,
its disasters innocuous, its brevity illusory—this new
sensation having had on me the effect which love has of filling
me with a precious essence; or rather this essence was not in
me, it was myself. I had ceased now to feel mediocre,
accidental, mortal. Whence could it have come to me, this all-
powerful joy? I was conscious that it was connected with the
taste of tea and cake, but that it infinitely transcended those       30
savours, could not, indeed, be of the same nature as theirs.
Whence did it come? What did it signify? How could I seize
upon and define it?

I drink a second mouthful, in which I find nothing more than
in the first, a third, which gives me rather less than the
second. It is time to stop; the potion is losing its magic. It is
plain that the object of my quest, the truth, lies not in the cup
but in myself. The tea has called up in me, but does not itself
understand, and can only repeat indefinitely with a gradual
loss of strength, the same testimony; which I, too, cannot       40
interpret, though I hope at least to be able to call upon the tea

for it again and to find it there presently, intact and at my disposal, for my final enlightenment. I put down my cup and examine my own mind. It is for it to discover the truth. But how? What an abyss of uncertainty whenever the mind feels that some part of it has strayed beyond its own borders; when it, the seeker, is at once the dark region through which it must go seeking, where all its equipment will avail it nothing. Seek? More than that: create. It is face to face with something which does not so far exist, to which it alone can give reality and **50** substance, which it alone can bring into the light of day.

And I begin again to ask myself what it could have been, this unremembered state which brought with it no logical proof of its existence, but only the sense that it was a happy, that it was a real state in whose presence other states of consciousness melted and vanished. I decide to attempt to make it reappear. I retrace my thoughts to the moment at which I drank the first spoonful of tea. I find again the same state, illumined by no fresh light. I compel my mind to make one further effort, to follow and recapture once again the **60** fleeting sensation. And that nothing may interrupt it in its course I shut out every obstacle, every extraneous idea, I stop my ears and inhibit all attention to the sounds which come from the next room. And then, feeling that my mind is growing fatigued without having any success to report, I compel it for a change to enjoy that distraction which I have just denied it, to think of other things, to rest and refresh itself before the supreme attempt. And then for the second time I clear an empty space in front of it. I place in position before my mind's eye the still recent taste of that first mouthful, and I feel **70** something start within me, something that leaves its resting-place and attempts to rise, something that has been embedded like an anchor at a great depth; I do not know yet what it is, but I can feel it mounting slowly; I can measure the resistance, I can hear the echo of great spaces traversed.

Undoubtedly what is thus palpitating in the depths of my being must be the image, the visual memory which, being linked to that taste, has tried to follow it into my conscious mind. But its struggles are too far off, too much confused; scarcely can I perceive the colorless reflection in which are **80** blended the uncapturable whirling medley of radiant hues, and I cannot distinguish its form, cannot invite it, as the one possible interpreter, to translate to me the evidence of its contemporary, its inseparable paramour, the taste of cake soaked in tea; cannot ask it to inform me what special circumstance is in question, of what period in my past life.

Will it ultimately reach the clear surface of my consciousness, this memory, this old, dead moment which the magnetism of an identical moment has travelled so far to importune, to disturb, to raise up out of the very depths of my being? I cannot tell. **90** Now that I feel nothing, it has stopped, has perhaps gone down again into its darkness, from which who can say whether it will ever rise? Ten times over I must essay the task, must lean down over the abyss. And each time the natural laziness which deters us from every difficult enterprise, every work of importance, has urged me to leave the thing alone, to drink my tea and to think merely of the worries of to-day and of my hopes for tomorrow, which let themselves be pondered over without effort or distress of mind.

And suddenly the memory returns. The taste was that of **100** the little crumb of madeleine which on Sunday mornings at Combray (because on those mornings I did not go out before church-time), when I went to say good day to her in her bedroom, my aunt Léonie used to give me, dipping it first in her own cup of real or of lime-flower tea. The sight of the little madeleine had recalled nothing to my mind before I tasted it; perhaps because I had so often seen such things in the interval, without tasting them, on the trays in pastry-cooks' windows, that their image had dissociated itself from those Combray days to take its place among others more recent; **110** perhaps because of those memories, so long abandoned and put out of mind, nothing now survived, everything was scattered; the forms of things, including that of the little scallop-shell of pastry, so richly sensual under its severe, religious folds, were either obliterated or had been so long dormant as to have lost the power of expansion which would have allowed them to resume their place in my consciousness. But when from a long-distant past nothing subsists, after the people are dead, after the things are broken and scattered, still, alone, more fragile, but with more vitality, more **120** unsubstantial, more persistent, more faithful, the smell and taste of things remain poised a long time, like souls, ready to remind us, waiting and hoping for their moment, amid the ruins of all the rest; and bear unfaltering, in the tiny and almost impalpable drop of their essence, the vast structure of recollection.

And once I had recognized the taste of the crumb of madeleine soaked in her decoction of lime-flowers which my aunt used to give me (although I did not yet know and must long postpone the discovery of why this memory made me so **130** happy) immediately the old grey house upon the street, where her room was, rose up like the scenery of a theatre to attach itself to the little pavilion, opening on to the garden, which had been built out behind it for my parents (the isolated panel which until that moment had been all that I could see); and with the house the town, from morning to night and in all weathers, the Square where I was sent before luncheon, the streets along which I used to run errands, the country roads we took when it was fine. And just as the Japanese amuse themselves by filling a porcelain bowl with water and steeping **140** in it little crumbs of paper which until then are without character or form, but, the moment they become wet, stretch themselves and bend, take on color and distinctive shape, become flowers or houses or people, permanent and recognisable, so in that moment all the flowers in our garden and in M. Swann's park, and the water-lilies on the Vivonne and the good folk of the village and their little dwellings and the parish church and the whole of Combray and of its surroundings, taking their proper shapes and growing solid, sprang into being, towns and gardens alike, from my cup of tea. . . . **150**

**Q** **What links does Proust draw between his unconscious and his conscious self?**

**Q** **What role does the madeleine play in these relationships?**

## The Nightmare Reality of Kafka

For Proust, memory was a life-enriching phenomenon, but for the German-Jewish novelist Franz Kafka (1883–1924), the subconscious life gave conscious experience bizarre and threatening gravity. Written in German, Kafka's novels and short stories take on the reality of dreams in which characters are nameless, details are precise but grotesque, and events lack logical consistency. In the nightmarish world of his novels, the central characters become victims of unknown or imprecisely understood forces. They may be caught in absurd but commonplace circumstances involving guilt and frustration, or they may be threatened by menacing events that appear to have neither meaning nor purpose. In *The Trial* (1925), for instance, the protagonist is arrested, convicted, and executed, without ever knowing the nature of his crime. In "The Metamorphosis," one of the most disquieting short stories of the twentieth century, the central character, Gregor Samsa, wakes one morning to discover that he has turned into a large insect. The themes of insecurity and vulnerability that recur in Kafka's novels reflect the mood that prevailed during the early decades of the century. Kafka himself was afflicted with this insecurity: shortly before he died in 1924, he asked a close friend to burn all of his manuscripts; the friend disregarded the request and saw to it that Kafka's works, even some that were unfinished, were published. Consequently, Kafka's style, which builds on deliberate ambiguity and fearful contradiction, has had a major influence on modern fiction. Although "The Metamorphosis" is too long to reproduce here in full, the excerpt that follows conveys some idea of Kafka's surreal narrative style.

### READING 33.3 From Kafka's "The Metamorphosis" (1915)

As Gregor Samsa awoke one morning from uneasy dreams he    1
found himself transformed in his bed into a gigantic insect. He
was lying on his hard, as it were armor-plated, back and when
he lifted his head a little he could see his dome-like brown belly
divided into stiff arched segments on top of which the bed quilt
could hardly keep in position and was about to slide off
completely. His numerous legs, which were pitifully thin
compared to the rest of his bulk, waved helplessly before
his eyes.

What has happened to me? he thought. It was no dream.    10
His room, a regular human bedroom, only rather too small, lay
quiet between the four familiar walls. Above the table on which
a collection of cloth samples was unpacked and spread out—
Samsa was a commercial traveler—hung the picture, which he
had recently cut out of an illustrated magazine and put into a
pretty gilt frame. It showed a lady, with a fur cap on and a fur
stole, sitting upright and holding out to the spectator a huge fur
muff into which the whole of her forearm had vanished!

Gregor's eyes turned next to the window, and the overcast    20
sky—one could hear raindrops beating on the window gutter—
made him quite melancholy. What about sleeping a little longer
and forgetting all this nonsense, he thought, but it could not be
done, for he was accustomed to sleep on his right side and in

his present condition he could not turn himself over. However
violently he forced himself towards his right side he always
rolled on to his back again. He tried it at least a hundred times,
shutting his eyes to keep from seeing his struggling legs, and
only desisted when he began to feel in his side a faint dull ache
he had never experienced before.    30

Oh God, he thought, what an exhausting job I've picked on!
Traveling about day in, day out. It's much more irritating work
than doing the actual business in the office, and on top of that
there's the trouble of constant traveling, of worrying about
train connections, the bed and irregular meals, casual
acquaintances that are always new and never become
intimate friends. The devil take it all! He felt a slight itching
upon his belly; slowly pushed himself on his back nearer to the
top of the bed so that he could lift his head more easily;
identified the itching place which was surrounded by many    40
small white spots the nature of which he could not understand
and made to touch it with a leg, but drew the leg back
immediately, for the contact made a cold shiver run through
him. . . .

He looked at the alarm clock ticking on the chest. Heavenly
Father! he thought. It was half-past six o'clock and the hands
were quietly moving on, it was even past the half-hour, it was
getting on toward a quarter to seven. Had the alarm clock not
gone off? From the bed one could see that it had been properly
set for four o'clock; of course it must have gone off. Yes, but    50
was it possible to sleep quietly through that ear-splitting noise?
Well, he had not slept quietly, yet apparently all the more
soundly for that. But what was he to do now? The next train
went at seven o'clock; to catch that he would need to hurry like
mad and his samples weren't even packed up, and he himself
wasn't feeling particularly fresh and active. And even if he did
catch the train he wouldn't avoid a row with the chief, since
the firm's porter would have been waiting for the five o'clock
train and would have long since reported his failure to turn
up. . . .    60

As all this was running through his mind at top speed without
his being able to decide to leave his bed—the alarm clock had
just struck a quarter to seven—there came a cautious tap at
the door behind the head of his bed. "Gregor," said a voice—it
was his mother's—"it's a quarter to seven. Hadn't you a train to
catch?" That gentle voice! Gregor had a shock as he heard his
own voice answering hers, unmistakably his own voice, it was
true, but with a persistent horrible twittering squeak behind it
like an undertone, that left the words in their clear shape only
for the first moment and then rose up reverberating round    70
them to destroy their sense, so that one could not be sure one
had heard them rightly. Gregor wanted to answer at length and
explain everything, but in the circumstances he confined
himself to saying: "Yes, yes, thank you, Mother, I'm getting up
now." The wooden door between them must have kept the
change in his voice from being noticeable outside, for his
mother contented herself with this statement and shuffled
away. Yet this brief exchange of words had made the other
members of the family aware that Gregor was still in the house,
as they had not expected, and at one of the side doors his    80
father was already knocking, gently, yet with his fist. "Gregor,
Gregor," he called, "what's the matter with you?" And after a

little while he called again in a deeper voice: "Gregor! Gregor!" At the other side door his sister was saying in a low, plaintive tone: "Gregor? Aren't you well? Are you needing anything?" He answered them both at once: "I'm just ready," and did his best to make his voice sound as normal as possible by enunciating the words very clearly and leaving long pauses between them. So his father went back to his breakfast, but his sister whispered: "Gregor, open the door, do.". . .                                     90
[Unexpectedly, the chief clerk arrives to find out why Gregor is not at work. He demands to see him.]

Slowly Gregor pushed the chair towards the door, then let go of it, caught hold of the door for support—the soles at the end of his little legs were somewhat sticky—and rested against it for a moment after his efforts. Then he set himself to turning the key in the lock with his mouth. It seemed, unhappily, that he hadn't really any teeth—what could he grip the key with?—but on the other hand his jaws were certainly very strong; with their help he did manage to set the key in            100 motion, heedless of the fact that he was undoubtedly damaging them somewhere, since a brown fluid issued from his mouth, flowed over the key and dripped on the floor. "Just listen to that," said the chief clerk next door; "he's turning the key." That was a great encouragement to Gregor; but they should all have shouted encouragement to him, his father and mother too: "Go on Gregor," they should have called out, "keep going, hold on to that key!" And in the belief that they were all following his efforts intently, he clenched his jaws recklessly on the key with all the force at his command. As the turning of the key        110 progressed he circled round the lock, holding on now only with his mouth, pushing on the key, as required, or pulling it down again with all the weight of his body. The louder click of the finally yielding lock literally quickened Gregor. With a deep breath of relief he said to himself: "So I didn't need the locksmith," and laid his head on the handle to open the door wide.

Since he had to pull the door towards him, he was still invisible when it was really wide open. He had to edge himself slowly round the near half of the double door, and to        120 do it very carefully if he was not to fall plump upon his back just on the threshold. He was still carrying out this difficult manoeuvre, with no time to observe anything else, when he heard the chief clerk utter a loud "Oh!"—it sounded like a gust of wind—and now he could see the man, standing as he was nearest to the door, clapping one hand before his open mouth and slowly backing away as if driven by some invisible steady pressure. His mother—in spite of the chief clerk's directions— first clasped her hands and looked at his father, then took two steps towards Gregor and fell on the floor among her            130 outspread skirts, her face quite hidden on her breast. His father knotted his fist with a fierce expression on his face as if he meant to knock Gregor back into his room, then looked uncertainly round the living room, covered his eyes with his hands and wept till his great chest heaved. . . .

Q  How would you describe Gregor Samsa's personality?

Q  What details in this story establish a sense of reality? Of unreality? Of fear?

## Joyce and Stream of Consciousness Prose

One of the most influential writers of the early twentieth century, and also one of the most challenging, was the Irish expatriate James Joyce (1882–1941). Born in Dublin and educated in Jesuit schools, Joyce abandoned Ireland in 1905 to live abroad. In Paris, he studied medicine and music but made his livelihood there and elsewhere by teaching foreign languages and writing short stories. Joyce's prose reflects his genius as a linguist and his keen sensitivity to the musical potential of words. His treatment of plot and character is deeply indebted to Freud, whose earliest publications Joyce had consumed with interest. From Freud's works, he drew inspiration for the **interior monologue**, a literary device consisting of the private musings of a character in the form of a "stream of consciousness"—a succession of images and ideas connected by free association rather than by logical argument or narrative sequence. The stream of consciousness device recalls the free association technique used by Freud in psychotherapy; it also recalls the discontinuous verse style of the Imagist poets (see chapter 32). In a stream of consciousness novel, the action is developed through the mind of the principal character as he or she responds to the dual play of conscious and subconscious stimuli. The following passage from Joyce's 600-page novel *Ulysses* (1922) provides a brief example:

He crossed to the bright side, avoiding the loose cellarflap of number seventy-five. The sun was nearing the steeple of George's church. Be a warm day I fancy, Specially in these black clothes feel it more. Black conducts, reflects (refracts is it?), the heat. But I couldn't go in that light suit. Make a picnic of it. His Boland's breadvan delivering with trays our daily but she prefers yesterday's loaves turnovers crisp crowns hot. Makes you feel young. Somewhere in the east: early morning: set off at dawn, travel round in front of the sun, steal a day's march on him. Keep it up for ever never grow a day older technically. . . . Wander along all day. Meet a robber or two. Well, meet him. Getting on to sundown. The shadows of the mosques along the pillars: priest with a scroll rolled up. A shiver of the trees, signal, the evening wind. I pass on. Fading gold sky. A mother watches from her doorway. She calls her children home in their dark language. High wall: beyond strings twanged. Night sky moon, violet, colour of Molly's new garters. Strings. Listen. A girl playing one of these instruments what do you call them: dulcimers. I pass. . . .

Joyce modeled his sprawling novel on the Homeric epic, the *Odyssey*. But Joyce's modern version differs profoundly from Homer's. Leopold Bloom, the main character of *Ulysses*, is as ordinary as Homer's Odysseus was heroic; his adventures seem trivial and insignificant by comparison with those of his Classical counterpart. Bloom's commonplace experiences, as he wanders from home to office, pub, and brothel, and then home again—a one-day "voyage" through the streets of Dublin—constitute the plot of the novel. The real "action," however, takes place in the minds of its principal characters: Bloom, his acquaintances, and his wife Molly. Their collective ruminations produce an overwhelming sense of desolation and a startling awareness that the human psyche can never extricate itself from the timeless blur of experience.

Joyce's stream of consciousness technique and his dense accumulation of unfamiliar and oddly compounded words make this monumental novel difficult to grasp—yet it remains more accessible than his experimental, baffling prose work, *Finnegans Wake* (1939). Initially, however, it was censorship that made *Ulysses* inaccessible to the public: since Joyce treated sexual matters as intimately as all other aspects of human experience, critics judged his language obscene. The novel was banned in the United States until 1933.

The combined influence of Freud and Joyce was visible in much of the first-ranking literature of the twentieth century. Writers such as Gertrude Stein (1874–1946) and the Nobel laureates Thomas Mann (1875–1955) and William Faulkner (1897–1962) extended the use of the stream of consciousness technique. In theater the American playwright Eugene O'Neill (1888–1953) fused Greek myth with Freudian concepts of guilt and repression in the dramatic trilogy *Mourning Becomes Electra* (1931). He devised dramatic techniques that revealed the characters' buried emotions, such as two actors playing different aspects of a single individual, the use of masks, and the embellishment of dialogue with accompanying asides.

The new psychology extended its influence to performance style as well: Freud's emphasis on the interior life inspired the development of **method acting**, a style of modern theatrical performance that tried to harness "true emotion" and "affective memory" (from childhood experience) in the interpretation of dramatic roles. The pioneer in method acting was the Russian director and actor Konstantin Stanislavsky (1863–1938), whose innovative techniques as head of the Moscow Art Theater spread to the United States in the early 1930s. There, his method inspired some of America's finest screen and stage actors, such as James Dean (1931–1955) and Marlon Brando (1924–2004).

## The New Freedom in Poetry

Modern poets avidly seized upon stream of consciousness techniques to emancipate poetry from syntactical and grammatical bonds—a mission that had been initiated by the Symbolists and refined by the Imagists. The French writer Guillaume Apollinaire (1880–1918), a close friend of Picasso and an admirer of Cubism, wrote poems that not only liberated words from their traditional placement in the sentence but also freed sentences from their traditional arrangement on the page. Inspired by the designs of ordinary handbills, billboards, and signs, Apollinaire created **concrete poems**, that is, poems produced in the shape of external objects, such as watches, neckties, and pigeons. He arranged the words in the poem "Il Pleut" ("It Rains"), for instance, as if they had fallen onto the page like raindrops from the heavens. Such word-pictures, which Apollinaire called "lyrical ideograms," inspired the poet to exult, "I too am a painter!"

The American poet E. E. Cummings (1894–1962) arrived in France in 1917 as a volunteer ambulance driver for the Red Cross. Like Apollinaire, Cummings wrote poems that violated the traditional rules of verse composition. To sharpen the focus of a poem, he subjected typography and syntax to acrobatic distortions that challenged the eye as well as the ear. Cummings poked fun at modern society by packing his verse with slang, jargon, and sexual innuendo. As the following poem suggests, his lyrics are often infused with large doses of playful humor.

---

**READING 33.4** Cummings' [she being Brand]
(1926)

| | |
|---|---:|
| she being Brand | 1 |
| -new;and you | |
| know consequently a | |
| little stiff i was | |
| careful of her and(having | 5 |
| thoroughly oiled the universal | |
| joint tested my gas felt of | |
| her radiator made sure her springs were O. | |
| | |
| K.)i went right to it flooded-the-carburetor cranked her | |
| up, slipped the | 10 |
| clutch(and then somehow got into reverse she | |
| kicked what | |
| the hell)next | |
| minute i was back in neutral tried and | |
| again slo-wly;bare,ly nudg.   ing(my | 15 |
| lev-er Right- | |
| oh and her gears being in | |
| A 1 shape passed | |
| from low through | |
| second-in-to-high like | 20 |
| greasedlightning) just as we turned the corner of Divinity | |
| avenue i touched the accelerator and give | |
| her the juice,good | |
| (it | |
| was the first ride and believe i we was | 25 |
| happy to see how nice she acted right up to | |
| the last minute coming back down by the Public | |
| Gardens i slammed on | |
| the | |
| internalexpanding | 30 |
| & | |
| externalcontracting | |
| brakes Bothatonce and | |
| brought allofher tremB | |
| -ling | 35 |
| to a: dead. | |
| stand- | |
| ;Still) | |

**Q**  Who is the "she" in this poem?

**Q**  What liberties does the poet take with form? With subject matter?

# The New Psychology and the Visual Arts

It was in the visual arts that the new psychology made its most dramatic and longlasting impact. As artists brought to their work their hidden emotions, repressed desires, and their dreams and fantasies, art became the vehicle of the subconscious. The irrational and antirational forces of the id was the subject and the inspiration for an assortment of styles. These include Expressionism, Metaphysical art, Dada, and Surrealism. Expressionism and Surrealism had particularly important effects on photography and film, as well as on the fields of commercial and applied arts. In every aspect of our daily life, from fashion designs to magazine and television advertisements, the evidence of the Freudian revolution is still visible.

## Expressionism

The pioneer Expressionist painter of the twentieth century was the Norwegian Edvard Munch (1863–1944). Munch was a great admirer of Henrik Ibsen, whose plays (see chapter 30) examine the inner conflicts and repressed desires of their characters. Obsessed with the traumas of puberty and frustrated sexuality, Munch was also deeply troubled by personal associations with illness and death—tuberculosis had killed both his mother and sister. Such subjects provided the imagery for his paintings and woodcuts; but it was in his style—a haunting synthesis of distorted forms and savage colors—that he captured the anguished intensity of the neurosis that led to his mental collapse in 1908.

*The Scream* (Figure **33.2**), a painting that has become a universal symbol of the modern condition, takes its mood of urgency and alarm from the combined effects of sinuous

**Figure 33.2 EDVARD MUNCH**, *The Scream*, 1893. Oil, pastel, and casein on cardboard, 35¾ × 29 in. The ghostly foreground figure (Munch himself) may have been inspired by an Inca mummy viewed by the artist in the Paris Exhibition of 1899. The blood-red sky may owe something to a volcanic eruption that took place in Indonesia in August 1883, the effects of which reached Munch's hometown in Norway.

**Figure 33.3 ERNST LUDWIG KIRCHNER,**
*Street, Berlin,* 1913. Oil on canvas, 3 ft. 11½ in.
× 35⅞ in. Two stylishly dressed prostitutes press
forward along a wildly tilted city street. Lurid
pinks, acid blues, and charcoal blacks add to the
claustrophobic atmosphere. Kirchner painted this
and similar scenes after moving from Dresden to
Berlin, during a time he described as being one
of loneliness and depression.

clouds, writhing blue-black waters, and a dramatically receding pier (a popular meeting spot near Munch's summer cottage). These visual rhythms suggest the resonating sound of the voiceless cry described by Munch in the notes to a preliminary drawing for the painting: "I walked with two friends. Then the sun sank. Suddenly the sky turned red as blood. . . . My friends walked on, and I was left alone, trembling with fear. I felt as if all nature were filled with one mighty unending shriek."

Munch's impassioned style foreshadowed German Expressionism. Like the Italian Futurists, young artists in Germany rebelled against the "old-established forces" of academic art. Influenced by Freud and by the arts of Africa and Oceania, two Modernist groups emerged: in Dresden, *Die Brücke* (The Bridge) was founded in 1905; the second, established in Munich in 1911, called itself *Der Blaue Reiter* (The Blue Rider). Though divided by strong personal differences, the artists of these two groups shared a style marked by pathos, violence, and emotional intensity. The German Expressionists inherited the brooding, romantic sensibility of Goethe, Nietzsche, and Wagner. They favored macabre and intimate subjects, which they rendered by means of distorted forms, harsh colors, and the bold and haunting use of black.

Led by Ernst Ludwig Kirchner (1880–1938), members of *Die Brücke*, including Erich Heckel (1883–1970), Karl Schmidt-Rottluff (1884–1976), and Emil Nolde (1867–1956), envisioned their movement as a "bridge" to Modernism. They embraced art as an outpouring of "inner necessity," emotion, and ecstasy. Seized by the prewar tensions of urban Germany, they painted probing self-portraits, tempestuous landscapes, and ominous cityscapes. In *Street, Berlin* (Figure **33.3**), Kirchner's jagged lines and dissonant colors, accented by aggressive areas of black, evoke the image of urban life as crowded, impersonal, and threatening. His convulsive distortions of figural form reveal the influence of African sculpture, while the nervous intensity of his line style reflects his indebtedness to the German graphic tradition pioneered by Albrecht Dürer (see chapter 19). Like Dürer, Kirchner rendered many of his subjects (including portraits and cityscapes) in woodcut—the favorite medium of German Expressionism.

**Figure 33.4 GIORGIO DE CHIRICO**, *The Nostalgia of the Infinite*, 1914; dated on painting 1911. Oil on canvas, 4 ft. 5¼ in. × 25½ in.

## Metaphysical Art and Fantasy

While the German Expressionists brought a new degree of subjective intensity to depictions of the visible world, other artists explored the life that lay beyond the senses. One of these artists was Giorgio de Chirico (1888–1978). Born in Greece, de Chirico moved to Italy in 1909. Rejecting the tenets of Italian Futurism (see chapter 32), he pioneered a style that he called "metaphysical," that is, "beyond physical reality." In canvases executed between 1910 and 1920, he introduced the landscape of the psyche into the realm of art. His sharply delineated images, contradictory perspectives, unnatural colors, and illogically cast shadows produced disturbing, dreamlike effects similar to those in Kafka's prose.

In *The Nostalgia of the Infinite* (Figure **33.4**) two figures, dwarfed by eerie shadows, stand in the empty courtyard; five flags flutter mysteriously in an airless, acid-green sky. The vanishing point established by the orthogonal lines of the portico on the right contradicts the low placement of the distant horizon. Of his disquieting cityscapes, de Chirico commented, "There are more enigmas in the shadow of a man who walks in the sun than in all the religions of past, present, and future." De Chirico anticipated a mode of representation known as *Magic Realism*, in which commonplace objects and events are exaggerated or juxtaposed in unexpected ways that evoke a mood of mystery or fantasy.

The Russian-born artist Marc Chagall (1887–1985) arrived in Paris in 1910. Like his countryman and fellow expatriate Igor Stravinsky, Chagall infused his first compositions with the folk tales and customs of his native land. His nostalgic recollection of rural Russia called *I and the Village* (Figure **33.5**) owes much to the lessons of Cubism and Fauvism. However, the disjunctive sizes and positions of the figures and the variety of arbitrary colors obey the whimsy of the unconscious. Chagall freely superimposed images upon one another or showed them floating in space, defying the laws of gravity. Autobiographical motifs, such as fiddle players and levitating lovers, became Chagall's hallmarks in the richly colored canvases, murals, and stained glass windows of his long and productive career.

### The Dada Movement

While Expressionism and fantasy investigated the Freudian unconscious, neither attacked nationalist tradition as aggressively as the movement known as *Dada*. Founded in 1916 in Zürich, Switzerland, the Dada movement consisted of a loosely knit group of European painters and poets who, perceiving World War I as evidence of a world gone mad, dedicated themselves to spreading the gospel of irrationality. The nonsensical name of the movement, "dada" ("hobbyhorse"), which was chosen by inserting a penknife at random into the pages of a dictionary, symbolized their irreverent stance. If the world had gone mad, should not its creative endeavors be equally mad? Dada answered with art that was the product of chance, accident, or outrageous behavior—with works that deliberately violated good taste, middle-class values, and artistic convention.

The Dadaists met regularly at the Café Voltaire in Zürich, where they orchestrated "noise concerts" and recited poetry created by way of **improvisation** and free association. The Romanian poet Tristan Tzara (1896–1963) produced poems from words cut out of newspapers and randomly scattered on a table, while the French sculptor and poet Jean Arp (1887–1966) constructed collages and relief sculptures from shapes dropped at random on a canvas and left "according to the laws of chance." Dada's attacks on

**Figure 33.5 MARC CHAGALL**, *I and the Village*, 1911. Oil on canvas, 6 ft. 3⅝ in. × 4 ft. 11⅝ in.

rationalist tradition and on modern technocracy in general reflected the spirit of <u>nihilism</u> (the denial of traditional and religious and moral principles) that flowered in the ashes of the war. In his "Lecture on Dada" in 1922, Tzara declared, "The acts of life have no beginning or end. Everything happens in a completely idiotic way. Simplicity is called dada. . . . Like everything in life, dada is useless."

As with poetry and painting, Dada theater paid homage to Freud by liberating "everything obscure in the mind, buried deep, unrevealed," as one French playwright explained. Narrative realism and traditional characterization gave way to improvisation and the performance of random and bizarre incidents. One form of Dada theater, the *theater of cruelty*, known for its violent and scatological themes, anticipated the theater of the absurd plays written during the 1950s and 1960s (see chapter 35).

The spirit of the Dadaists was most vividly realized in the work of the French artist Marcel Duchamp (1887–1968). Early in his career, Duchamp had flirted with Cubism and Futurism, producing the influential *Nude Descending a Staircase, No. 2* (see Figure 32.11); but after 1912, he abandoned professional painting and turned to making—or remaking—art objects. In 1913 he mounted a bicycle wheel atop a barstool, thus producing the first "ready-made," as well as the first **mobile** (a sculpture with moving parts). Four years later, Duchamp would launch the landmark ready-made of the century: he placed a common factory-produced urinal on a pedestal, signed the piece with the fictitious name, "R. Mutt," and submitted it for an exhibition held by the American Society of Independent Artists (Figure **33.6**). The piece, which he called *Fountain*, was rejected, but its long-term impact was enormous. By calling the "found object" a work of art, Duchamp mocked conventional techniques of making art. Moreover, by

L.H.O.O.Q.

**Figure 33.7 MARCEL DUCHAMP**, *L.H.O.O.Q.*, 1919. Rectified ready-made, pencil on a reproduction of the *Mona Lisa*, 7¾ × 4⅛ in.

**Figure 33.6 MARCEL DUCHAMP**, *Fountain (Urinal)*, 1917. Ready-made, height 24 in. There are eight factory-made replicas of *Fountain*, "signed" by Duchamp in 1964. In 1993, an artist attacked the piece on display in Nîmes, France. Claiming the right to use it for its original purpose, he urinated in it.

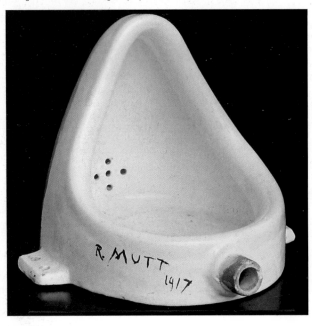

wrenching the object out of its functional context, he suggested that the image obeyed a logic of its own, a logic whose "rules" flouted traditional aesthetic norms. *Fountain* not only attacked the barrier between art and life, but called for art that exalted the nonsensical, the accidental, and the absurd.

Perhaps most important, however, *Fountain* introduced to modern art the revolutionary notion that a work of art was first and foremost about an artist's *idea*. *Fountain* was not art because Duchamp had "made" it, but because he had chosen to remove it from the context of everyday life and had given it a whole new identity (as art). Pursuing this logic, the artist might also alter (or "remake") existing art, as for example, when Duchamp drew a mustache on a reproduction of Leonardo da Vinci's venerable *Mona Lisa*, adding a series of letters at the bottom that, when recited rapidly (in French), describe the sitter in lusty street slang (Figure **33.7**). This "corrected ready-made," as Duchamp called the piece, expressed the Dada disdain for Western high art. It established the modern artist as maverick—the self-appointed prophet and defiler of tradition.

Moving to New York City in 1918, Duchamp labored for ten years on his magnum opus, a large glass and wire assemblage filled with esoteric sexual symbolism. He called it *The Bride Stripped Bare by Her Bachelors, Even*. After 1920, Duchamp went "underground," spending as much time perfecting his chess game (his favorite pastime) as making art. Nevertheless, his small, pioneering body of work and his irreverent view that art "has absolutely no existence as . . . truth" have had a powerful influence on scores of poets, painters, and composers even into the twenty-first century.

## Surrealism and Abstract Surrealists: Picasso, Miró, and Klee

One of Modernism's most distinctive movements, *Surrealism* (the term coined by Guillaume Apollinaire in 1917), was devoted to giving physical expression to the workings of the unconscious mind. The Surrealists paid explicit homage to Freud and his writings, especially those on free association and dream analysis. In the first "Surrealist Manifesto" (1924), the French critic and spiritual godfather of Surrealism, André Breton (1896–1966) proclaimed the artist's liberation from reason and from the demands of conventional society. Having visited Freud in Vienna in 1921, Breton described the Surrealist commitment to the irrational as follows:

> We are still living under the reign of logic. . . . But in this day and age logical methods are applicable only to solving problems of secondary interest. The absolute rationalism that is still in vogue allows us to consider only facts relating directly to our experience. . . . [Experience] is protected by the sentinels of common sense. Under the pretense of civilization and progress, we have managed to banish from the mind everything that may rightly or wrongly be termed superstition, or fancy; forbidden is any kind of search for truth which is not in conformance with accepted practices. It was, apparently, by pure chance, that a part of our mental world which we pretended not to be concerned with any longer—and, in my opinion, by far the most important part—has been brought back to light. For this we must give thanks to the discoveries of Sigmund Freud. . . . The imagination is perhaps on the point of reasserting itself, of reclaiming its rights.

Breton defined Surrealism as "psychic automatism, in its pure state," that is, creative effort guided by thought functions free of rational control and "exempt from any aesthetic or moral concern." He emphasized the omnipotence of the dream state in guiding the Surrealist enterprise.

Just as writers developed new literary techniques to achieve freedom from rational control, so visual artists devised new methods and processes to liberate the visual imagination. Some explored psychic automatism, allowing the hand to move spontaneously and at random, as if casually doodling or improvising. Others tried to recover a sense of childlike spontaneity by filling their paintings with free-spirited, biomorphic shapes. Fundamentally, however, the paradox of Surrealist art rested on the artist's *conscious* effort to capture *unconscious* experience.

Breton recognized Picasso as one of the pioneers of Surrealist art. As early as 1907, in *Les Demoiselles d'Avignon* (see Figure 32.3), Picasso had begun to radicalize the image of the human figure; by the mid-1920s, brutal dissection and savage distortion dominated his art. In 1927, Picasso painted the *Seated Woman* (Figure **33.8**), the image of a "split personality" that seemed to symbolize Freud's three-part psyche. The head of the female consists of a frontal view, as well as at least two profile views, each of which

**Figure 33.8 PABLO PICASSO**, *Seated Woman*, Paris, 1927. Oil on wood, 4 ft. 3⅛ in. × 3 ft. 2¼ in.

reveals a different aspect of her personality. The "split personality" motif continued to preoccupy Picasso throughout his long artistic career. In scores of paintings and sculptures, as well as in the stream of consciousness prose he wrote during the 1930s, Picasso pursued double meanings and visual puns, thus securing his reputation as the master of metamorphosis in twentieth-century art.

In the paintings of the Spanish artist Joan Miró (1893–1983), the Surrealist's search for subconscious experience kindled the artist's personal mythology. Miró's simple, childlike figures, his biomorphic creatures and spiny, abstract organisms became the denizens of a fantastic universe. The creatures in *The Harlequin's Carnival*—amoeba, snakes, and insects—cavort in unbounded space (Figure **33.9**). A ladder leads to an eyelash; a window opens onto a pyramid. "In my pictures," explained Miro, "there are tiny forms in vast, empty spaces. Empty space, empty horizons, empty plains, everything that is stripped has always impressed me."

The Swiss-born painter Paul Klee (1879–1940) stood on the fringes of Surrealism. One of the most sophisticated artists of the century, Klee was a brilliant draftsman who created physically small artworks that resemble

hieroglyphic puzzles. His abstractions, like the entries in his personal diaries, are characterized by gentle humor and exquisite finesse; they belong to the substratum of the mind—the subconscious repository of mysterious symbols. "Art does not represent the visible," Klee insisted, "rather, it renders visible [the invisible]."

Klee's *Fish Magic* (see Figure 33.1), painted during his tenure as a teacher at the Bauhaus, consists of a group of carefully arranged organic motifs that resemble sacred signs. Flowers, fish, and human figure, all executed with pictographic simplicity, share the ambient space of planets whose rhythms are measured by a mysteriously suspended clock. Klee was among the first artists to recognize the art of the untutored and the mentally ill. "Only children, madmen, and savages," he wrote, "truly understand the 'in-between' world of spiritual truth."

## Visionary Surrealists: Magritte and Dali

While Picasso, Miró, and Klee favored abstract and biomorphic images, other Surrealists juxtaposed meticulously painted objects in ways that were often shocking or unexpected. The most notable of these visionary Surrealists were René Magritte and Salvador Dali. Both were superb

**Figure 33.9 JOAN MIRÓ**, *The Harlequin's Carnival*, 1924. Oil on canvas, 26 × 36½ in. Years after painting this picture, Miró claimed that some of the imagery in his early art was inspired by hallucinations brought on by hunger and by staring at the cracks in the plaster walls of his shabby Paris apartment.

draftsmen whose *trompe l'oeil* skills elicited a disquieting dream reality.

Profoundly influenced by de Chirico, the Belgian artist Magritte (1898–1967) combined realistically detailed objects in startling and irrational ways. In one of his paintings, a coffin takes the place of a reclining figure; in another, a bird cage is substituted for the head of the sitter; and in still another, human toes appear on a pair of leather shoes. In such discordant images, Magritte brought mystery to the objects of everyday experience. "I don't paint visions," Magritte wrote, "I describe objects—and the mutual relationships of objects—in such a way that none of our habitual concepts or feelings is necessarily linked with them." The small piece entitled *The Betrayal of Images* (1928) depicts with crisp and faultless accuracy a briar pipe, beneath which appears the legend "This is not a pipe" (Figure **33.10**). The painting addresses the age-old distinction between the real world—the world of the *actual* pipe—and the painted image, whose reality is the virtual *illusion* of a pipe. At the same time, it anticipates Modernist efforts to determine how words and images differ in conveying information.

The Spanish painter and impresario Salvador Dali (1904–1989) was as much a showman as an artist. Cultivating the bizarre as a lifestyle, Dali exhibited a perverse desire to shock his audiences. Drawing motifs from his own erotic dreams and fantasies, he executed both natural and unnatural images with meticulous precision, combining them in unusual settings or giving them grotesque attributes.

**Figure 33.10 RENÉ MAGRITTE**, *The Betrayal of Images*, ca. 1928–1929. Oil on canvas, 25⅛ × 37 in. "People who look for symbolic meanings fail to grasp the inherent poetry and mystery of the image," complained Magritte. "By asking, 'What does this mean,' they express a wish that everything be understandable."

Dali's infamous *The Persistence of Memory* (Figure **33.11**) consists of a broad and barren landscape occupied by a leafless tree, three limp watches, and a watchcase crawling with ants. One of the timepieces plays host to a fly, while another rests upon a mass of brain matter resembling a profiled self-portrait—a motif that the artist frequently featured in his works. To seek an explicit message in this painting—even one addressing modern notions of time—would be to miss the point, for, as Dali himself warned, his "hand-painted dream photographs" were merely designed to "stamp themselves indelibly upon the mind."

**Figure 33.11 SALVADOR DALI**, *The Persistence of Memory* (*Persistance de la Mémoire*), 1931. Oil on canvas, 9½ × 13 in. One of the most deceptive aspects of this painting is its size: while it appears to be a large canvas, it is actually not much larger than this page.

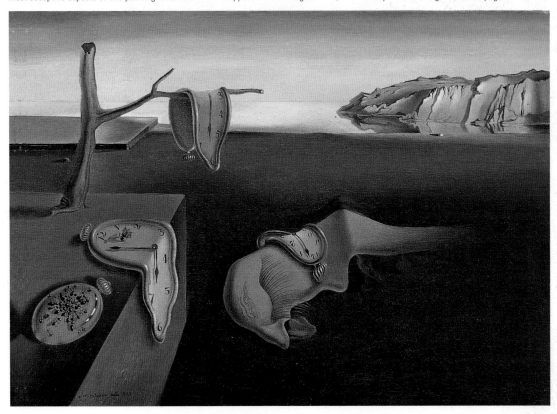

## The Women of Surrealism

Perhaps more than any other movement in the history of early Modernism, Surrealism attracted a good many women artists. Arguably the most celebrated of these was Mexico's Frida Kahlo (1907–1954). Kahlo's paintings, of which more than one-third are self-portraits, reflect the determined effort (shared by many feminists) to present the female image as something other than the object of male desire. Her art bears testimony to what she called the "two great accidents" of her life: a bus crash that at the age of eighteen left her disabled, and her stormy marriage to the notorious Mexican mural painter Diego Rivera (see chapter 34). Like Rivera, Kahlo was a fervent Marxist and a nationalist who supported the revolutionary government that took control of Mexico in 1921. But the principal subject matter of Kahlo's art is Frida herself: "I am the subject I know best," she explained. Her paintings bring to life the experience of chronic pain, both physical (her accident required some thirty surgeries and ultimately involved the amputation of her right leg) and psychic (repeated miscarriages, for example, left her incapable of bearing a child).

Kahlo's canvases reveal her close identification with Mexican folk art, which traditionally features visceral and diabolical details. At the same time, her taste for realistically conceived but shockingly juxtaposed images reflects her debt to de Chirico and the Magic Realist style. In *The Broken Column* (Figure **33.12**), Kahlo pictures herself as sufferer and savior, an emblematic figure that recalls the devotional icons of Mexico's religious shrines.

A pioneer Modernist on the American scene, Georgia O'Keeffe (1887–1986) is often classified with America's regional painters. However, her treatment of haunting, biomorphic images abstracted from greatly enlarged flowers and bleached animal bones gives her early paintings a menacing presence (Figure **33.13**). In a fluid line style that distills the essence of the subject, the so-called "high priestess" of early Modernism brought a visionary clarity to the most ordinary ingredients of the American landscape.

The unorthodox combination of commonplace objects—the hallmark of the visionary Surrealists—was a particularly effective strategy for Surrealist sculptors; and in this domain as well, women made notable contributions. The fur-lined cup and saucer (Figure **33.14**) conceived by the Swiss-German sculptor Meret Oppenheim (1913–1985) is shocking in its union of familiar but disparate elements. Conceived in the irreverent spirit of Duchamp's modified ready-mades, Oppenheim's *Object: Breakfast in Fur* provokes a sequence of discomfiting narrative associations.

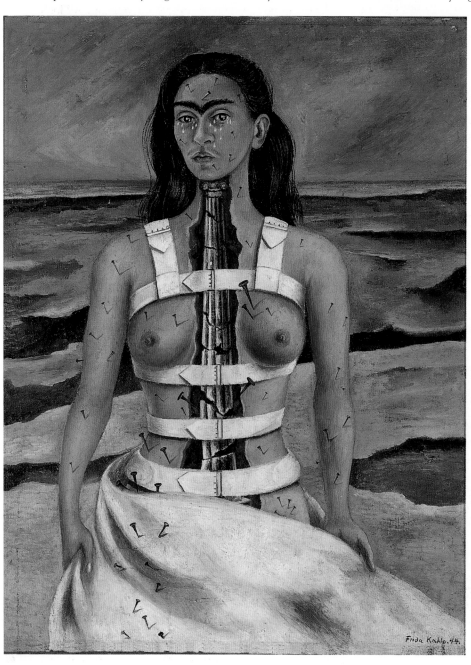

**Figure 33.12 FRIDA KAHLO**, *The Broken Column*, 1944. Oil on canvas, 15¾ × 12¼ in. Visiting Mexico, André Breton declared Kahlo to be a superb Surrealist; but Kahlo protested, "I never painted dreams. I painted my own reality."

## Dada and Surrealist Photography

Photography was an ideal medium with which to explore the layers of the unconscious mind. Modernist photographers experimented with double exposure and unorthodox darkroom techniques to create unusual new effects similar to those of visionary Surrealist painters and sculptors. Liberating photography from traditional pictorialism, a group of Berlin Dadaists invented a new kind of collage called **photomontage**. The photomontage consisted of "found" photographic images cut from books, magazines, and newspapers, and pasted on a flat surface. A champion of the technique, Raoul Hausmann (1886–1971), called photomontage "the 'alienation' of photography." By this, he implied that photomontage destroyed the role of photography as a medium for recreating physical reality. But the statement also suggests that by its dependence on fragmentation and dislocation, photomontage offered "a visually and conceptually new image of the chaos of an age of war and revolution."

The only female member of the group, Hannah Höch (1889–1979), was schooled in the visual arts and advertising. Her early training in Berlin, preparing advertising brochures directed at a female audience, opened her eyes to the way in which mass media targeted women. To her photomontages she brought sensitivity to feminist issues and wary recognition of the growing corruption and militarism of Weimar Germany (the period between 1919 and Hitler's seizure of power in 1933). Her disjunctive *Cut with the Kitchen Knife through the Last Weimar Beer Belly Cultural Epoch of Germany* consists of bits and pieces clipped from newspapers and magazines: the wheels and cogs of military technology, the faces of German celebrities, and androgynous figures that reference her own bisexuality (Figure **33.15**). The series of "quick cuts" between the images anticipated experiments in cinematic montage that were to transform the history of film (see chapter 34).

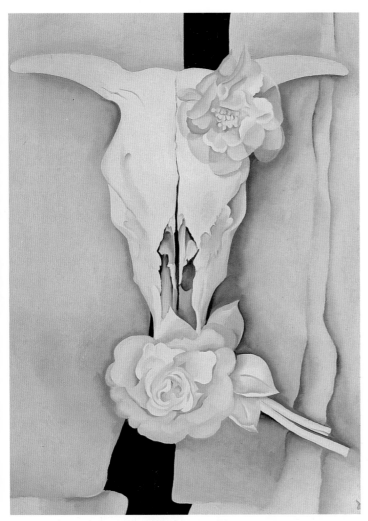

**Figure 33.13 GEORGIA O'KEEFFE**, *Cow's Skull: with Calico Roses*, 1931. Oil on canvas, 3 ft. ⁵⁄₁₆ in. × 24⅛ in. After an early career aided by the American photographer, Alfred Stieglitz (whom she later married), O'Keeffe left New York City, settling in New Mexico in 1934. Her earliest abstract drawings were inspired by her reading of Wassily Kandinsky's *On the Spiritual in Art.*

**Figure 33.14 MERET OPPENHEIM**, *Object: Breakfast in Fur (Object: Le Déjeuner en fourrure)*, 1936. Fur-covered cup, saucer, and spoon; cup 4⅜ in. diameter; saucer 9⅜ in. diameter; spoon 8 in. long; overall height 2⅞ in.

**Figure 33.15 HANNAH HÖCH**, *Cut with the Kitchen Knife*, 1919. Collage of pasted papers,
3 ft. 8⅜ in. × 35½ in. In this allegorical critique of Weimar culture, Höch irreverently assembles
photographic images of political leaders, sports stars, Dada artists, and urban political events.

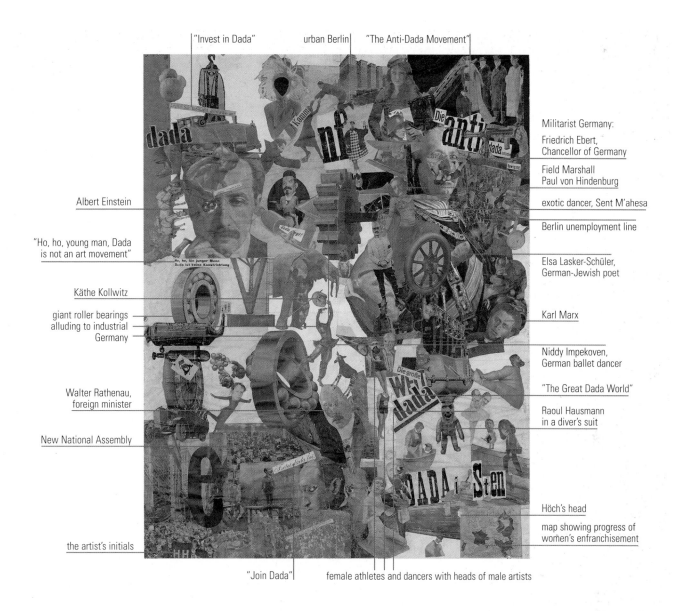

"Invest in Dada"  urban Berlin  "The Anti-Dada Movement"

Militarist Germany:
Friedrich Ebert,
Chancellor of Germany

Field Marshall
Paul von Hindenburg

Albert Einstein

exotic dancer, Sent M'ahesa

Berlin unemployment line

"Ho, ho, young man, Dada
is not an art movement"

Elsa Lasker-Schüler,
German-Jewish poet

Käthe Kollwitz

giant roller bearings
alluding to industrial
Germany

Karl Marx

Niddy Impekoven,
German ballet dancer

Walter Rathenau,
foreign minister

"The Great Dada World"

Raoul Hausmann
in a diver's suit

New National Assembly

Höch's head

map showing progress of
women's enfranchisement

the artist's initials

"Join Dada"  female athletes and dancers with heads of male artists

## Dada and Surrealist Film

The pranksters of Dada looked to film as a vehicle of the nonsensical. Duchamp and the American photographer Man Ray (1890–1976) matched wits in New York City to make one of the earliest Dada films, the entire action of which showed a courtesan, who called herself the baroness Elsa von Freytag-Loringhoven, shaving her pubic hair. In 1928, Salvador Dali teamed up with the Spanish filmmaker Luis Buñuel (1900–1983) to create the pioneer Surrealist film, *Un Chien Andalou*. Violence and eroticism are the dominant motifs of this film, whose more famous scenes include ants crawling out of a hole in a man's palm (an oblique reference to Christ's stigmata), a man bleeding from the mouth as he fondles a woman, a woman poking a stick at an amputated hand that lies on the street, an eyeball being sliced with a razor blade, and two pianos filled with the mutilated carcasses of donkeys. Such special techniques as slow motion, close-up, and quick cuts from scene to scene work to create jolting, dreamlike effects. It is no surprise that Surrealist film had a formative influence on some of the twentieth century's most imaginative filmmakers, including Jean Cocteau, Jean Renoir, Ingmar Bergman, and Federico Fellini.

# The New Psychology and Music

During the 1920s, composers moved beyond the exotic instrumental forays of Stravinsky's *Rite of Spring* to explore even more unorthodox experiments in sound. A group of six artists that included the French composer Eric Satie (1866–1925) incorporated into their music such "instruments" as doorbells, typewriters, and roulette wheels. Satie's style, which is typically sparse, rhythmic, and witty, has much in common with the poetry of Apollinaire and E. E. Cummings. His compositions, to which he gave such titles as *Flabby Preludes*, *Desiccated Embryos*, and *Three Pieces in the Form of a Pear*, were, however, less eccentric than was his lifestyle—he ate nothing but white foods and wore only gray suits.

## Strauss and Bartók

The Freudian impact on music was most evident in the medium of musical drama, which, by the second decade of the century, incorporated themes of sexuality, eroticism, female hysteria, and the life of dreams. In the opera *Salome* (1905), a modern interpretation of the martyrdom of John the Baptist, the German composer Richard Strauss (1864–1949) dramatized the obsessive erotic attachment of King Herod's beautiful niece to the Christian prophet. Revolutionary in sound (in some places the meter changes in every bar) and in its frank treatment of a biblical subject, *Salome* shocked critics so deeply that a performance slated for Vienna in 1905 was cancelled; in America, the opera was banned for almost thirty years after its New York performance in 1907.

*Bluebeard's Castle* (1918), a one-act opera by the leading Hungarian composer of the twentieth century, Béla Bartók (1881–1945), did not suffer so harsh a fate, despite the fact that the composer had boldly recast a popular fairy tale into a parable of repressed tensions and jealousy between the sexes.

## Schoenberg

The mood of anxiety and apprehension that characterized Expressionist and Surrealist art was, however, most powerfully realized in the compositions of Arnold Schoenberg, whose experiments in atonality were introduced in chapter 32. Schoenberg's song cycles, or **monodramas**, were dramatic pieces written for a single (usually deeply disturbed) character. In the monodrama *Erwartung* (*Expectation*), Schoenberg took as his subject a woman's frenzied search for the lover who has deserted her. In *Pierrot Lunaire* (*Moonstruck Pierrot*) of 1912, a cycle of twenty-one songs for female voice and small instrumental ensemble, Schoenberg brought to life the dreamworld of a mad clown.

The texts of his atonal and harshly dissonant song cycles resemble stream of consciousness monologues. They are performed in **Sprechstimme** (or "speech-song"), a style in which words are spoken at different pitches. Neither exclusively song nor speech, *Sprechstimme* is a kind of operatic recitation in which pitches are approximated and the voice may glide in a wailing manner from note to note. Many of the critics found *Pierrot Lunaire* "depraved" and "ugly." But despite the controversy ignited by his disquieting music, Schoenberg attracted a large following. Even after he moved to the United States in 1933, young composers—including many associated with Hollywood films—flocked to study with him. And, modern movie audiences were quick to accept the jolting dissonances of scores that worked to lend emotional expressiveness to the cinematic narrative.

## Berg

Schoenberg's foremost student, Alban Berg (1885–1935), produced two of the most powerful operas of the twentieth century. Though less strictly atonal than Schoenberg's song cycles, Berg's operas *Wozzeck* (1921) and *Lulu* (1935) make use of serial techniques and the *Sprechstimme* style. Thematically, they feature the highly charged motifs of sexual frustration, murder, and suicide.

The unfinished *Lulu* is the story of a sexually dominated woman who both destroys and is destroyed by her lovers. *Lulu* has been called "sordid," "psychotic," and "shocking." It explores such Freudian subjects as female hysteria and repressed sexuality, while at the same time it exploits the age-old image of woman-as-serpent. Both the music and the story of *Lulu* evoke a nightmarelike atmosphere, which, in modern multimedia productions, has been enhanced by the use of onstage film and slide projections.

See Music Listening Selections at end of chapter.

# LOOKING BACK

### Freud

- Sigmund Freud's theories concerning the nature of the human psyche, the significance of dreams, and the dominating role of human sexuality had a revolutionary effect on modern society and on the arts.
- As the events of the two world wars would confirm Freud's pessimistic analysis of human nature, so the arts of the twentieth century acknowledged his view that human reason was not the "keeper of the castle"; the castle itself was perilously vulnerable to the dark forces of the human mind.

### The New Psychology and Literature

- Proust, Kafka, and Joyce are representative of the modern novelist's preoccupation with the unconscious mind and with the role of memory and dreams in shaping reality.
- Stream of consciousness narrative and the interior monologue are among the modernist literary techniques used to develop plot and character.
- American playwrights responded to the stream of consciousness technique, even as modern theater and film investigated a new performance style based on method acting.
- The poetry of E. E. Cummings reveals the influence of free association in liberating words from the bounds of syntax and conventional transcription.

### The New Psychology and the Visual Arts

- In the visual arts, Freud's impact generated styles that gave free play to fantasy and dreams: the Expressionism of Munch and Kirchner, the Metaphysical art of de Chirico, and the colorful fantasies of Chagall.
- Marcel Duchamp, the most outrageous of the Dada artists, championed a nihilistic, antibourgeois, anti-art spirit that had far-reaching effects in the second half of the century.
- In 1924, André Breton launched Surrealism, an international movement to liberate the life of the mind from the bonds of reason. Strongly influenced by Freud, the Surrealists viewed the unconscious realm as a battleground of conflicting forces dominated by the instincts.
- Picasso, Miró, and Klee explored the terrain of the interior life in abstract paintings filled with both playful and ominous images, while Dali and Magritte questioned illusion itself by way of realistically detailed, yet irrationally juxtaposed objects.
- Kahlo, O'Keeffe, Oppenheim, and Höch were among the female Surrealists who manipulated the stuff of the real world so as to evoke jolting dreamlike effects and disquieting personal truths.

### The New Psychology and Music

- In music, Eric Satie made use of mundane sounds with the same enthusiasm that E. E. Cummings brought to slang and Duchamp exercised for "found objects."
- Freud's impact was most powerfully realized in the Expressionistic monodramas of Schoenberg and the sexually charged operas of Strauss, Bartók, and Berg.

### Music Listening Selections

**CD Two Selection 17** Schoenberg, *Pierrot Lunaire*, Op. 21, Part 3, No. 15, "Heimweh," 1912.

## Glossary

**archetype** the primal patterns of the collective unconscious, which Carl Jung described as "mental forms whose presence cannot be explained by anything in the individual's own life and which seem to be aboriginal, innate, and inherited shapes of the human mind"

**collective unconscious** according to Jung, the universal realm of the unconscious life, which contains the archetypes

**concrete poetry** poetry produced in the shape of ordinary, external objects

**improvisation** the invention of the work of art as it is being performed

**interior monologue** a literary device by which the stream of consciousness of a character is presented; it records the internal, emotional experience of the character on one or more levels of consciousness

**method acting** a modern style of theatrical performance that tries to harness childhood emotions and memories in the service of interpreting a dramatic role

**mobile** a sculpture constructed so that its parts move by natural or mechanical means

**monodrama** in music, a dramatic piece written for only one character

**nihilism** a viewpoint that denies objective moral truths and traditional religious and moral principles

**photomontage** the combination of freely juxtaposed and usually heterogeneous photographic images (see also Glossary, chapter 34, "montage")

***Sprechstimme*** (German, "speech-song") a style of operatic recitation in which words are spoken at different pitches

**sublimation** the positive modification and redirection of primal urges that Freud identified as the work of the ego

# Chapter

# 34

## Total War, Totalitarianism, and the Arts

**ca. 1900–1950**

*"Where is God now?"*
Elie Wiesel

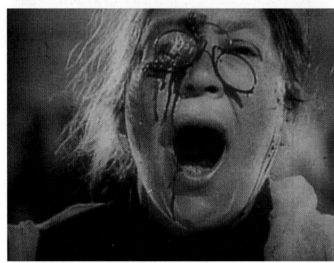

**Figure 34.1 SERGEI M. EISENSTEIN**, *The Battleship Potemkin*, 1925.
Film stills from Act IV, "The Odessa Steps Massacre."

# LOOKING AHEAD

Two fundamentally related calamities afflicted the twentieth century: total war and totalitarian dictatorship. The consequences of both were so great that the world has still not recovered from them. Total war and totalitarianism, facilitated by sophisticated military technology and electronic forms of mass communication, caused the twentieth century to be the bloodiest in world history. Unlike the Black Death, the Lisbon earthquake, and other natural disasters the wars and totalitarian regimes of the Modern Era were perpetrated *on* human beings *by* human beings. These human-made disasters not only challenged the belief that technology would improve the quality of human life, they seemed to validate Freud's theory that mortals are driven by base instincts and the dark forces of self-destruction.

The two world wars of the twentieth century provide the context for the arts of this era. Many writers, painters, and composers responded directly with visceral antiwar statements. Others, acknowledging the requirements of totalitarian regimes, those of Hitler in Germany, Stalin in Russia, and Mao in China, produced works that responded to the revolutionary ideologies of the state. Photography and film—media that appealed directly to the masses—became important wartime vehicles, functioning both as propaganda and as documentary evidence of brutality and despair. The era inspired two of the twentieth century's leading artists to produce landmark Modernist works: T. S. Eliot's *The Waste Land* and Pablo Picasso's *Guernica*.

## Total Wars

In the West, the end of the nineteenth century was a time of relative peace and optimistic faith in the progress of humankind. Throughout the world, however, sharp contrasts existed between rich and poor, and between technologically backward and technologically advanced nations. As the more powerful states jockeyed for political and economic primacy, and as Europe and the United States continued to build their industrial and military strength, few anticipated the possibility of widespread armed conflict. In 1914, however, that possibility became a reality with the outbreak of the first of two world wars. World War I, the first *total* war in world history, ended forever the so-called "age of innocence." And by the end of World War II in 1945, nothing would ever seem certain again.

The Great War of 1914, as World War I was called, and World War II, which followed in 1939, are called "total" not only because they involved more nations than

had ever before been engaged in armed combat, but because they killed—along with military personnel—large numbers of civilians. Further, they were total in the sense that they were fought with a "no holds barred" attitude—all methods of destruction were utilized in the name of conquest.

The weapons of advanced technology made warfare more impersonal and more devastating than ever before. World War I combatants used machine guns, heavy artillery, hand grenades, poison gas, flame throwers, armored tanks, submarines, dirigibles (airships), and airplanes. From their open cockpits, pilots fired on enemy aircraft, while on land soldiers fought from lines of trenches dug deep into the ground. The rapid-firing, fully automatic machine gun alone caused almost 80 percent of the casualties. The cost of four years of war was approximately $350 billion, and the death tolls were staggering. In all, seventy million armed men fought in World War I, and more than eight million of them died. In World War II, airplanes and aerial bombs (including, ultimately, the atomic bomb) played major roles; war costs tripled those of World War I, and casualties among the Allied forces alone rose to over eighteen million people.

The underlying cause of both wars was aggressive rivalry between European powers. During the nineteenth century, nationalism and industrialism had facilitated militant competition for colonies throughout the world (see chapter 30); the armed forces became the embodiment of a nation's sovereign spirit and the primary tool for imperialism. National leaders fiercely defended the notion that military might was the best safeguard of peace: *"Si vis pacem, para bellum"*—"if you want peace, prepare for war," they argued. Nations believed their safety lay in defensive alliances. They joined with their ideological or geographic neighbors to create a system of alliances that, by the early twentieth century, divided Europe into two potentially hostile camps, each equipped to mobilize their armies if threatened.

### World War I

The circumstances that led to World War I involved the increasingly visible efforts of Austria-Hungary and Germany to dominate vast portions of Eastern Europe. Germany, having risen to power during the nineteenth century, rivaled all other European nations in industrial might. By the early twentieth century, German efforts to colonize markets for trade took the form of militant imperialism in Eastern Europe. In July of 1914, Austria-Hungary, seeking to expand Austrian territory to the south, used the political assassination of Archduke Francis Ferdinand (heir to the throne of Austria-Hungary) as a pretext to declare war on Serbia. Almost immediately, two opposing alliances came into confrontation: the Central Powers of Austria-Hungary, Germany, and the Ottoman Empire versus the Allied forces of Serbia, Belgium, France, Great Britain, and Russia. Clearly, the policy of peace through military strength had not prevented war but actually encouraged it.

At the beginning of the war, the Central Powers won early victories in Belgium and Poland, but the Allies stopped the German advance at the First Battle of the Marne in September of 1914 (Map **34.1**). The opposing armies settled down to warfare along the western front—a solid line of two opposing trenches that stretched 500 miles from the English Channel to the Swiss border. At the same time, on the eastern front, Russian armies lost over a million men in combat against the combined German and Austrian forces. In the early years of the war, the United States remained neutral, but when German submarines began sinking unarmed passenger ships in 1917, the American president Woodrow Wilson opted to aid the Allies in order to "make the world safe for democracy." Fortified by American supplies and troops, the Allies moved toward victory. In November 1918, the fighting ended with an armistice.

# World War I Literature

## World War I Poetry

Writers responded to the war with sentiments ranging from buoyant idealism and militant patriotism to frustration and despair. The most enduring literature of the era, however, expressed the bitter anguish of the war experience itself. The poetry of the young British officer Wilfred Owen (1893–1918) reflects the sense of cynicism and futility that was voiced toward the end of the war. Owen viewed war as a senseless waste of human resources and a barbaric form of human behavior. His poems, which question the meaning of wartime heroism, unmask "the old Lie" that it is "fitting and proper to die for one's country." The poet was killed in combat at the age of twenty-five, just one week before the armistice was signed.

**Map 34.1** World War I, 1914–1918.

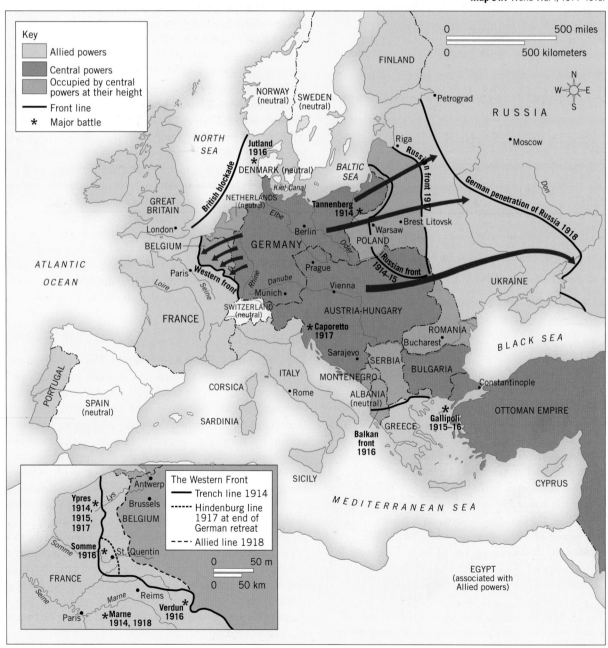

## READING 34.1 Owen's "Dulce Et Decorum Est"[1] (1918)

Bent double, like old beggars under sacks,                    1
Knock-kneed, coughing like hags, we cursed through sludge,
Till on the haunting flares we turned our backs,
And towards our distant rest began to trudge.
Men marched asleep. Many had lost their boots,               5
But limped on, blood-shod. All went lame, all blind;
Drunk with fatigue; deaf even to the hoots
Of tired, outstripped Five-Nines[2] that drop behind.

Gas! GAS! Quick, boys!—An ecstasy of fumbling
Fitting the clumsy helmets just in time,                     10
But someone still was yelling out and stumbling
And flound'ring like a man in fire or lime.—
Dim through the misty panes and thick green light,
As under a green sea, I saw him drowning.

In all my dreams before my helpless sight                    15
He plunges at me, guttering, choking, drowning.

If in some smothering dreams, you too could pace
Behind the wagon that we flung him in,
And watch the white eyes writhing in his face,
His hanging face, like a devil's sick of sin,                20
If you could hear, at every jolt, the blood
Come gargling from the froth-corrupted lungs
Bitter as the cud
Of vile, incurable sores on innocent tongues,—
My friend, you would not tell with such high zest            25
To children ardent for some desperate glory,
The old Lie: *Dulce et decorum est*
*Pro patria mori.*

**Q** Why does the poet try to reconcile the technology of modern war with traditional ideals of patriotism?

Other poets viewed the war as symbolic of a dying Western civilization. The poet T. S. Eliot, whom we met in chapter 32, summed up this view in his classic poem *The Waste Land* (1922). This requiem for a dry and sterile culture is structured like a collection of individual poems, each narrated by a different speaker at a different time, but all evoking the themes of loss and hope for redemption. Incorporating quotations in Greek, Italian, German, and Sanskrit, the poem makes reference to Classical and Celtic mythology, the Bible, Saint Augustine, Dante, Chaucer, Shakespeare, Whitman, Wagner, the Hindu Upanishads, the sermons of the Buddha, James Frazer's The Golden Bough (see chapter 31), and other canonic works. The inclusion of such references, while indicative of Eliot's erudition, required that the poet himself append footnotes to the text. *The Waste Land* became the single most influential poem in early modern literature. Its incantatory rhythms and profound allusions established the idiom of modern poetry as compressed, complex, and serious.

---

[1] "It is fitting and proper to die for one's country." A line from "Ode III" by the Roman poet Horace (see chapter 6).
[2] Gas shells.

## READING 34.2 From Eliot's *The Waste Land* (1922)

**V. *What the Thunder Said***

After the torchlight red on sweaty faces
After the frosty silence in the gardens
After the agony in stony places
The shouting and the crying
Prison and palace and reverberation
Of thunder of spring over distant mountains
He who was living is now dead
We who were living are now dying
With a little patience
    Here is no water but only rock
Rock and no water and the sandy road
The road winding above among the mountains
Which are mountains of rock without water
If there were water we should stop and drink
Amongst the rock one cannot stop or think
Sweat is dry and feet are in the sand
If there were only water amongst the rock
Dead mountain mouth of carious teeth that cannot spit
Here one can neither stand nor lie nor sit
There is not even silence in the mountains
But dry sterile thunder without rain
There is not even solitude in the mountains
But red sullen faces sneer and snarl
From doors of mudcracked houses
                              If there were water
    And no rock
    If there were rock
    And also water
    And water
    A spring
    A pool among the rock
    If there were the sound of water only
    Not the cicada
    And dry grass singing
    But sound of water over a rock
    Where the hermit-thrush sings in the pine trees
    Drip drop drip drop drop drop drop
    But there is no water

. . . . . . . . . .

**Q** It has been said that Eliot favored "biblical rhythms." Do you detect any in this excerpt? What effects do they achieve?

Eliot's contemporary and one of the greatest lyricists of the century, William Butler Yeats (1865–1939), responded to the violence of World War I and to the prevailing mood of unrest in his native Ireland with the apocalyptic poem "The Second Coming." The title of the poem alludes both to the long-awaited Second Coming of Jesus and to the nameless force that, in Yeats' view, threatened to enthrall the world in darkness.

Turning and turning in the widening gyre[1]                                1
The falcon cannot hear the falconer;
Things fall apart; the center cannot hold;
Mere anarchy is loosed upon the world,
The blood-dimmed tide is loosed, and everywhere          5
The ceremony of innocence is drowned;
The best lack all conviction, while the worst
Are full of passionate intensity.

Surely some revelation is at hand;
Surely the Second Coming is at hand.                            10
The Second Coming! Hardly are those words out
When a vast image out of Spiritus Mundi[2]
Troubles my sight: somewhere in sands of the desert
A shape with lion body and the head of a man,
A gaze blank and pitiless as the sun,                              15
Is moving its slow thighs, while all about it
Reel shadows of the indignant desert birds.
The darkness drops again; but now I know
That twenty centuries of stony sleep
Were vexed to nightmare by a rocking cradle,              20
And what rough beast, its hour come round at last,
Slouches towards Bethlehem to be born?

**Q** **Is the Second Coming Yeats describes one of deliverance or destruction?**

## World War I Fiction

World War I also inspired some of this century's most outstanding fiction—much of it written by men who had engaged in field combat. The American Ernest Hemingway (1899–1961) immortalized the Allied offensive in Italy in *A Farewell to Arms* (1929). The novel, whose title reflects the desperate hope that World War I would be "the war to end all wars," is a study in disillusionment and a testament to the futility of armed combat. Hemingway's prose is characterized by understatement and journalistic succinctness. His profound respect for physical and emotional courage, apparent in all his novels, was forged on the battlefields of the war, which he observed firsthand.

Armed conflict had a similar influence on the life and work of the novelist Erich Maria Remarque (1898–1970). Remarque, a German soldier who was wounded in combat several times, brought first-hand experience of World War I to his book *All Quiet on the Western Front*. Perhaps the finest war novel of the twentieth century, it portrays with horrifying clarity the brutal realities of trench warfare and poison gas, two of the most chilling features of the war. Remarque tells the story in first-person, present-tense narrative, a style that compels the reader to share the

---

[1] A circular course traced by the upward sweep of a falcon. The image reflects Yeats' cyclical view of history.

[2] World Spirit, similar to the Jungian Great Memory of shared archetypal images.

apprehension of the protagonist. Over one million copies of Remarque's novel were sold in Germany during the year of its publication, and similar success greeted it in translation and in its three movie versions. In 1939, however, the Nazi regime in Germany condemned Remarque's outspoken antimilitarism by publicly burning his books and depriving him of German citizenship. Shortly thereafter, Remarque moved to the United States, where he became an American citizen.

An indigent looking wood receives us. We pass by the soup-       1
kitchens. Under cover of the wood we climb out. The lorries
turn back. They are to collect us again in the morning, before
dawn.

Mist and the smoke of guns lie breast-high over the fields.
The moon is shining. Along the road troops file. Their helmets
gleam softly in the moonlight. The heads and the rifles stand
out above the white mist, nodding heads, rocking carriers of
guns.

Farther on the mist ends. Here the heads become figures;         10
coats, trousers, and boots appear out of the mist as from a
milky pool. They become a column. The column marches on,
straight ahead, the figures resolve themselves into a block,
individuals are no longer recognizable, the dark wedge presses
onward, fantastically topped by the heads and weapons
floating off on the milky pool. A column—not men at all.

Guns and munition wagons are moving along a crossroad.
The backs of the horses shine in the moonlight, their
movements are beautiful, they toss their heads, and their eyes
gleam. The guns and the wagons float before the dim            20
background of the moonlit landscape, the riders in their steel
helmets resemble knights of a forgotten time; it is strangely
beautiful and arresting.

We push on to the pioneer dump. Some of us load our
shoulders with pointed and twisted iron stakes; others thrust
smooth iron rods through rolls of wire and go off with them.
The burdens are awkward and heavy.

The ground becomes more broken. From ahead come
warnings: "Look out, deep shell-holes on the left"—"Mind,
trenches"— — —                                                           30

Our eyes peer out, our feet and our sticks feel in front of us
before they take the weight of the body. Suddenly the line halts;
I bump my face against the roll of wire carried by the man in
front and curse.

There are some shell-smashed lorries in the road. Another
order: "Cigarettes and pipes out." We are getting near the line.

In the meantime it has become pitch dark. We skirt a small
wood and then have the front-line immediately before us.

An uncertain, red glow spreads along the skyline from one
end to the other. It is in perpetual movement, punctuated with     40
the bursts of flame from the muzzles of the batteries. Balls of
light rise up high above it, silver and red spheres which
explode and rain down in showers of red, white, and green
stars. French rockets go up, which unfold a silk parachute to
the air and drift slowly down. They light up everything as

bright as day, their light shines on us and we see our shadows sharply outlined on the ground. They hover for the space of a minute before they burn out. Immediately fresh ones shoot up to the sky, and again, green, red, and blue stars.

"Bombardment," says Kat.                                                              50

The thunder of the guns swells to a single heavy roar and then breaks up again into separate explosions. The dry bursts of the machine-guns rattle. Above us the air teems with invisible swift movements, with howls, piping, and hisses. They are the smaller shells;—and amongst them, booming through the night like an organ, go the great coal-boxes and the heavies. They have a hoarse, distant bellow like a rutting stag and make their way high above the howl and whistle of the smaller shells. It reminds me of flocks of wild geese when I hear them. Last autumn the wild geese flew day after day       60 across the path of the shells.

The searchlights begin to sweep the dark sky. They slide along it like gigantic tapering rulers. One of them pauses, and quivers a little. Immediately a second is beside him, a black insect is caught between them and tries to escape—the airman. He hesitates, is blinded and falls. . . .

We go back. It is time we returned to the lorries. The sky is become a bit brighter. Three o'clock in the morning. The breeze is fresh and cool, the pale hour makes our faces look grey.

We trudge onward in single file through the trenches and       70 shell-holes and come again to the zone of mist. Katczinsky is restive, that's a bad sign.

"What's up, Kat?" says Kropp.

"I wish I were back home." Home—he means the huts.

"It won't last much longer, Kat."

He is nervous. "I don't know, I don't know— — —"

We come to the communication-trench and then to the open fields. The little wood reappears; we know every foot of ground here. There's the cemetery with the mounds and the black crosses.                                                             80

That moment it breaks out behind us, swells, roars, and thunders. We duck down—a cloud of flame shoots up a hundred yards ahead of us.

The next minute under a second explosion part of the wood rises slowly in the air, three or four trees sail up and then crash to pieces. The shells begin to hiss like safety-valves—heavy fire— —

"Take cover!" yells somebody—"Cover!"

The fields are flat, the wood is too distant and dangerous— the only cover is the graveyard and the mounds. We stumble       90 across in the dark and as though spirited away every man lies glued behind a mound.

Not a moment too soon. The dark goes mad. It heaves and raves. Darkness blacker than the night rushes on us with giant strides, over us and away. The flames of the explosions light up the graveyard.

There is no escape anywhere. By the light of the shells I try to get a view of the fields. They are a surging sea, daggers of flame from the explosions leap up like fountains. It is impossible for anyone to break through it.                                          100

The wood vanishes, it is pounded, crushed, torn to pieces. We must stay here in the graveyard.

The earth bursts before us. It rains clods. I feel a smack. My

sleeve is torn away by a splinter. I shut my fist. No pain. Still that does not reassure me: wounds don't hurt till afterwards. I feel the arm all over. It is grazed but sound. Now a crack on the skull, I begin to lose consciousness. Like lightning the thought comes to me: Don't faint, sink down in the black broth and immediately come up the top again. A splinter slashes into my helmet, but has travelled so far that it does not go through. I       110 wipe the mud out of my eyes. A hole is torn up in front of me. Shells hardly ever land in the same hole twice, I'll get into it. With one bound I fling myself down and lie on the earth as flat as a fish; there it whistles again, quickly I crouch together, claw for cover, feel something on the left, shove in beside it, it gives way, I groan, the earth leaps, the blast thunders in my ears, I creep under the yielding thing, cover myself with it, draw it over me, it is wood, cloth, cover, cover, miserable cover against the whizzing splinters.

I open my eyes—my fingers grasp a sleeve, an arm. A       120 wounded man? I yell to him—no answer—a dead man. My hand gropes farther, splinters of wood—now I remember again that we are lying in the graveyard.

But the shelling is stronger than everything. It wipes out the sensibilities, I merely crawl still deeper into the coffin, it should protect me, and especially as Death himself lies in it too.

Before me gapes the shell-hole. I grasp it with my eyes as with fists. With one leap I must be in it. There, I get a smack in the face, a hand clamps on to my shoulder—has the dead man waked up?—The hand shakes me, I turn my head, in the       130 second of light I stare into the face of Katczinsky, he has his mouth wide open and is yelling. I hear nothing, he rattles me, comes nearer, in a momentary lull his voice reaches me: "Gas—Gaas—Gaaas—Pass it on."

I grab for my gas-mask. Some distance from me there lies someone. I think of nothing but this: That fellow there must know: Gaaas—Gaaas— — —

I call, I lean toward him, I swipe at him with the satchel, he doesn't see—once again, again—he merely ducks—it's a recruit—I look at Kat desperately, he has his mask ready—I       140 pull out mine too, my helmet falls to one side, it slips over my face, I reach the man, his satchel is on the side nearest me, I seize the mask, pull it over his head, he understands, I let go and with a jump drop back into the shell-hole.

The dull thud of the gas-shells mingles with the crashes of the high explosives. A bell sounds between the explosions, gongs, and metal clappers warning everyone—Gas—Gas— Gaas.

Someone plumps down behind me, another. I wipe the goggles of my mask clear of the moist breath. It is Kat, Kropp,       150 and someone else. All four of us lie there in heavy, watchful suspense and breathe as lightly as possible.

These first minutes with the mask decide between life and death: is it tightly woven? I remember the awful sights in the hospital: the gas patients who in day-long suffocation cough their burnt lungs up in clots.

Cautiously, the mouth applied to the valve, I breathe. The gas still creeps over the ground and sinks into all hollows. Like a big, soft jelly-fish it floats into our shell-hole and lolls there obscenely. I nudge Kat, it is better to crawl out and lie on top       160 than to stay here where the gas collects most. But we don't get as far as that; a second bombardment begins. It is no longer as though the shells roared; it is the earth itself raging.

With a crash something black bears down on us. It lands close beside us; a coffin thrown up.

I see Kat move and crawl across. The coffin has hit the fourth man in our hole on his outstretched arm. He tries to tear off his gas-mask with the other hand. Kropp seizes him just in time, twists the hand sharply behind his back and holds it fast.

Kat and I proceed to free the wounded arm. The coffin lid is **170** loose and bursts open, we are easily able to pull it off, we toss the corpse out, it slides to the bottom of the shell-hole, then we try to loosen the under-part.

Fortunately the man swoons and Kropp is able to help us. We no longer have to be careful, but work away till the coffin gives with a sigh before the spade that we have dug in under it.

It has grown lighter. Kat takes a piece of the lid, places it under the shattered arm, and we wrap all our bandages round it. For the moment we can do no more.

Inside the gas-mask my head booms and roars—it is nigh **180** bursting. My lungs are tight, they breathe always the same hot, used-up air, the veins on my temples are swollen, I feel I am suffocating.

A grey light filters through to us. I climb out over the edge of the shell-hole. In the dirty twilight lies a leg torn clean off; the boot is quite whole, I take that all in at a glance. Now someone stands up a few yards distant. I polish the windows, in my excitement they are immediately dimmed again, I peer through them, the man there no longer wears his mask.

I wait some seconds—he has not collapsed—he looks **190** around and makes a few paces—rattling in my throat I tear my mask off too and fall down, the air streams into me like cold water, my eyes are bursting, the wave sweeps over me and extinguishes me. . . .

**Q** **What elements contribute to a sense of the macabre in this piece?**

**Q** **How does Remarque achieve cinematic momentum?**

## World War I Art

### Ernst

In Germany, World War I brought impassioned protests from many visual artists. One of the most outspoken was Max Ernst (1891–1976), whose career flowered in the Dada and Surrealist movements. Shortly after the war, Ernst began to create unsettling visual fantasies assembled from bits of photographs and prints that he cut from magazines, books, and newspapers. In the collage-painting *Two Ambiguous Figures* (Figure **34.2**), he combined the paraphernalia of modern warfare with the equipment of the scientist's laboratory.

Ernst's machinelike monsters are suspiciously reminiscent of the gas-masked soldiers that he encountered during his four-year stint in the German infantry. Sadly enough, Ernst's demons have become prophetic icons of modern warfare. Poison gas, used by the Iraqis in the 1980s war

**Figure 34.2 MAX ERNST**, *Two Ambiguous Figures*, 1919. Collage with gouache and pencil, 9½ × 6½ in. Ernst produced this provocative image by painting over a page torn from a teaching aids catalogue for scientific equipment used in chemistry and biology.

with Iran, received renewed international attention during the widely televised Gulf War of 1991, when images of both soldiers and civilians donning gas masks were a common, if appalling, sight.

### Grosz

The art of George Grosz (1893–1959) was unique in its imaginative blend of social criticism and biting satire. Discharged from the army in 1916 after a brief experience at the front, Grosz mocked the German military and its corrupt and mindless bureaucracy in sketchy, brittle compositions filled with pungent caricatures. For example, the wartime pen and ink drawing, *Fit for Active Service* (Figure **34.3**), shows a fat German army doctor pronouncing a skeletal cadaver "O.K.," hence, fit to serve in combat. Here, Grosz makes pointed reference to the prevailing military practice of drafting old (and even ill) recruits. In a trenchant line style, he evokes a sense of the macabre similar to that captured by Remarque in *All Quiet on the Western Front*. Like Remarque (and hundreds of other European artists and writers), Grosz fled Nazi Germany for the

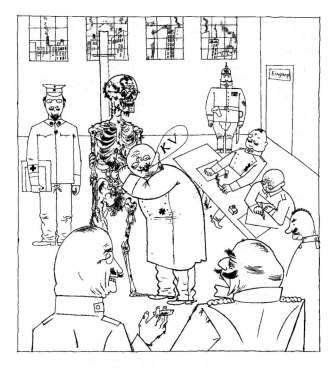

**Figure 34.3 GEORGE GROSZ**, *Fit for Active Service*, 1916–1917. Pen and brush and ink on paper, 20 × 14⅜ in. Grosz delighted in mocking the corrupt "fat cats" of Weimar society. At the top of this drawing, he shows factory chimneys spewing smoke that polluted the already tainted political environment of his native Berlin.

United States in the 1930s, where he eventually became an American citizen.

## Léger

Fernand Léger's art (1881–1955) is usually classed with that of the Cubists, but it was the French artist's wartime experience that actually shaped his long and productive career. During his four years on the front, Léger came to appreciate both the visual eloquence of modern machinery and the common humanity of the working-class soldiers with whom he shared the trenches. "Dazzled" (as he put it) by the breech of a 75-millimetre gun as it stood in the sunlight, Léger discovered similar kinds of beauty in ordinary human beings and in everyday objects—"the pots and pans on the white wall of your kitchen." "I invent images from machines," he claimed. The anonymity of urban life and the cold monumentality of the city—gray, hard, and sleek—became major themes for Léger in the postwar years. This "mechanical" aesthetic is visible in his painting *Three Women* (Figure **34.4**). Robust and robotic, the near-identical nudes (and their cat) share a common, austere geometry.

**Figure 34.4 FERNAND LÉGER**, *Three Women (Le Grand Déjeuner)*, 1921. Oil on canvas, 6 ft. ½ in. × 8 ft. 3 in. Sturdy women share the objectlike quality of a breakfast still life. "I have made use of the machine as others have used the nude body or the still life," explained Léger.

## Experimental Film

Fernand Léger produced one of the earliest and most influential abstract films in the history of motion pictures. Developed in collaboration with the American journalist Dudley Murphy, *Ballet mécanique* (*Mechanical Ballet*, 1923–1924) puts into motion a series of abstract shapes and mundane objects (such as bottles and kitchen utensils), which, interspersed with human elements, convey a playful but dehumanized sense of everyday experience. The rhythms and juxtapositions of the images suggest—without any narrative—the notion of modern life as mechanized, routine, standardized, and impersonal. The repeated image of a laundry woman, for instance, alternating with that of a rotating machine part, plays on the associative qualities of visual motifs in ways that would influence filmmakers for decades.

## The Russian Revolution

One of the last of the European powers to become industrialized, Russia entered World War I in 1914 under the leadership of Tzar Nicholas II (1868–1918). Russian involvement in the war, compounded by problems of government corruption and a weak and essentially agrarian economy, reduced the nation to desperate straits. Within a single year, the Russian army lost over one million men; a million more soldiers deserted. Food and fuel shortages threatened the entire civilian population. By 1917, a full-scale revolution was underway: strikes and riots broke out in the cities, while in the countryside peasants seized the lands of their aristocratic landlords. The revolution of 1917 forced the abdication of the tzar and ushered in a new regime, which, in turn, was seized by members of the Russian socialist party under the leadership of the Marxist revolutionary Vladimir Ilyich Lenin (1870–1924).

Between 1917 and 1921, by means of shrewd political manipulation and a reign of terror conducted by the Red Army and the secret police, Lenin installed the left-wing faction of the Marxist socialists—the Bolsheviks—as the party that would govern a nation of more than 150 million people. Tailoring Marxist ideas to the needs of revolutionary Russia, Lenin became the architect of Soviet communism.

In his treatise *Imperialism, the Highest Stage of Capitalism* (1916), Lenin followed Marx in describing imperialism as an expression of the capitalist effort to monopolize raw materials and markets throughout the world. He agreed that a "dictatorship of the proletariat" was the first step in liberating the workers from bourgeois suppression. While condemning the state as "the organ of class domination," he projected the transition to a classless society in a series of phases, which he outlined in the influential pamphlet "The State and Revolution" (1917). According to Lenin, in the first phase of communist society (generally called socialism), private property would be converted into property held in common and the means of production and distribution would belong to the whole of society. Every member of society would perform a type of labor and each would be entitled to a "quantity of products" (drawn from public warehouses) that corresponded to his or her "quantity of work." (A favorite

**Figure 34.5 A.I. STRAKHOV**, *Emancipated Women Build Socialism! 8th March, Day of the Liberation of Women*, 1920. Colored lithograph, 3 ft. 6½ in. × 26¾ in. Strong, simple forms, flat, bright colors, and short, easily memorized texts were the main characteristics of the Bolshevik political posters produced in the early decades of the twentieth century.

Lenin slogan ran, "He who does not work does not eat.") In the first phase of communism, the socialist state prevailed. As Lenin explained, "a form of state is still necessary, which, while maintaining public ownership of the means of production, would preserve the equality of labor and equality in the distribution of products."

In the second phase of communism, however, the state would disappear altogether:

> The state will be able to wither away completely when society has realized the rule: "From each according to his ability; to each according to his needs," *i.e.*, when people have become accustomed to observe the fundamental rules of social life, and their labor is so productive that they voluntarily work *according to their ability*. . . . There will then be no need for any exact calculation by society of the quantity of products to be distributed to each of its members; each will take freely according to his needs.

Lenin was aware that such a social order might be deemed "a pure Utopia"; yet, idealistically, he anticipated the victory of communist ideals throughout the world. The reality was otherwise. In early twentieth-century Russia, the Bolsheviks created a dictatorship *over* rather than *of* the proletariat. In 1918, when the Constituent Assembly refused to approve Bolshevik power, Lenin dissolved the assembly. (In free elections Lenin's party received less than a quarter of one percent of the vote.) He then eliminated all other parties and consolidated the Communist Party in the hands of five men—an elite committee called the Politburo, which Lenin himself chaired. Russia was renamed the Union of Soviet Socialist Republics (U.S.S.R.) in 1922, and in 1924 the constitution established a sovereign Congress of Soviets. But this body was actually governed by the leadership of the Communist Party, which maintained absolute authority well after Lenin's death.*

The Communist Party established the first **totalitarian** regime of the twentieth century. Totalitarianism subordinated the life of the individual to the needs of the state. Through strict control of political, economic, and cultural life, and by means of coercive measures such as censorship and terrorism, Soviet communists persecuted those whose activities they deemed threatening to the state. Using educational propaganda and the state-run media, they worked tirelessly to indoctrinate Soviet citizens with the virtues of communism.

Under the rule of Joseph Stalin (1879–1953), who took control of the communist bureaucracy in 1926, the Soviets launched vast programs of industrialization and agricultural collectivization (the transformation of private farms into government-run units) that demanded heroic sacrifice among the Soviet people. Peasants worked long hours on state-controlled farms, earning a bare subsistence wage.

---

* The Communist Party ceased to rule upon the collapse of the Soviet Union in 1991.

Stalin crushed all opposition: his secret police "purged" the state of dissidents, who were either imprisoned, exiled to *gulags* (labor camps), or executed. Between 1928 and 1938, the combination of severe famine and Stalin's inhuman policies (later known as "the great terror") took the lives of fifteen to twenty million Russians.

Communism enforced totalitarian control over all aspects of cultural expression. In 1934, the First All-Union Congress of Soviet Writers officially approved the style of *socialist realism* in the arts. It condemned all manifestations of "Modernism" (from Cubist painting to hot jazz) as "bourgeois decadence." The congress called upon Soviet artists to create "a true, historically concrete portrayal of reality in its revolutionary development." Artists—including Malevich and the pioneer Russian constructivists—were instructed to communicate simply and directly, to shun all forms of decadent (that is, modern) Western art, and to describe only the positive aspects of socialist society. In realistically conceived posters, the new Soviet man and woman were portrayed earnestly operating tractors or running factory machinery (Figure **34.5**). Thus the arts served to reinforce in the public mind the ideological benefits of communism. Socialist realism and the philosophy of art as mass propaganda lent support to almost every totalitarian regime of the twentieth century.

# The Great Depression and the American Scene

 World War I left Europe devastated, and massive economic problems burdened both the Central Powers and the Allied nations. In the three years following the war, world industrial production declined by more than a third, prices dropped sharply, and over thirty million people lost their jobs. The United States emerged from the war as the great creditor nation, but its economy was inextricably tied to world conditions. Following the inevitable crash of inflated stock prices in 1929, a growing paralysis swept through the American economy that developed into the Great Depression—a world crisis that lasted until the 1940s.

## Literature

The Great Depression inspired literary descriptions of economic oppression and misery that were often as much social documents as fictional narratives. The most memorable of these is the American novel *The Grapes of Wrath*, written in 1939 by John Steinbeck (1902–1968). The story recounts the odyssey of a family of Oklahoma migrant farmers who make their way to California in search of a living. In straightforward and photographically detailed prose, Steinbeck describes courageous encounters with starvation, injustice, and sheer evil. Like the soldiers in Remarque's regiment, the members of the Joad family (and especially the matriarch, Ma Joad) display heroism in sheer survival.

**Figure 34.6 THOMAS HART BENTON**, *City Activities with Dance Hall*, from the mural series *America Today*, 1930. Distemper and egg tempera on gessoed linen with oil glaze, 7 ft. 8 in. × 11 ft. 2½ in. Benton's *America Today* murals are set in the Prohibition Era: effective January 16, 1920, the eighteenth amendment to the United States Constitution prohibited the manufacture and sale of alcohol. Unpopular and unenforceable, the amendment was repealed in 1933.

beer, bootlegged during Prohibition

ticker-tape machine and Wall Street traders

trapeze artist and circus performers

cigarettes advertisement

Jazz Age dance hall

soda "jerk" in drugstore ice-cream parlor

sign above books alluding to popular mystery novels of "S. S. Van Dine"

Elizabeth Pollock, wife of Benton's student

Benton with paintbrush and highball, toasting Director of New School for Social Research who commissioned the murals

whiskey (illicit at the time), and shot glass

homemade still for making "bathtub gin"

woman reading cinema handbill

Benton's wife and son with Caroline Pratt, progressive educator and founder of the first nursery school in America

The *Grapes of Wrath* is an example of *Social Realism*, a style that presents socially significant subject matter in an objective and lifelike manner. Not to be confused with socialist realism, which operated to glorify the socialist state, Social Realism was a vehicle of criticism and political protest. A writer, declared Steinbeck, is "the watchdog of society"; he must "set down his time as nearly as he can understand it."

## The Visual Arts

During the Depression, Social Realism also dominated America's visual arts. In opposition to Modernism, which sacrificed subject matter to formal abstraction, Social Realism made use of recognizable imagery that communicated the concerns of the masses. The Missouri-born Thomas Hart Benton (1889–1975) devoted his career to depicting scenes that called into question the political and economic policies leading to the Great Depression. Benton aimed to commemorate "true" American values by immortalizing the lives of ordinary men and women, whom he pictured as rugged and energetic. In three sets of public **murals** completed between 1930 and 1933, he created an extraordinary pictorial history of the United States. He portrayed steelworking, mining, farming, and other working-class activities, as well as bootlegging, gospel singing, crap shooting, and a wide variety of essentially familiar pastimes.

Benton's *City Activities*, one section from *America Today*, a larger set of murals depicting American life during the Prohibition era, is a montage of "vignettes" from such popular urban entertainments as the circus, the movie theater, and the dance hall (Figure **34.6**). A ticker-tape machine—the symbol of Wall Street commercialism and American greed—appears in the upper part of the mural; it is balanced in the lower foreground by another instrument of commercialism—bootlegging equipment. Benton, who appears with paintbrush in hand in the lower right of the painting, admired the purity of Midwestern rural life. His assessment of America's urban centers as "nothing but coffins for living and thinking" is powerfully conveyed in *America Today*. In Benton's hands the mural was not mere decoration. It was a major form of public art, one that

## Science and Technology

| | |
|---|---|
| **1927** | the first television transmission is viewed in America |
| **1930** | the British invent a workable jet engine |
| **1938** | the Germans split the atom to achieve nuclear fission |
| **1939** | British scientists produce pure penicillin |
| **1945** | the first experimental atomic bomb is exploded at Alamogordo, New Mexico |

revealed ordinary American life as vividly as Renaissance murals mirrored the elitist world of sixteenth-century Italy.

## Mexico's Mural Renaissance

Benton drew inspiration from the work of two great Mexican muralists: José Clemente Orozco (1883–1949) and Diego Rivera (1886–1957). Their paintings, characterized by simple yet powerful forms and bold colors, capture the vitality and the futility of the Mexican Revolution—one of many militant efforts at reforming economic and social conditions in Central and South America during the first half of the twentieth century (Figure **34.7**).

**Figure 34.7 DIEGO RIVERA**, *Liberation of the Peon*, 1931. Fresco, 6 ft. 2 in. × 7 ft. 11 in. Rivera helped to launch Mexico's Mural Renaissance. His large, simplified figures and bold colors look back to Maya relief sculptures and frescoes.

The Mexican Revolution (1910–1920) was particularly significant as the first social revolution of the century to engage the active participation of great masses of peasants and urban workers. United under the banner of "Land Liberty," Mexico's farmers and laborers opposed the promotion of industry and the reallocation of farmland at their expense. Rivera championed their cause in murals that featured sympathetic depictions of peasants, often inspired by the art of their Maya and Aztec forebears. By emphasizing the Amerindian aspect of Mexico's history, Rivera's art—like the revolution itself—helped to effect a change in Mexico's self-image.

## Photography

During the Great Depression, photography was pressed into political service. United States federal agencies sponsored a program to provide a permanent record of economic and social conditions in rural America. Migration and rural poverty—bread lines, beggars, and the shanty towns of America's impoverished classes—became the primary subjects of *documentary photography*. The New York photographer Dorothea Lange (1895–1965) traveled across the country to record the conditions of destitute farmers who had fled the Midwestern dust bowl for the fields of California. *Migrant Mother* (Figure **34.8**), which Lange photographed at a farm camp in Nipomo, California, is the portrait of a gaunt thirty-two-year-old woman who had become the sole supporter of her six children. Forced to sell her last possessions for food, the anxious but unconquerable heroine in this photograph might have stepped out of the pages of Steinbeck's *Grapes of Wrath*. Lange's moving image reaches beyond a specific time and place to universalize the twin evils of poverty and oppression.

## Totalitarianism and World War II

In Germany, widespread discontent and turmoil followed the combined effects of the Great Depression and the humiliating peace terms dictated by the victorious Allies. Crippling debts forced German banks to close in 1931, and at the height of the Depression only one-third of all Germany's workers were fully employed. In the wake of these conditions, the young ideologue Adolf Hitler (1889–1945) rose to power. By 1933, Hitler was chancellor of Germany and the leader (in German, *Führer*) of the National Socialist German Workers' party (the *Nazi* party), which would lead Germany again into a world war.

A fanatic racist, Hitler shaped the Nazi platform. He blamed Germany's ills on the nation's internal "enemies," whom he identified as Jews, Marxists, bourgeois liberals, and "social deviates." Hitler promised to "purify" the German state of its "threatening" minorities and rebuild the country into a mighty empire. He manipulated public opinion by using all available means of propaganda—especially the radio, which brought his voice into every German home.

**Figure 34.8 DOROTHEA LANGE**, *Migrant Mother, Nipomo, California*, 1936. Gelatin-silver print. *Migrant Mother* has been hailed as the Depression era equivalent of the medieval Madonna: an image of protective anguish and despair.

In his autobiographical work *Mein Kampf* (*My Struggle*), published in 1925, Hitler set forth a misguided theory of "Aryan racial superiority" that would inspire some of the most malevolent episodes in the history of humankind, including genocide: the systematic extermination of millions of Jews, along with thousands of Roman Catholics, gypsies, homosexuals, and other minorities. Justifying his racist ideology, he wrote:

> What we must fight for is to safeguard the existence and reproduction of our race and our people, the sustenance of our children and the purity of our blood, the freedom and independence of the fatherland so that our people may mature for the fulfillment of the mission allotted to it by the creator of the universe.

*Mein Kampf* exalted the totalitarian state as "the guardian of a millennial future in the face of which the wishes and the selfishness of the individual must appear as nothing and submit." "The state is a means to an end," insisted Hitler. "Its end lies in the preservation and advancement of physically and psychically homogeneous creatures."

Less than twenty years after the close of World War I the second, even more devastating, world war threatened. The conditions that contributed to the outbreak of World War II included the failure of the peace settlement that had ended World War I and the undiminished growth of nationalism and militarism. But the specific event that initiated a renewal of hostilities was Hitler's military advance into Poland in 1939.

Once again, two opposing alliances were formed: Germany, Italy, Bulgaria, and Hungary comprised the Axis powers (the term describing the imaginary line between Rome and Berlin), while France and Britain and, in 1941, the United States and the Soviet Union, constituted the major Allied forces. Germany joined forces with totalitarian regimes in Italy (under Benito Mussolini) and in Spain (under General Francisco Franco), and the hostilities quickly spread into North Africa, the Balkans, and elsewhere. The fighting that took place during the three-year civil war in Spain (1936–1939) and in the German attack on the Netherlands in 1940 anticipated the merciless aspects of total war. In Spain, Nazi dive-bombers destroyed whole cities, while in the Netherlands, German tanks, parachute troops, and artillery overran the country in less than a week. The tempo of death was quickened as German air power attacked both military and civilian targets. France fell to Germany in 1940, and Britain became the target of systematic German bombing raids. At the same time, violating a Nazi–Soviet pact of 1939, Hitler invaded the Soviet Union, only to suffer massive defeat in the Battle of Stalingrad in 1942 (Map **34.2**).

The United States, though supportive of the Allies, again tried to hold fast to its policy of "benevolent neutrality." It was brought into the war nevertheless by Japan, which had risen rapidly to power in the late nineteenth century. Japan had defeated the Russians in the Russo–Japanese War of 1904. The small nation had successfully invaded Manchuria in 1931 and established a foothold in China and Southeast Asia. In December 1941, in opposition to United States efforts at restricting Japanese trade, the Japanese naval air service dropped bombs on the American air base at Pearl Harbor in Hawaii. The United States, declaring war on Japan, joined the twenty-five other nations that opposed the Axis powers and sent combat forces to fight in both Europe and the Pacific.

The war against Japan was essentially a naval war, but it involved land and air attacks as well. Its terrible climax was America's attack on two Japanese cities, Hiroshima and Nagasaki, in August of 1945. The bombing, which annihilated over 120,000 people (mostly civilians) and forced the Japanese to surrender within a matter of days, ushered in the atomic age. Just months before, as German forces had given way to Allied assaults on all fronts, Hitler

**Map 34.2** World War II: The Defeat of the Axis, 1942–1945.

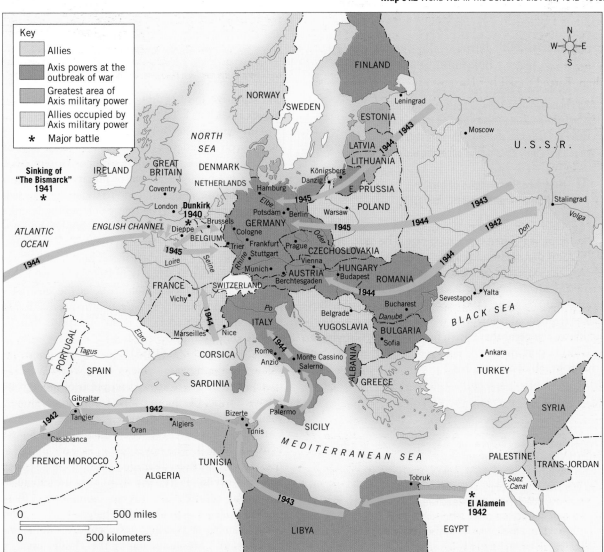

had committed suicide. World War II came to a close with the surrender of both Germany and Japan in 1945.

## World War II Poetry

Around the globe World War II poetry carried to new extremes the sentiments of despair and futility. The American poet and critic Randall Jarrell (1914–1965), who served in the US Army Air Corps from 1942 to 1946, condemned military combat as dehumanizing and degrading. In the short poem "The Death of the Ball Turret Gunner," a World War II airman, speaking from beyond the grave, recounts his fatal experience as an air force gunner. Encased in the Plexiglas bubble dome of an airplane ball turret—like an infant in his mother's womb—he "wakes" to "black flak" and dies; the startling image of birth in death conflates dreaming and waking. Jarrell observed that modern combat, fueled by sophisticated technical instruments, neither fostered pride nor affirmed human nobility. Rather, such combat turned the soldier into a technician and an instrument of war. It robbed him of personal identity and reduced him to the level of an object—a thing to be washed out by a high-pressure steam hose. The note to the title of the poem was provided by the poet himself.

---

### READING 34.5 Jarrell's "The Death of the Ball Turret Gunner"[1] (1945)

From my mother's sleep I fell into the State,
And I hunched in its belly till my wet fur froze.[2]
Six miles from earth, loosed from its dream of life,
I woke to black flak and the nightmare fighters.
When I died they washed me out of the turret with a hose.

**Q** How are the images of birth and death conflated by Jarrell?

---

In Japan, lamentation preceded rage. The *haiku*, the light verse form that had traditionally enshrined such images as cherry blossoms and spring rain, now became the instrument by which Japanese poets evoked the presence of death. Kato Shuson (1905–1993) introduced the three *haikus* reproduced below with the following words: "In the middle of the night there was a heavy air raid. Carrying my sick brother on my back I wandered in the flames with my wife in search of our children."

---

[1] "A ball turret was a Plexiglas sphere set into the belly of a B-17 or B-24 and inhabited by two .50 caliber machine-guns and one man, a short, small man. When this gunner traced with his machine-guns a fighter attacking his bomber from below, he revolved with the turret; hunched upside-down in his little sphere, he looked like the fetus in the womb. The fighters which attacked him were armed with cannon firing explosive shells. The hose was a steam hose."
[2] The airman's fur-lined flight jacket.

---

### READING 34.6 Shuson's *haikus* (ca. 1945)

| | |
|---|---|
| *Hi no oku ni* | In the depths of the flames |
| *Botan kuzururu* | I saw how a peony |
| *Sama wo mitsu* | Crumbles to pieces. |
| | |
| *Kogarashi ya* | Cold winter storm— |
| *Shōdo no kinko* | A safe-door in a burnt-out site |
| *Fukinarasu* | Creaking in the wind. |
| | |
| *Fuyu kamome* | The winter sea gulls— |
| *Sei no ie nashi* | In life without a house, |
| *Shi no haka nashi* | In death without a grave. |

**Q** What effects are achieved by verbal compression?

## World War II Fiction

As in the poetry of Jarrell, the novels of World War II were characterized by nihilism and resignation, their heroes robbed of reason and innocence. In *From Here to Eternity* (1951) by James Jones (1921–1977) and *The Naked and the Dead* (1948) by Norman Mailer (1923–2007), war makes men and machines interchangeable—the brutality of total war dehumanizes its heroes. Mailer's raw, naturalistic novels, which are peppered with the four-letter words that characterize so much modern fiction, portray a culture dominated by violence and sexuality. Stylistically, Mailer often deviated from the traditional beginning-middle-and-end narrative format, using instead such cinematic techniques as flashback.

This episodic technique also prevails in the novels of Joseph Heller (1923–1999), Kurt Vonnegut (1922–2007), and other **gallows humor** writers. "Gallows" (or "black") humor is a form of literary satire that mocks modern life by calling attention to situations that seem too ghastly or too absurd to be true. Such fiction describes the grotesque and the macabre in the passionless and nonchalant manner of a contemporary newspaper account. Like an elaborate hate joke, the gallows humor novel provokes helpless laughter at what is hideous and awful. Modern war, according to these humorists, is the greatest of all hate jokes: dominated by bureaucratic capriciousness and mechanized destruction, it is an enterprise that has no victors, only victims.

Heller's *Catch-22* (1955), one of the most popular gallows humor novels to emerge from World War II, marks the shift from the realistic description of modern warfare (characteristic of the novels of Remarque, Jones, and Mailer) to its savage satirization. Heller based the events of *Catch-22* on his own experiences as an air force bombardier in World War II. The novel takes place on an air base off the coast of Italy, but its plot is less concerned with the events of the war than with the dehumanizing operations of the vast military bureaucracy that runs the war. Heller describes this bureaucracy as symbolic of "the humbug, hypocrisy, cruelty and sheer stupidity of our mass society." His rendering of the classic armed forces condolence form-letter satirizes the impersonal character of modern war and provides a brief example of his biting style:

> Dear Mrs.,/Mr.,/Miss,/or Mr. and Mrs.— — —:
> Words cannot express the deep personal grief I experienced when your husband,/son,/father,/or brother was killed,/wounded,/or reported missing in action.

*Catch-22* is a caustic blend of nihilism and forced cheerfulness. The characters in the novel—including a navigator who has no sense of direction and an aviator who bombs his own air base for commercial advantage—operate at the mercy of a depersonalizing system. As they try their best to preserve their identity and their sanity, they become the enemies of the very authorities that sent them to war.

## Responses to Totalitarianism

While total war became a compelling theme in twentieth-century fiction, so too did totalitarianism, especially as it was described by those who had experienced it first-hand. Until Stalin's death in 1953, a reign of terror prevailed in the Soviet Union. As many found out, the slightest deviation from orthodox Marxist-Stalinist decorum resulted in imprisonment, slave labor, or execution. Between 1929 and 1953 some eighteen million people were sent to prison camps and another six million were exiled to remote parts of the Soviet Union. Aleksandr Solzhenitsyn (1918–2008) served in the Russian army during World War II, and although he had twice received recognition for bravery in combat, Solzhenitsyn was arrested in 1945 for veiled anti-Stalinist comments that he had made in a letter to a friend. He was sentenced to eight years of imprisonment, spending half the term in a *gulag* in Siberia and the other half teaching mathematics in a Moscow prison. His Siberian experience provided the eyewitness material for his first novel, *One Day in the Life of Ivan Denisovich* (1962). It was followed in 1973–1976 by *The Gulag Archipelago*, a documentary description of Soviet prison life. These dispassionate accounts of the grim conditions of totalitarianism are searing indictments of inhumanity, and testaments to the heroism of the victims of Soviet political oppression.

Like Stalin, Hitler wielded unlimited and often ruthless authority. He destroyed democratic institutions in Germany, condemned avant-garde art, modern architecture, atonal music, and jazz as "degenerate," attacked Einstein's theories as "Jewish physics," and proceeded to eliminate—by means of the *Gestapo* (the Nazi secret police)—all opposition to his program of mass conformity. In 1933, over 35,000 Germans died either by suicide or from "unexplained causes." Over the next ten years, concentration camps arose in Austria, Poland, and Germany to house Hitler's "impure" minorities. It is estimated that six million Jews and five million non-Jews were put to death in Nazi gas chambers—a hideous episode in European history known as the Holocaust.

In Germany, the voices of actual witnesses to the atrocities of the Holocaust were for the most part silenced by death, but drawings by camp inmates and documentary photographs taken just after the war (see Figure 34.11) provide shocking visual evidence of modern barbarism. One of the most eloquent survivors of the Holocaust is the writer Elie Wiesel (b. 1928), recipient of the Nobel Peace Prize in 1986. At the age of fifteen, Wiesel, a Romanian Jew, was shipped with his entire family to the concentration camp at Auschwitz, Poland. From there the family was split up, and Wiesel and his father were sent to a labor camp in Buchenwald, Germany, where the youth saw his father and hundreds of others killed by the Nazis. Liberated in 1945, Wiesel transmuted the traumatic experiences of his childhood into prose. "Auschwitz," wrote Wiesel, "represents the negation and failure of human progress: it negates the human design and casts doubts on its validity." *Night*, Wiesel's autobiographical record of the Nazi terrors, is a graphic account of Hitler's barbarism. The brief excerpt that follows reveals the anguish Wiesel and other Jews experienced in confronting what appeared to be God's silence in the face of brutal injustice.

### READING 34.7 From Wiesel's *Night* (1958)

One day, the electric power station at Buna was blown up. The [1] Gestapo, summoned to the spot, suspected sabotage. They found a trail. It eventually led to the Dutch Oberkapo.[1] And there, after a search, they found an important stock of arms.

The Oberkapo was arrested immediately. He was tortured for a period of weeks, but in vain. He would not give a single name. He was transferred to Auschwitz. We never heard of him again.

But his little servant had been left behind in the camp in prison. Also put to torture, he too would not speak. Then the SS[2] sentenced him to death, with two other prisoners who had [10] been discovered with arms.

One day when we came back from work, we saw three gallows rearing up in the assembly place, three black crows. Roll call. SS all round us, machine guns trained: the traditional ceremony. Three victims in chains—and one of them, the little servant, the sad-eyed angel.

The SS seemed more preoccupied, more disturbed than usual. To hang a young boy in front of thousands of spectators was no light matter. The head of the camp read the verdict. All eyes were on the child. He was lividly pale, almost calm, [20] biting his lips. The gallows threw its shadow over him.

This time the Lagerkapo[3] refused to act as executioner. Three SS replaced him.

The three victims mounted together onto the chairs.

The three necks were placed at the same moment within the nooses.

"Long live liberty!" cried the two adults.

But the child was silent.

"Where is God? Where is He?" someone behind me asked.

At a sign from the head of the camp, the three chairs tipped [30]

---

[1] The foreman of the prisoners, selected from among them by the Nazis.

[2] A special police force that operated the camps.

[3] The prisoner who acted as foreman of the warehouse.

**Figure 34.9 LEE MILLER**, *Buchenwald, Germany,* 30 April 1945. Photograph.

over.

Total silence throughout the camp. On the horizon, the sun was setting.

"Bare your heads!" yelled the head of the camp. His voice was raucous. We were weeping.

"Cover your heads!"

Then the march past began. The two adults were no longer alive. Their tongues hung swollen, blue-tinged. But the third rope was still moving; being so light, the child was still alive. . . .

For more than half an hour he stayed there, struggling    40
between life and death, dying in slow agony under our eyes. And we had to look him full in the face. He was still alive when I passed in front of him. His tongue was still red, his eyes were not yet glazed.

Behind me, I heard the same man asking:

"Where is God now?"

And I heard a voice within me answer him:

"Where is He? Here He is—He is hanging here on this gallows. . . ."

That night the soup tasted of corpses. . . .    50

**Q** **What similarities and differences do you detect between the circumstances described here and those described by Remarque (Reading 34.4)?**

**Q** **How do the styles of Wiesel and Remarque compare?**

## The Visual Arts in the War Era

### Photojournalism

The realities of World War II were recorded by an international array of photojournalists. One of the most gifted was Lee Miller (1907–1977), an American debutante who became the first female wartime photojournalist and an early witness to the horrors of the German concentration camps (Figure **34.9**). The American photographer Robert Capa (1897–1954) produced notable pictures of World War II paratroopers, and the French photographer Henri Cartier-Bresson (1908–2004) immortalized the plight of war-torn Europe in hundreds of aesthetically compelling social realist photographs.

In the Soviet Union, photography came under the totalitarian knife, as Stalin's propagandists carefully excised from official photographs unseemly images of political brutality. The "remaking" of history via photomanipulation— a technique that would become popular among American filmmakers at the end of the century—had its ignoble beginnings in the war era.

### Picasso's *Guernica*

On the afternoon of April 26, 1937, during the Spanish Civil War (1936–1939) that pitted republican forces against the Fascist dictatorship of General Francisco Franco, the German air force (in league with the Spanish Fascists) dropped incendiary bombs on Guernica, a small Basque market town in northeast Spain. During three and a half hours of bombing, the town was leveled and hundreds of people were killed. News of the event—the world's first aerial bombardment of a civilian target—reached Paris, where the horrified Pablo Picasso read illustrated newspaper accounts of the attack as the death toll mounted. Earlier in the year, the artist had been invited to contribute a painting for the Spanish Pavilion of the Paris World's Fair. The bombing of Guernica provided him with inspiration for the huge mural that would become the twentieth century's most memorable antiwar image (see Figure 34.10).

More powerful than any literary description, *Guernica* captures the grim brutality and suffering of the wartime era. For the painting, as wide as the 26 feet of his studio wall, Picasso chose monochromatic tones—the ashen grays of incineration—which also call to mind the documentary media of mass communication: newspapers, photographs, and film. However, *Guernica* is far from documentary. Its flat, abstract figures and airless spatial field, distilled from the language of Cubism, provide a sharp contrast with the Social Realist style that dominated much of the art produced in Europe and America between the wars. Distinct from a true-to-life rendering, the painting conflates the actual event of the bombing with an assortment of images drawn from Picasso's personal pictorial vocabulary, especially those of the Spanish bullfight, the ancient ritual of sacrificial death that intrigued the artist. The bull, at once hero and victim of the traditional combat, stands at the left of the shallow stage; the horse, whose body bears the gaping wound of a spear, rears its head in an agonized cry, its role in this massacre no less devastating than the one it

often plays in the bullring, when attacked by the bull itself. Four women—one carrying a dead infant, a second holding a lamp, a third consumed in the flames of a burning building—issue voiceless screams configured to repeat that of the wounded horse. The dead warrior at the bottom of the composition—actually a broken statue—makes reference to war's corrupting effect on the artifacts of high culture, while mocking the militant idealism represented by traditional war monuments. By the unique conjunction of powerful images—a screaming woman, a dead baby, a severed arm, a victimized animal—Picasso created a universal icon for the inhuman atrocities of war, one that has made good his claim that art is "a weapon against the enemy."

# MAKING CONNECTIONS

**Figure 34.10 PABLO PICASSO** (above), *Guernica*, 1937. Oil on canvas, 11 ft. 5½ in. × 25 ft. 5¾ in.

Picasso regarded himself as heir to the historical giants of world art, and especially those who came from his own native Spain. Familiar with Goya's painting, *The Third of May, 1808* (Figure **34.11**), which immortalizes the massacre of Madrid's citizens by the invading forces of France, he expropriated some of its most effective devices, such as the triangular beam of light that unifies the composition and sharp light/dark contrasts that create dramatic tension. In the image of the burning woman in *Guernica* (Figure **34.10**), Picasso makes reference to the unforgettable figure of Goya's protagonist, who, facing the French firing squad, flings his arms above his head in a gesture of rage and despair. Since the return of *Guernica* to Spain in 1981, it has become, like Goya's *Third of May*, a national monument.

**Figure 34.11 FRANCISCO GOYA** (below), *The Third of May, 1808: The Execution of the Defenders of Madrid*, 1814. Oil on canvas, 8 ft. 6 in. × 10 ft. 4 in.

**Figure 34.12 SERGEI M. EISENSTEIN**, *The Battleship Potemkin*, 1925. Film stills from Act IV, "The Odessa Steps Massacre." A woman, whose face will be slashed by a soldier, watches the careening baby carriage as it rolls down the steps. The Odessa Steps sequence, whose rapidly increasing tempo evokes apprehension and terror, is an ingenious piece of editing that has been imitated with great frequency by modern filmmakers.

## Film in the War Era

### Eisenstein

Film provided a permanent historical record of the turbulent military and political events of the early twentieth century. It also became an effective medium of political propaganda. In Russia, Lenin envisioned film as an invaluable means of spreading the ideals of communism. Following the Russian Revolution, he nationalized the fledgling motion-picture industry. In the hands of the Russian filmmaker Sergei Eisenstein (1898–1948), film operated both as a vehicle for political persuasion and as a fine art. He shaped the social and artistic potential of cinema by combining realistic narrative with symbolic imagery.

In *The Battleship Potemkin* (1925), his silent film masterpiece, Eisenstein told the story of a 1905 mutiny led by the crew of a Russian naval vessel, and the subsequent massacre of their sympathizers—the citizens of Odessa. While this singular event did not actually occur, Eisenstein drew on similar brutalities described in the Russian press. To recreate the effect of an on-the-spot documentary, he made use of **montage**, the cinematic technique that depends on a rapid succession of images. The so-called "Odessa Steps sequence" at the end of the film interposes 155 separate images in less than five minutes; the footage shows the advancing tzarist soldiers attacking their civilian victims, including a mother who is killed trying to save her infant in a baby carriage that slowly careens down a broad flight of stairs (Figure **34.12**).

Alternating close-ups (see Figure 34.1) and long shots, shots from below and above, fixed shots and traveling shots, the Odessa Steps sequence gave the fictional massacre of Odessa's civilian victims unprecedented dramatic authenticity.

Two years later, in 1927, Eisenstein made the Russian Revolution itself the subject of the film *Ten Days That Shook the World*. Both in his silent movies and in those he made later with sound, Eisenstein developed techniques that drew the viewer into the space of the film. He deliberately cut off parts of faces to bring attention to the eyes, played one shot off the next to build a conflicting and often discontinuous sequence, and devised visual angles that, in true constructivist fashion, produced startling asymmetrical abstractions.

The masterpiece of Eisenstein's post-silent film career was *Alexander Nevsky* (1938), a film that exalted the thirteenth-century Russian prince who defended the motherland against the onslaught of the Teutonic Knights. Here Eisenstein linked the musical score (composed by Sergei Prokofiev) to the pacing of the cinematic action: specifically, to the compositional flow of individual shots in the visual sequence—a technique known as "vertical montage." In place of the operatic crowd scenes of his earlier films, he framed the protagonist within landscapes and battle scenes that were as gloriously stylized as monumental paintings. *Alexander Nevsky* earned the approval of Joseph Stalin and the acclaim of the Russian people. It survives as a landmark in the history of inventive filmmaking.

### Riefenstahl

While Eisenstein used film to glorify the collective and individual heroism of the Soviet people, German filmmakers working for Hitler turned motion pictures into outright vehicles of state propaganda. The filmmaker and former actress Leni Riefenstahl (1902–2003) received unlimited state subsidies to produce the most famous propaganda film of all time, *The Triumph of the Will* (1934). She engaged a crew of 135 people to film the huge rallies and ceremonies staged by Hitler and the Nazi party, including their first meeting in Nuremberg. *The Triumph of the Will* is a synthesis of documentary fact and sheer artifice. Its bold camera angles and stark compositions seem in themselves totalitarian—witness the absolute symmetry and exacting conformity of the masses of troops that frame the tiny figures of Hitler and his compatriots at the Nuremberg rally (Figure **34.13**).

### Film in America

In America, film served to inform, to boost morale, and to propagandize for the Allied cause; but it also served as entertainment and escape. At the height of the Depression as well as during the war era millions of Americans flocked to movie theaters each week. While such prize-winning movies as *All Quiet on the Western Front* (1930) and *From Here to Eternity* (1953) were painfully realistic, numerous other films romanticized and glamorized the war. An exception to the standard war-movie fare was *The Great Dictator* (1940), which was directed by the multitalented British-born actor and filmmaker Charlie Chaplin (1889–1977). In this hilarious satire of Fascist dictatorship, Adolf Hitler (known in the film as Adenoid Hynkel and played by Chaplin) rises to power as head of the "Double Cross Party," only to be arrested by his own troops, who mistake him for a Jewish barber.

**Figure 34.13 LENI RIEFENSTAHL**, *The Triumph of the Will*, 1934. Film still showing Himmler, Hitler, and Lutze framed by columns of people as they approach the memorial monument in Nuremberg, Germany.

# Music in the War Era

Every totalitarian government in history has feared the power of music. In Nazi Germany, jazz was forbidden on the basis of its free and improvised style and its association with black musicians; in communist China, Beethoven's music was banned as the sound of the independent spirit. In Soviet Russia, Lenin's regime laid down the specific rule that composers write only music that "communicated" to the people. Atonality, associated with elitism and inscrutability, was to be avoided, along with other expressions of Western "decadence." "Music," observed Lenin, "is a means of unifying great masses of people."

## Shostakovich

The career of the eminent Russian composer Dmitri Shostakovich (1906–1975) illustrates the challenges faced by Soviet composers in the time of Stalin. Enrolled at thirteen in the Leningrad Conservatory, Shostakovich was the product of rigorous classical training. His compositions, including fifteen symphonies, fifteen string quartets, and numerous scores for ballet, opera, plays, and motion pictures, incorporate songlike melodies and insistent rhythmic repetition. They are essentially tonal, but they make dramatic use of dissonance. One of his first operas, *Lady Macbeth of Mtsensk* (1934), was hailed by the Soviet press as a loyal expression of socialist ideology. However, within two years, *Pravda*, the official Soviet newspaper, condemned it as "*antinarodnaya*," that is, "antipeople." In 1941, the Seventh ("Leningrad") Symphony was hailed as a celebration of the Soviet triumph against the Nazi invasion of Leningrad. Nevertheless, in 1948, it received harsh criticism for its "bourgeois formalism." That same year, Shostakovich was denounced by the government and dismissed from his posts at the Moscow and Leningrad Conservatories.

The fact that music rarely has meaning beyond sound itself worked, however, in the composer's favor: passages featuring militaristic rhythms might be taken as a sign of militant triumph, but they might also be heard as a reference to freedom from oppression. Only after 1979, when the memoirs of Shostakovich were smuggled out of the Soviet Union, did it become apparent that the composer intended the symphony as an attack on Stalin's inhumanity toward his own people.

## Prokofiev

The career of the Russian composer Sergei Prokofiev (1891–1953) was equally turbulent. Permitted to leave Russia in 1918, he was persuaded to return in 1936. Defending Soviet principles, he proclaimed ". . . the composer . . . is in duty bound to serve man, the people. He must be a citizen first and foremost, so that his art may consciously extol human life and lead man to a radiant future." In 1948, the Soviets nevertheless denounced Prokofiev's music as "too modern"; and, along with Shostakovich, Prokofiev was relieved of his position at the Soviet music conservatories.

Prokofiev's compositions, most of which reveal his preference for classical form, are tonal and melodic, but they are boldly inventive in modulation and harmonic dissonance. In his scores for the ballets *Romeo and Juliet* (1935) and *Cinderella* (1944), and in his cantata for the Eisenstein film *Alexander Nevsky* (1938), Prokofiev demonstrated a talent for driving rhythms, sprightly marches, and unexpected, often whimsical shifts of tempo and melody. These features are found as well in his two modern-day classics: the witty *Lieutenant Kije Suite* (1934) and the symphonic fairy tale, *Peter and the Wolf* (1936).

## Britten

Twentieth-century composers were frequently moved to commemorate the horrors of war. The most monumental example of such music is the *War Requiem* (1963) written by the British composer Benjamin Britten (1913–1976) to accompany the consecration of England's new Coventry Cathedral, built alongside the ruins of the fourteenth-century cathedral that had been virtually destroyed by German bombs in World War II. Britten was a master at setting text to music. In the *War Requiem* he juxtaposed the Roman Catholic Mass for the Dead (the Latin Requiem Mass) with lines from the poems of Wilfred Owen. The latter convey the composer's antiwar convictions. Britten's imaginative union of sacred ritual and secular song calls for orchestra, chorus, boys' chorus, and three soloists. Poignant in spirit and dramatic in effect, this oratorio may be seen as the musical analogue of Picasso's *Guernica*.

## Penderecki

If it were possible to capture in music the agony of war, the Polish composer Krzysztof Penderecki (b. 1933) has come closest to doing so. His *Threnody in Memory of the Victims of Hiroshima* (1960) consists of violent torrents of dissonant, percussive sound, some of which is produced by beating on the bodies of the fifty-two stringed instruments for which the piece is scored. The ten-minute song of lamentation for the dead begins with a long, screaming tone produced by playing the highest pitches possible on the violins; it is followed by passages punctuated by **tone clusters** (groups of adjacent dissonant notes). The rapid shifts in densities, timbres, rhythms, and dynamics are jarring and disquieting—effects consistent with the subject matter of the piece.

*Threnody* was said to be the "anguished cry" that proclaimed the birth of the musical avant-garde behind the Iron Curtain. Penderecki's angry blurring of tones also characterizes his *Dies Irae* (1967), subtitled *Oratorio Dedicated to the Memory of those Murdered at Auschwitz*. Like Britten's *War Requiem*, Penderecki's composition draws on Christian liturgy—here the traditional hymn of Last Judgment (the "Day of Wrath")—to convey a mood of darkness and despair. The *Dies Irae*, first performed on the grounds of a former concentration camp, is punctuated by clanking chains and piercing sirens. Harsh and abrasive, it remains a symbol of the Holocaust's haunting impact.

## Copland and the American Sound

One of America's finest twentieth-century composers, Aaron Copland (1900–1990) turned away from the horrors of war; however, just as the music of Shostakovich and Prokofiev was rooted in Russian soil, so that of Copland drew nourishment from native American idioms. The New York composer spiced his largely tonal compositions with the simple harmonies of American folk songs, the clarity of Puritan hymns, and the lively and often syncopated rhythms of jazz and Mexican dance. In 1941, Copland advised American composers to find alternatives to the harsh and demanding serialism of their European colleagues: "The new musical audiences will have to have music they can comprehend," he insisted. "It must therefore be simple and direct . . . Above all, it must be fresh in feeling." Copland achieved these goals in all his compositions, especially in the ballet scores *Billy the Kid* (1938), *Rodeo* (1940), and *Appalachian Spring* (1944).

🎵 *Appalachian Spring*, commissioned by the Martha Graham Dance Company, was originally called "Ballet for Martha." The choreographer chose its title, which is based on the first line of a poem by the American writer, Hart Crane (1899–1932). (The "spring" in the title refers not to a season but to a source of water.) Graham's ballet tells the story of a newly betrothed Pennsylvania frontier couple, who are welcomed to their new community by a revivalist preacher and his congregation. An orchestral suite for small chamber orchestra, it features five variations on the familiar Shaker song, "'Tis the Gift to Be Simple." In directing an orchestral rehearsal for the piece in 1974, Copland urged, "Make it more American in spirit, in that the sentiment isn't shown on the face." Copland also composed for film, winning an Oscar in 1949 for his score for *The Heiress*. Like the murals of Thomas Hart Benton, Copland's music wedded American themes to a vigorous and readily accessible language of form.

# The Communist Revolution in China

The history of totalitarianism is not confined to the West. In the course of the twentieth century, modern tyrants wiped out whole populations in parts of Cambodia, Vietnam, Iraq, Africa, and elsewhere. Of all the Asian countries, however, China experienced the most dramatic changes. In 1900, less than 10 percent of the Chinese population owned almost 80 percent of the land. Clamoring for reform, as well as for independence from foreign domination, nationalist forces moved to redistribute land among the enormous peasant population. By 1911, the National People's Party had overthrown the Manchu leaders (see chapter 21) and established a republican government. But the Nationalists failed to provide an efficient program for land redistribution. Consequently, after 1937, they lost much of their popular support. Following World War II, the communist forces under the leadership of Mao Zedong (1893–1976) rose to power. In 1949 they formed the People's Republic of China.

In China as in Russia, the Communist Party gained exclusive control of the government, with Mao serving as both chairman of the party and head of state. Mao called upon the great masses of citizens to work toward radical reform. "The theory of Marx, Engels, Lenin and Stalin is universally applicable," wrote Mao. However, he added, "We should regard it not as a dogma, but as a guide to action." A competent poet and scholar, Mao drew up the guidelines for the new society of China, a society that practiced cooperative endeavor and self-discipline. These guidelines were published in 1963 as the *Quotations from Chairman Mao*. Mao's "little red book" soon became the "bible" of the Chinese Revolution. On youth, Mao wrote, "The world is yours, as well as ours, but in the last analysis, it is yours. You young people, full of vigor and vitality, are in the bloom of life, like the sun at eight or nine in the morning. Our hope is placed in you." On women: "In order to build a great socialist society, it is of the utmost importance to arouse the broad masses of women to join in productive activity. Men and women must receive equal pay for equal work in production." And on the masses: "The masses have boundless creative power . . . the revolutionary war is a war of the masses; it can be waged only by mobilizing the masses and relying on them."

Mao's ambitious reforms earned the support of the landless masses, but his methods for achieving his goals struck at the foundations of traditional Chinese culture. He moved to replace the old order, and especially the Confucian veneration of the family, with new socialist values that demanded devotion to the local economic unit—and ultimately to the state. To carry out his series of five-year plans for economic development in industry and agriculture, he instituted iron-handed totalitarian practices, including indoctrination, exile, and repeated purges of the voices of opposition. Between 1949 and 1952, Mao authorized the execution of some two to five million people, including the wealthy landowners themselves.

Like the century's other totalitarian leaders, Mao directed writers to infuse their works with ideological content that celebrated the creative powers of the masses. To some extent, however, the movement for a "people's literature" advanced reforms that already had been launched during the political revolution of 1911: at that time, traditional styles of writing, including the "book language" of the classics, gave way to the language of common, vernacular speech. The new naturalistic style was strongly influenced by Western literature and journalism. Chinese writers responded enthusiastically to modern European novels, short stories, and psychological dramas—poets even imitated such Western forms as the sonnet.

In the visual arts, the influence of late nineteenth-century Western printmakers such as Käthe Kollwitz (see chapter 30), helped to shape the powerful realism of many

---

🎵 See Music Listening Selections at end of chapter.

Chinese artists, including Li Hua (1907–1994). Li's stark and searing woodcut of a bound man (Figure **34.14**)—a metaphor for modern China—reiterates the silent scream of Munch (see Figure 33.2) and Eisenstein (see Figure 34.12). During the Cultural Revolution (1966–1976) China's communist regime reinstated the official policy of socialist realism as it had been defined by the First All-Union Congress of Soviet Writers in 1934. The consequences of this policy would work to foment the liberation movements of the last decades of the century.

**Figure 34.14 LI HUA**, *Roar!* 1936. Woodcut, 8 × 6 in. Li Hua's woodcut is representative of the modern woodcut movement that flourished in China during the 1930s. The movement was a significant expression of China's avant-garde.

## Chronology

| | |
|---|---|
| 1910–1920 | Mexican Revolution |
| 1911 | Nationalist Revolution in China |
| 1914–1918 | World War I |
| 1917 | Russian Revolution |
| 1926 | Stalin becomes Soviet dictator |
| 1929 | Stock market crashes |
| 1936–1939 | Spanish Civil War |
| 1939–1945 | World War II |
| 1949 | People's Republic of China formed under Mao |

# LOOKING BACK

## Total Wars

- The twentieth century was molded in the crucible of total war and totalitarianism.
- World Wars I and II were more devastating in nature and effect than any preceding wars in world history. They involved numerous nations, killed unprecedented numbers of civilians, and employed the weapons of modern technology: machine guns, poison gas, tanks, and finally, atomic bombs.

## World War I Literature

- Writers responded to total war and totalitarianism with rage, disbelief, and compassion.
- Bitter indictments of World War I are found in the poetry of Owen, Eliot, and Yeats, who viewed war as an indication of the decay of Western civilization.
- The novelist Erich Remarque portrayed a firsthand account of trench warfare and the devastating nature of World War I.

## World War I Art

- Visual artists also protested against the calamities of war. Max Ernst used collage-paintings to create bizarre dehumanized images, while George Grosz produced mocking depictions of the German military machine.
- Léger's Cubist paintings reflect his appreciation of modern weaponry and machinery. He produced one of the first abstract films, *Ballet mécanique*, which pictured modern life as mechanized and impersonal.

## The Russian Revolution

- World War I, a corrupt tsarist government, and a weak economy led to discontent in Russia. The Russian Revolution of 1917 marked the beginnings of Soviet communism and ushered in decades of totalitarian rule inspired by the Marxist ideology of Vladimir Lenin.
- Following Lenin, Stalin took control of Russia. Under his totalitarian regime dissidents were imprisoned, executed, or exiled, and all expressions of "Modernism" were condemned.

In the arts, socialist realism promoted the ideological benefits of communism.

## The Great Depression and the American Scene

- America's economy, like that of the rest of the world, suffered after World War I, and the country was swept into the Great Depression.
- Social Realism, often a vehicle of social criticism and protest, dominated the novels of John Steinbeck and the murals of Thomas Hart Benton. As with the mural paintings of revolutionary Mexico, Benton's murals depicting American occupations and pastimes became a major form of public art.
- Dorothea Lange and other photographers of the Great Depression left a documentary record of rural poverty and oppression.

## Totalitarianism and World War II

- Under Adolf Hitler, the Nazi policy of militant racism brought about the brutal deaths of millions throughout Europe.
- In the poems of Randall Jarrell, the fiction works of Norman Mailer, and the gallows humor novels of Joseph Heller, World War II literature emphasized the dehumanizing effects of war.
- The firsthand experiences of Solzhenitsyn in the Russian *gulags* and Wiesel in Nazi concentration camps are shocking records of totalitarian inhumanity.

## The Visual Arts in the War Era

- Photography documented the horrifying realities of World War II. The first female war photojournalist Lee Miller made moving images of Nazi concentration camps.
- Working in Paris, Picasso responded to news reports of the German aerial bombing of a Spanish market town; *Guernica* has become the quintessential antiwar painting of the twentieth century.

## Film in the War Era

- The Russian filmmaker Sergei Eisenstein pioneered the technique of cinematic montage to brilliant effect in the classic film *The Battleship Potemkin*.
- American films generally served as morale boosters and vehicles of Allied propaganda; the British actor Charlie Chaplin satirized Fascist dictatorship.

## Music in the War Era

- Living under the critical eye of the communist regime, Dmitri

Shostakovich and Sergei Prokofiev composed in distinctly different but memorable musical styles.
- In England, Benjamin Britten commemorated World War II in his *War Requiem*, while in Poland Krzysztof Penderecki immortalized the harsh realities of twentieth-century genocide in atonal compositions.
- Native idioms, such as folk songs and Mexican dance, were integrated into the readily accessible music of one of America's most notable composers, Aaron Copland.

## The Communist Revolution in China

- After Nationalist forces in China failed to provide much-needed land reforms, the Communist Party, under the leadership of Mao Zedong, gained control, forming the People's Republic of China in 1949.
- Economic reform went hand in hand with the eradication of age-old traditions and the execution of dissidents and landowners. Mao's "little red book," which encouraged the empowerment of the masses, became the "bible" of the Chinese Revolution.

### Music Listening Selections

**CD Two Selection 19** Copland, *Appalachian Spring*, excerpt, 1944.

# Glossary

**gallows humor** (or "black humor") the use of morbid and absurd situations for comic and satirical purposes in modern fiction and drama

**montage** in art, music, or literature, a composite made by freely juxtaposing usually heterogeneous images; in cinema, the production of a rapid succession of images to present a stream of interconnected ideas

(see also Glossary, chapter 33 "photomontage")

**mural** a painting applied to a large wall or ceiling

**tone cluster** a group of adjacent dissonant notes, such as the notes of a scale, sounded together

**totalitarian** a political regime that imposes the will of the state upon the life and conduct of the individual

# Chapter

# 35

## The Quest for Meaning
### ca. 1940–1960

*"Man is nothing else but what he makes of himself."*
Jean-Paul Sartre

**Figure 35.1 HELEN FRANKENTHALER**, *Before the Caves*, 1958.
Oil on canvas, 8 ft. 6⅛ in. × 8 ft. 8⅜ in.

# LOOKING AHEAD

The nightmare of World War II left the world's population in a state of shock and disillusion. The Western democracies had held back the forces of totalitarian aggression, but the future seemed as threatening as ever. The treaty settlements that ended World War II left two large blocs of powerful nations ranged against each other in an effort to further their individual political, social, and ideological ends. The largest of these ideological power blocs, the nations led by the United States and its democratic/capitalistic ideology, stood opposed to the Soviet/communist bloc, which came to include most of the East European countries adjacent to Russia. Communism and capitalist democracy now confronted one another in hostile distrust. And both possessed nuclear capability with the potential to extinguish the human race.

The pessimism that accompanied the two world wars was compounded by a loss of faith in the bedrock beliefs of former centuries. The realities of trench warfare, the Holocaust, and Hiroshima made it difficult to maintain that human beings were rational by nature, that technology would work to advance human happiness, and that the universe was governed by a benevolent God. There is little wonder that the events of the first half of the twentieth century caused a loss of confidence in moral absolutes. The sense of estrangement from God and reason produced a condition of anxious withdrawal that has been called "alienation." By mid-century, the quest for meaning had produced the philosophy of Existentialism, while the mood of alienation and anxiety pervaded the literature of dystopia, the personality of the fictional antihero, and a host of new directions in the arts. Avant-garde movements in painting, music, and dance launched America to a position of cultural leadership in the West.

## The Cold War

The contest for world domination—the so-called "cold war" that followed World War II—determined the course of international relations during the second half of the twentieth century. In Europe, postwar Germany was politically divided, most visibly by the Berlin Wall that separated Soviet-dominated East Germany from the West German Democratic Republic. As "power vacuums" occurred in the post-colonial regions of East Asia, the cold war grew hot. In the Korean peninsula, the two superpowers, the Soviet Union and the United States, wrestled diplomatically but unsuccessfully for dominion in what would ultimately become all-out war. The Korean War (1950–1953), fought virtually to a standoff with both sides suffering terrible losses (three million Koreans, mostly civilians, died), ended with the division of the country into a northern communist state (the Korean People's Democratic Republic) and a southern democratic state (the Republic of Korea). The destabilized circumstances of the lingering cold war contributed to the anxieties of the postwar era.

## Existentialism

 Existentialism, the most important philosophic movement of the twentieth century, examined the unique nature of individual experience within an indifferent universe. Focusing on matters of human freedom, choice, and responsibility, it had its roots in the late nineteenth century, most notably in the writings of the Danish philosopher Søren Kierkegaard (1813–1855). But it rose to prominence through the efforts of the French left-wing intellectual, Jean-Paul Sartre.

### The Philosophy of Sartre

Jean-Paul Sartre (1905–1980), the leading philosopher of the twentieth century, made significant contributions as a playwright, novelist, journalist, and literary critic. Sartre fought in World War II and was active in the French resistance to the German occupation of France. Committed to social reform, he supported the working-class ideals of Marxist communism, but never became a member of the French Communist Party.

Sartre's philosophy, as expounded in his classic work *Being and Nothingness* (1943), took as its basic premise the idea that existence precedes essence, that is, that one's material being exists prior to and independent of any intrinsic factors. Sartre's premise challenged the fundamentals of traditional philosophy: Plato had identified "essence" as Forms (or Ideas) that were eternal and unchanging. For Aristotle, reason—humankind's capacity for rational thought—was the "essence" that separated human beings from the lower animals. Philosophers from Descartes through Kant followed the ancients by defending the notion that primary internal principles of being preceded being itself—a view that was metaphysically compatible with Christian theology.

Sartre proposed, however, that human beings have no fixed nature. They are not imbued with any special divinity, nor are they (by nature) rational. They are neither imprisoned by unconscious forces (as Freud had held) nor are they determined by specific economic conditions (as Marx had maintained). Born into the world as body/matter, they proceed to make the choices by which they form their own natures. In Sartre's analysis, each individual is the sum of his or her actions. "We are what we choose to be," he insisted. Because we must choose at every turn between a variety of possibilities, we are "condemned to be free." Moreover, since every choice implies a choice for all humankind, we bear the overwhelming burden of total responsibility—a condition that Sartre called "anguish."

## Communism versus Capitalism

For roughly a half century following World War II, the great powers of the world were divided into two opposing ideological camps, popularly known as "communism" and "capitalism." Each of these power blocs fervently defended its superiority, and the necessity of its success in the world struggle for dominance. "Communism"—in reality one of several forms of Marxist–Leninist socialism—describes a social and political system committed to the principle that the central state should own and operate the nation's means of production and distribution of goods, with the entire population sharing the resulting wealth equally (see chapters 30 and 34). "Capitalism" describes a system based in the principle that the world's economic capital should function according to free market

forces, described by Adam Smith (see chapter 24), and that government should have little to do with regulation of the economic and financial world. Individual initiative and enterprise would then function to produce and distribute goods among the population.

These two seemingly incompatible and competing ideologies fueled the cold war of the postwar years. While the cold war has only occasionally turned hot in the past half century—most recently in the Vietnam War (see chapter 37)—the competing ideologies of communism and capitalism, and the policies guided by these ideas, worked to destabilize international relations during most of the twentieth century.

---

Sartre's viewpoint struck a balance between optimism and despair. While freedom and meaning depend on human action, said Sartre, all human actions, by necessity, are played out within a moral void—that is, within a universe lacking divine guidance and absolute values. To our profound despair, we seek meaning in a meaningless world. Yet, because human life is all there is, it must be cherished. According to Sartre, the human condition is one of anxiety experienced in the face of nothingness and the inevitability of death. Such anxiety is compounded because we alone are responsible for our actions. To disclaim responsibility for those actions by blaming external causes—"the Devil made me do it," "The ghetto turned me into a criminal," or "My parents were too lenient"—is to act in "bad faith." For Sartre, no forms of human engineering, technocratic or otherwise, can usurp the human potential for free action. To fly from freedom and responsibility is a form of self-deception and inauthenticity. "We are alone, with no excuses," according to Sartre.

In addition to his major philosophic work, Sartre wrote a number of significant novels, short stories, and plays. The most gripping of his plays, *No Exit* (1945), features three characters trapped in a "hell" they have created by their efforts to justify the acts of bad faith that have shaped their lives. The principal ideas set forth in these most famous of Sartre's writings are summarized in the lecture entitled "Existentialism," which Sartre presented in Paris in 1945. In the following excerpt from this essay, Sartre discusses Existentialism as an ethics of action and involvement and explores the meaning of existential anguish.

### READING 35.1 From Sartre's "Existentialism" (1945)

. . . Atheistic existentialism . . . states that if God does not    1
exist, there is at least one being in whom existence precedes
essence, a being who exists before he can be defined by any
concept, and that this being is man, or, as Heidegger[1] says,

human reality. What is meant here by saying that existence
precedes essence? It means that, first of all, man exists, turns
up, appears on the scene, and, only afterwards, defines
himself. If man, as the existentialist conceives him, is
indefinable, it is because at first he is nothing. Only afterward
will he be something, and he himself will have made what he    10
will be. Thus, there is no human nature, since there is no God
to conceive it. Not only is man what he conceives himself to
be, but he is also only what he wills himself to be after this
thrust toward existence.

Man is nothing else but what he makes of himself. Such is
the first principle of existentialism. It is also what is called
subjectivity, the name we are labeled with when charges are
brought against us. But what do we mean by this, if not that
man has a greater dignity than a stone or table? For we mean
that man first exists, that is, that man first of all is the being    20
who hurls himself toward a future and who is conscious of
imagining himself as being in the future. Man is at the start a
plan which is aware of itself, rather than a patch of moss, a
piece of garbage, or a cauliflower; nothing exists prior to this
plan; there is nothing in heaven; man will be what he will
have planned to be. Not what he will want to be. Because by
the word "will" we generally mean a conscious decision,
which is subsequent to what we have already made of
ourselves. I may want to belong to a political party, write a
book, get married; but all that is only a manifestation of an    30
earlier, more spontaneous choice that is called "will." But if
existence really does precede essence, man is responsible for
what he is. Thus, existentialism's first move is to make every
man aware of what he is and to make the full responsibility of
his existence rest on him. And when we say that a man is
responsible for himself, we do not only mean that he is
responsible for his own individuality, but that he is responsible
for all men.

---

[1] A German philosopher (1889–1976) whose writings had a major influence on Sartre and other Existentialists.

The word subjectivism has two meanings, and our opponents play on the two. Subjectivism means, on the one hand, that an individual chooses and makes himself; and, on the other, that it is impossible for man to transcend human subjectivity. The second of these is the essential meaning of existentialism. When we say that man chooses his own self, we mean that every one of us does likewise; but we also mean by that that in making this choice he also chooses all men. In fact, in creating the man that we want to be, there is not a single one of our acts which does not at the same time create an image of man as we think he ought to be. To choose to be this or that is to affirm at the same time the value of what we choose, because we can never choose evil. We always choose the good, and nothing can be good for us without being good for all.

If, on the other hand, existence precedes essence, and if we grant that we exist and fashion our image at one and the same time, the image is valid for everybody and for our whole age. Thus, our responsibility is much greater than we might have supposed, because it involves all mankind. If I am a workingman and choose to join a Christian trade-union rather than be a communist, and if by being a member I want to show that the best thing for man is resignation, that the kingdom of man is not of this world, I am not only involving my own case—I want to be resigned for everyone. As a result, my action has involved all humanity. To take a more individual matter, if I want to marry, to have children; even if this marriage depends solely on my own circumstances or passion or wish, I am involving all humanity in monogamy and not merely myself. Therefore, I am responsible for myself and for everyone else. I am creating a certain image of man of my own choosing. In choosing myself, I choose man.

This helps us understand what the actual content is of such rather grandiloquent words as anguish, forlornness, despair. As you will see, it's all quite simple.

First, what is meant by anguish? The existentialists say at once that man is anguish. What that means is this: the man who involves himself and who realizes that he is not only the person he chooses to be, but also a lawmaker who is, at the same time, choosing all mankind as well as himself, cannot escape the feeling of his total and deep responsibility. Of course, there are many people who are not anxious; but we claim that they are hiding their anxiety, that they are fleeing from it. Certainly, many people believe that when they do something, they themselves are the only ones involved, and when someone says to them, "What if everyone acted that way?" they shrug their shoulders and answer, "Everyone doesn't act that way." But really, one should always ask himself, "What would happen if everybody looked at things that way?" There is no escaping this disturbing thought except by a kind of double-dealing. A man who lies and makes excuses for himself by saying "not everybody does that," is someone with an uneasy conscience, because the act of lying implies that a universal value is conferred upon the lie. . . .

The existentialist . . . thinks it very distressing that God does not exist, because all possibility of finding values in a heaven of ideas disappears along with Him; there can no longer be an *a priori* Good, since there is no infinite and perfect

consciousness to think it. Nowhere is it written that the Good exists, that we must be honest, that we must not lie; because the fact is we are on a plane where there are only men. Dostoevsky said, "If God didn't exist, everything would be possible." That is the very starting point of existentialism. Indeed, everything is permissible if God does not exist, and as a result man is forlorn, because neither within him nor without does he find anything to cling to. He can't start making excuses for himself.

If existence really does precede essence, there is no explaining things away by reference to a fixed and given human nature. In other words, there is no determinism, man is free, man is freedom. On the other hand, if God does not exist, we find no values or commands to turn to which legitimize our conduct. So, in the bright realm of values, we have no excuse behind us, nor justification before us. We are alone, with no excuses.

That is the idea I shall try to convey when I say that man is condemned to be free. Condemned, because he did not create himself, yet, in other respects is free; because, once thrown into the world, he is responsible for everything he does. The existentialist does not believe in the power of passion. He will never agree that a sweeping passion is a ravaging torrent which fatally leads a man to certain acts and is therefore an excuse. He thinks that man is responsible for his passion.

The existentialist does not think that man is going to help himself by finding in the world some omen by which to orient himself. Because he thinks that man will interpret the omen to suit himself. Therefore, he thinks that man, with no support and no aid, is condemned every moment to invent man. Ponge,[2] in a very fine article, has said, "Man is the future of man." That's exactly it. But if it is taken to mean that this future is recorded in heaven, that God sees it, then it is false, because it would really no longer be a future. If it is taken to mean that whatever a man may be, there is a future to be forged, a virgin future before him, then this remark is sound. But then we are forlorn. . . .

Now, for the existentialist there is really no love other than one which manifests itself in a person's being in love. There is no genius other than one which is expressed in works of art; the genius of Proust is the sum of Proust's works; the genius of Racine is his series of tragedies. Outside of that, there is nothing. Why say that Racine could have written another tragedy, when he didn't write it? A man is involved in life, leaves his impress on it, and outside of that there is nothing. To be sure, this may seem a harsh thought to someone whose life hasn't been a success. But, on the other hand, it prompts people to understand that reality alone is what counts, that dreams, expectations, and hopes warrant no more than to define a man as a disappointed dream, as miscarried hopes, as vain expectations. In other words, to define him negatively and not positively. However, when we say, "You are nothing else than your life," that does not imply that the artist will be judged solely on the basis of his works of art; a thousand other things will contribute toward summing him up. What we

---

[2] Francis Ponge (1899–1987) was a French poet and critic.

mean is that a man is nothing else than a series of undertakings, that he is the sum, the organization, the ensemble of the relationships which make up these undertakings. . . .

If it is impossible to find in every man some universal essence which would be human nature, yet there does exist a universal human condition. It's not by chance that today's thinkers speak more readily of man's condition than of his nature. By condition they mean, more or less definitely, the *a* **160** *priori* limits which outline man's fundamental situation in the universe. Historical situations vary; a man may be born a slave in a pagan society or a feudal lord or a proletarian. What does not vary is the necessity for him to exist in the world, to be at work there, to be there in the midst of other people, and to be mortal there. . . .

But there is another meaning of humanism. Fundamentally it is this: man is constantly outside of himself; in projecting himself, in losing himself outside of himself, he makes for man's existing; and, on the other hand, it is by pursuing **170** transcendent goals that he is able to exist; man, being this state of passing-beyond, and seizing upon things only as they bear upon this passing-beyond, is at the heart, at the center of this passing-beyond. There is no universe other than a human universe, the universe of human subjectivity. This connection between transcendency, as a constituent element of man—not in the sense that God is transcendent, but in the sense of passing beyond—and subjectivity, in the sense that man is not closed in on himself but is always present in a human universe, is what we call existentialist humanism. Humanism, **180** because we remind man that there is no lawmaker other than himself, and that in his forlornness he will decide by himself; because we point out that man will fulfill himself as man, not in turning toward himself, but in seeking outside of himself a goal which is just this liberation, just this particular fulfillment.

From these few reflections it is evident that nothing is more unjust than the objections that have been raised against us. Existentialism is nothing else than an attempt to draw all the consequences of a coherent atheistic position. It isn't trying to plunge man into despair at all. But if one calls every attitude **190** of unbelief despair, like the Christians, then the word is not being used in its original sense. Existentialism isn't so atheistic that it wears itself out showing that God doesn't exist. Rather, it declares that even if God did exist, that would change nothing. There you've got our point of view. Not that we believe that God exists, but we think that the problem of His existence is not the issue. In this sense existentialism is optimistic, a doctrine of action, and it is plain dishonesty for Christians to make no distinction between their own despair and ours and then to call us despairing. **200**

**Q** In your own words, explain: "existence precedes essence" and "existential anguish."

**Q** Evaluate Sartre's claims: "You are nothing else than your life," and "Man is condemned to be free."

## Christian Existentialism

While Sartre excluded the question of God's existence from his speculations, Christian Existentialists saw little contradiction between the belief in a Supreme Being and the ethics of human freedom and responsibility. They held that religious philosophy need not concern itself with the proof or disproof of God's existence; rather, it should focus on the moral life of the individual. Beyond what Kierkegaard had called the "leap of faith" from which all religious belief proceeded, there lay a continuing moral responsibility for one's own life. According to the philosophers Karl Jaspers (1883–1969) and Gabriel Marcel (1889–1973), God had challenged human beings to act as free and responsible creatures.

Among Christian theologians, a similar concern for the moral life of the individual moved religion out of the seminaries and into the streets. The Protestant theologian Reinhold Niebuhr (1892–1971) criticized doctrinaire theology and called for the revival of moral conduct in an immoral society. Convinced that human participation was essential to social redemption, Niebuhr urged Christians to cultivate humility and advance justice in modern society. Niebuhr's contemporary and fellow Lutheran Paul Tillich (1886–1965) boldly rejected the concept of a *personal* god. For Tillich, anxiety and alienation were conditions preliminary to the mystical apprehension of a "God above the God of theism."

# Literature at Mid-Century

## Utopias and Dystopias

In the postwar era, the breach between humanism and science seemed wider than ever. Increasingly, intellectuals questioned the social value of scientific knowledge as it applied to human progress. Optimists still envisioned modern technology as a liberating force for humankind. The American behavioral psychologist B. F. Skinner (1904–1990), for instance, anticipated a society in which the behavior of human beings might be scientifically engineered for the benefit of both the individual and the community. In the futuristic novel *Walden Two* (1948), Skinner created a fictional society in which the "technology of behavior" replaced traditional "prescientific" views of freedom and dignity. *Walden Two* is typical of a large body of *utopian literature* that exalted science as a positive force in shaping the future.

Pessimists, on the other hand, feared—and still fear—that modern technology might produce catastrophes ranging from a nuclear holocaust to the absolute loss of personal freedom. *Dystopian literature*, that is, works that picture societies in which conditions are dreadful and bleak, reflect this negative outlook. The most notable of these are *Brave New World* (1932) by the British writer Aldous Huxley (1894–1963), *1984* (1949) by England's George Orwell (the pen name of Eric Arthur Blair, 1903–1950), and *Fahrenheit 451* (1953) by the American Ray Bradbury (b. 1920). All three of the novels present fictional totalitarian societies in which modern technology and the techniques of human engineering operate to destroy human freedom.

*Brave New World* describes an imaginary society of the seventh century "A.F." ("after Henry Ford," the early twentieth-century American automobile manufacturer). In Huxley's futuristic society, babies are conceived in test tubes and, following the assembly line methods invented by Henry Ford for the manufacture of cars, individuals are behaviorally conditioned to perform socially beneficial tasks. From this "brave new world," the concept and practice of family life have been eradicated; human anxieties are quelled by means of *soma* (a mood-altering drug); and art, literature, and religion—all of which, according to the custodians of technology, threaten communal order and stability—have been ruthlessly purged.

## The Literary Antihero

The postwar era witnessed the birth of a new kind of literary hero: a hero who, deprived of traditional values and religious beliefs, bears the burden of freedom and the total responsibility for his actions. The existential hero—or, more exactly, antihero—takes up the quest for meaning: alienated by nature and circumstance, he makes choices in a world lacking moral absolutes, a world in which no act might be called "good" unless it is chosen in conscious preference to its alternatives. Unlike the heroes of old, the modern antihero is neither noble nor sure of purpose. He might act decisively, but with full recognition of the absence of shared cultural values or personal reward. Trapped rather than liberated by freedom, he might have trouble getting along with others or simply making it through the day—"Hell," says one of Sartre's characters in *No Exit*, "is other people." Confronting meaninglessness and irrationality, the antihero might achieve nothing other than the awful recognition of life's absurdity.

Twentieth-century literature is filled with antiheroes—characters whose lives illustrate the absurdity of the human condition. Sartre's compatriot Albert Camus (1913–1960) defined the absurd as the "divorce between man and life, actor and setting." In Camus' short stories and novels, the antihero inevitably confronts the basic existential imperatives: "Recognize your dignity as a human being"; "Choose and commit yourself to action." The central character of Camus' classic work *The Stranger* (1942) is the quintessential alienated man: he is estranged from traditional social values and unable to establish his sense of being except through continual rebellion. Camus' view of human nature was less cynical than Sartre's and more concerned with the value of benevolent reconciliation between individuals. At the same time, the situations described in his novels—and his own death in an automobile crash—seem inescapably arbitrary and absurd.

Although Existentialism was an essentially European phenomenon, the existential hero appears in the literature of twentieth-century writers throughout the world, most notably in the novels of Argentina's Jorge Luis Borges (see chapter 37) and Japan's Oē Kenzaburo (b. 1935). In

### Science and Technology

| 1944 | a Canadian bacteriologist proves DNA is fundamental in determining heredity |
| 1946 | the first functional electronic digital computer is tested in America |
| 1947 | quantum electrodynamics (QED) studies "irregular" behavior of subatomic particles |
| 1948 | Bell Laboratories develop the transistor |
| 1951 | nuclear reactors are utilized successfully to produce electricity |

postwar America, the existential perspective cut across regional lines, from the deep South of William Faulkner (1897–1962) and Walker Percy (1916–1990) to John Cheever's (1912–1982) New England and Bernard Malamud's (1914–1986) New York: and from the urban Midwest of Saul Bellow (1915–2005) to California's Beat Generation. The Beat Generation were a group of writers who prized bohemian creativity, anticonformity, and a spontaneous lifestyle. They are best represented by Jack Kerouac's *On the Road* (1951), a saga of youthful restlessness that Kerouac called his "true-story novel"; and by Allen Ginsberg's long, in-your-face poem *Howl* (1955). The latter, a ranting lament on America's loss of values, makes notorious reference to illicit drugs, to sexuality and homosexuality, and to the evils of American commercialism. It opens with these angry lines:

> I saw the best minds of my generation destroyed by
> madness, starving hysterical naked,
> dragging themselves through the negro streets at
> dawn looking for an angry fix;
> angel-headed hipsters burning for the ancient
> heavenly connection
> to the starry dynamo in the machinery of night, . . . .

Postwar dramatists also treated the existential experience: in the Pulitzer prize-winning play *Death of a Salesman* (1949) by Arthur Miller (1915–2005), the antihero is a quintessentially American figure. Miller's protagonist, Willy Loman, is a salesman, a "little man" who has met failure at every turn, but he cannot recognize the inauthenticity of his false claims to material success nor escape the futility of his self-deception. An American classic, *Salesman* depends on traditional dramatic structure in bringing to life a complex but ultimately sympathetic existential figure. An entirely different type of theater, however, would come to dominate the postwar era.

## Theater of the Absurd

The international movement known as *theater of the absurd* so vividly captured the anguish of modern society that late twentieth-century critics called it "the true theater of our time." Abandoning Classical theater from Sophocles and Shakespeare through Ibsen and Miller, Absurdist playwrights rejected traditional dramatic structure (in which action moves from conflict to resolution), along with traditional modes of character development. The Absurdist play, which drew stylistic inspiration from Dada performance art and Surrealist film, lacks dramatic progression, direction, and resolution. Its characters undergo little or no change, dialogue contradicts actions, and events follow no logical order. Dramatic action, leavened with gallows humor, may consist of irrational and grotesque situations that remain unresolved at the end of the performance—as is often the case in real life.

The principal figures of Absurdist theater reflect the international character of the movement: they include Samuel Beckett (Irish), Eugène Ionesco (Romanian), Harold Pinter (British), Fernando Arrabal (Spanish), Jean Genet (French), and Edward Albee (American). Of these, Samuel Beckett (1906–1989), recipient of the Nobel Prize in 1969, earned the greatest distinction. Early in his career, Beckett came under the influence of James Joyce, parts of whose novel *Finnegans Wake* he recorded from dictation, as the aging Joyce was losing his eyesight. Beckett admired Joyce's experimental use of language. He also shared the views of the Austrian linguistic philosopher Ludwig Wittgenstein (see chapter 37), who held that human beings were imprisoned by language and consequently cut off from the possibility of true understanding.

The concept of language as the prisonhouse of the mind—a point of view that had far-reaching consequences in Postmodern philosophy—was fundamental to Beckett's dramatic style. It is particularly apparent in his most notable work, *Waiting for Godot*, written in 1948 and first staged in 1952. The main "action" of the play consists of a running dialogue—terse, repetitious, and often comical—between two tramps as they await the mysterious "Godot" (who, despite their anxious expectations, never arrives). Some find in Godot a symbol of salvation, revelation, or, most commonly, God—an interpretation that Beckett himself rejected. Nevertheless, the absent "deliverer" (perhaps by his very absence) gives a modicum of meaning to the lives of the central characters. Their longings and delusions, their paralysis and ignorance, are anticipated in the play's opening line, "Nothing to be done." The progress of the play, animated by an extraordinary blend of biblical references, broad slapstick, comic wordplay, Zenlike propositions, and crude jokes, gives life to Sartre's observation that "man first of all is the being who hurls himself toward a future" (see Reading 35.1). A parable of the existential condition, *Waiting for Godot* dwells on the divorce between expectation and event. At the same time (and as the brief excerpt from the end of Act Two illustrates), the play underscores the futility of communication between frail creatures who cling (and wait) together.

## READING 35.2 From Beckett's *Waiting for Godot*
(1948)

**Estragon:** Where shall we go?                                          1
**Vladimir:** Not far.
**Estragon:** Oh yes, let's go far away from here.
**Vladimir:** We can't.
**Estragon:** Why not?
**Vladimir:** We have to come back to-morrow.
**Estragon:** What for?
**Vladimir:** To wait for Godot.
**Estragon:** Ah! *(Silence.)* He didn't come?
**Vladimir:** No.                                                        10
**Estragon:** And now it's too late.
**Vladimir:** Yes, now it's night.
**Estragon:** And if we dropped him. *(Pause.)* If we dropped him?
**Vladimir:** He'd punish us. *(Silence. He looks at the tree.)* Everything's dead but the tree.
**Estragon** *(Looking at the tree)*: What is it?
**Vladimir:** It's the tree.
**Estragon:** Yes, but what kind?
**Vladimir:** I don't know. A willow.                                    20
*(Estragon draws Vladimir towards the tree. They stand motionless before it. Silence.)*
**Estragon:** Why don't we hang ourselves?
**Vladimir:** With what?
**Estragon:** You haven't got a bit of rope?
**Vladimir:** No.
**Estragon:** Then we can't.
*(Silence.)*
**Vladimir:** Let's go.
**Estragon:** Wait, there's my belt.
**Vladimir:** It's too short.
**Estragon:** You could hang on to my legs.
**Vladimir:** And who'd hang on to mine?                                 30
**Estragon:** True.
**Vladimir:** Show all the same. *(Estragon loosens the cord that holds up his trousers which, much too big for him, fall about his ankles. They look at the cord.)* It might do at a pinch. But is it strong enough?
**Estragon:** We'll soon see. Here.
*(They each take an end of the cord and pull. It breaks. They almost fall.)*
**Vladimir:** Not worth a curse.
*(Silence.)*
**Estragon:** You say we have to come back to-morrow?
**Vladimir:** Yes.
**Estragon:** Then we can bring a good bit of rope.                      40
**Vladimir:** Yes.
*(Silence.)*
**Estragon:** Didi.
**Vladimir:** Yes.
**Estragon:** I can't go on like this.
**Vladimir:** That's what you think.
**Estragon:** If we parted? That might be better for us.
**Vladimir:** We'll hang ourselves tomorrow. *(Pause.)* Unless Godot comes.
**Estragon:** And if he comes?
**Vladimir:** We'll be saved.                                            50
*(Vladimir takes off his hat (Lucky's), peers inside it, feels about inside it, shakes it, knocks on the crown, puts it on again.)*
**Estragon:** Well? Shall we go?
**Vladimir:** Pull on your trousers.
**Estragon:** What?

**Vladimir:** Pull on your trousers.

**Estragon:** You want me to pull off my trousers?

**Vladimir:** Pull ON your trousers.

**Estragon** (*Realizing his trousers are down*): True. (*He pulls up his trousers.*)

**Vladimir:** Well? Shall we go?

**Estragon:** Yes, let's go.                                                      60

(*They do not move.*)

(*Curtain.*)

**Q** What aspects of "the absurd" are communicated in this reading?

**Q** Do the two protagonists differ in personality?

## Poetry at Mid-Century: Dylan Thomas

Dylan Thomas (1914–1953) took a thoughtful attitude toward the modern condition, which he viewed as a mere stopping point between birth and death. Calling himself a Welshman first and a drunkard second, he became famous in America for his rhapsodic public readings and for the sheer musicality of his poetry. His poem "Do Not Go Gentle Into That Good Night," published just after the death of his father in 1951, makes a plea for life-affirming action even in the face of death. Thomas creates a rhythmic litany with the phrases "wise men," "good men," "wild men," "grave men"—resolving four of the six stanzas with the imperative: "rage against the dying of the light." The reference to those "who see with blinding sight" was probably inspired by the loss of vision that the poet's schoolteacher father suffered during his last years of life, but it also may be taken as an allusion to his father's agnosticism, that is, to his spiritual blindness—and, more generally, to the mood of alienation afflicting a generation of modern disbelievers. In 1954, Igor Stravinsky used this poem as the basis for *In Memoriam Dylan Thomas*, a piece written for tenor, string orchestra, and two trombones.

**READING 35.3** Thomas' "Do Not Go Gentle Into That Good Night" (1951)

Do not go gentle into that good night,                                     1
Old age should burn and rave at close of day;
Rage, rage against the dying of the light.

Though wise men at their end know dark is right,
Because their words had forked no lightning they      5
Do not go gentle into that good night.

Good men, the last wave by, crying how bright
Their frail deeds might have danced in a green bay,
Rage, rage against the dying of the light.

Wild men who caught and sang the sun in flight,      10
And learn, too late, they grieved it on its way,
Do not go gentle into that good night.

Grave men, near death, who see with blinding sight
Blind eyes could blaze like meteors and be gay,
Rage, rage against the dying of the light.               15

And you, my father, there on the sad height,
Curse, bless, me now with your fierce tears, I pray.
Do not go gentle into that good night.
Rage, rage against the dying of the light.

**Q** How does Thomas use the imagery of light and dark in this poem?

**Q** Does religious faith play any part here?

## Rabindranath Tagore

In contrast with Thomas, the Bengali poet Rabindranath Tagore (1861–1941) saw a world in spiritual deterioration. For Tagore, the crisis of modern society lay in a set of misplaced values that prized the rush of business and the acquisition of material comforts at the expense of beauty, creativity, and spiritual harmony. Born in Bengal, India (while the province was still under British control), Tagore was raised in a family of artists, musicians, and social reformers. After a brief stay in England, he returned to India, where he became a prolific writer, publishing some sixty volumes of poetry, plays, stories, and novels.

In India, Tagore pursued his ambition to foster a "spiritual unity of all races" by founding an international educational institute for the exchange of ideas between Western scholars and Indian students. Awarded the Nobel Prize in literature in 1913, Tagore left a body of writings that offers an Eastern, and specifically Hindu, approach to the modern quest for meaning. In his narrative poem, "The Man Had No Useful Work," he deals with the existential responsibility for individual choice. This provocative allegory questions the value of the practical, goal-oriented pursuits that drive most modern societies. It also plays on the ironic possibility that works of art may be both meaningless and essential.

**READING 35.4** Tagore's "The Man Had No Useful Work" (1921)

The man had no useful work, only vagaries of various kinds.     1
Therefore it surprised him to find himself in Paradise after a
    life spent perfecting trifles.
Now the guide had taken him by mistake to the wrong
    Paradise—one meant only for good, busy souls.

In this Paradise, our man saunters along the road only to
    obstruct the rush of business.
He stands aside from the path and is warned that he tramples
    on sown seed. Pushed, he starts up: hustled, he moves on.     5
A very busy girl comes to fetch water from the well. Her feet
    run on the pavement like rapid fingers over harp-strings.
    Hastily she ties a negligent knot with her hair, and loose
    locks on her forehead pry into the dark of her eyes.
The man says to her, "Would you lend me your pitcher?"
"My pitcher?" she asks, "to draw water?"
"No, to paint patterns on."
"I have no time to waste," the girl retorts in contempt.     10

Now a busy soul has no chance against one who is supremely
    idle.
Every day she meets him at the well, and every day he repeats
    the same request, till at last she yields.
Our man paints the pitcher with curious colors in a mysterious
    maze of lines.
The girl takes it up, turns it round and asks, "What does it
    mean?"
"It has no meaning," he answers.       15

The girl carries the pitcher home. She holds it up in different
    lights and tries to con its mystery.
At night she leaves her bed, lights a lamp, and gazes at it from
    all points of view.
This is the first time she has met with something without
    meaning.

On the next day the man is again near the well.
The girl asks, "What do you want?"       20
"To do more work for you!"
"What work?" she enquires.
"Allow me to weave colored strands into a ribbon to bind your
    hair."
"Is there any need?" she asks.
"None whatever," he allows.       25
The ribbon is made, and thenceforward she spends a great
    deal of time over her hair.

The even stretch of well-employed time in that Paradise
    begins to show irregular rents.
The elders are troubled; they meet in council.
The guide confesses his blunder, saying that he has brought
    the wrong man to the wrong place.
The wrong man is called. His turban, flaming with color,
    shows plainly how great that blunder has been.       30
The chief of the elders says, "You must go back to the earth."
The man heaves a sigh of relief: "I am ready."
The girl with the ribbon round her hair chimes in: "I also!"
For the first time the chief of the elders is faced with a
    situation which has no sense in it.

**Q** **What does each figure in Tagore's**
    **allegory represent?**

**Q** **Is there a "moral" to this story?**

# The Visual Arts at Mid-Century

The major figure in postwar European art was the Dublin-born painter Francis Bacon (1909–1992). Self-trained, Bacon infused European Expressionism with an eccentric approach to form that turned human and animal figures into flayed carcasses and mangled skeletons. Like a sorcerer, he transformed his favorite images from film, magazine illustrations, and the history of art into grotesque and deformed (but sensuously painted) icons.

Bacon had never seen the original portrait of Pope Innocent X, executed in 1650 by Diego Velázquez (see chapter 21); however, he owned many reproductions of the painting and was haunted by the lonely presence of its subject. Painting more than twenty-five versions of the work, Bacon imprisoned the figure in a transparent cage, immobilized by ambiguous lines of force (Figure **35.2**). The venerable pope became a visceral expression of anguish and alienation. His silent scream, a logo for despiritualized Modernism, looks back to Munch (Figure 33.2), Eisenstein (Figure 34.1), and Picasso (Figure 34.10), all of whom Bacon admired.

## Abstract Expressionism

For hundreds of years, almost all important new styles in painting had originated in Paris or other European cities. After 1945, however, the United States, and New York City in particular, took the lead with a radical new style called *Abstract Expressionism*. Abstract Expressionism had its roots in the Modernist assault on traditional, representational art. It took inspiration from the reductionist abstractions of Picasso and Matisse, the colorist experiments of Wassily Kandinsky, the nonsensical performances of Dada, and the "automatic" art of the Surrealists. The new style embraced the role of chance with existential fervor; it also seemed resonant of the quantum physicist's description of the universe as a series of continuously shifting random patterns. Whether or not such theories directly influenced the visual arts, they paralleled the experiments in random art that occurred at this time.

**Figure 35.2 FRANCIS BACON**, *Head VI*, 1949. Oil on canvas, 36¾ × 30¼ in. The painting has become an icon of existential despair. The pope's gaping mouth was inspired by the screaming woman from the Odessa Steps sequence in Eisenstein's *Battleship Potemkin* (see Figure 34.12), and by graphic illustrations of diseases of the mouth in a book the artist had purchased in Paris.

**Figure 35.3 WILLEM DE KOONING**,
*Woman and Bicycle,* 1952–1953. Oil on canvas,
6 ft. 4½ in. × 4 ft. 1 in. Despite what seem to be
urgent and spontaneous brushstrokes, the painting
required more than eighteen months of effort, during
which the artist repeatedly laid on, scraped away, and
restored color to the canvas.

In America, Abstract Expressionism ushered in the so-called "heroic age" of American painting. The pioneers of the movement were a group of talented immigrants who had escaped Nazi oppression and the perils of war-torn Europe. These artists included Arshile Gorky (1905–1948), Hans Hofmann (1880–1966), and Willem de Kooning (1904–1997), all of whom moved to New York between 1920 and 1930. Working on large canvases and using oversized brushes, paint was applied in a loose, free, and instinctive manner that emphasized the physical gesture—the very *act* of painting.

Abstract Expressionist paintings are usually nonrepresentational, but where recognizable subject matter appears, as in de Kooning's series of fierce, totemic women—one of his favorite subjects—it is rendered with frenzied, subjective urgency (Figure **35.3**). De Kooning's wide-eyed females, with their huge breasts and toothy grins, were thought by some to reflect a negative view of women. Actually, however, they took their inspiration from Sumerian votive sculptures and Earth Mother images (see Figures 0.5 and 1.2). De Kooning joked that his women were the sisters of popular pin-ups and billboard goddesses, celebrated for their vacant "American smile."

By contrast, the huge black-and-white canvases of Franz Kline (1910–1962) consist entirely of imposing, abstract shapes. Though wholly nonrepresentational, they call to mind the powerful angularity of bridges, steel mills, and other monuments of postwar urban expansion (see Figure

35.4). Kline, who used housepainters' brushes on canvases that often measured over 10 feet square, achieved a sense of rugged immediacy (which he called "snap").

## Pollock

The best known of the Abstract Expressionists is Wyoming-born Jackson Pollock (1912–1956). His early paintings reveal a coarse figural style and brutal brushwork similar to de Kooning's, but by 1945 Pollock had devised a technique that made action itself the subject of the painting. Instead of mounting the canvas on an easel, he strapped it to the floor of his studio and proceeded to drip, splash, pour, and spread oil, enamel, and commercial aluminum paints across its surface (Figure **35.6**). Layered filaments of paint—the artist's seductive "handwriting"—mingled with sand, nails, matches, bottle shards, and occasional cigarette butts.

**Figure 35.4 FRANZ KLINE**, *Mahoning*, 1956. Oil and paper collage on canvas, 6 ft. 8 in. × 8 ft. 4 in.

**Figure 35.5 TOREI ENJI**, *Calligraphic Talisman*, late eighteenth century. Sumi on paper, 4 ft. 2¾ in. × 10⅛ in.

For centuries, Japan's Zen masters practiced the art of calligraphy, an art whose practice was revived in the eighteenth century (see chapter 21). Executed with large brushes dipped in black ink, Zen paintings were acts of meditation that required concentration and focus, and an intuitive balance of improvisation and control (Figure **35.5**). Usually confined to silk or paper scrolls no more than 4 or 5 feet in length, these calligraphic works convey the vigor of larger paintings like those of the Abstract Expressionists (Figure **35.4**). While the latter may not have been directly influenced by the Zen masters, they were probably aware of the radical Japanese postwar group known as the Gutai Bijutsu Kyokai (Concrete Art Association). The indirect heirs of the Zen masters, the Gutai sponsored "action events" that harnessed physical action to chance. Their performances featured the spontaneous and occasionally outrageous manipulation of paint, which might be flung or hurled at the canvas. Like the abstract expressionists, the Gutai united improvisation and control in the tradition of Japan's Zen masters.

Pollock's daring new method, which came to be called *action painting*, allowed him (as he explained) "to walk around [the canvas], work from the four sides and literally be *in* the painting," a method inspired by the healing rituals of Navajo sand painting whose union of intuition, improvisation, and rigorous control he admired. "It seems to me," he observed, "that the modern painter cannot express his age, the airplane, the atom bomb, the radio, in the old forms of the Renaissance or of any other past culture. Each age finds its own technique." Pollock's canvases are baffling studies in sensation, density, and rhythm, but they are apt metaphors for an age that defined physical reality in terms of process, uncertainty, and chance. Like the currents in some cosmic whirlpool, the galactic paint threads of *Lavender Mist* (Figure **35.7**) seem to expand beyond the limits of the canvas, as if to mirror postwar theories of quantum forces in an expanding universe. Pollock viewed each of his works of art as having a life of its own, but he insisted that *he* controlled its direction: "There is no accident, just as there is no beginning and no end."

**Figure 35.6** Jackson Pollock at work in his Long Island studio, 1950.

**Figure 35.7 JACKSON POLLOCK**, *Number 1, 1950* (*Lavender Mist*), 1950. Oil, enamel, and aluminum on canvas, 7ft. 3in. × 9ft. 10in. Compositions like this one anticipated some of the photographs of outer space taken in the mid 1990s by the Hubble space telescope.

## Color-Field Painting

One variety of Abstract Expressionism, known as *color-field painting*, involved the application of large, often transparent, layers of paint to the surface of the canvas. The paintings of Mark Rothko (1903–1970) consist of translucent, soft-edged blocks of color that float mysteriously on the surfaces of yet other fields of color (Figure **35.8**). These huge, sensuous compositions derive their power from the subtle interaction of rich layers of paint, which seem to glow from within. Rothko himself insisted that his subject matter was "tragedy, ecstasy, and doom," states of mind that are best appreciated by close—18 inches, advised the artist—contemplation of the luminous originals, whose subtlety is lost in photographic reproduction. "The people who weep before my pictures are having the same religious experience I had when I painted them," he contended; "and if you . . . are moved only by their color relationships, then you miss the point." Rothko took his own life in 1970.

While Rothko's abstract shapes are usually self-contained, those of Helen Frankenthaler (b. 1928) tend to swell and expand like exotic blooms (see Figure 35.1). Frankenthaler cultivated the practice of pouring thin washes of paint directly from coffee tins onto raw or **unprimed** (without gesso undercoat) canvas. Her lyrical compositions, often heroic in scale, capture the transparent freshness of watercolors.

In a culture increasingly dominated by mass mechanization, American Abstractionists asserted their preference for an art that was gestural, personal, and spontaneous. The *process* of making art was becoming as important as the

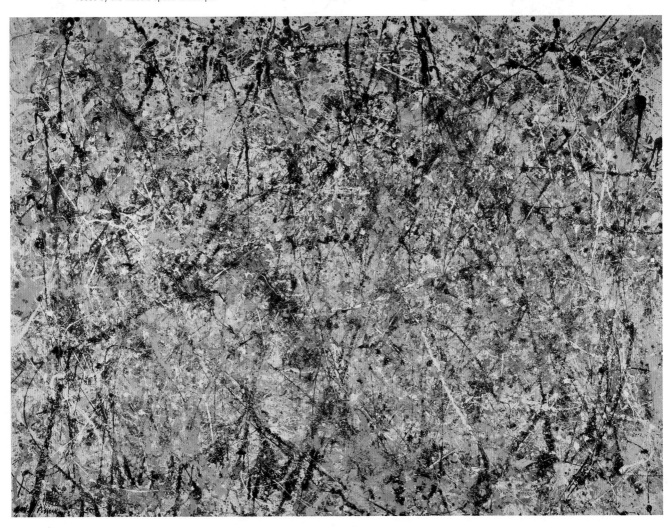

**Figure 35.8 MARK ROTHKO**, *Untitled*, 1960.
Oil on canvas, 5 ft. 9 in. × 4 ft. 2⅛ in.

*product.* At the same time, these artists seemed to turn their backs on bourgeois taste by creating artworks that were simply too large to hang in the average living room. As the movement developed, in fact, the size of the canvas grew as if to accommodate the heroic ambitions of the artists themselves. Ironically, however, these artworks, which scorned the depersonalizing effects of capitalist technology, came to be prized by the guardians of that very technology. Abstract Expressionist paintings, which now hang in corporate offices, hotels, banks, and sanctuaries (such as Houston's nondenominational Rothko Chapel), have become hallmarks of modern sophistication.

## Hopper's America

The Abstract Expressionists represented a decisive break with the Realist tradition in American painting and with Social Realism in particular. Nevertheless, throughout the century, representational art continued to flourish. The paintings of the New York artist Edward Hopper (1882–1967), for instance, present a figurative view of an urban America that is bleak and empty of meaningful relationships. Hopper's fondness for American cinema and theater is reflected in oddly cropped, artificially lit compositions that often resemble film stills. Like the film still, Hopper's frozen moments seem to belong to a larger, existential narrative. In *Nighthawks* (Figure **35.9**), Hopper depicts a harshly lit all-night diner, whose occupants share the same small space but little intimacy. His characters, estranged and isolated in the mundane interiors of "one-night cheap hotels" and "sawdust restaurants," call to mind Eliot's Prufrock.

**Figure 35.9 EDWARD HOPPER**, *Nighthawks*, 1942. Oil on canvas, 33 ⅛ in. × 5 ft. ⅛ in. Hopper was notorious for painting the joyless, mundane activities of everyday urban life. A native New Yorker, he reported that his inspiration for this melancholy scene was a corner restaurant on Greenwich Avenue.

**Figure 35.10 ALBERTO GIACOMETTI**, *City Square (La Place)*, 1948. Bronze, 8½ × 25⅜ × 17¼ in. The isolation of each individual (on what might be an urban street) is conveyed by the fact that no figure, if extended in its forward movement, would encounter another figure in the spatial field.

# Sculpture at Mid-Century

## Giacometti

The mood of existential anxiety also dominated international sculpture. What the art critic Herbert Read called a "geometry of fear" is evident in the figurative and the nonfigurative sculpture of the Swiss artist Alberto Giacometti (1901–1966). In 1930 Giacometti came under the influence of Surrealism, but in the postwar era he devised a new language with which to describe the human figure and the human condition. In both small and large clay works, thereafter cast in bronze, he transformed figurative subjects into haunting, spindly creatures that seem to symbolize existential solitude (Figure **35.10**). Giacometti's disengaged and ravaged figures were greatly admired by Sartre, who wrote the introduction to the catalogue for the artist's one-man exhibition in New York City in 1948. Giacometti's ties to Existentialist writers secured his commission to design the set for the original production of Beckett's *Waiting for Godot*.

## Segal

In America, the haunting works of George Segal (1924–2000) captured the modern mood of alienation. Segal devised a unique method of constructing life-sized figures from plaster casts of live models—often friends and members of his own family. He installed these ghostly replicas in mundane settings staged with ordinary, uncast props: barstools, streetlights, beds, bus seats (Figure **35.11**). These "assembled environments," as he called them, allowed Segal to comment on

matters of alienation, social injustice, and the failure of communication in modern life. Stylistically, Segal's tableaux link the tradition of Realist sculpture to the pop and performance art movements of the later twentieth century (see chapter 37).

## Smith

The nonfigurative sculpture of the postwar era shared the improvisatory vitality of Abstract Expressionist painting. American sculptors, exploiting such industrial materials as welded iron and steel, constructed iconic abstractions that were monumental in size and dynamic in spirit. Among the pioneers of *constructed sculpture* was the Midwestern artist David Smith (1906–1965). Smith learned to weld while in college during a summer job at an automobile plant. He mastered a variety of other industrial processes while working in a wartime locomotive factory. His early pieces were large, welded iron forms sprayed with multiple layers of automobile enamel. During the 1950s, he began to construct

**Figure 35.11 GEORGE SEGAL**, *Bus Riders*, 1962. Plaster, cottongauze, steel, wood, and vinyl, 5 ft. 10 in. × 3 ft. 6¾ in. × 7 ft. 6¾ in. Segal used actual plaster-bandage casts of the models in his early sculptures. Later, he began painting them with bright colors; and finally, they were cast in bronze with a white patina to resemble the original ghostly plaster.

**Figure 35.12 DAVID SMITH**, *Cubi XVII*, 1963. Stainless steel, height 9 ft. Dallas Museum of Fine Arts. Smith made cardboard maquettes of each *Cubi* from old liquor cartons before transposing them into stainless steel forms. He likened the marks on the burnished surfaces to brushstrokes.

boxlike stainless steel forms whose surfaces he burnished and scraped with motorized tools so that they reflected the colors of their surroundings (Figure **35.12**).

Smith forged a new structural style based on industrial techniques. His heroic forms share the calligraphic energy of Franz Kline's gestural abstractions: they capture a sense of aggressive movement that animates the space around them. While the efforts of Giacometti and Segal may reflect existential despair, Smith's sculptures symbolize the optimistic spirit of postwar America. "The metal itself," he insisted, "possesses little art history. What associations it possesses are those of this century: power, structure, movement, progress, suspension, destruction, brutality."

## Calder

The American sculptor Alexander Calder (1898–1976) was a contemporary of the Surrealists, whom he met in Paris in 1926. Influenced by the work of Duchamp and Miró, Calder created abstract wire constructions. These he motorized or hung from ceilings so that they floated freely in the air. Calder's wind-driven mobiles, which range from a few inches in size to enormous proportions, take advantage of the "chance" effects of air currents to create constantly changing relationships between volumes and voids, that is, between brightly colored, biomorphic aluminum shapes and the surrounding space (Figure **35.13**).

**Figure 35.13 ALEXANDER CALDER**, *Big Red*, 1959. Sheet metal and steel wire, 6 ft. 2 in. × 9 ft. 6 in.

## Film at Mid-Century

In the postwar era, filmmakers took a number of new directions. In Italy, the *Neorealism* of Roberto Rossellini (1906–1977) probed the bitter consequences of fascism. With the film *Open City* (1945), Rossellini replaced the cinema of entertainment with a brutal new genre that chronicled human tragedies as if they were natural disasters. Wedded to Realism in both style and substance, Rossellini employed nonprofessional actors and filmed entirely on location. Neorealist cinema self-consciously rejected the artifice of cinematic moralizing and Hollywood "staging," seeking instead to depict the harsh realities of commonplace existence.

A second direction in postwar film appeared in the form of *film noir*, a cinematic style (especially popular in Germany, France, and America) that dealt with the dark world of crime and intrigue. Unlike the gangster movies of the 1930s, *film noir* conveyed a mood of disillusion and resignation proceeding from moral ambiguities between good and evil. In the American film *Double Indemnity* (1944), the *femme fatale* (the dangerous, seductive woman) made one of her earliest cinematic appearances. And in the *film noir* classic, *A Touch of Evil* (1958), the multitalented director and actor Orson Welles (1915–1985) used long takes (shots of twenty or more seconds), high and low camera positions, and off-center compositions to create sinister characters and ominous settings.

A third film genre, the *thriller*, dominated by the impresario Alfred Hitchcock (1899–1980), depended for its impact on suspense rather than graphic violence. Hitchcock's unique combination of story and style—quick shots that alternate between the character and the (often fearful) object of his gaze—were particularly successful in such films as *Rear Window* (1954) and *Psycho* (1960).

Postwar cinema took up the quest for meaning by way of films that challenged traditional moral values. The pioneer Japanese filmmaker Akira Kurosawa (1910–1998) explored the complexities of modern life by revisiting traditional *samurai* legends. A highly skilled director, he used unusual camera angles, flashbacks, and a stringent economy of expression in the classics *Rashōmon* (1950) and *The Seven Samurai* (1954). These films convey Kurosawa's utopian view that positive social action can redeem the world's evils.

### Bergman

Less optimistic concerning the fate of humankind was the Swedish cinematic giant Ingmar Bergman (1918–2007). In his almost four dozen films, Bergman probed the troubled lives of modern men and women. The loss of God, the acknowledgment of spiritual and emotional alienation, and the anxieties that accompany self-understanding are his principal themes. Bergman's most notable films are *The Seventh Seal* (1956), *Wild Strawberries* (1957), and *Persona* (1966). His landmark work, *The Seventh Seal*, is an allegorical tale of despair in the face of impending death. Set in medieval Europe (and inspired by the Revelation of Saint John in the New Testament), it is the story of a knight who returns home from the Crusades, only to confront widespread plague and human suffering. Disillusioned, he ultimately challenges Death to a game of chess, the stakes of which are life itself. Bergman compared filmmaking to composing music: a non-narrative and largely intuitive enterprise. His apocalyptic visions, translated to film, proceeded from what he called "the administration of the unspeakable."

## Architecture at Mid-Century

By the middle of the twentieth century, public architecture assumed a distinctly international character. The principles of International Style architecture, based on the use of structural steel, ferroconcrete, and glass, had gained popularity through the influence of Bauhaus-trained architects and Le Corbusier (see chapter 32). Standardization and machinelike efficiency became the hallmarks of high-rise urban apartment buildings, constructed in their thousands to provide low-rent housing in the decades after 1930. In the building of schools, factories, and offices, the simplicity and austerity of the International Style echoed the mood of depersonalization that prevailed in the arts. International Style skyscrapers became symbols of corporate wealth and modern technocracy. They reflected the materialism of the twentieth century as powerfully as the Gothic cathedral summed up the spirituality of the High Middle Ages.

### Van der Rohe

Among the most daring of the International Style proponents was the Dutch architect (and the last director of the Bauhaus) Ludwig Mies van der Rohe (1886–1969). Mies' credo "less is more" inspired austere structures such as the Seagram Building in New York City, designed in partnership with Philip Johnson (1906–2005) in 1958 (Figure 35.14). This sleek, unadorned slab of metallic bronze and amber glass was "the last word" in sophisticated machine engineering and a monument to the "form follows function" credo of the International Style. The proportions of the building are as impeccable as those of any Classical structure: the raised level at the bottom is balanced at the top by a four-story band of darker glass. For decades, the Seagram Building influenced glass-and-steel-box architecture; unfortunately, in many of its imitators, it was the cool, impersonal quality of the building and not its poetic simplicity that prevailed.

At mid-century, some of the world's leading architects reacted against the strict geometry and functional purism of International Style architecture. Instead, they provided subjective, personal, and even romantic alternatives to the cool rationalism of the International Style. Using the medium of cast concrete, they created organically shaped structures that were as gestural as the sculptures of Smith and as lyrical as the paintings of Frankenthaler. The Trans World Airlines Terminal at New York's Kennedy Airport (Figure 35.15), for example, designed by the Finnish architect Eero Saarinen (1910–1961), is a metaphor for flight: its cross-vaulted roof—a steel structure surfaced with concrete—flares upward like a gigantic bird. The interior

**Figure 35.14 LUDWIG MIES VAN DER ROHE**, Seagram Building, New York, 1954–1958. Metallic bronze and amber glass.

**Figure 35.15 EERO SAARINEN**, Trans World Airlines Terminal, Kennedy Airport, New York, 1962.

of the terminal unfolds gradually and mysteriously to embrace fluid, uninterrupted space.

## Wright at Mid-Century

One of the most original minds of the twentieth century, Frank Lloyd Wright had produced notable examples of domestic architecture as early as 1909 (see Figures 32.22 and 32.23). At mid-century, he designed one of the most unique buildings in America: the Guggenheim Museum. An architectural landmark that contrasts vividly with Manhattan's typically boxy vertical buildings, the museum is configured as a ribbon of white ferroconcrete that winds into a cylindrical shape, narrowing from top to bottom. Its interior, which resembles the inside of a huge snail shell, consists of a continuous spiral ramp fixed around an open, central well (Figure **35.16**). A clear glass dome at the top allows natural light to bathe interior space, whose breathtaking enclosure competes seductively with most of the artwork exhibited therein. A ten-story limestone extension added in 1992 has reduced the dramatic contrast between the rotunda and its urban setting, but it does not destroy the eloquence of the original design (Figure **35.17**). The Guggenheim remains the definitive example of the modern architectural imagination.

## Fuller

The architectural visionary and pioneer environmentalist, Richard Buckminster Fuller (1895–1983), saw few of his futuristic ideas realized in tangible form. Fuller was ahead of his time in realizing that the earth's resources are finite and the planet (which he called "spaceship Earth") is a fragile entity. His campaigns for energy-efficient, affordable housing inspired one of the earliest prefabricated house

**Figure 35.16 FRANK LLOYD WRIGHT**, The Solomon R. Guggenheim Museum interior, 1957–1959. Objecting to the problems associated with hanging paintings on walls that are not strictly vertical, Willem de Kooning and twenty other artists wrote a letter refusing to show their works in the museum. Traditionally configured rooms have been added to Wright's original design.

**Figure 35.17 FRANK LLOYD WRIGHT**, The Solomon R. Guggenheim Museum, New York, 1957–1959.

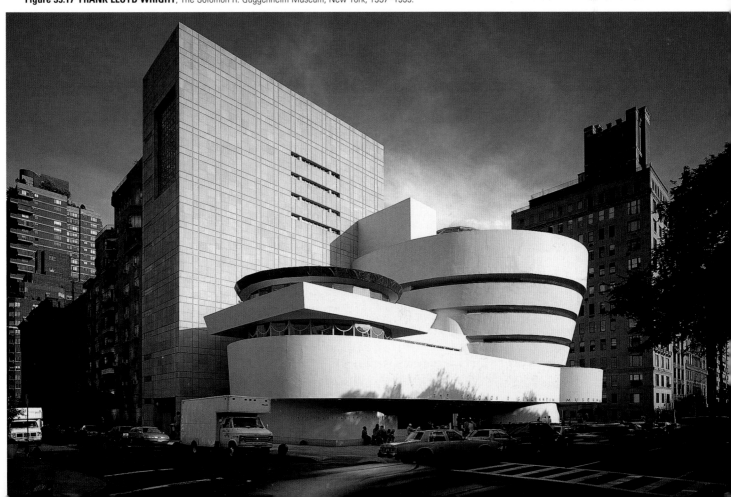

**Figure 35.18 RICHARD BUCKMINSTER FULLER**, geodesic dome, U.S. Pavilion, Montreal International Exposition, 1967. The original dome, which served as the United States Pavilion at Expo '67, was 250 feet in diameter and 200 feet high. In 1976, a fire destroyed the acrylic surface but left the lattice frame of the dome, which has since been restored.

designs: the Dymaxion (1927) was a metal structure hung from a central mast with outer walls of continuous glass.

Fuller is best known for his **geodesic domes**, which depend on the tensile properties of lightweight triangular elements. This type of construction, which uses a minimum of structure to create maximum strength, could be mass-produced cheaply and flown anywhere by helicopter to provide instant shelter. Like the Dymaxion, the geodesic dome that he designed for the 1967 International Exposition in Montreal (Figure **35.18**) had little impact on architectural construction until the end of the twentieth century (see Figure 37.22).

## Music and Dance at Mid-Century

### Cage

The most inventive figure in mid twentieth-century music was the American composer John Cage (1912–1992). Cage styled himself a student of architecture and gardening, and a devotee of Zen Buddhism. He studied with Arnold Schoenberg (see chapter 32), who described him as an inventor, rather than a composer. A leading spokesman for experimentation, Cage once defined music as a combination of sounds (specific pitches), noise (nonpitched sounds), and silence, with rhythm as the common denominator. "Everything we do is music," he insisted.

In 1938 Cage invented the prepared piano, a traditional Steinway piano modified by attaching to its strings pieces of rubber, bamboo slats, bolts, and other objects. When played, the prepared piano becomes something like a percussion instrument, the sounds of which resemble those of a Balinese orchestra; as Cage observed, "a percussive orchestra under the control of a single player." The *Sonata* 🎼 V (1948), written for the prepared piano, belongs to a series of sixteen sonatas and four interludes that reflect the composer's introduction to Indian music and philosophy. These early compositions are delicate in timbre and texture and elegant in percussive rhythms.

🎼 See Music Listening Selections at end of chapter.

Cage's later works were radically experimental, especially in their effort to accommodate silence and nonpitched sound. In 1953, Cage composed *4' 33"*, a piece in which a performer sits motionless before the piano for four minutes and thirty-three seconds. The "music" of *4' 33"* consists of the fleeting, random sounds that occur during the designated time period—the breathing of the pianist, the shuffling of the audience's feet, or the distant hum of traffic outside of the concert hall.

Much of Cage's music is **aleatory**, that is, based on chance or random procedures. To determine the placement of notes in a musical composition, Cage might apply the numbers dictated in a throw of the dice or incorporate the surface stains and imperfections on an otherwise blank piece of sheet music. He found inspiration for these techniques in Zen Buddhism, in the *I jing* (China's ancient oracular *Book of Changes*), and in the psychic automatism of the Surrealists. Accident and chance were basic to his *Imaginary Landscape No. 4* (1951), a composition that calls for twelve radios playing simultaneously with twenty-four performers (two at each radio) randomly turning the volume and selector controls. Such antimusical music celebrates the absurd and random nature of the modern experience. At the same time, it blurs the traditional relationship between composers and performers, and between artistic conception and execution. Nevertheless, despite Cage's chance methods, each of his compositions is fully scored: even the most unconventional passages follow his explicit directions. These "scored improvisations" acknowledge the existential credo that every creative act involves choice. The decision to operate at random (whether by a roll of the dice, a toss of coins, or some other method), even the decision *not* to act, represents a choice.

Cage's avant-garde methods, as publicized in his numerous essays and lectures, had an enormous influence on younger artists. His "chance" aesthetic inspired the international Neodada movement known as *Fluxus*. Fluxus artists, writers, filmmakers, and musicians experimented with minimal, performance-oriented works that left the viewer to complete the work of art (see chapter 38).

## Cunningham

In the mid 1940s, Cage met the American choreographer Merce Cunningham (1922–2009) and the young painter Robert Rauschenberg (1925–2008; see chapter 37). At Black Mountain College in Asheville, North Carolina, they collaborated in staging performances that employed improvisational techniques and inventive combinations of dance, mime, poetry, music, slide projections, and film.

Cunningham's contribution to modern choreography stems from his radical disassociation of music and dance. Rejecting the representational, storytelling dance style of his teacher, Martha Graham (see chapter 32), he concentrated exclusively on movement and form. In a Cunningham piece, dance may proceed without music, or music may coexist with dance, but the tempo of the music may be wholly irrelevant to the movements of the dancers. Cunningham disclaims traditional dance positions and ignores traditional staging (whereby dancers are assigned to specific spaces). His choreography calls for clean, expansive body gestures that occupy large, spatial fields. Like a Pollock painting or a Cage composition, a Cunningham dance may unfold along a broad continuum, lacking a fixed center. It treats all body movements (even the ordinary actions of running, jumping, and falling) equally; and such movements may occur by way of improvisation or—as with the music of Cage—by chance. Nevertheless, as with Cage's compositions, even improvisation is planned (or choreographed) by the artist.

One of Cunningham's early works, entitled *Summerspace* (1958), shares the raw energy and spontaneity that typify the canvases of the Abstract Expressionists (Figure **35.19**). In this multimedia piece Cunningham explores the tensions between chance and choice and between freedom and control, that lie at the heart of existential expression.

**Figure 35.19 MERCE CUNNINGHAM**, *Summerspace*, 1958. Cage became director of Cunningham's dance company, founded in 1953. With Rauschenberg, who designed the sets and costumes for *Summerspace*, he and Cunningham produced some of the most innovative mixed-media performances of the predigital era.

# LOOKING BACK

### The Cold War

- Alienation and anxiety were two principal conditions of the postwar mentality.
- Following World War II, a contest for world domination known as the "cold war" determined the course of international relations. Two seemingly incompatible ideologies, communism and capitalism, competed for prominence in the global arena.
- Capitalism found its roots in Adam Smith's free market philosophy, while communism gave a central state the power to distribute wealth equally.

### Existentialism

- Existentialism, a humanistic philosophy formulated by Jean-Paul Sartre, emphasized the role of individual choice in a world that lacked moral absolutes.
- Both secular and Christian Existentialism charged human beings with full responsibility for their freely chosen actions.

### Literature at Mid-Century

- Twentieth-century writers gave voice to the existential challenge and to the anguish produced by the individual's freedom to choose. Pessimists feared the destructive potential of modern technology and anticipated the demise of human freedom.
- Modern antiheroes, such as the burlesque tramps in Samuel Beckett's theater-of-the-absurd *Waiting for Godot*, contend with the despair of making choices in an essentially meaningless universe. Their survival seems to depend upon an authentic commitment to action.
- Asian writers such as Rabindranath Tagore pursued the quest for meaning in parts of the world where Modernism did as much to threaten as to reshape tradition.

### The Visual Arts at Mid-Century

- In the visual arts, the center of gravity shifted from Paris to New York City. The movement known as Abstract Expressionism marked a heroic effort at self-actualization through the gestural and often brutal application of paint to canvas.
- The action paintings of Jackson Pollock and the color-field paintings of Frankenthaler and Rothko explore the dynamic balance between chance and choice.

### Sculpture at Mid-Century

- Existential anxiety characterizes the sculptures of Alberto Giacometti and George Segal whose figures evoke a mood of alienation, even as they occupy the crowded urban environment.
- David Smith's large-scale works introduced industrial

techniques to abstract sculptures fabricated in iron and stainless steel.

### Film at Mid-Century

- Italian director Roberto Rossellini's Neorealist style used nonprofessional actors and on-site filming to depict reality at its fullest.
- The *film noir* genre dealt with the dark, moral ambiguities of the criminal world. Alfred Hitchcock thrillers focused on suspense rather than graphic violence.
- Masters of postwar films, Akira Kurosawa and Ingmar Bergman questioned traditional moral values, often using allegory to probe states of disillusion and despair.

### Architecture at Mid-Century

- The International Style in architecture culminated in classic glass-box skyscrapers; despite some exceptions, these buildings reinforced the impersonal nature of the modern urban community.
- Buckminster Fuller's geodesic dome and a new wave of seductive ferroconcrete buildings, exemplified in Frank Lloyd Wright's Guggenheim Museum, challenged the austerity of the International Style.

### Music and Dance at Mid-Century

- In the domains of music and dance, as in the visual arts, the postwar generation took the absence of absolutes as the starting point for free experimentation.
- John Cage, the foremost member of the musical avant-garde, integrated silence, noise, and chance into his compositions.
- Merce Cunningham redefined modern dance as movement stripped of both thematic and musical associations.

## Music Listening Selections

**CD Two Selection 20**   Cage, *Sonata V*, 1948, excerpt.

## Glossary

**aleatory** (Latin, *alea*, "dice") any kind of music composed according to chance or random procedures

**geodesic dome**  a spherical structure formed by lightweight elements held in tension

**unprimed**  lacking the gesso undercoat normally applied to the surface of the canvas

# Chapter 36

## Liberation and Equality
### ca. 1930–2000

*"This world is white no longer, and it will never be white again."*
James Baldwin

**Figure 36.1 JEFF WALL**, *After* Invisible Man *by Ralph Ellison, "The Preface," Edition of 2*, 1999–2000. Cibachrome transparency, aluminum light box, fluorescent bulbs, 75¼ × 106¼ × 10¼ in. Wall made this large-scale backlit cibachrome photograph from a scene he himself staged with a hired actor and a fabricated set. He is inspired by subjects and images drawn from the history of art and literature.

# LOOKING AHEAD

While the mood of despair pervaded much of the postwar era, a second, more positive spirit fueled movements to achieve liberation and equality in many parts of the world. Two major liberation movements marked the second half of the twentieth century. The first involved efforts on the part of colonial nations to secure political, economic, religious, and ethnic independence. It also aimed to reduce poverty and raise standards of living in the world's industrially underdeveloped nations, thus bringing them to the productive status of nations with more highly developed economies.

The second movement for liberation, fired by opposition to age-old social injustices and ingrained prejudice, involved the demand for racial, ethnic, and gender equality. Engaging worldwide participation, the movement embraced a lengthy struggle for civil rights in the African-American population of the United States, the demand for equality among feminists throughout the West, and a recognition of the inequalities suffered by those of untraditional sexual orientation.

The movements for liberation and equality—colonial, racial, and sexual—provided the context for some of the most significant literature, art, and music of the twentieth century. In the long run, all artworks must be judged without reference to the politics, race, or gender of the artists who created them. Nevertheless, the works included in this chapter are better understood as expressions of a unique time and place in the history of the humanistic tradition.

## Anticolonialism and Liberation

In the postwar era, the weakened European nations were unable to maintain the military and economic forces necessary to sustain their empires. At the same time, their colonial subjects increased their efforts to free themselves of Western rulers.

One of the earliest revolts against colonial rule took place in India. During World War I, the Indian National Congress came under the influence of the Hindu Mohandas Gandhi (1869–1948). Gandhi, whose followers called him "Mahatma," or "great soul," led India's struggle for independence from Great Britain. Guided by the precepts of Hinduism, as well as by the Sermon on the Mount and the writings of Thoreau and Tolstoy, Gandhi initiated a policy of peaceful protest against colonial oppression. His program of nonviolent resistance, including fasting and peaceful demonstrations, influenced subsequent liberation movements throughout the world. Gandhi's involvement was crucial to India's emancipation from British control,

which occurred in 1947, only one year before he was assassinated by a Hindu fanatic who opposed his conciliatory gestures toward India's Muslim minority.

Between 1944 and 1960, many nations, including Jordan, Burma, Palestine, Sri Lanka, Ghana, Malaya, Cyprus, and Nigeria, freed themselves from British rule. Syria, Lebanon, Cambodia, Laos, North and South Vietnam, Morocco, Tunisia, Cameroon, Mali, and other African states won independence from France. And still other territories claimed their freedom from the empires of the United States, Japan, the Netherlands, Belgium, and Italy.

In Central America, Southeast Asia, and elsewhere, however, internal conflicts provoked military intervention by First World powers, that is, the industrialized capitalist nations, including the United States, most of Western Europe, Japan, and Canada. Between 1964 and 1975, the United States succeeded France in an unsuccessful effort to defend South Vietnam from communist control. The Vietnam War—the longest war in American history—cost the lives of some 50,000 Americans and more than fifteen million Vietnamese. More recently, in Eastern Europe, the demise of Soviet authority has unleashed age-old ethnic conflicts, producing fragmentation and bloodshed.

### Liberation and Literature in the Islamic World

While India achieved its emancipation from British control, a related drive for liberation was underway among the members of the country's Muslim minority. The quest for an autonomous Muslim state on the Indian subcontinent resulted in the creation of an independent Pakistan in 1947. Other parts of the Islamic world, however, were not so successful. For instance, brutal massacres, riots, and revolution plagued Egypt for decades before it became an independent nation in 1971. Impeding the success of independent Muslim states was the fact that the West, even after granting them their independence, continued to influence key aspects of their economies, such as the production of oil.

Equally challenging was the process of modernization itself: specifically, the incompatibility between the agenda of modernization, focused on Western-style capitalism and democratic reform, and the fundamentals of Muslim tradition based in the Qur'an and a governing theocracy. In most parts of the Islamic world, the difficulties of introducing modern legal and constitutional innovations into centuries-old Islamic societies proved overwhelming. To this day, in fact, minority elements within the Islamic world remain in violent opposition to the culture of modernization and to Western intrusion in Muslim affairs.

If Western technology and imperialism have weighed heavily in the transition from ancient to modern times, Muslim culture has nonetheless flourished. In India, the poet and philosopher Muhammad Iqbal (1876–1938) envisioned Islam as the leading moral force in South Asia. While supporting the formation of an independent Muslim state in Pakistan, he emphasized the importance of achieving brotherhood among India's Muslim, Christian, and Hindu populations. Educated in law and philosophy at Oxford, England, Iqbal anticipated a pan-Islamic community that transcended ethnic, racial, and national loyalties. He urged his followers to replace Islamic mysticism and passive contemplation with an activist spirit. In his poems, he gave voice to the despair felt by Muslims who viewed imperialism and Modernism as twin threats to spirituality and divine law.

---

## READING 36.1 Islamic Poems

**Iqbal's "Revolution" (1938)**

Death to man's soul is Europe, death is Asia
To man's will: neither feels the vital current.
In man's hearts stirs a revolution's torrent;
Maybe our old world too is nearing death.

**Iqbal's "Europe and Syria" (1936)**

This land of Syria gave the West a Prophet
Of purity and pity and innocence;
And Syria from the West as recompense
Gets dice and drink and troops of prostitutes.          10

**Q** Based on the evidence of these two poems, how would you describe the Muslim response to Western values?

---

## Liberation and Literature in Latin America

From the time of Christopher Columbus, the peoples of Latin America have served the political and economic interests of First World countries more powerful than their own. And even after the European nations departed from the shores of Argentina, Brazil, Mexico, Peru, and other Latin American states in the early nineteenth century, the intolerable conditions that had prevailed in the long era of colonialism persisted: the vast majority of Latin Americans, including great masses of peasants of Native American descent, lived in relative poverty, while small, wealthy, landowning elites held power. These elites maintained their position by virtue of their alliance with the financial and industrial interests of First World nations, including (especially since the 1890s) the United States.

Spanish-speaking and predominantly Catholic, the rapidly growing populations of the more than two dozen nations of Latin America have suffered repeated social upheaval in their attempts to cope with persistent problems of inequality, exploitation, and underdevelopment. The long and bitter history of the Mexican Revolution, commemorated in the murals of Diego Rivera (see Figure 34.7), provides a vivid example. From country to country, political and social reformers have struggled to revolutionize the socioeconomic order, to liberate Latin America from economic colonialism, and to bring about a more equitable distribution of wealth. Support for these essentially socialist movements has come from representatives of the deprived elements of society, including organized labor

and, often enough, from the Catholic Church, which has acted on behalf of the masses as an agent of social justice. The "liberation theology" preached by reformist elements in the clergy advanced a powerful new rendering of Christian dogma.

Latin America's artists rallied to support movements for liberation. During the 1960s, the outpouring of exceptionally fine Latin American prose and poetry constituted a literary boom, the influence of which is still being felt worldwide. Among the champions of reform was the Chilean Pablo Neruda (1904–1973), one of Latin America's most prolific Spanish-language poets. His poems, often embellished with violent, Surrealist images, endorse a radical, populist ideology. In "The United Fruit Co." he describes the corruption of justice and freedom in the "Banana Republics" of Latin America. The poem, phrased as a mock Last Judgment, smolders with indignation at the United States' policies of commercial exploitation in the nations south of its borders.

---

## READING 36.2 Neruda's "United Fruit Co." (1950)

When the trumpets had sounded and all          1
was in readiness on the face of the earth,
Jehovah divided his universe:
Anaconda, Ford Motors,
Coca-Cola Inc., and similar entities:          5
the most succulent item of all,
The United Fruit Company Incorporated
reserved for itself: the heartland
and coasts of my country,
the delectable waist of America.          10
They rechristened their properties:
the "Banana Republics"—
and over the languishing dead,
the uneasy repose of the heroes
who harried that greatness,          15
their flags and their freedoms,
they established an *opéra bouffe*:
they ravished all enterprise,
awarded the laurels like Caesars,
unleashed all the covetous, and contrived          20
the tyrannical Reign of the Flies—
Trujillo the fly, and Tacho the fly,
the flies called Carias, Martinez,
Ubico[1]—all of them flies, flies
dank with the blood of their marmalade          25
vassalage, flies buzzing drunkenly

---

[1] The twentieth-century dictators of Latin America: Rafael Molina Trujillo brutally dominated the Dominican Republic from 1930 to 1961; "Tacho" was the nickname for Anastasio Somoza, who controlled Nicaragua from 1937 until his assassination in 1956; Tiburcio Carias, self-styled dictator of Honduras, was supported during the 1930s and 1940s by the United Fruit Company; Maximilian Martinez was the ruthless dictator of El Salvador during the 1930s and 1940s; Jorge Ubico seized power in Guatemala in 1931 and served as a puppet of the United States until 1944.

on the populous middens:
the fly-circus fly and the scholarly
kind, case-hardened in tyranny.
Then in the bloody domain of the flies          30
The United Fruit Company Incorporated
sailed off with a booty of coffee and fruits
brimming its cargo boats, gliding
like trays with the spoils
of our drowning dominions.                       35
And all the while, somewhere in the sugary
hells of our seaports,
smothered by gases, an Indian
fell in the morning:
a body spun off, an anonymous                    40
chattel, some numeral tumbling,
a branch with its death running out of it
in the vat of the carrion, fruit laden and foul.

**Q** **What sentiments dominate this poem?**

**Q** **What is the function of Neruda's mock Last Judgment?**

## The Quest for Racial Equality

The most turbulent liberation movement of the twentieth century addressed the issue of racial equality—an issue so dramatically reflected in the African-American experience that some observers have dubbed the century "The Race Era." Since the days of slavery, millions of black Americans had existed as an underprivileged minority population living within an advanced industrial state.

The Dutch took the first Africans to America in 1619, and during the late seventeenth and eighteenth centuries, thousands of slaves were imported to the American colonies, especially those in the South. For 250 years, until the end of the Civil War, slavery was a fact of American life. The Emancipation Proclamation issued by Abraham Lincoln in 1863 facilitated the liberation of the slaves, but it was not until 1865—with the Thirteenth Amendment to the United States Constitution—that all slaves were finally freed. This and other constitutional amendments guaranteed the rights of black people; nevertheless, the lives of African-Americans continued to be harsh and poor by comparison with those of their former white masters. Separation of the races by segregated housing, inferior schools, and exclusion from voting and equal employment were only a few of the inequities suffered by this minority in the post-emancipation United States. It was to these issues and to the more general problem of racism that many African-Americans addressed themselves after World War I.

### The Harlem Renaissance

World War I provided African-Americans with new opportunities in education and employment. During and after the war, over five million African-Americans migrated from the South to the northern states. New York City

**Figure 36.2 JACOB LAWRENCE**, "Race riots were numerous. White workers were hostile toward the migrants who had been hired to break strikes." Panel 50 from "The Migration" series, 1940–1941; text and title revised by the artist, 1993. Tempera on gesso on composition board, 18 × 12 in.

became the center of economic opportunity, as well as the melting pot for black people from other parts of the world. But white frustration and fear of black competition for jobs led to race riots in over twenty-five cities during the "bloody summer" of 1919 (Figure **36.2**).

Between 1920 and 1940, the quest for racial equality and a search for self-identity among African-Americans inspired an upsurge of creative expression in the arts. Centered in Harlem—a part of Manhattan occupied largely by African-Americans—poets, painters, musicians, and dancers forged the movement that came to be called the Harlem Renaissance.

The Harlem Renaissance made the self-conscious "rebirth" of the African heritage the principal part of an intellectual and cultural quest for racial identity and equality. A leading figure of the movement was the writer, folklorist, and anthropologist Zora Neale Hurston (1891–1960). Hurston made use of African-American dialect to create some of the strongest female characters in early twentieth-century fiction. Her novel, *Their Eyes Were Watching God*, is widely regarded as a classic of black literature.

Hurston's contemporary, Langston Hughes (1902–1967), was one of the most eloquent voices of the Harlem Renaissance. Hughes was born in Missouri and moved to New York in 1921, where he became the first African-American to support himself as a professional writer. A musician as well as a journalist and a novelist, Hughes was the rare poet whose powerful phrases ("a dream deferred," "a raisin in the sun," and "black like me") are enshrined in the canon of American literature and in the English language. His poems, which capture the musical qualities of the African oral tradition, fuse everyday speech with the rhythms of blues and jazz. Hughes, who regarded poets as "lyric historians," drew deeply on his own experience: his "Theme for English B" records his response to the education of black students in a dominantly white culture. In "Harlem," a meditation on the "bloody summer" of 1919, Hughes looks to the immediate past to presage the angry riots that have recurred regularly since the 1960s in America's black ghettos.

Like the writers of the Harlem Renaissance, the Chicago-born poet Gwendolyn Brooks (1917–2000) drew upon the idioms of jazz and street slang to produce a vivid picture of the black ghettos in her city. The first African-American to receive the Pulitzer Prize for poetry (1949), Brooks brought to attention the plight of black people—especially young black men and women—in American society. The two poems in Reading 36.4 are representative of the early part of her long and productive career.

---

┌─ **READING 36.3** The Poems of Hughes

**Hughes' "Theme for English B" (1949)**

The instructor said,                                                  1

   *Go home and write*
   *a page tonight.*
   *And let that page come out of you—*
   *Then, it will be true.*                                  5

I wonder if it's that simple?

I am twenty-two, colored, born in Winston-Salem.
I went to school there, then Durham, then here
to this college on the hill above Harlem.
I am the only colored student in my class.                           10
The steps from the hill lead down into Harlem,
through a park, then I cross St. Nicholas,
Eighth Avenue, Seventh, and I come to the Y,
the Harlem Branch Y, where I take the elevator
up to my room, sit down, and write this page:                        15

It's not easy to know what is true for you or me
at twenty-two, my age. But I guess I'm what
I feel and see and hear, Harlem, I hear you:
hear you, hear me—we two—you, me, talk on this page.
(I hear New York, too.) Me—who?                                      20
Well, I like to eat, sleep, drink, and be in love.
I like to work, read, learn, and understand life.
I like a pipe for a Christmas present,

or records—Bessie, bop, or Bach.
I guess being colored doesn't make me *not* like                     25
the same things other folks like who are other races.
So will my page be colored that I write?
Being me, it will not be white.
But it will be
a part of you, instructor.                                           30
You are white—
yet a part of me, as I am a part of you.
That's American.
Sometimes perhaps you don't want to be a part of me.
Nor do I often want to be a part of you.                             35
But we are, that's true!
I guess you learn from me—
although you're older—and white—
and somewhat more free.

This is my page for English B.                                       40

**Hughes' "Harlem" (1951)**

What happens to a dream deferred?                                     1

Does it dry up
like a raisin in the sun?
Or fester like a sore—
And then run?                                                         5
Does it stink like rotten meat?
Or crust and sugar over—
like a syrupy sweet?
Maybe it just sags
like a heavy load.                                                   10

*Or does it explode?*

└─ **Q** To what extent do the circumstances described in these poems (written fifty years ago) still pertain?

---

┌─ **READING 36.4** The Poems of Brooks

**Brooks' "The Mother" (1945)**

Abortions will not let you forget.                                    1
You remember the children you got that you did not get,
The damp small pulps with a little or with no hair,
The singers and workers that never handled the air.
You will never neglect or beat                                        5
Them, or silence or buy with a sweet.
You will never wind up the sucking-thumb
Or scuttle off ghosts that come.
You will never leave them, controlling your luscious sigh,
Return for a snack of them, with gobbling mother-eye.                 10

I have heard in the voices of the wind the voices of my
   dim killed children.
I have contracted. I have eased
My dim dears at the breasts they could never suck.
I have said, Sweets, if I sinned, if I seized
Your luck                                                            15
And your lives from your unfinished reach,

If I stole your births and your names,
Your straight baby tears and your games,
Your stilted or lovely loves, your tumults, your marriages,
  aches, and your deaths,

If I poisoned the beginnings of your breaths,                    20
Believe that even in my deliberateness I was not deliberate.
Though why should I whine,
Whine that the crime was other than mine?—
Since anyhow you are dead.
Or rather, or instead,                                            25
You were never made.

But that too, I am afraid,
Is faulty: oh, what shall I say, how is the truth to be said?
You were born, you had body, you died.
It is just that you never giggled or planned or cried.            30

Believe me, I loved you all.
Believe me, I knew you, though faintly, and I loved,
  I loved you
All.

### Brooks' "We Real Cool" (1959)

The Pool Players.
Seven at the Golden Shovel.

  We real cool. We
  Left school. We

  Lurk late. We
  Strike straight. We

  Sing sin. We
  Thin gin. We

  Jazz June. We
  Die soon.

**Q** In what ways are these poems descriptive?
Are they also didactic? How so?

## Richard Wright and the Realities of Racism

Richard Wright (1908–1960) was born on a cotton plantation in Mississippi and came to New York City in 1937,
just after the heyday of the Harlem Renaissance. Wright
brought to his writings the anger of a man who had known
physical punishment and repeated injustice at the hands of
white people. In his novel *Native Son* (1940), the nightmarish story of a poor, young black man who kills his white
employer's daughter, Wright examined the ways in which
the frustrated search for identity led some African-
Americans to despair, defiance, and even violent crime.
The novel won Wright immediate acclaim and was rewrit-
ten for the New York stage in 1941.

In the autobiographical sketch *The Ethics of Living Jim
Crow* (1938), Wright records with grim frankness the experience of growing up in a racially segregated community in
the American South. "Jim Crow," the stage name of a popular nineteenth-century minstrel performer, Thomas D.
Rice, had come to describe anything pertaining to African-
Americans, including matters of racial segregation.

─ **READING 36.5** From Wright's *The Ethics
            of Living Jim Crow* (1938)

My first lesson in how to live as a Negro came when I was      1
quite small. We were living in Arkansas. Our house stood
behind the railroad tracks. Its skimpy yard was paved with
black cinders. Nothing green ever grew in that yard. The only
touch of green we could see was far away, beyond the tracks,
over where the white folks lived. But cinders were good
enough for me and I never missed the green growing things.
And anyhow cinders were fine weapons. You could always
have a nice hot war with huge black cinders. All you had to do
was crouch behind the brick pillars of a house with your hands  10
full of gritty ammunition. And the first woolly black head you
saw pop out from behind another row of pillars was your
target. You tried your very best to knock it off. It was great
fun.  I never fully realized the appalling disadvantages of a
cinder environment till one day the gang to which I belonged
found itself engaged in a war with the white boys who lived
beyond the tracks. As usual we laid down our cinder barrage,
thinking that this would wipe the white boys out. But they
replied with a steady bombardment of broken bottles. We
doubled our cinder barrage, but they hid behind trees, hedges, 20
and the sloping embankment of their lawns. Having no such
fortifications, we retreated to the brick pillars of our homes.
During the retreat a broken milk bottle caught me behind the
ear, opening a deep gash which bled profusely. The sight of
blood pouring over my face completely demoralized our ranks.
My fellow-combatants left me standing paralyzed in the center
of the yard, and scurried for their homes. A kind neighbor saw
me, and rushed me to a doctor, who took three stitches in my
neck.

I sat brooding on my front steps, nursing my wound and        30
waiting for my mother to come from work. I felt that a grave
injustice had been done me. It was all right to throw cinders.
The greatest harm a cinder could do was leave a bruise. But
broken bottles were dangerous; they left you cut, bleeding, and
helpless.

When night fell, my mother came from the white folks'
kitchen. I raced down the street to meet her. I could just feel
in my bones that she would understand. I knew she would tell
me exactly what to do next time. I grabbed her hand and
babbled out the whole story. She examined my wound, then     40
slapped me.

"How come yuh didn't hide?" she asked me. "How come yuh
awways fightin'?"

I was outraged, and bawled. Between sobs I told her that I
didn't have any trees or hedges to hide behind. There wasn't a
thing I could have used as a trench. And you couldn't throw
very far when you were hiding behind the brick pillars of a
house. She grabbed a barrel stave, dragged me home, stripped
me naked, and beat me till I had a fever of one hundred and
two. She would smack my rump with the stave, and, while the   50
skin was still smarting impart to me gems of Jim Crow
wisdom. I was never to throw cinders any more. I was never
to fight any more wars. I was never, never, under any
conditions, to fight *white* folks again. And they were
absolutely right in clouting me with the broken milk bottle.

Didn't I know she was working hard every day in the hot kitchens of the white folks to make money to take care of me? When was I ever going to learn to be a good boy? She couldn't be bothered with my fights. She finished by telling me that I ought to be thankful to God as long as I lived that they didn't kill me. 60

All that night I was delirious and could not sleep. Each time I closed my eyes I saw monstrous white faces suspended from the ceiling, leering at me.

From that time on, the charm of my cinder yard was gone. The green trees, the trimmed hedges, the cropped lawns grew very meaningful, became a symbol. Even today when I think of white folks, the hard, sharp outlines of white houses surrounded by trees, lawns, and hedges are present somewhere in the background of my mind. Through the years 70 they grew into an overreaching symbol of fear.

It was a long time before I came in close contact with white folks again. We moved from Arkansas to Mississippi. Here we had the good fortune not to live behind the railroad tracks, or close to white neighborhoods. We lived in the very heart of the local Black Belt. There were black churches and black preachers; there were black schools and black teachers; black groceries and black clerks. In fact, everything was so solidly black that for a long time I did not even think of white folks, save in remote and vague terms. But this could not last 80 forever. As one grows older one eats more. One's clothing costs more. When I finished grammar school I had to go to work. My mother could no longer feed and clothe me on her cooking job.

There is but one place where a black boy who knows no trade can get a job, and that's where the houses and faces are white, where the trees, lawns, and hedges are green. My first job was with an optical company in Jackson, Mississippi. The morning I applied I stood straight and neat before the boss, answering all his questions with sharp yessirs and nosirs. I 90 was very careful to pronounce my *sirs* distinctly, in order that he might know that I was polite, that I knew where I was, and that I knew he was a *white* man. I wanted that job badly.

He looked me over as though he were examining a prize poodle. He questioned me closely about my schooling, being particularly insistent about how much mathematics I had had. He seemed very pleased when I told him I had had two years of algebra.

"Boy, how would you like to try to learn something around here?" he asked me. 100

"I'd like it fine, sir," I said, happy. I had visions of "working my way up." Even Negroes have those visions.

"All right," he said. "Come on."

I followed him to the small factory.

"Pease," he said to a white man of about thirty-five, "this is Richard. He's going to work for us."

Pease looked at me and nodded.

I was then taken to a white boy of about seventeen.

"Morrie, this is Richard, who's going to work for us."

"Whut yuh sayin' there, boy!" Morrie boomed at me. 110

"Fine!" I answered.

The boss instructed these two to help me, teach me, give me jobs to do, and let me learn what I could in my spare time.

My wages were five dollars a week.

I worked hard, trying to please. For the first month I got along O.K. Both Pease and Morrie seemed to like me. But one thing was missing. And I kept thinking about it. I was not learning anything and nobody was volunteering to help me. Thinking they had forgotten that I was to learn something about the mechanics of grinding lenses, I asked Morrie one 120 day to tell me about the work. He grew red.

"Whut yuh tryin' t' do, nigger, get smart?" he asked.

"Naw; I ain' tryin' t' git smart," I said.

"Well, don't, if yuh know whut's good for yuh!"

I was puzzled. Maybe he just doesn't want to help me, I thought. I went to Pease.

"Say, are yuh crazy, you black bastard?" Pease asked me, his gray eyes growing hard.

I spoke out, reminding him that the boss had said I was to be given a chance to learn something. 130

"Nigger, you think you're *white*, don't you?

"Naw, sir!"

"Well, you're acting mighty like it!"

"But, Mr. Pease, the boss said . . ."

Pease shook his fist in my face.

"This is a *white* man's work around here, and you better watch yourself!"

From then on they changed toward me. They said good-morning no more. When I was just a bit slow in performing some duty, I was called a lazy black son-of-a-bitch. 140

Once I thought of reporting all this to the boss. But the mere idea of what would happen to me if Pease and Morrie should learn that I had "snitched" stopped me. And after all the boss was a white man, too. What was the use?

The climax came at noon one summer day. Pease called me to his workbench. To get to him I had to go between two narrow benches and stand with my back against a wall.

"Yes, sir," I said.

"Richard, I want to ask you something," Pease began pleasantly, not looking up from his work. 150

"Yes, sir," I said again.

Morrie came over, blocking the narrow passage between the benches. He folded his arms, staring at me solemnly.

I looked from one to the other, sensing that something was coming.

"Yes, sir," I said for the third time.

Pease looked up and spoke very slowly.

"Richard, *Mr.* Morrie here tells me you called me *Pease.*"

I stiffened. A void seemed to open up in me. I knew this was the showdown. 160

He meant that I had failed to call him Mr. Pease. I looked at Morrie. He was gripping a steel bar in his hands. I opened my mouth to speak, to protest, to assure Pease that I had never called him simply *Pease*, and that I had never had any intentions of doing so, when Morrie grabbed me by the collar, ramming my head against the wall.

"Now be careful, nigger!" snarled Morrie, baring his teeth. "*I* heard yuh call 'im *Pease*! 'N' if yuh say yuh didn't, yuh're callin' me a *lie*, see?" He waved the steel bar threateningly.

If I had said: No, sir, Mr. Pease, I never called you *Pease* I 170 would have been automatically calling Morrie a liar. And if I said: Yes, sir, Mr. Pease, I called you *Pease*, I would have been pleading guilty to having uttered the worst insult that a Negro can utter to a southern white man. I stood hesitating, trying to frame a neutral reply.

"Richard, I asked you a question!" said Pease. Anger was creeping into his voice.

"I don't remember calling you *Pease*, Mr. Pease," I said cautiously. "And if I did, I sure didn't mean . . ."

"You black son-of-a-bitch! You called me *Pease*, then!" he 180 spat, slapping me till I bent sideways over a bench. Morrie was on top of me, demanding:

"Didn't you call 'im *Pease*? If yuh say yuh didn't, I'll rip yo' gut string loose with this bar, yuh black granny dodger! Yuh can't call a white man a lie 'n' git erway with it, you black son-of-a-bitch!"

I wilted. I begged them not to bother me. I knew what they wanted. They wanted me to leave.

"I'll leave," I promised. "I'll leave right *now*."

They gave me a minute to get out of the factory. I was 190 warned not to show up again, or tell the boss.

I went.

When I told the folks at home what had happened, they called me a fool. They told me that I must never again attempt to exceed my boundaries. When you are working for white folks, they said, you got to "stay in your place" if you want to keep working. . . .

**Q.** Which of the details in this selection bring to life the plight of young blacks in the American South?

**Q.** Describe the character, Pease: is he a believable figure?

## The Civil Rights Movement

Well after World War II, racism remained an undeniable obstacle to equality. Ironically, while Americans had fought to oppose Nazi racism in Germany, black Americans endured a system of inferior education, restricted jobs, ghetto housing, and generally low living standards. High crime rates, illiteracy, and drug addiction were evidence of affluent America's awesome failure to assimilate a population that suffered in its midst. The fact that African-Americans had served in great numbers in World War II inspired a redoubled effort to end persistent discrimination and segregation in the United States. During the 1950s and 1960s, that effort came to flower in the civil rights movement.

Civil rights leaders of the 1950s demanded enforcement of all the provisions for equality promised in the United States Constitution. Their demands led to a landmark Supreme Court decision in 1954 that banned school segregation; by implication, the ruling undermined the entire system of legalized segregation in the United States. Desegregation was met with fierce resistance, especially in the American South. In response, the so-called "Negro Revolt" began in 1955 and continued for over a decade. It took the form of nonviolent, direct-action protests, including boycotts of segregated lunch counters, peaceful "sit-ins," and protest marches. Leading the revolt was Dr. Martin Luther King, Jr. (1929–1968), a Protestant pastor and civil rights activist who modeled his campaign of peaceful protest on the example of Gandhi. As president of the Southern Christian Leadership Conference, King served as an inspiration to all African-Americans.

The urgency of their cause is conveyed in a letter King wrote while confined to jail for marching without a permit in the city of Birmingham, Alabama. It addressed a group of local white clergy, who had publicly criticized King for breaking laws that prohibited black people from using public facilities and for promoting "untimely" demonstrations. After King's letter was published in *The Christian Century* (June 12, 1963), it became (in a shorter version edited by King himself) the key text in a nationwide debate over civil rights: it provided philosophic justification for the practice of civil disobedience as a means of opposing injustice. King's measured eloquence and reasoned restraint stand in ironic contrast to the savagery of the opposition, who had used guns, hoses, and attack dogs against the demonstrators, 2400 of whom were jailed along with King.

### READING 36.6 From King's *Letter from Birmingham Jail* (1963)

My dear Fellow Clergymen,
While confined here in the Birmingham City Jail, I came     1
across your recent statement calling our present activities
"unwise and untimely." Seldom, if ever, do I pause to answer
criticism of my work and ideas. But since I feel that you are
men of genuine goodwill and your criticisms are sincerely set
forth, I would like to answer your statement in what I hope
will be patient and reasonable terms.

I think I should give the reason for my being in Birmingham,
since you have been influenced by the argument of "outsiders
coming in." Several months ago our local affiliate here in     10
Birmingham invited us to be on call to engage in a nonviolent
direct action program if such were deemed necessary. We
readily consented and when the hour came we lived up to our
promises. So I am here, along with several members of my
staff, because we were invited here. Beyond this, I am in
Birmingham because injustice is here.

Moreover, I am cognizant of the interrelatedness of all
communities and states. I cannot sit idly by in Atlanta and not
be concerned about what happens in Birmingham. Injustice
anywhere is a threat to justice everywhere. We are caught in   20
an inescapable network of mutuality tied in a single garment
of destiny. Never again can we afford to live with the narrow,
provincial "outsider agitator" idea. Anyone who lives inside the
United States can never be considered an outsider anywhere
in this country.

You deplore the demonstrations that are presently taking
place in Birmingham. But I am sorry that your statement did not
express a similar concern for the conditions that brought the
demonstrations into being. I would not hesitate to say that
it is unfortunate that so-called demonstrations are taking      30

place in Birmingham at this time, but I would say in more emphatic terms that it is even more unfortunate that the white power structure of this city left the Negro community with no other alternative.

In any nonviolent campaign there are four basic steps: 1) collection of the facts to determine whether injustices are alive; 2) negotiation; 3) self-purification; and 4) direct action.

You may well ask, "Why direct action? Why sit-ins, marches, etc.? Isn't negotiation a better path?" You are exactly right in your call for negotiation. Indeed, this is the purpose of 40 direct action. Nonviolent direct action seeks to create such a crisis and establish such creative tension that a community that has constantly refused to negotiate is forced to confront the issue. So the purpose of the direct action is to create a situation so crisis-packed that it will inevitably open the door to negotiation.

My friends, I must say to you that we have not made a single gain in civil rights without determined legal and nonviolent pressure. History is the long and tragic story of the fact that privileged groups seldom give up their privileges 50 voluntarily. Individuals may see the moral light and voluntarily give up their unjust posture; but as Reinhold Niebuhr[1] has reminded us, groups are more immoral than individuals.

We know through painful experience that freedom is never voluntarily given by the oppressor; it must be demanded by the oppressed. For years now I have heard the word "Wait!" It rings in the ear of every Negro with a piercing familiarity. This "wait" has almost always meant "never." We must come to see with the distinguished jurist of yesterday that "justice too long delayed is justice denied." We have waited for more than 60 three hundred and forty years for our constitutional and God-given rights.

You express a great deal of anxiety over our willingness to break laws. This is certainly a legitimate concern. Since we so diligently urge people to obey the Supreme Court's decision of 1954 outlawing segregation in the public schools, it is rather strange and paradoxical to find us consciously breaking laws. One may well ask, "How can you advocate breaking some laws and obeying others?" The answer is found in the fact that there are two types of laws. There are *just* laws and 70 there are *unjust* laws. One has not only a legal but a moral responsibility to obey just laws. Conversely, one has a moral responsibility to disobey unjust laws.

Now what is the difference between the two? A just law is a man-made code that squares with the moral law or the law of God. An unjust law is a code that is out of harmony with the moral law. Any law that degrades human personality is unjust. All segregation statutes are unjust because segregation distorts the soul and damages the personality. It gives the segregator a false sense of superiority and the 80 segregated a false sense of inferiority.

Let us turn to a more concrete example of just and unjust laws. An unjust law is a code that a majority inflicts on a minority that is not binding on itself. This is *difference* made legal. On the other hand a just law is a code that a majority

compels a minority to follow and that it is willing to follow itself. This is *sameness* made legal.

I hope you can see the distinction I am trying to point out. In no sense do I advocate evading or defying the law as the rabid segregationist would do. This would lead to anarchy. One who 90 breaks an unjust law *openly*, *lovingly*, and with a willingness to accept the penalty by staying in jail to arouse the conscience of the community over its injustice, is in reality expressing the very highest respect for law.

Of course there is nothing new about this kind of civil disobedience. It was seen sublimely in the refusal of Shadrach, Meshach, and Abednego to obey the laws of Nebuchadnezzar[2] because a higher moral law was involved. It was practiced superbly by the early Christians.

We can never forget that everything Hitler did in Germany 100 was "legal" and everything the Hungarian freedom fighters did in Hungary was "illegal." It was "illegal" to aid and comfort a Jew in Hitler's Germany.

In your statement you asserted that our actions, even though peaceful, must be condemned because they precipitate violence. But can this assertion be logically made? Isn't this like condemning the robbed man because his possession of money precipitated the evil act of robbery? We must come to see, as federal courts have consistently affirmed, that it is immoral to urge an individual to withdraw his efforts to gain 110 his basic constitutional rights because the quest precipitates violence. Society must protect the robbed and punish the robber.

Over the last few years I have consistently preached that nonviolence demands that the means we use must be as pure as the ends we seek. So I have tried to make it clear that it is wrong to use immoral means to gain moral ends. But now I must affirm that it is just as wrong, or even more so, to use moral means to preserve immoral ends. T. S. Eliot has said that there is no greater treason than to do the right deed for 120 the wrong reason.

I wish you had commended the Negro sit-inners and demonstrators of Birmingham for their sublime courage, their willingness to suffer, and their amazing discipline in the midst of the most inhuman provocation. One day the South will recognize its real heroes. They will include old, oppressed, battered Negro women, symbolized in a seventy-two-year-old woman of Montgomery, Alabama, who rose up with a sense of dignity and with her people decided not to ride the segregated buses, and responded to one who inquired about 130 her tiredness with ungrammatical profundity: "My feets is tired, but my soul is rested." One day the South will know that when these disinherited children of God sat down at the lunch counters they were in reality standing up for the best in the American dream and the most sacred values in our Judeo-Christian heritage, and thus carrying our whole nation back to great wells of democracy which were dug deep by the

---

[1] An American Protestant theologian (1892–1971) who urged ethical realism in Christian approaches to political debate (see chapter 35).

[2] The Chaldean king of the sixth century B.C.E., who, according to the Book of Daniel, demanded that these Hebrew youths worship the Babylonian gods. Nebuchadnezzar cast them into a fiery furnace, but they were delivered unhurt by an angel of God (see Figure 9.7).

founding fathers in the formulation of the Constitution and the Declaration of Independence.

I hope this letter finds you strong in the faith. I also hope 140 that circumstances will soon make it possible for me to meet each of you, not as an integrationist or a civil rights leader, but as a fellow clergyman and a Christian brother. Let us hope that the dark clouds of racial prejudice will soon pass away and the deep fog of misunderstanding will be lifted from our fear-drenched communities and in some not too distant tomorrow the radiant stars of love and brotherhood will shine over our great nation with all of their scintillating beauty.

> *Yours for the cause of*
> *Peace and Brotherhood* 150
> Martin Luther King, Jr.

**Q** **What arguments does Dr. King make for nonviolence and negotiation?**

**Q** **Evaluate the claim (line 53) that "groups are more immoral than individuals."**

While Dr. King practiced the tactics of nonviolence to achieve the goals of racial integration and civil rights in America, another protest leader took a very different tack: Malcolm Little (1925–1965), who called himself "Malcolm X," experienced firsthand the inequities and degradation of life in white America. For a time he turned to crime and drugs as a means of survival. Arrested and sentenced to prison in 1946, he took the opportunity to study history and religion, and most especially the teachings of Islam. By the time he was released in 1952, he had joined the Nation of Islam and was prepared to launch his career as a Muslim minister.

Malcolm and other "Black Muslims" despaired over persistent racism in white America. They determined that black people should pursue a very different course from that of Dr. King and the Southern Christian Leadership Conference. African-Americans, argued Malcolm, should abandon aspirations for integration. Instead, they should separate from white Americans in every feasible way; they should create a black nation in which—through hard work and the pursuit of Muslim morality—they might live equally, in dignity, free of the daily affronts of white racism. These goals should be achieved by all available means, violent if necessary (armed self-defense was a first step). Only by fighting for black nationalism would African-Americans ever gain power and self-respect in racist America. Little wonder that Malcolm was feared and reviled by white Americans and deemed a dangerous radical by more moderate black people as well.

In 1963, Malcolm addressed a conference of black leaders in Detroit, Michigan. In this speech, which later came to be called "Message to the Grass Roots," Malcolm addressed a large audience representing a cross section of the African-American community. The power and immediacy of his style is best captured on the tape of the speech published by the African-American Broadcasting and Record Company. Nevertheless, the following brief excerpt

provides a glimpse into the ferocious eloquence that Malcolm exhibited throughout his brief career—until his death by assassination in 1965.

┌─ **READING 36.7** From Malcolm X's *Message*
│ *to the Grass Roots* (1963)

. . . America has a very serious problem. Not only does 1 America have a very serious problem, but our people have a very serious problem. America's problem is us. We're her problem. The only reason she has a problem is she doesn't want us here. And every time you look at yourself, be you black, brown, red or yellow, a so-called Negro, you represent a person who poses such a serious problem for America because you're not wanted. Once you face this as a fact, then you can start plotting a course that will make you appear intelligent, instead of unintelligent. 10

What you and I need to do is learn to forget our differences. When we come together, we don't come together as Baptists or Methodists. You don't catch hell because you're a Baptist, and you don't catch hell because you're a Methodist. You don't catch hell because you're a Methodist or Baptist, you don't catch hell because you're a Democrat or a Republican, you don't catch hell because you're a Mason or an Elk, and you sure don't catch hell because you're an American; because if you were an American, you wouldn't catch hell. You catch hell because you're a black man. You catch hell, all of us catch 20 hell, for the same reason.

So we're all black people, so-called Negroes, second- class citizens, ex-slaves. You're nothing but an ex-slave. You don't like to be told that. But what else are you? You are ex-slaves. You didn't come here on the "Mayflower." You came here on a slave ship. In chains, like a horse, or a cow, or a chicken. And you were brought here by the people who came here on the "Mayflower," you were brought here by the so-called Pilgrims, or Founding Fathers. They were the ones who brought you here. 30

We have a common enemy. We have this in common: We have a common oppressor, a common exploiter, and a common discriminator. But once we all realize that we have a common enemy, then we unite—on the basis of what we have in common. And what we have foremost in common is that enemy—the white man. . . .

As long as the white man sent you to Korea, you bled. He sent you to Germany, you bled. He sent you to the South Pacific to fight the Japanese, you bled. You bleed for white people, but when it comes to seeing your own churches being 40 bombed and little black girls murdered, you haven't got any blood. You bleed when the white man says bleed; you bite when the white man says bite; and you bark when the white man says bark. I hate to say this about us, but it's true. How are you going to be nonviolent in Mississippi, as violent as you were in Korea? How can you justify being nonviolent in Mississippi and Alabama, when your churches are being bombed, and your little girls are being murdered, and at the same time you are going to get violent with Hitler, and Tojo, and somebody else you don't even know? 50

If violence is wrong in America, violence is wrong abroad. If it is wrong to be violent defending black women and black children and black babies and black men, then it is wrong for America to draft us and make us violent abroad in defense of her. And if it is right for America to draft us, and teach us how to be violent in defense of her, then it is right for you and me to do whatever is necessary to defend our own people right here in this country. . . .

Q How does Malcolm justify black violence?

Q How do his perceptions differ from King's?

## The Literature of the Black Revolution

The passage of the Civil Rights Act in America in 1964 provided an end to official segregation in public places; but continuing discrimination and the growing militancy of some civil rights groups provoked a more violent phase of the protests during the late 1960s and thereafter. Even before the assassination of Martin Luther King, Jr., in 1968, the black revolution had begun to assume a transnational fervor. American voices joined those of their black neighbors in West India, South Africa, and elsewhere in the world. Fired by **apartheid**, the system of strict racial segregation that prevailed legally in South Africa until 1994, the poet Bloke Modisane (1923–1986) lamented:

> it gets awful lonely,
> lonely;
> like screaming,
> screaming lonely
> screaming down dream alley,
> screaming blues, like none can hear

In *Black Skin, White Masks* (1958)—the handbook for African revolution—the West Indian essayist and revolutionary Franz Fanon (1925–1961) defended violence as necessary and desirable in overcoming the tyranny of whites over blacks in the colonial world. "At the level of individuals," he wrote, "violence is a cleansing force." In the United States, where advertising media made clear the disparity between the material comforts of black and white Americans, the black revolution swelled on a tide of rising expectations. LeRoi Jones (b. 1934), who in 1966 adopted the African name Imamu Amiri Baraka, echoed the message of Malcolm X in poems and plays that advocated militant action and pan-Africanism. Rejecting white Western literary tradition, Baraka called for "poems that kill"; "Let there be no love poems written," he entreats, "until love can exist freely and cleanly."

***Baldwin and Ellison*** Two luminaries of American black protest literature were James Baldwin (1924–1987) and Ralph Ellison (1914–1994). Baldwin, the eldest of nine children raised in Harlem in conditions of poverty, began writing when he was fourteen years old. Encouraged early in his career by Richard Wright, he became a formidable preacher of the gospel of equality. For Baldwin, writing was a subversive act. "You write," he insisted, "in order to change the world, knowing perfectly well that you probably can't, but also knowing that literature is indispensable to the world. In some way, your aspirations and concern for a single man in fact do begin to change the world. The world changes according to the way people see it, and if you alter, even by a millimeter, the way a person looks or people look at reality, then you can change it."

In his novels, short stories, and essays, Baldwin stressed the affinity African-Americans felt with other poverty-stricken populations. Yet, as he tried to define the unique differences between black and white people, he observed that the former were strangers in the modern world—a world whose traditions were claimed by those who were white. As he explained in the essay "Stranger in the Village" (1953):

> [European Whites] cannot be, from the point of view of power, strangers anywhere in the world; they have made the modern world, in effect, even if they do not know it. The most illiterate among them is related, in a way that I am not, to Dante, Shakespeare, Michelangelo, Aeschylus, da Vinci, Rembrandt, and Racine; the cathedral at Chartres says something to them which it cannot say to me . . . . Out of their hymns and dances come Beethoven and Bach. Go back a few centuries and they are in their full glory—but I am in Africa, watching the conquerors arrive.

But Baldwin uncovered a much overlooked truth about the character of the modern world: that black culture has influenced white culture, and especially American culture, in a profound and irreversible manner:

> The time has come to realize that the interracial drama acted out on the American continent has not only created a new black man, it has created a new white man, too. . . . One of the things that distinguishes Americans from other people is that no other people has ever been so deeply involved in the lives of black men, and vice versa. . . . It is precisely this black–white experience which may prove of indispensable value to us in the world we face today. This world is white no longer, and it will never be white again.

Baldwin's contemporary, Ralph Ellison, a native of Oklahoma and an amateur jazz musician, came to Harlem during the 1930s to study sculpture and musical composition. He was influenced by both Hughes and Wright and soon turned to writing short stories and newspaper reviews. In 1945, he began the novel *Invisible Man*, a fiction masterpiece that probes the black estrangement from white culture. The prologue to the novel, an excerpt of which follows, offers a glimpse into the spiritual odyssey of the "invisible" protagonist, an unnamed black man who lives rent-free in a Harlem basement flat illuminated by 1369 light bulbs he has connected (illegally) to the city's electrical grid (see Figure 36.1). It broaches, with surrealistic intensity, some of Ellison's most important themes: the nightmarish quality of urban life and the alienation experienced by both black and white Americans in the modern United States.

## READING 36.8 From Ellison's *Invisible Man* (1952)

I am an invisible man. No, I am not a spook like those who      1
haunted Edgar Allan Poe;[1] nor am I one of your Hollywood-
movie ectoplasms. I am a man of substance, of flesh and
bone, fiber and liquids—and I might even be said to possess a
mind. I am invisible, understand, simply because people refuse
to see me. Like the bodiless heads you see sometimes in circus
sideshows, it is as though I have been surrounded by mirrors of
hard, distorting glass. When they approach me they see only
my surroundings, themselves, or figments of their
imagination—indeed, everything and anything except me.       10
   Nor is my invisibility exactly a matter of a bio-chemical
accident to my epidermis. That invisibility to which I refer
occurs because of a peculiar disposition of the eyes of those
with whom I come in contact. A matter of the construction of
their *inner* eyes, those eyes with which they look through their
physical eyes upon reality. I am not complaining, nor am I
protesting either. It is sometimes advantageous to be unseen,
although it is most often rather wearing on the nerves. Then
too, you're constantly being bumped against by those of poor
vision. Or again, you often doubt if you really exist. You       20
wonder whether you aren't simply a phantom in other people's
minds. Say, a figure in a nightmare which the sleeper tries
with all his strength to destroy. It's when you feel like this
that, out of resentment, you begin to bump people back. And,
let me confess, you feel that way most of the time. You ache
with the need to convince yourself that you do exist in the real
world, that you're a part of all the sound and anguish, and you
strike out with your fists, you curse and you swear to make
them recognize you. And, alas, it's seldom successful.
   One night I accidentally bumped into a man, and perhaps       30
because of the near darkness he saw me and called me an
insulting name. I sprang at him, seized his coat lapels and
demanded that he apologize. He was a tall blond man, and as
my face came close to his he looked insolently out of his blue
eyes and cursed me, his breath hot in my face as he struggled.
I pulled his chin down sharp upon the crown of my head,
butting him as I had seen the West Indians do, and I felt his
flesh tear and the blood gush out, and I yelled, "Apologize!
Apologize!" But he continued to curse and struggle, and I
butted him again and again until he went down heavily, on his       40
knees, profusely bleeding. I kicked him repeatedly, in a frenzy
because he still uttered insults though his lips were frothy
with blood. Oh yes, I kicked him! And in my outrage I got out
my knife and prepared to slit his throat, right there beneath
the lamplight in the deserted street, holding him by the collar
with one hand, and opening the knife with my teeth—when it
occurred to me that the man had not *seen* me, actually; that he,
as far as he knew, was in the midst of a walking nightmare!
And I stopped the blade, slicing the air as I pushed

him away, letting him fall back to the street. I stared at him       50
hard as the lights of a car stabbed through the darkness. He lay
there, moaning on the asphalt; a man almost killed by a
phantom. It unnerved me. I was both disgusted and ashamed. I
was like a drunken man myself, wavering about on weakened
legs. Then I was amused. Something in this man's thick head
had sprung out and beaten him within an inch of his life. I
began to laugh at this crazy discovery. Would he have
awakened at the point of Death? Would Death himself have
freed him for wakeful living? But I didn't linger. I ran away into
the dark, laughing so hard I feared I might rupture myself. The       60
next day I saw his picture in the *Daily News*, beneath a
caption stating that he had been "mugged." Poor fool, poor
blind fool, I thought with sincere compassion, mugged by an
invisible man! . . .

**Q  What does Ellison's protagonist mean
    when he says he is "an invisible man"?**

***Morrison and Walker*** In the literature of the black
revolution, especially that of the last three decades of the
twentieth century, many of the most powerful voices were
female. Succeeding such notable Harlem Renaissance
writers as Zora Neale Hurston (1891–1960) and Dorothy
West (1912–1998), two contemporary figures—Toni
Morrison (b. 1931) and Alice Walker (b. 1944)—have
risen to eminence.

Toni Morrison is celebrated as one of the century's finest
writers. Her novels, rich in epic themes, memorable characters, and vivid oral rhythms, examine the long-range
consequences of slavery in America. Many of her characters, Afro-American women, suffer displacement and
despair in their homes and communities. The Pulitzer
Prize-winning *Beloved* (1988), inspired by the true story of
an African-American slave, is a story of racism's power to
destroy the natural impulses of human love. In 1993,
Morrison became the first black woman to be honored
with the Nobel Prize in literature.

Alice Walker, whose novel *The Color Purple* won the
Pulitzer Prize in fiction in 1982, is celebrated for her can-
did characterizations of black women facing the perils of
racism, domestic violence, and sexual abuse. Her short
story "Elethia" probes the dual issues of identity and liberation as they come to shape the destiny of a young black
female.

## READING 36.9 Walker's "Elethia" (1981)

A certain perverse experience shaped Elethia's life, and made       1
it possible for it to be true that she carried with her at all
times a small apothecary jar of ashes.
   There was in the town where she was born a man whose
ancestors had owned a large plantation on which everything
under the sun was made or grown. There had been many
slaves, and though slavery no longer existed, this grandson of
former slaveowners held a quaint proprietary point of view
where colored people were concerned. He adored them, of

---

[1] A leading American poet, literary critic, and short-story writer (1809–
    1849), noted for his tales of terror and his clever detective stories.

course. Not in the present—it went without saying—but at that time, stopped, just on the outskirts of his memory: his grandfather's time.

This man, whom Elethia never saw, opened a locally famous restaurant on a busy street near the center of town. He called it "Old Uncle Albert's." In the window of the restaurant was a stuffed likeness of Uncle Albert himself, a small brown dummy of waxen skin and glittery black eyes. His lips were intensely smiling and his false teeth shone. He carried a covered tray in one hand, raised level with his shoulder, and over his other arm was draped a white napkin.

Black people could not eat at Uncle Albert's, though they worked, of course, in the kitchen. But on Saturday afternoons a crowd of them would gather to look at "Uncle Albert" and discuss how near to the real person the dummy looked. Only the very old people remembered Albert Porter, and their eyesight was no better than their memory. Still there was a comfort somehow in knowing that Albert's likeness was here before them daily and that if he smiled as a dummy in a fashion he was not known to do as a man, well, perhaps both memory and eyesight were wrong.

The old people appeared grateful to the rich man who owned the restaurant for giving them a taste of vicarious fame. They could pass by the gleaming window where Uncle Albert stood, seemingly in the act of sprinting forward with his tray, and know that though niggers were not allowed in the front door, ole Albert was already inside, and looking mighty pleased about it, too.

For Elethia the fascination was in Uncle Albert's fingernails. She wondered how his creator had got them on. She wondered also about the white hair that shone so brightly under the lights. One summer she worked as a salad girl in the restaurant's kitchen, and it was she who discovered the truth about Uncle Albert. He was not a dummy; he was stuffed. Like a bird, like a moose's head, like a giant bass. He was stuffed.

One night after the restaurant was closed someone broke in and stole nothing but Uncle Albert. It was Elethia and her friends, boys who were in her class and who called her "Thia." Boys who bought Thunderbird and shared it with her. Boys who laughed at her jokes so much they hardly remembered she was also cute. Her tight buddies. They carefully burned Uncle Albert to ashes in the incinerator of their high school, and each of them kept a bottle of his ashes. And for each of them what they knew and their reaction to what they knew was profound.

The experience undercut whatever solid foundation Elethia had assumed she had. She became secretive, wary, looking over her shoulder at the slightest noise. She haunted the museums of any city in which she found herself, looking, usually, at the remains of Indians, for they were plentiful everywhere she went. She discovered some of the Indian warriors and maidens in the museums were also real, stuffed people, painted and wigged and robed, like figures in the Rue Morgue. There were so many, in fact, that she could not possibly steal and burn them all. Besides, she did not know if these figures—with their valiant glass eyes—would wish to be burned.

About Uncle Albert she felt she knew.

What kind of man was Uncle Albert?

Well, the old folks said, he wasn't nobody's uncle and wouldn't sit still for nobody to call him that, either.

Why, said another old-timer, I recalls the time they hung a boy's privates on a post at the end of the street where all the black folks shopped, just to scare us all, you understand, and Albert Porter was the one took 'em down and buried 'em. Us never did find the rest of the boy though. It was just like always—they would throw you in the river with a big old green log tied to you, and down to the bottom you sunk.

He continued.

Albert was born in slavery and he remembered that his mama and daddy didn't know nothing about slavery'd done ended for near 'bout ten years, the boss man kept them so ignorant of the law, you understand. So he was a mad so-an'-so when he found out. They used to beat him *severe* trying to make him forget the past and grin and act like a nigger. (Whenever you saw somebody acting like a nigger, Albert said, you could be sure he seriously disremembered his past.) But he never would. Never would work in the big house as head servant, neither—always broke up stuff. The master at that time was always going around pinching him too. Looks like he hated Albert more than anything—but he never would let him get a job anywhere else. And Albert never would leave home. Too stubborn.

Stubborn, yes. My land, another one said. That's why it do seem strange to see that dummy that sposed to be old Albert with his mouth open. All them teeth. Hell, all Albert's teeth was knocked out before he was grown.

Elethia went away to college and her friends went into the army because they were poor and that was the way things were. They discovered Uncle Alberts all over the world. Elethia was especially disheartened to find Uncle Alberts in her textbooks, in the newspapers and on t.v.

Everywhere she looked there was an Uncle Albert (and many Aunt Albertas, it goes without saying).

But she had her jar of ashes, the old-timers' memories written down, and her friends who wrote that in the army they were learning skills that would get them through more than a plate glass window.

And she was careful that, no matter how compelling the hype, Uncle Alberts, in her own mind, were not permitted to exist.

Q  What are "Uncle Alberts"?

Q  What social contradictions does Walker attack in this story?

## African-Americans and the Visual Arts

During the Harlem Renaissance, African-American painters and sculptors made public the social concerns of black poets and writers. In picturing their experience, they drew on African folk idioms and colloquial forms of native expression; but they also absorbed the radically new styles of European Modernism. Among these painters, there emerged a "blues aesthetic" that featured bold colors, angular forms, and rhythmic, stylized compositions.

**Figure 36.3 ROMARE BEARDEN**, *Empress of the Blues*, 1974. Acrylic and pencil on paper and printed paper on paperboard, 3 ft. 10 in. × 4 ft. 2 in. Bearden depicts Bessie Smith, the singer known as the "Empress of the Blues." The artist's working methods gave visual substance to the "call and response" patterns in African music and jazz: "You put down one color, and it calls for an answer," he explained.

One of the most notable artists of the twentieth century, Jacob Lawrence (1917–2000) migrated to Harlem with his family in 1930. Lawrence's powerful style features flat, local colors and angular, abstract forms that owe as much to African art as to Synthetic Cubism and Expressionism. At the same time, his lifelong commitment to social and racial issues made him heir to the nineteenth-century artist–critics Goya and Daumier, whom he admired. Painting in tempera on masonite panels, Lawrence won early acclaim for serial paintings that deal with black history and with the lives of black American heroes and heroines. Among the most famous of these is a series of sixty panels known as "The Migration of the Negro" (1940–1941). For "The Migration"—an expressionistic narrative of the great northward movement of African-Americans after World War I—Lawrence drew on textual sources rather than firsthand visual experience. The drama of each episode (see Figure 36.2) is conveyed by means of bold rhythms and vigorous, geometric shapes that preserve what Lawrence called "the magic of the picture plane."

Lawrence's contemporary, Romare Bearden (1916–1988), was born in North Carolina, but grew up in Harlem. He knew the major figures of the Harlem Renaissance, including Lawrence himself, Langston Hughes, and the leading jazz musicians of New York. Bearden's favorite medium was collage. The earliest of these emerged against the backdrop of the civil rights movement and took as their theme the African-American struggle. Much like Hannah Höch (see Figure 33.15), Bearden cut bits and pieces of images from popular magazines; but his semi-abstract compositions developed narrative themes drawn from everyday life. Their abrupt shifts in scale and strident colors call to mind the improvisational phrasing and syncopated rhythms of jazz. Music, in fact, provided the subject matter for some of his most notable works, such as *Train Whistle Blues* (1964), *Three Folk Musicians* (1967), *New Orleans Ragging Home* (1974), and *Empress of the Blues* (1974, Figure **36.3**).

Since the mid-twentieth century, African-American artists have taken ever more cynical approaches to themes of race discrimination and racial stereotyping. The sculptor Betye Saar (b. 1926) abandoned the African-inspired fetishlike sculptures of her early career and turned to fabricating boxed constructions that attacked the icons of commercial white culture. In the mixed-media sculpture entitled *The Liberation of Aunt Jemima*, Saar transforms the familiar symbol of American pancakes and cozy kitchens into a gun-toting version of the "mammy" stereotype (Figure **36.4**).

The satirist–artist Robert Colescott (1925–2009) creates parodies of famous paintings in which whites are recast as cartoon-style, stereotyped black men and women. In doing so, Colescott calls attention to their exclusion from Western art history. His bitter parody of Delacroix's *Liberty Leading the People* (1976) features a crew of brashly painted African-American rebels commanded by a black-faced Liberty. Colescott's *Les Demoiselles d'Alabama* (Figure **36.5**), an obvious funk-art clone of Picasso's landmark painting (see Figure 32.2), slyly challenges contemporary definitions of Primitivism and Modernism. Colescott observes, "Picasso started with European art and abstracted through African art, producing 'Africanism' but keeping one foot in European art. I began with Picasso's Africanism and moved toward European art, keeping one foot in Africanism. . . ."

**Figure 36.4 BETYE SAAR**,
*The Liberation of Aunt Jemima*,
1972. Mixed media, 11¾ × 8 × 2¾ in.
Saar drew attention to unflattering
stereotypes of African Americans:
Uncle Tom, Little Black Sambo, and Aunt
Jemima. Her version of the trademark
figure associated with a popular pancake
mix is seen here as a domestic servant
with a rifle, a pistol, and a broom.
A second version shows her as a nanny,
holding a squalling white baby.

The American artist Kara Walker (b. 1969) appreciates the fact that liberation and racial freedom are ongoing processes. Using her trademark silhouettes, she brings to contemporary art a subtle and complex examination of the tangled relationships between white and black Americans, especially as they played out between the male masters and female slaves of the nineteenth-century American South. In the piece *A Work on Progress* (Figure **36.6**) she pictures a stereotypical African-American housemaid sweeping out a sister figure whose chains are newly broken. The liberated female may represent the end of slavery, but like the trash she sweeps from the house, she holds an undefined (and unwelcome) place in society.

## African-Americans and Jazz

Possibly the most important contribution made by African-Americans to world culture occurred in the area of music, specifically in the birth and development of that unique form of modern music known as jazz. Jazz is a synthesis of diverse musical elements that came together in the first two decades of the twentieth century, but it was after World War I that jazz came to full fruition as an artform. Although some music historians insist that jazz is the product of place, not race, the primary role of African-Americans in the origins and evolution of jazz is indisputable.

Jazz is primarily a performer's rather than a composer's art. Dominated by Afro-Caribbean rhythmic styles, it

**Figure 36.5 ROBERT COLESCOTT**,
*Les Demoiselles d'Alabama (Vestidas)*,
1985. Acrylic on canvas, 8 ft. × 7 ft. 8 in.

**Figure 36.6 KARA WALKER**, *A Work on Progress*, 1998. Cut paper and adhesive, 5 ft. 9 in. × 6 ft. 8 in. Installation view at The Walker Art Center, 2007. Walker made use of the popular folk-art tradition of cut-paper silhouettes, which were often used for late eighteenth-century portraits. She recently employed this technique to illustrate the poems of Toni Morrison.

incorporates a wide range of European and African-American concepts of harmony, melody, and tone color. In its evolution, jazz absorbed the musical idioms of the marching brass band, the minstrel stage, the blues, and the piano style known as *ragtime*. Ragtime is a form of piano composition and performance featuring highly syncopated rhythms and simple, appealing melodies. It apparently originated in the lower Mississippi valley, but it migrated north after the Civil War and became popular during the 1890s. Its most inspired proponent (if not its inventor) was the black composer and popular pianist Scott Joplin (1868–1917). Early jazz performers, like "Jelly Roll" Morton (Ferdinand Joseph LaMonthe, 1885–1941), who claimed to have invented jazz, utilized ragtime rhythms in developing the essential features of the new form.

*Blues*, a formative element in the evolution of jazz, had begun as a vocal rather than an instrumental genre. Native to the United States, but possibly stemming from African

song forms and harmonics, it is an emotive type of individual expression for lamenting one's troubles, loneliness, and despair. A blues song may recall the wailing cries of plantation slaves; it may describe the anguish of separation and loss or the hope for deliverance from oppression. Such classics as W. C. Handy's "St. Louis Blues" (1914) begin with a line that states a simple plaint ("I hate to see the evening sun go down"); the plaint is repeated in a second line, and it is "answered" in a third ("It makes me think I'm on my last go-round")—a pattern derived perhaps from African call and response chants (see chapter 18). Technically, blues makes use of a special scale known as a "blues scale," which features (among other things) the flatted forms of E, G, and B within the standard scale.

Both ragtime and blues contributed substantially to the development of jazz as a unique musical idiom. But if jazz manifests any single defining quality, that quality would have to be improvisation—individual and collective. Most jazz performances are based in standard melodies—often familiar popular tunes; the individual performers (and sometimes a group of performers within an ensemble) "improvise" on the base melody. They invent passages while in the process of performing them—a form of "composing as you go"—or they incorporate bits of other (often familiar) melodies into their solos. Most scholars agree that improvisation, either individual or collective, constitutes the single element that most distinguishes jazz from other musical idioms.

Finally, jazz employs a unique variation on standard rhythms that performers and aficionados term "**swing.**" While it is virtually impossible to define the concept of "swing," it may best be described as the practice of playing just off the beat—slightly ahead or behind. "Swinging" normally involves achieving a certain rhythmic "groove"—a combination of rhythm and harmony that vitalizes the ensemble and propels the performance forward. (In the words of a 1940s popular song, "It don't mean a thing if it ain't got that swing!")

## African-Americans and Film

The first African-American to establish himself as a major Hollywood filmmaker, Shelton Jackson "Spike" Lee (b. 1957) has won international acclaim for films that explore race conflicts in the inner city (*Do the Right Thing*, 1989), modern black history (*Malcolm X*, 1992), the black minstrel tradition (*Bamboozled*, 2000), drug-dealing (*25th Hour*, 2002), and the black infantrymen, the so-called "buffalo soldiers" of World War II (*Miracle at St. Anna*, 2008). Lee uses the camera inventively to underline social conflicts, as in his radical close-ups of faces caught in bitter, heated disputes. He favors short, disconnected scenes, the "accidental" effects of the handheld camera, and editing techniques that often leave the narrative themes of his films unresolved but filled with implications. Lee opened the door to a new wave of black filmmakers that includes John Singleton (*Boyz in the Hood*, 1991) and Julie Dash (*Daughters of the Dust*, 1991).

See Music Listening Selections at end of chapter.

**Figure 36.7** King Oliver's Creole Jazz Band, 1923. Honore Dutrey, Warren "Baby" Dodds, Joe Oliver, Louis Armstrong, Lil Hardin, Bill Johnson, and Johnny Dodds.

As a performance art, jazz depends on the interaction of the ensemble's members as they create an essentially new composition in the very act of performing it. Although syncopated rhythms, the blues motif, harmonic flexibility, and improvisation were not in themselves new, their combination—when vitalized by a "swinging" performance—produced an essentially new artform, one that would have a major impact on Western music for years to come.

**Armstrong** The beginnings of American jazz are found in New Orleans, Louisiana, a melting pot for the rich heritage of Spanish, French, African, Caribbean, Indian, and Black Creole musical traditions. Here, black and white musicians drew on the intricate rhythms of African tribal dance and the European harmonies of traditional marching bands. The street musicians who regularly marched behind funeral or wedding processions, many of whom were neither formally trained nor could read music, might play trumpets, trombones, and clarinets; rhythm was provided by tubas as well as snare and bass drums. These musicians made up the "front line" of the parade; the crowd that danced behind them was called the "second line."* Parade bands performed perhaps the earliest version of what became jazz. Similar bands also played the popular music of the time in nightclubs and dance halls.

Louis Armstrong (1900–1971), a native of New Orleans began playing the cornet at the age of twelve. By the 1920s he had emerged as the foremost jazz musician of the period. Armstrong's innovative solos provided the breakthrough by which solo improvisation became central to jazz performance. His ability to redirect harmonies and to invent reworkings of standard melodies in his solos—all performed with breathtaking virtuosity—elevated the jazz soloist to the foremost role in ensemble performance.

"Satchmo" ("Satchelmouth") Armstrong was also a jazz singer with formidable musical gifts. He often embellished jazz with **scat singing**—an improvised set of nonsense syllables. His compelling personality and unfailing good spirits brought joy to millions and turned jazz into an internationally respected musical form. "Hotter Than That" (1927), a composition by Lillian Hardin (Armstrong's wife), exemplifies the style termed "hot jazz" (Figure **36.7**)—a style that the French in particular elevated to the status of a craze.

**The Jazz Age** In the 1920s jazz spread north to the urban centers of Chicago, Kansas City, and New York. Armstrong moved to Chicago in 1922. In New York, extraordinary jazz and blues singers like Bessie Smith (1898–1937), known by her fans as the "Empress of the Blues" (see Figure 36.3) and Billie Holiday (1915–1959)—"Lady Day"—drew worldwide acclaim through the phenomena of radio and phonograph records. In the so-called "Jazz Age," jazz had a major impact on other musical genres. The American composer George Gershwin (1898–1937) incorporated the rhythms of jazz into the mesmerizing *Rhapsody in Blue* (1924), a concert piece for piano and orchestra. Gershwin's *Porgy and Bess* (1935), a fully composed opera dealing with the life of poverty-stricken Charleston African-Americans, combined jazz, blues, and spiritual and folk idioms to produce a new style of American musical theater featuring an all-black cast.

Popular music of the 1930s and 1940s was closely tied to the vogue for big band jazz and the danceable rhythms of swing, a big-band jazz style that fed the dance craze of the 1940s. The white swing bands of Tommy Dorsey, Glenn Miller, and Benny Goodman (who later integrated his band—the first bandleader to do so) played a mix of instrumental swing and popular ballads, while black swing bands like that of William "Count" Basie (1904–1984) leaned more toward blues and a dynamic big-band sound.

---

* Not to be confused with a variant usage of the term which distinguishes the rhythm section of a band from the "front line" of reed and brass solo instrumentalists.

♪ See Music Listening Selections at end of chapter.

## Chronology

**Postwar Jazz** In the years following World War II, jazz took on some of the complex and sophisticated characteristics of "art music." The beguiling suite *Black, Brown, and Beige* (1948) composed by Edward Kennedy "Duke" Ellington (1899–1974) paved the way for concert hall jazz, a form that has enjoyed a revival since the 1990s. Ellington was a prolific musician, unquestionably the foremost composer in the jazz idiom (and arguably in *any* idiom) that the United States has produced.

On a smaller scale, among groups of five to seven instruments, the jazz of the late 1940s and 1950s engaged the unique improvisational talents of individual performers. New forms included "bebop" (or "bop")—a jazz style characterized by frenzied tempos, complex chord progressions, and dense polyrhythms—and "cool" jazz, a more restrained and gentler style associated with the West Coast. "Koko," performed by the saxophonist Charlie Parker (1920–1955) and the trumpeter John "Dizzy" Gillespie (1917–1993), epitomizes the bebop style of the 1940s: the piece is an improvised version of the popular jazz standard, "Cherokee," by the British composer, Ray Noble (1903–1978).

Since the jazz renaissance of the 1980s, the New Orleans composer, trumpet prodigy, and teacher Wynton Marsalis (b. 1961) has reconfirmed the role of jazz as America's classical music. Awarded the Pulitzer Prize in 1995 for his jazz oratorio on slavery, *Blood on the Field*, Marsalis has become the world's most articulate spokesperson for the jazz genre. Likening jazz to the open exchange of ideas, Marsalis holds, "Jazz is more than the best expression there is of American culture; it is the most democratic of arts." To this day, jazz remains a unique kind of chamber music that combines the best of classical and popular musicianship.

**Hip-Hop** Like the "blues aesthetic" in the poetry and painting of the Harlem Renaissance, a "jazz aesthetic" featuring spontaneity and improvisation infused the 1970s performance phenomenon known as *hip-hop*. A product of the inner-city American subculture, hip-hop brings together loud, percussive

♪ See Music Listening Selections at end of chapter.

music (often electronically "mixed" by disc jockeys), the spoken word, and street-dance, generating a raw vitality that borders on the violent (see chapter 38).

The paintings of the short-lived Jean-Michel Basquiat (1960–1988) embrace the free improvisations and borrowed "riffs" of modern jazz, even as they infuse the staccato rhythms and jarring lyrics of hip-hop. Basquiat's artworks conflate crude, childlike but familiar images, grim cartoon logos, and scrawled graffiti—an urban folk-art style that vents the rage and joy of inner-city youths (like Basquiat himself). *Horn Players* (Figure **36.8**), executed with portable oil sticks on a blackboardlike surface, pays homage to the jazz giants Dizzy Gillespie and Charlie Parker—the word "ornithology" a witty reference to the latter's nickname: "Bird".

## African-Americans and Dance

The African-American impact on twentieth-century dance rivaled that of music. For centuries, dance served African-Americans as a primary language of religious expression and as a metaphor of physical freedom. By the

**Figure 36.8 JEAN-MICHEL BASQUIAT**, *Horn Players,* 1983. Acrylic and mixed media on canvas, 8 ft. × 6 ft. 3 in. The death's head at the center of the piece, a favorite motif of the artist, appears in many of his works. It is seen by some to have anticipated Basquiat's death of an overdose of cocaine and heroin at the age of twenty-eight.

late nineteenth century, as all-black theatrical companies and minstrel shows toured the United States, black entertainment styles began to reach white audiences. Popular black dances such as the high-kicking cakewalk became the international fad of the early 1900s, and dances such as the black bottom and lindy hop came to influence both social and theatrical performance.

With the pioneer African-American choreographer Katherine Dunham, introduced in chapter 32, black dance moved beyond the level of stage entertainment. After completing her doctorate in anthropology at the university of Chicago in 1939, she traveled to Jamaica, Trinidad, Martinique, and Haiti to do research, some of which explored the relationship between dance and voodoo practice. An avid student of Caribbean dance, Dunham drew heavily on Afro-Caribbean and African culture in both choreography and the sets and costumes designed by her husband, John Pratt (Figure **36.9**). Dunham's troupe borrowed from Caribbean music the rhythms of the steel band, an instrumental ensemble consisting entirely of steel drums fashioned from oil containers. Originating in Trinidad, steel bands provided percussive accompaniment for calypso and other kinds of improvised dance forms. In her book *Dances of Haiti*, Dunham examines the sociological function of dance—for instance, how communal dance captures the spirit of folk celebrations and how African religious dance interacts with European secular dance.

Dunham's work inspired others. Born in Trinidad and raised in New York City, Pearl Primus (1919–1994) used her studies in choreography and anthropology (like Dunham, she earned a doctorate in this field) to become the world's foremost authority on African dance. Following a trip to Africa in the 1940s, she brought to modern dance the spirit and substance of native tribal rituals. She also choreographed theatrical versions of African-American spirituals and poems, including those of Langston Hughes. In her book *African Dance*, Primus declared: "The dance is strong magic. . . . It turns the body to liquid steel. It makes it vibrate like a guitar. The body can fly without wings. It can sing without voice."

**Figure 36.9** Katherine Dunham in the 1945–1946 production of *Tropical Revue*. While working on her master's degree, the "dancing anthropologist" had to choose between dance and an academic career. While she went on to complete the doctorate, she ultimately chose dance, establishing in 1945 her own dance company, with which she toured the world.

The achievements of Dunham and Primus gave African-American dance theater international stature. Since 1950, such outstanding choreographers as Alvin Ailey (1931–1989), Donald McKayle (b. 1930), and Arthur Mitchell (b. 1934) have graced the history of American dance. Ailey's *Revelations* (1960), a suite that draws on his Texas roots and his affection for African-American spirituals, song-sermons, and gospel music, is an enduring tribute to the cultural history of the American South.

## The Quest for Gender Equality

Throughout history, misogyny (the hatred of women) and the perception of the female sex as inferior in intelligence and strength have enforced conditions of gender inequality. While women make up the majority of the population in many cultures, they have exercised little significant political or economic power. Like many ethnic minorities, women have long been relegated to the position of second-class citizens. In 1900, women were permitted to vote in only one country in the world: New Zealand. By mid-century, women in most First World countries had gained voting rights; nevertheless, their social and economic status has remained far below that of men. As recently as 1985, the World Conference on Women reported that while women represent 50 percent of the world's population and contribute nearly two-thirds

| Science and Technology | |
|---|---|
| 1953 | biophysicists determine the molecular structure of DNA |
| 1953 | Jonas Salk (American) tests an effective polio vaccine |
| 1955 | an American endocrinologist produces a successful birth control pill |
| 1982 | the fatal immune system disorder AIDS (Acquired Immune Deficiency Syndrome) is diagnosed |

of all working hours, they receive only one-tenth of the world's income and own less than one percent of the world's property. Though female inequality has been a fact of history, it was not until the twentieth century that the quest for female liberation took the form of an international movement.

## The Literature of Feminism: Woolf

The history of **feminism** (the principle advocating equal social, political, and economic rights for men and women) reaches back at least to the fourteenth century, when the French poet Christine de Pisan took up the pen in defense of women (see chapter 15). Christine had sporadic followers among Renaissance and Enlightenment humanists. The most notable of these was Mary Wollstonecraft (1759–1797), who published her provocative *Vindication of the Rights of Woman* in London in 1792 (see chapter 24). During the nineteenth century, Condorcet and Mill wrote reasoned pleas for female equality, as did the female novelist George Sand (see chapters 28 and 30). In America, the eloquence of Angelina Grimké (1805–1879) and other *suffragettes* (women advocating equality for women) was instrumental in winning women the right to vote in 1920.

Among the most impassioned advocates of the feminist movement was the novelist Virginia Woolf (1882–1941). Woolf argued that equal opportunity for education and economic advantage were even more important than the right to vote (British women gained the vote in 1918). In her novels and essays, Woolf proposed that women could become powerful only by achieving financial and psychological independence from men. Freedom, argued Woolf, is the prerequisite for creativity: for a woman to secure her own creative freedom, she must have money and the privacy provided by "a room of her own." The essay "A Room of One's Own" voices a response to a clergyman's remark that no female could have matched the genius of William Shakespeare. In the excerpt below, Woolf envisions Shakespeare's imaginary sister, Judith, in her sixteenth-century setting. She uses this fictional character to raise some challenging questions concerning the psychological aspects of female creativity.

---

### READING 36.10 From Woolf's "A Room of One's Own" (1929)

. . . Let me imagine, since facts are so hard to come by, what     1
would have happened had Shakespeare had a wonderfully
gifted sister, called Judith, let us say. Shakespeare himself
went, very probably—his mother was an heiress—to the
grammar school, where he may have learnt Latin—Ovid, Virgil
and Horace—and the elements of grammar and logic. He was,
it is well known, a wild boy who poached rabbits, perhaps
shot a deer, and had, rather sooner than he should have done,
to marry a woman in the neighbourhood, who bore him a child
rather quicker than was right. That escapade sent him to seek     10
his fortune in London. He had, it seemed, a taste for the
theatre; he began by holding horses at the stage door. Very

soon he got work in the theatre, became a successful actor,
and lived at the hub of the universe, meeting everybody,
knowing everybody, practising his art on the boards, exercising
his wits in the streets, and even getting access to the palace of
the queen. Meanwhile his extraordinarily gifted sister, let
us suppose, remained at home. She was as adventurous, as
imaginative, as agog to see the world as he was. But she was
not sent to school. She had no chance of learning grammar     20
and logic, let alone of reading Horace and Virgil. She picked
up a book now and then, one of her brother's perhaps, and
read a few pages. But then her parents came in and told her
to mend the stockings or mind the stew and not moon about
with books and papers. They would have spoken sharply but
kindly, for they were substantial people who knew the
conditions of life for a woman and loved their daughter—
indeed, more likely than not she was the apple of her father's
eye. Perhaps she scribbled some pages up in an apple loft on
the sly, but was careful to hide them or set fire to them. Soon,     30
however, before she was out of her teens, she was to be
betrothed to the son of a neighbouring wool-stapler. She cried
out that marriage was hateful to her, and for that she was
severely beaten by her father. Then he ceased to scold her. He
begged her instead not to hurt him, not to shame him in this
matter of her marriage. He would give her a chain of beads or a
fine petticoat, he said; and there were tears in his eyes.
How could she disobey him? How could she break his heart?
The force of her own gift alone drove her to it. She made up a
small parcel of her belongings, let herself down by a rope one     40
summer's night and took the road to London. She was not
seventeen. The birds that sang in the hedge were not more
musical than she was. She had the quickest fancy, a gift like
her brother's, for the tune of words. Like him, she had a taste
for the theatre. She stood at the stage door; she wanted to
act, she said. Men laughed in her face. The manager—a fat,
loose-lipped man—guffawed. He bellowed something about
poodles dancing and women acting—no woman, he said, could
possibly be an actress. He hinted—you can imagine
what. She could get no training in her craft. Could she even     50
seek her dinner in a tavern or roam the streets at midnight?
Yet her genius was for fiction and lusted to feed abundantly
upon the lives of men and women and the study of their ways.
At last—for she was very young, oddly like Shakespeare the
poet in her face, with the same grey eyes and rounded
brows—at last Nick Greene the actor-manager took pity on
her; she found herself with child by that gentleman and so—
who shall measure the heat and violence of the poet's heart
when caught and tangled in a woman's body?—killed herself
one winter's night and lies buried at some cross-roads where     60
the omnibuses now stop outside the Elephant and Castle.

. . . any woman born with a great gift in the sixteenth
century would certainly have gone crazed, shot herself, or
ended her days in some lonely cottage outside the village, half
witch, half wizard, feared and mocked at. For it needs little
skill in psychology to be sure that a highly gifted girl who had
tried to use her gift for poetry would have been so thwarted
and hindered by other people, so tortured and pulled asunder
by her own contrary instincts, that she must have lost her
health and sanity to a certainty. No girl could have walked to     70

London and stood at a stage door and forced her way into the presence of actor-managers without doing herself a violence and suffering an anguish which may have been irrational—for chastity may be a fetish invented by certain societies for unknown reasons—but were none the less inevitable. Chastity had then, it has even now, a religious importance in a woman's life, and has so wrapped itself round with nerves and instincts that to cut it free and bring it to the light of day demands courage of the rarest. To have lived a free life in London in the sixteenth century would have meant for a **80** woman who was poet and playwright a nervous stress and dilemma which might well have killed her. Had she survived, whatever she had written would have been twisted and deformed, issuing from a strained and morbid imagination. And undoubtedly, I thought, looking at the shelf where there are no plays by women, her work would have gone unsigned. That refuge she would have sought certainly. It was the relic of the sense of chastity that dictated anonymity to women even so late as the nineteenth century. Currer Bell,[1] George Eliot, George Sand, all the victims of inner strife as their **90** writings prove, sought ineffectively to veil themselves by using the name of a man. Thus they did homage to the convention, which if not implanted by the other sex was liberally encouraged by them (the chief glory of a woman is not to be talked of, said Pericles, himself a much-talked-of man), that publicity in women is detestable. Anonymity runs in their blood. . . .

— **Q** **How does the figure of Shakespeare's fictional sister work to make Woolf's point?**

— **Q** **How fragile, according to Woolf, is female creativity?**

## Postwar Feminism: de Beauvoir

The two world wars had a positive effect on the position of women. In the absence of men during wartime, women assumed many male jobs in agriculture and in industry. As Woolf predicted, the newly found financial independence of women gave them a sense of freedom and stimulated their demands for legal and social equality. In the Soviet Union, the communist regime put women to work in industry and on the battlefields. Women's roles in other regions beyond the West were also changing. In China, where women had been bought and sold for centuries, the People's Republic in 1949 closed all brothels, forbade arranged marriages, and enforced policies of equal pay for equal work.

Leaders of the feminist movement in the West demanded psychological independence as well as job equality; their goals involved raising the consciousness of *both* sexes. The new woman must shed her passivity and achieve independence through responsible action insisted the French novelist, social critic, and existentialist Simone de Beauvoir

---

[1] Currer Bell was the pseudonym for the British novelist Charlotte Brontë (1816–1855); for Eliot and Sand, see chapter 28.

---

(1908–1986). In the classic feminist text *The Second Sex*, de Beauvoir dethroned the "myth of femininity"—the false and disempowering idea that women possess a unique and preordained "feminine" essence, which condemns them to a role of social and intellectual subordination to men. Reassessing the biological, psychological, and political reasons for women's dependency, she concluded that while Man defines Woman as "the Other" (or *second* sex), it is women themselves who complacently accept their subordinate position. De Beauvoir called on women everywhere "to renounce all advantages conferred upon them by their alliance" with men. She pursued this goal (unsuccessfully, according to some critics) in her own life: her fifty-year liaison with Jean-Paul Sartre constitutes one of the most intriguing partnerships of the century. Although both enjoyed love affairs with other people, they shared a lifelong marriage of minds.

In the following brief excerpt from *The Second Sex*, de Beauvoir explores the nature of female dependency upon men and the "metaphysical risk" of liberty.

— **READING 36.11** From de Beauvoir's
*The Second Sex* (1949)

If woman seems to be the inessential which never becomes **1** the essential, it is because she herself fails to bring about this change. Proletarians say "We"; Negroes also. Regarding themselves as subjects, they transform the bourgeois, the whites, into "others." But women do not say "We," except at some congress of feminists or similar formal demonstration; men say "women," and women use the same word in referring to themselves. They do not authentically assume a subjective attitude. The proletarians have accomplished the revolution in Russia, the Negroes in Haiti, the Indo-Chinese are battling for **10** it in Indo-China; but the women's effort has never been anything more than a symbolic agitation. They have gained only what men have been willing to grant; they have taken nothing, they have only received.

The reason for this is that women lack concrete means for organizing themselves into a unit which can stand face to face with the correlative unit. They have no past, no history, no religion of their own; and they have no such solidarity of work and interest as that of the proletariat. They are not even promiscuously herded together in the way that creates **20** community feeling among the American Negroes, the ghetto Jews, the workers of Saint-Denis, or the factory hands of Renault. They live dispersed among the males, attached through residence, housework, economic condition, and social standing to certain men— fathers or husbands—more firmly than they are to other women. If they belong to the bourgeoisie, they feel solidarity with men of that class, not with proletarian women; if they are white, their allegiance is to white men, not to Negro women. The proletariat can propose to massacre the ruling class, and a sufficiently **30** fanatical Jew or Negro might dream of getting sole possession of the atomic bomb and making humanity wholly Jewish or black; but woman cannot even dream of exterminating the males. The bond that unites her to her oppressors is not comparable to any other. The division of the sexes is a biological fact, not an event in human history. Male and female stand opposed within a primordial *Mitsein*,[1] and woman has not broken it. The couple is a fundamental unity with two halves riveted together, and the cleavage of society along the line of sex is impossible. Here is to be found the basic trait of woman: she is the *Other* in a totality of which the two components are necessary to one another. . . . 40

Now, woman has always been man's dependant, if not his slave; the two sexes have never shared the world in equality. And even today woman is heavily handicapped, though her situation is beginning to change. Almost nowhere is her legal status the same as man's, and frequently it is much to her disadvantage. Even when her rights are legally recognized in the abstract, long-standing custom prevents their full expression in the mores. In the economic sphere men and women can almost be said to make up two castes; other things being equal, the former hold the better jobs, get higher wages, and have more opportunity for success than their new competitors. In industry and politics men have a great many more positions and they monopolize the most important posts. In addition to all this, they enjoy a traditional prestige that the education of children tends in every way to support, for the present enshrines the past—and in the past all history has been made by men. At the present time, when women are beginning to take part in the affairs of the world, it is still a 60 world that belongs to men— they have no doubt of it at all and women have scarcely any. To decline to be the Other, to refuse to be a party to the deal—this would be for women to renounce all the advantages conferred upon them by their alliance with the superior caste. Man-the-sovereign will provide woman-the-liege with material protection and will undertake the moral justification of her existence; thus she can evade at once both economic risk and the metaphysical risk of a liberty in which ends and aims must be contrived without assistance. Indeed, along with the ethical urge of 70 each individual to affirm his subjective existence, there is also the temptation to forego liberty and become a thing. This is an inauspicious road, for he who takes it—passive, lost, ruined—becomes henceforth the creature of another's will, frustrated in his transcendence and deprived of every value. But it is an easy road; on it one avoids the strain involved in undertaking an authentic existence. When man makes of woman the *Other*, he may, then, expect her to manifest deep-seated tendencies toward complicity. Thus, woman may fail to lay claim to the status of subject because she lacks definite 80 resources, because she feels the necessary bond that ties her to man regardless of reciprocity, and because she is often very well pleased with her role as the *Other*. . . .

**Q** **What circumstances, according to de Beauvoir, work to make the female "the Other"?**

**Q** **Is it still "a world that belongs to men"? (line 61).**

[1] German for "co-existence."

## America's Feminist Writers

During the 1960s, and especially in the United States, the struggle for equality between the sexes assumed a strident tone. Gender discrimination in both education and employment triggered demands for federal legislation on behalf of women. Even as new types of contraceptives gave women control over their reproductive functions and greater sexual freedoms, the campaign to secure legal and political rights continued, generating protest marches and a spate of consciousness-raising literature. In 1963, Betty Friedan (1921–2006) published *The Feminine Mystique*, which claimed that American society—and commercial advertising in particular—had brainwashed women to prefer the roles of wives and mothers to other positions in life. Friedan was one of the first feminists to attack the theories of Sigmund Freud (see chapter 33), especially Freud's patriarchal view of women as failed men. She challenged women to question the existing order and to seek careers outside the home. With the founding of the National Organization for Women (NOW) in 1966, radical feminists called for a restructuring of all Western institutions.

Since the 1960s, there has been a virtual renaissance of poetry and fiction focused on the twin themes of gender equality and the search for female self-identity. As with the literature of black liberation, feminist writing often seethes with repressed rage and anger. Clearly, not all modern literature written by women addresses exclusively female issues—contemporary female writers have dealt with subjects as varied as boxing and the plight of the environment. Yet, in much of the postwar literature produced by women, three motifs recur: the victimization of the female, her effort to define her role in a society traditionally dominated by men, and her displacement from her ancient role as goddess and matriarch.

The first generation of feminist poets includes Sylvia Plath (1932–1963) and Anne Sexton (1928–1975). Plath's searing verse reflects her sense of dislocation in male-dominated society. Much like Plath, Sexton probes problems related to the socialization of women and the search for female identity. Deeply confessional, her verse often reflects upon her own troubled life, which (like Plath's) ended in suicide—an ironic fulfillment of Woolf's prophecy concerning the fate of Shakespeare's imaginary sister. In the autobiographical poem "Self in 1958," Sexton explores the images that traditionally have defined women: dolls, apparel, kitchens, and, finally, herself as an extension of her mother. Sexton's poem, which contemplates the female struggle for self-identity in modern society, recalls both Nora's plight in Ibsen's *A Doll's House* (see chapter 30) and Woolf's observation that women "think through their mothers."

The African-American poet Sonia Sanchez (b. 1935) deals with the interrelated questions of racism and identity. Sanchez's poetry is more colloquial than Sexton's, and (like Baraka's) it is often fiercely confrontational. In the poem "Woman" Sanchez draws on the literary tradition in which eminent (and usually male) writers call upon the Classical gods for inspiration: she invokes the spiritual powers of mother earth to infuse her with courage and creative energy.

The poems of Adrienne Rich (b. 1929) are among the most challenging in the feminist canon. They are, to a large extent, impassioned responses to her shifting and often conflicting roles as American, Southerner, Jew, wife, mother, teacher, civil rights activist, feminist, and lesbian. Many of Rich's poems explore the complexities of personal and political relationships, especially as they are affected by gender. In the poem "Translations," she draws attention to the ways in which traditional gender roles polarize the sexes and potentially disempower women.

The youngest of the feminist poets in this group, Rita Dove (b. 1952), is the first African-American woman to have served as poet laureate in the United States (1993–1995). Dove's six collections of poetry, one of which was awarded the Pulitzer Prize (1987), reach into the domains of the black feminist experience. In the short poem "Rosa," from the sequence of poems entitled "On the Bus with Rosa Parks," Dove pays homage to the heroism of the black woman who, riding a Montgomery, Alabama, bus, refused to give up her seat to a white man. (The incident triggered one of the earliest civil rights protests, a citywide boycott led by Martin Luther King.)

## READING 36.12 Feminist Poems

### Sexton's "Self in 1958" (1966)

What is reality? 　　　　　　　　　　　　　　　　1
I am a plaster doll; I pose
with eyes that cut open without landfall or nightfall
upon some shellacked and grinning person,
eyes that open, blue, steel, and close. 　　　　　　　5
Am I approximately an I. Magnin[1] transplant?
I have hair, black angel,
black-angel-stuffing to comb,
nylon legs, luminous arms
and some advertised clothes. 　　　　　　　　　　10

I live in a doll's house
with four chairs,
a counterfeit table, a flat roof
and a big front door.
Many have come to such a small crossroad. 　　　15
There is an iron bed,
(Life enlarges, life takes aim)
a cardboard floor,
windows that flash open on someone's city,
and little more. 　　　　　　　　　　　　　　　20
Someone plays with me,
plants me in the all-electric kitchen,
Is this what Mrs. Rombauer[2] said?
Someone pretends with me—
I am walled in solid by their noise— 　　　　　　25
or puts me upon their straight bed.

They think I am me!
Their warmth? Their warmth is not a friend!
They pry my mouth for their cups of gin
and their stale bread. 　　　　　　　　　　　　　30

What is reality
to this synthetic doll
who should smile, who should shift gears,
should spring the doors open in a wholesome disorder,
and have no evidence of ruin or fears? 　　　　　35
But I would cry,
rooted into the wall that
was once my mother,
if I could remember how
and if I had the tears. 　　　　　　　　　　　　40

### Sanchez's "Woman" (1978)

Come ride my birth, earth mother 　　　　　　　1
tell me how i have become, became
this woman with razor blades between
her teeth.
　　　　sing me my history O earth mother
about tongues multiplying memories 　　　　　　5
about breaths contained in straw.
pull me from the throat of mankind
where worms eat, O earth mother.
come to this Black woman. you.
rider of earth pilgrimages. 　　　　　　　　　　10
tell me how i have held five bodies
in one large cocktail of love
and still have the thirst of the beginning sip.
tell me. tellLLLLLL me. earth mother
for i want to rediscover me. the secret of me 　15
the river of me. the morning ease of me.
i want my body to carry my words like aqueducts.
i want to make the world my diary
and speak rivers.

rise up earth mother 　　　　　　　　　　　　20
out of rope-strung-trees
dancing a windless dance
come phantom mother
dance me a breakfast of births
let your mouth spill me forth 　　　　　　　　25
so i creak with your mornings.
come old mother, light up my mind
with a story bright as the sun.

### Rich's "Translations" (1972)

You show me the poems of some woman 　　　　1
my age, or younger
translated from your language

Certain words occur: *enemy, oven, sorrow*
enough to let me know 　　　　　　　　　　　　5
she's a woman of my time

obsessed

---

[1] A fashionable department store.

[2] Irma S. Rombauer, author of the popular cookbook, *The Joy of Cooking*.

with Love, our subject:
we've trained it like ivy to our walls
baked it like bread in our ovens　　　　　　10
worn it like lead on our ankles
watched it through binoculars as if
it were a helicopter
bringing food to our famine
or the satellite　　　　　　　　　　　　15
of a hostile power

I begin to see that woman
doing things: stirring rice
ironing a skirt
typing a manuscript till dawn　　　　　　20

trying to make a call
from a phonebooth

The phone rings unanswered
in a man's bedroom

she hears him telling someone else　　　　25
*Never mind. She'll get tired.*
hears him telling her story to her sister
who becomes her enemy
and will in her own time
light her own way to sorrow　　　　　　30

ignorant of the fact this way of grief
is shared, unnecessary
and political

### Dove's "Rosa" (1998)

How she sat there,　　　　　　　　　　1
the time right inside a place
so wrong it was ready.

That trim name with
its dream of a bench　　　　　　　　　　5
to rest on. Her sensible coat.

Doing nothing was the doing:
the clean flame of her gaze
carved by a camera flash.

How she stood up　　　　　　　　　　10
when they bent down to retrieve
her purse. That courtesy.

**Q**　**What aspects of the female experience do each of these poems address?**

**Q**　**How might these poems "empower" women?**

# MAKING CONNECTIONS

**Figure 36.10 NIKI DE SAINT PHALLE**, *Black Venus*, 1965–1967. Painted polyester, 9 ft. 2 in. × 35 in. × 24 in.

Niki de Saint Phalle's *Black Venus*, a hugely proportioned polyester "earth mother," wears a large red heart on her belly and flowers on her hips (Figure **36.10**). This exuberant creature is Saint Phalle's answer to the Western stereotypes of female beauty. She is more closely related to the ponderous fertility figures of prehistory, such as the Venus of Willendorf (Figure **36.11**), than to the refined, Classical goddesses of the ancient Greeks and Romans. Indeed, she is the feminist reproof to the idealized female figure that dominated mainstream art through the nineteenth century.

**Figure 36.11** "Venus" of Willendorf, from Lower Austria, ca. 25,000–20,000 B.C.E. Limestone, height 4⅜ in.

## Feminist Art

The history of world art includes only a small number of female artists. Addressing this fact, the Australian-born feminist Germaine Greer (b. 1939) explained,

> There is . . . no female Leonardo, no female Titian, no female Poussin, but the reason does not lie in the fact that women have wombs, that they can have babies, that their brains are smaller, that they lack vigor, that they are not sensual. The reason is simply that you cannot make great artists out of egos that have been damaged, with wills that are defective, with libidos that have been driven out of reach and energy diverted into neurotic channels.

A sure indication of change, however, is the fact that, since the middle of the twentieth century, the number of women in the visual arts (and in music as well) has been greater than ever before in history. And, as with feminist poetry, much of the painting and sculpture produced by women artists since the 1960s has been driven by feminist concerns. A few representative examples will suffice to make this point.

Bringing a feminist attention to the female body, the internationally acclaimed French sculptor Niki de Saint Phalle (1930–2003) fabricated gigantic sculptures that she called "Nanas." In 1963 Saint Phalle exhibited a monumental 80-foot-long, 20-foot-high, and 30-foot-wide Nana that viewers might enter through a doorway between the figure's legs. Inside was a cinema with Greta Garbo movies, a telephone, a refreshment bar, and taped voices of romantic conversations between a man and a woman.

The militant American feminist Judy Gerowitz (b. 1939), who in 1969 assumed the surname of her native city (hence, Judy Chicago), has been a lifelong advocate of women's art. Chicago pioneered some of the first art

**Figure 36.12  JUDY CHICAGO**, *The Dinner Party*, 1974–1979. Multimedia, 48 × 48 × 48 ft. With the ambitious combination of ceramics and textiles, Chicago introduced craft techniques into the arts of the 1970s. Each plate here is an independent artwork; each runner bears embroidery that includes the name of the honoree and her identifying symbol.

communities in which women worked together to produce, exhibit, and sell art. Her efforts ignited the visual arts with the consciousness-raising politics of the feminist movement. Between 1974 and 1979, Chicago directed a project called *The Dinner Party*, a room-size sculpture consisting of a triangular table with thirty-nine place settings, each symbolizing a famous woman in myth or history (Figure **36.12**). The feminist counterpart of the Last Supper, *The Dinner Party* pays homage to such immortals as Nefertiti, Sappho, Queen Elizabeth I, and Virginia Woolf. To carry out this monumental project, Chicago studied the traditionally female arts of embroidery and china painting, inventing at the same time new techniques for combining such dissimilar materials as ceramics and lace. Over 300 men and women contributed to this cooperative enterprise, which brought international attention to the cultural contributions of women in world history.

In searching for a feminist aesthetic, women artists have brought attention to the female body as representative of nature's procreative forces. The Cuban-born Ana Mendieta (1948–1985) used photography and film to document performances inspired by Afro-Caribbean fertility rituals. For the series known as *Silhouettes*, Mendieta immersed herself in pools of water, sand, and mud, and recorded 200 images of her body or its physical impressions on various earth surfaces. In the photograph *Tree of Life* from this series, the artist, encrusted with grass and mud, appears in the dual guises of dryad (a Classical tree nymph) and ancient priestess (Figure **36.13**). She stated: "My art is the way I establish the bonds that unite me to the universe."

**Figure 36.13 Ana Mendieta,** *Tree of Life* from the Silvetas series, 1977. Color photographs, 20 × 13¾ in. Mendieta integrated the performance traditions of Afro-Caribbean religions in her feminist pieces. After 1980, she distanced herself from the feminist art movement, which she felt was too closely tied to white, middle-class values.

The career of the American photographer Cindy Sherman (b. 1954) addresses one of the more recent concerns of feminist artists: the fact that the traditional Western *image* of the female—sweet, sexy, and servile—has been shaped by male needs and values. Such images, say contemporary feminists, reflect the controlling power of the (male) "gaze." The theory of the "male gaze," which emerged among feminist critics of the 1960s, holds that the female image, usually conceived by male artists and rendered exclusively from the male perspective, reduces women to the status of objects. Just as Colescott and Saar use art to attack racial stereotypes, so Sherman makes visual assaults on gender stereotypes—those projected by the collective body of "great art" and by the modern-day phenomena of television, "girlie" magazines, and other mass media. Sherman's large, glossy studio photographs of the 1970s feature the artist herself in poses and attire that call attention to the body as a political or sexual object. In personalized narratives that resemble black-and-white movie stills, she recreates commercial stereotypes that mock the subservient roles that women play: the "little woman," the *femme fatale*, the baby doll, the "pin-up," and the lovesick teenager. Since the 1980s, Sherman has used the newest techniques in color photography to assault—

often in visceral terms—sexual and historical stereotypes of women. She may replace the male image in a world-famous painting with a female image (often Sherman herself), use artificial body parts to "remake" the traditional nude, or flagrantly recast famous females from Western myth, history, and religion (Figure **36.14**).

Well aware of the extent to which commercialism shapes identity, Barbara Kruger (b. 1945) creates photographs that deftly unite word and image to resemble commercial billboards. "Your Body is a Battleground," insists Kruger; by superimposing the message over the divided (positive and negative) image of a female face, the artist calls attention to the controversial issue of abortion in contemporary society (Figure **36.15**).

## Gender Identity

The dual quest for racial and gender equality has also worked to raise public consciousness concerning the ways sex is used as a structuring principle in human culture and society. Distinct from *gender*, which is a culturally prescribed construct of masculine or feminine identity, *sex*, a biologically determined construct, distinguishes the individual as either male or female. Assumptions concerning the sexual and social roles of males and females are rooted in traditions as old as Paleolithic culture and as venerated as the Bible. For many, sexual roles are fixed and

**Figure 36.14 CINDY SHERMAN**, *Untitled #276*, 1993. Color photograph, edition of six, 6 ft. 8½ in. × 5 ft. 1 in. framed. Sitting in a curtained space, on a low throne, this flaxen-haired "Cinderella" assumes a vulgar pose. She holds, however, three stems of lilies, a symbol of purity traditionally associated with the Virgin Mary. Sherman underscores the ambiguity of her photographs' contents by deliberately leaving them untitled.

**Figure 36.15 BARBARA KRUGER**, *Untitled ("Your Body is a Battleground")*, 1989. Photographic silkscreen on vinyl, 9 ft. 4 in. × 9 ft. 4 in.

unchanging. However, these assumptions, like so many others in the cultural history of the twentieth century, came to be challenged and reassessed.

Gender issues accompanied a demand for equality on the part of those of untraditional sexual orientation—bisexuals, homosexuals (gays and lesbians), and other transgendered individuals. In America homosexuals date the birth of their "liberation" to June 1969, when they openly and violently protested a police raid on the Stonewall Inn, a gay bar in New York's Greenwich Village. Thereafter, the call for protection against harassment shifted to litigated demands for gender equality. While all societies have included a transgendered subculture, it was not until the last decades of the twentieth century that sexual and public issues intersected to produce some highly controversial questions. Should homosexuals serve in the armed forces? Should homosexual marriage be legalized? How does homosexuality affect the future of the traditional family? Should sexually explicit art receive public funding? The resolution of these and other gender-related questions continues to impact the progress of the humanistic tradition.

There are a number of reasons why issues of human sexuality became so visible in the culture of the late twentieth century: increasing sexual permissiveness (the consequence of improved pharmaceutical methods of contraception); the activity of the media (especially TV and film) in broadcasting sexually explicit entertainment; and the appearance of the devastating pandemic called AIDS (Acquired Immune Deficiency Syndrome), a life-threatening disease resulting from a retrovirus named HIV that attacks the blood cells of the body, thus causing a failure of the autoimmune system. Collectively, these phenomena have represented an overwhelming challenge to

traditional concepts of sexuality, sexual behavior, and (more generally) to conventional morality. They have also generated a provocative blurring of sex roles (which has been increasingly exploited in commercial advertising and the popular media). And they continue to complicate the task of distinguishing between forms of expression that have mere shock value and those that represent a substantial creative achievement.

The photographs of Robert Mapplethorpe (1946–1989) are significant in this regard. Mapplethorpe's fine-grained silver gelatin prints display exquisitely composed images ranging from still life subjects to Classically posed nudes. Although usually lacking explicit narrative, they reflect the artist's preoccupation with physical and sexual themes: male virility, sadomasochism, androgyny, and sexual identity. A sculptor in his early training, Mapplethorpe presents his subjects as pristine objects, occasionally transforming them into erotic symbols. His photographs depict contemporary sexuality in a manner that is at once detached and impassioned, but they often gain added power as gender-bending parodies of sexual stereotypes—witness the startling union of masculine and feminine cues in the portrait of Lisa Lyon—herself a weight-lifter (Figure **36.16**; see also Figure 38.17). Mapplethorpe fulfills the artist's mission to see things (in his words) "like they haven't been seen before."

Themes of human sexuality have also increasingly preoccupied twentieth- and twenty-first-century writers. In her science fiction fantasy *The Left Hand of Darkness* (1969), American writer Ursula LeGuin (b. 1929) describes a distant planet, home to creatures with the sexual potential of both males and females. The ambisexuality of the characters in this fictional utopia calls into question human preconceptions about the defined roles of behavior for men and women. Through the device of science fiction, LeGuin suggests a shift in focus from the narrow view of male–female dualities (or opposites) to larger, more urgent matters of interdependence.

While LeGuin examines bisexuality in imaginary settings, others, and in particular gay artists, have dealt with the experience of homosexuality in their day-to-day lives. Sexual "otherness" and the gay sensibility are themes that appear regularly in the popular entertainment media of television and film. They are also the subject of inquiry among scholars of a new discipline known as "queer representation."*

By drawing attention to the ways in which matters of sexuality affect society and its institutions, contemporary art asserts that sexuality and power are as closely related as race and power or gender and power. Tony Kushner's Pulitzer Prize-winning play *Angels in America: A Gay Fantasia on National Themes* (written in two parts: *Millennium Approaches*, 1990, and *Perestroika*, 1993) presents a radical vision of American society set against the

---

* See Martin Duberman, ed., *Queer Representations: Reading Lives, Reading Cultures.* New York: City University of New York Center for Lesbian and Gay Studies, 1997.

**Figure 36.16 ROBERT MAPPLETHORPE**, *Lisa Lyon*, 1982. Silver gelatin print. Mapplethorpe focused on the body as a site of pain and pleasure. Gallery exhibitions of his photographs offering a frank treatment of alternative lifestyles and sexual practices have caused intense public controversy.

AIDS epidemic and the politics of conservatism. Kushner (b. 1957) urges the old America—"straight," Protestant, and white—to look with greater objectivity at "the fringe" (the variety of ethnic, racial, and sexual minorities), which demands acceptance and its share of power. Kushner's landmark drama represents the movement for body-conscious politics and socially responsible art that animated the last decade of the twentieth century.

Beyond issues of sexual orientation and the struggle against discrimination on the part of the transgendered minority, the more immediate issue of the AIDS pandemic left its mark on the late twentieth century. The *Aids Memorial Quilt*, begun in 1985, engaged 20,000 ordinary individuals, each of whom created a single 3- by 6-foot fabric panel in memory of someone who had died of an HIV-related disease. In 1992, AIDS activists assembled the panels in 16-foot squares and took them from San Francisco to Washington, D.C., to protest governmental inaction with regard to the AIDS crisis. Commemorating the deaths of some 150,000 Americans, the *Aids Memorial Quilt* covered 15 acres of ground between the Washington Monument and Lincoln Memorial. The Names Project continues: in 2004, the quilt panels numbered 44,000, that is, more than double the figure of the original.

One of the most moving monuments to the AIDS crisis is the controversial *Still/Here* (1994), a performance work conceived by the African-American dancer Bill T. Jones (b. 1952). For the piece Jones, who is himself HIV-positive, combined choreography and vocal music with video imagery derived in part from workshops he conducted with AIDS victims. *Still/Here* has provoked heated debate concerning the artistic value of issue-driven art: does art that showcases sickness and death serve merely to manipulate viewers? This is only one of many questions that probe current efforts to wed art to social action.

## Chronology

| | |
|---|---|
| 1918 | British women granted the right to vote |
| 1920 | American women granted the right to vote |
| 1966 | Founding of National Organization for Women (NOW) |
| 1969 | Police raid Stonewall Inn, a gay bar in New York City |

# EXPLORING ISSUES

### Issue-Driven Art

One of the most moving responses to the AIDS crisis is *Still/Here* (1994), a two-act dance-theater work produced by the African-American dancer/choreographer Bill T. Jones. Jones conceived the piece in part as a memorial to his partner, Arnie Zane, who died of AIDS in 1988. For the work, Jones combined dance and a vocal score with video imagery derived in part from workshops he conducted with AIDS victims. When it was first performed in 1994, *Still/Here* provoked heated criticism and debate. Critics questioned the value of art that showcased sickness and death. Others

defended the right as well as the responsibility of the artist to put art at the service of social action and reform. More than ten years later, many regard *Still/Here* as a tribute to the resilience of the human spirit in the face of life-threatening illness. But the work raises important questions. What role should issue-driven art play in contemporary life? If such art takes meaning and authority exclusively from its immediate context, can it be evaluated objectively for its broader aesthetic value?

# LOOKING BACK

## Anticolonialism and Liberation

- The quest for liberation from poverty, oppression, and inequality was a prevailing theme in twentieth-century history. In dozens of countries, movements for decolonization followed World War II.
- At the same time, racial and ethnic minorities fought valiantly to oppose discrimination as practiced by the majority culture. These crusades are yet ongoing among the populations of Eastern Europe, Latin America, the Middle East, Africa, and elsewhere.
- Western intrusion in Muslim lands has provoked protest, as evidenced in the poetry of Muhammad Iqbal.
- Liberation movements in Latin America were supported by the Catholic Church and by such writers as Pablo Neruda, whose poems condemn colonialism and commercial exploitation.

## The Quest for Racial Equality

- The struggle of African-Americans to achieve freedom from the evils of racism has a long and dramatic history. From the Harlem Renaissance in the early twentieth century through the civil rights movement of the 1960s, the arts have mirrored that history.
- In the poems of Langston Hughes and Gwendolyn Brooks, and in the novels of Richard Wright, James Baldwin, Ralph Ellison, and Alice Walker, the plight and identity of African-Americans in white America have been central themes.
- Visual artist Romare Bearden engaged the world of jazz in collage; Betye Saar, Robert Colescott, and Kara Walker, have tested the stereotypes of American racism by way of parody and satire.
- The impact of black culture in music and dance has been formidable. Blues and jazz giants from Louis Armstrong to Wynton Marsalis have produced a living body of popular music, while choreographers from Katherine Dunham to Alvin Ailey have inspired generations of dancers to draw on their African heritage.

## The Quest for Gender Equality

- During the postwar era, women throughout the world worked to gain political, economic, and social equality.
- The writings of feminists Virginia Woolf and Simone de Beauvoir influenced women to examine the psychological conditions of their oppression.

- In America, the feminist movement elicited a virtual golden age in literature. The self-conscious poetry of Anne Sexton, Sonia Sanchez, Rita Dove, and Adrienne Rich is representative of this phenomenon.
- In the visual arts, at least two generations of women have redefined traditional concepts of female identity: first, by celebrating womanhood itself, and, more recently, by attacking outworn stereotypes.
- One of the most controversial of the twentieth century's liberation movements centered on issues of gender identity. Amidst the AIDS pandemic, Robert Mapplethorpe and Tony Kushner brought candor and perceptivity to matters of sexuality and sexual behavior.

## Music Listening Selections

**CD Two Selection 21** Handy, "St. Louis Blues," 1914.
**CD Two Selection 22** Hardin/Armstrong, "Hotter Than That," 1927.
**CD Two Selection 23** Parker/Gillespie, "Koko," 1945.

## Glossary

**apartheid** a policy of strict racial segregation and political and economic discrimination against the black population in South Africa

**feminism** the doctrine advocating equal social, political, and economic rights for women

**scat singing** a jazz performance style in which nonsense syllables replace the lyrics of a song

**swing** the jazz performer's practice of varying from the standard rhythms by playing just ahead of, or just behind, the beat; also, a big-band jazz style developed in the 1920s and flourishing in the age of large dance bands (1932–1942)

# Chapter

# 37

## The Information Age

### ca. 1960–present

*"In America, advertising enjoys universal popular adherence and the American way of life is fashioned by it."*
Ellul

**Figure 37.1 ROBERT RAUSCHENBERG**, *Buffalo II*, 1964. Oil on canvas with silkscreen, 8 ft. × 6 ft. Rauschenberg used solvent transfer and screen-printing techniques to reproduce images from magazines and newspapers. The central strategy of his work, that of collecting and combining, informed both his prints and his three-dimensional pieces.

# LOOKING AHEAD

Some historians date the end of Modernism from the decade of the Holocaust and the devastation of World War II, a period that saw the obliteration of utopian ideals and the rise of cynicism and doubt. But these sobering realities also formed the background for the Postmodern shift from an Industrial Age (dominated by farming and manufacturing) to an Information Age (dominated by radical changes in the technology of communication and the ways we receive and process information). The agents of high technology, the mass media, and electronic modes of communication have facilitated this shift. In the fifteenth century, movable type brought about the print revolution, which transformed an essentially oral culture into one that depended on the book. In our own time, electronic forms of communication have had an equally revolutionary effect: they have made more information available to greater numbers of people at greater speeds than ever before. And they have delivered much of that information in a visual form.

The information explosion had massive effects on the culture of the late twentieth century. It encouraged unusual literary styles modeled on electronic modes of communication. Along with high technology materials and digital techniques, it contributed to a wealth of new visual art styles and forms, many of which are conceptual and interactive. In music and film, digital technology affected everything from the production of sound to its storage and distribution. The culture of Postmodernism is challenging not only because of its diversity of styles and opinions, but because it embraces the historical past with stark objectivity and skepticism.

## The Information Explosion

Television and computers—the primary vehicles of the information explosion—have altered almost every aspect of life in our time. The wonderchild of electronics and the quintessential example of modern mass media, television transmits sound and light by electromagnetic waves that carry information instantaneously into homes across the face of the earth. The very name "television" comes from the Greek word *tele*, meaning "far," and the Latin *videre*, meaning "to see"; hence "to see far." Television did not become common to middle-class life in the West until the 1950s, although it had been invented decades before then. By the 1960s, the events of a war in the jungles of Vietnam were being relayed via electronic communications satellite into American living rooms. In 1969, in a live telecast, the world saw the first astronauts walk on the surface of the moon. And in the early 1990s, during the Middle Eastern conflict triggered by the Iraqi invasion of Kuwait, those with access to television witnessed the first "prime-time

| Science and Technology | |
|---|---|
| 1950 | commercial color television becomes available |
| 1953 | first commercially successful computer introduced |
| 1959 | American engineers produce the first microchip (made from a silicon wafer) |
| 1970 | fiber optics technology is perfected to carry information thousands of times faster than copper cables |
| 1972 | first commercial videogame introduced |
| 1975 | first personal computer available |
| 1979 | first portable music device (the Walkman) produced |
| 1983 | first commercial cellular (wireless) phones produced |

war"—a war that was "processed" by censorship and television newscasting.

The second major technological phenomenon of the Information Age is the computer. Digital computers—machines that process information in the form of numbers—were first used widely in the 1950s. By the 1960s, computers consisting of electronic circuits were able to perform millions of calculations per second. Smaller and more reliable than ever before, computers have come to facilitate a vast range of functions from cellphone communication to rapid prototyping, a digital process that "prints" objects in three dimensions. Computer technology accelerated the process of information production, storage, and retrieval. A single computer chip is capable of storing an entire encyclopedia. Virtually unlimited amounts of information are available in various data banks, united by the World Wide Web, a system of electronically linked texts (or hypertexts) accessed by way of a series of interconnected computer networks known as the Internet.

Since the 1990s, information technology has rapidly proliferated. The world's first online, nonprofit English-language encyclopedia, Wikipedia, was launched in 2001. Publicly edited and continuously updated, it contained (in 2009) almost three million articles. Equally ambitious are current projects to create a universal literary archive by putting all existing printed matter into an electronic library. The website YouTube invites a polyglot audience to post video "clips," while the image-hosting website, Flickr, provides a community resource for millions of photos and videos. Online postings—web-logs ("blogs")—exchange information and personal opinions on everything from current fashion fads to political policy.

### From Book to Screen

Book culture and the written language depend on linearity, syntactical order, and precision. By contrast, the culture of the Information Age is increasingly image-oriented (Figure 37.1). By way of screens—television, computer, telephone, or camera—we receive ideas configured as pictures and logos, symbols and signs. Visual information (like

The French sociologist Jacques Ellul (1912–1994) blamed television for creating what he called, a society of "mass man." He singled out advertising as the most pernicious condition assaulting human dignity. In *The Technological Society* (1964), Ellul observed,

> Advertising [affects] all people; or at least an overwhelming majority. Its goal is to persuade the masses to buy. . . . The inevitable consequence is the creation of the mass man. As advertising of the most varied products is concentrated, a new type of human being, precise and generalized, emerges. We can get a general impression of this new human type by studying America, where human beings tend clearly to become identified with the ideal of advertising. In America, advertising enjoys

## Victims of Mass Persuasion?

universal popular adherence and the American way of life is fashioned by it.

Ellul's view of advertising as a form of "psychological collectivism" that robs human beings of freedom and self-esteem dates from a time in which commercial advertising was dominated by printed media and television. However, today's computerized forms of communication, such as Internet websites and web-logs, empower individuals to respond to mass advertising. The newest digital technologies provide a free resource for interactive, individual expression. Nevertheless, in a society whose consumers are targeted regularly by computer software programs that analyze their buying habits, the possibility of techno-structural threats to human dignity remains an issue.

---

music or film) is manipulated by dozens of electronic processes: clipping, combining, distorting, mixing, and remixing. In contrast with the linear medium of print, electronic images are generated in diffuse, discontinuous bundles and rapidly dispatched fragments. The electronic media tend to homogenize images, that is, to make all images uniform and alike. Product and message fall to process and medium. (Or, as communications theorist Marshall McLuhan famously observed, "the medium is the message.") Electronic processing and the rapid diffusion of images via television and the Internet have worked to reduce distinctions between different types of information: the stuff of "popular" culture is often indistinguishable from that of "high" culture. Moreover, the world of the screen has turned information, from protest marches to breakfast cereals, into marketable commodities, transforming culture into (what one critic calls) "a vast garage sale."

### Science and Technology

|  | |
|------|--|
| **1990** | the internationally linked computer network (the Internet) becomes accessible to personal computers |
| **1995 +** | advances in nanotechnology and microprocessing make possible minicomputers, palm TVs, smart bombs, etc. |
| **2000 +** | wireless networks, broadband, digital TV and satellite radio become mainstream |
| **2001** | Apple releases its first generation iPod (portable digital music device) |
| **2007** | wireless electronic reading devices become available |

## New Directions in Science and Philosophy

The major developments of the last half-century followed from scientific advances that have made possible investigations into outer space—the universe at large—and inner space, the province of our own bodies. Science and techno-logy have propelled humankind beyond planet earth and into the cosmos. At the same time, they have provided an unprecedented understanding of the genetic patterns that govern life itself. These phenomena have worked to make the planet smaller, the universe larger, and methods of navigating the two ever more promising.

### String Theory

Since the middle of the twentieth century, physicists have tried to reconcile the insights of the two great intellectual systems advanced early in the century: Einstein's theory of relativity, which applies to vast, cosmological space, and quantum physics, which describes the realms of the very small. They seek to establish "a theory of everything," one that might explain the "fundamental of fundamentals" that governs the organization and complexity of matter. A new (but yet unproven) theory proposes that all matter—from the page of this book to the skin of a peach—consists of tiny loops of vibrating strings. *String* (or *Superstring*) *Theory*, most eloquently explained by the American physicist Brian Greene (b. 1962), describes a multidimensional universe in which loops of strings and oscillating globules of matter unite all of creation into vibrational patterns.* While the workings of such a universe can be simulated on a computer, language—other than the language of mathematics—is

---

* Brian Greene, *The Elegant Universe: Superstrings, Hidden Dimensions and the Quest for the Ultimate Theory.* New York, Norton, 1999.

too frail to serve as an explanatory medium. Yet it is in the arts, and possibly in aesthetic theory, that the design of this elegant universe may be approximated. As the Norwegian physicist Niels Bohr observed, "When it comes to atoms, language can be used only as in poetry."

## Chaos Theory

Equally fascinating are the speculations of those who explore the shape and structure of matter itself. The proponents of *Chaos Theory* find that universal patterns underlie the seemingly random operations of nature. The catalyst for the development of chaos theory was the electronic computer, by which the mathematics of random patterns (applied to such matters as air turbulence and weather predictions) was first calculated. Predictable patterns repeat themselves in physical phenomena ranging from the formation of a snowflake to the rhythms of the human heart. Chaos theorists (not only physicists, but also astronomers, mathematicians, biologists, and computer scientists) observe that while these patterns appear random, unstable, and disorderly, they are actually self-similar in scale, like the zigs and zags of a lightning bolt, or the oscillating motions of electric currents. To Einstein's famous assertion, "God does not play dice with the universe," these theorists might respond: "Not only does God play dice; but they are loaded."

## The Human Genome

One of the major projects of the late twentieth century was the successful mapping of the *human genome*. By the year 2000, molecular biologists had been able (with the help of computers) to ascertain the order of nearly three billion units of DNA, thereby locating genes and determining their functions in the human cellular system. Ultimately, this enterprise is expected to revolutionize the practice of medicine, in both the preventive treatment of gene-related diseases and in the repair and regeneration of tissues. (Already, such gene-related research has diminished the number of AIDS deaths internationally.)

The tools of genetic engineering have also given scientists the ability to clone life forms. They also promise the mitigation of what Freud described as one of humankind's greatest threats: the suffering "from our own body, which is doomed to decay and dissolution." From sports medicine to psychoanalysis, society has come to perceive human beings as mechanisms that can be improved, if not perfected, by the right diet, drugs, exercise, and a healthy life-style. The 1990s brought exciting breakthroughs in the area of *cognitive neuroscience*, as new imaging technologies showed how brain waves can influence matter. In recent German experiments in neural consciousness, patients wearing electrodes on their scalps modulate electrical signals to choose letters from a video screen—thus communicating with nothing but their own brains. These biofeedback experiments are reinforced by neurochemical research: the American biochemist Candace Pert (b. 1946) writes in her groundbreaking book *Molecules of Emotion* (1997), "We know that the immune system, like the central nervous system, has

| Science and Technology | |
|---|---|
| 1953 | DNA discovered |
| 1967 | Christian Barnard (South African) performs the first human heart transplant |
| 1973 | American biochemists isolate genes to make genetic engineering possible |
| 1978 | the world's first test-tube baby is born |
| 1983 | the first commercial use of MRI (Magnetic Resonance Imaging) |
| 1996 | Dolly, a cloned sheep, is born in Scotland |
| 2000 | scientists complete the mapping of the human genome |
| 2005 | first publicly available personal genetic blueprints |
| 2007 | human skin cells are found to be reprogrammable as stem cells |

memory and the capacity to learn. Thus, it could be said that intelligence is located not only in the brain but in cells that are distributed throughout the body, and that the traditional separation of mental processes, including emotions, from the body, is no longer valid." As the gap between mind and body grows narrower, Eastern notions of the symbiosis of matter and spirit have received increased attention in the West. By way of popular literature (such as *Quantum Healing: Exploring the Frontier of Mind/Body Medicine*, 1990), the Indian-born endocrinologist Deepak Chopra (b. 1946) introduced Western audiences to holistic models of meditation and body control that have flourished in India for 2000 years.

## Language Theory

While science moves forward optimistically to reveal the underlying natural order, philosophy has entered a phase of radical skepticism that denies the existence of any true or uniform system of thought. Contemporary philosophers have fastened on the idea, first popularized by the Austrian Ludwig Wittgenstein (1889–1951), that all forms of expression, and, indeed, all truths, are dominated by the limits of language as a descriptive tool. Wittgenstein, whose life's work was an inquiry into the ways in which language represents the world, argued that sentences (or propositions) were "pictures of reality." His groundbreaking theories on the philosophy of language were published two years after his death under the title *Philosophical Investigations*.

Following Wittgenstein, philosophers tried to unlock the meaning of the *text* (that is, any mode of cultural expression) by way of a close analysis of its linguistic structure. Language theorists suggested that one must "deconstruct" or "take apart" discourse in order to "unmask" its many meanings. The leaders of *Deconstruction*, the French philosophers Jacques Derrida (1930–2004) and Michel Foucault (1926–1984), were influential in arguing that all human beings are prisoners of the very language they use to think and to describe the world. In *Of Grammatology* (1967), Derrida examined the relationship between speech and writing, and their roles in the effectiveness of communication. In a similar direction, Foucault's *The Archeology of Knowledge* (1969) suggests that language is not the servant, but the master, of those who use it; we fail to realize that we are forever submitting to its demands. Philosophers, he asserted, should abandon the search for absolute truths and concentrate on the discovery of meaning(s). "Deconstruction" became the popular method of analysis in philosophy, linguistics, and literary criticism in the late twentieth century.

The American philosopher Richard Rorty (1931–2007) was deeply troubled by the limits of both linguistic inquiry and traditional philosophy. Rorty argued that the great thinkers of the postphilosophical age are not the metaphysicians or the linguists but, rather, those artists whose works provide others with insights into achieving Postmodern self-transformation. What Rorty called the "linguistic turn" describes the move (among writers and philosophers) to rethink language as verbal coding.

# Literature in the Information Age

## Postmodernism

The term "Postmodernism" came into use shortly before World War II to describe the reaction to or against Modernism, but by the late 1960s it had come to designate the cultural condition of the late twentieth century. Whether defined as a reaction against Modernism or as an entirely new form of Modernism, Postmodernism is a phenomenon that occurred principally in the West. As a style, it is marked by a bemused awareness of a historical past whose "reality" has been processed by mass communication and information technology.

Postmodern artists appropriate (or borrow) pre-existing texts and images from history, advertising, and the media. They offer alternatives to the high seriousness and introversion of Modernist expression, and move instead in the direction of parody (burlesque imitation), whimsy, paradox, and irony. Their playful amalgam of disparate styles mingles the superficial and the profound. Their seemingly incongruous "layering" of images calls to mind the fundamentals of Chaos Theory, which advances a geometry of the universe that is "broken up, twisted, tangled, intertwined."

In contrast with elitist Modernism, Postmodernism is self-consciously populist, even to the point of inviting the active participation of the beholder. Whereas Modern artists (consider Eliot or Kandinsky) exalt the artist as visionary and rebel, Postmodern artists bring wry skepticism to the creative act. Less preoccupied than the Modernists with formal abstraction and its redeeming power, Postmodernists acknowledge art as an information system and a commodity shaped by the electronic media, its messages, and its modes of communication. The Postmodern stance is more disengaged than authorial, its message often enigmatic. Finally, Postmodernism is pluralistic, that is, it

suggests that meaning is many-faceted and fleeting, rather than absolute and fixed; and that the individual has numerous (and often contradictory) identities.

## Postmodern Fiction

Postmodern writers share the contemporary philosopher's disdain for rational structure and the Deconstructionist's fascination with the function of language. They tend to bypass traditional narrative styles in favor of techniques that parody the writer's craft, mingle past, present, and future events, leave situations unresolved, and freely mix the ordinary and the bizarre. This genre has been called "Metafiction"—fiction about fiction. It takes fragments of information out of their original literary/historical context and juxtaposes them with little or no commentary on their meaning. In a single story, a line from a poem by T. S. Eliot or a Shakespeare play may appear alongside a catchy saying or banal slogan from a television commercial, a phrase from a national anthem, or a shopping list, as if the writer were claiming all information as equally valuable. In Postmodern fiction, characters undergo little or no development, plots often lack logical direction, and events—whether ordinary, perverse, or fantastic—may be described in the detached tone of a newspaper article. Like the television newscast, the language of Postmodern fiction is often diffuse, discontinuous, and filled with innuendo and "commentary." The American novelist Kurt Vonnegut (1922–2007) favored clipped sentences framed in the present tense. He created a kind of "videofiction" that seemed aimed at readers whose attention spans have been dwarfed by commercial television programming. The Italian novelist Italo Calvino (1923–1985) engages the reader in a hunt for meanings that lie in the spaces between the act of writing and the events the words describe. Calvino interrupts the story line of his novel *If On a Winter's Night a Traveler* (1979) to confront the reader, thus:

> For a couple of pages now you have been reading on, and this would be the time to tell you clearly whether this station where I have got off is a station of the past or a station of today; instead the sentences continue to move in vagueness, grayness, in a kind of no man's land of experience reduced to the lowest kind of denominator. Watch out: it is surely a method of involving you gradually, capturing you in the story before you realize it—a trap. Or perhaps the author still has not made up his mind, just as you, reader, for that matter, are not sure what you would most like to read.

While Vonnegut and Calvino are representative of twentieth-century Metafiction, they are by no means the only writers whose prose works have a Postmodern stamp. The Nobel Prize-winning author Doris Lessing (b. 1919) conceived *The Golden Notebook* (1962) as a series of interwoven narrative fragments, diary entries, and personal notes. Her voice is that of a middle-aged female writer who struggles with the political and personal traumas of a postwar, Postmodern society.

It is too soon to determine which of the internationally renowned writers of the last half-century will leave landmarks in the history of culture. The following are likely candidates: Joan Didion (b. 1934), Tom Wolfe (b. 1930), and Don DeLillo (b. 1936). All three American authors employ the events of their time to produce *docufiction*— a literary genre that gives an original (and fictionalized) narrative context to contemporary events and situations. DeLillo captures the cinematic rush of American life in the compelling novel *Underworld*, which connects major worldwide phenomena—the atomic bomb, the cold war— to such everyday events as baseball and waste management. His style, in which the narrative moves back and forth in time, parallels a Postmodern propensity for disordering time sequences, readily apparent in contemporary cinema. DeLillo's concerns for international terrorism, the ecology of the planet, urban violence, and the loss of spiritual and moral values are shared by many contemporary novelists. Most, however, such as Philip Roth (b. 1933), John Updike (1932–2009), and Margaret Atwood (b. 1939), have maintained a traditional narrative style.

## Postmodern Poetry

As with Postmodern fiction, so too with poetry; parody and ambivalence dominate. Multiple meanings or the absence of meaning itself are related to language, its ambiguities, and its role in shaping the self. In the poem "To Talk," the Mexican poet and critic Octavio Paz (1914–1999) deals with the idea of language as both self-defining and sacred. More opaque are the poems of the American writer John Ashbery (b. 1927). While his verses are often playful, they are also usually cryptic and inscrutable. In the poem "Paradoxes and Oxymorons" Ashbery suggests that both language and life are incongruous, contradictory, and intrinsically human.

---

**READING 37.1** Paz's "To Talk" (1987)

I read in a poem:                                                      1
*to talk is divine.*
But gods don't speak:
they create and destroy worlds
while men do the talking,                                             5
Gods, without words,
play terrifying games.

The spirit descends,
untying tongues,
but it doesn't speak words:                                           10
it speaks flames.
Language, lit by a god
is a prophecy
of flames and a crash
of burnt syllables:                                                   15
meaningless ash.

Man's word
is the daughter of death.
We talk because we are
mortal: words                                                         20

are not signs, they are years.
Saying what they say,
the names we speak
say time: they say us,
we are the names of time.                                             25
To talk is human.

**Q** **What insights concerning the powers and perils of language does Paz convey in this poem?**

---

**READING 37.2** Ashbery's "Paradoxes and Oxymorons"[1] (1981)

This poem is concerned with language on a very plain level.         1
Look at it talking to you. You look out a window
Or pretend to fidget. You have it but you don't have it.
You miss it, it misses you. You miss each other.

This poem is sad because it wants to be yours, and cannot.           5
What's a plain level? It is that and other things,
Bringing a system of them into play. Play?
Well, actually, yes, but I consider play to be

A deeper outside thing, a dreamed role-pattern,
As in the division of grace these long August days                  10
Without proof. Open-ended. And before you know it
It gets lost in the steam and chatter of typewriters.

It has been played once more. I think you exist only
To tease me into doing it, on your level, and then you aren't there
Or have adopted a different attitude. And the poem                   15
Has set me softly down beside you. The poem is you.

**Q** **To what does "it" refer at each use here? Can you find any paradoxes or oxymorons in this poem?**

## Magic Realism

The term "Magic Realism" originated in the context of the visual arts where it characterized the paintings of Giorgio de Chirico and Magritte (see chapter 33). As a literary term, it describes a genre in which magical elements appear in an otherwise realistic setting. Magical Realism dominated Latin American fiction from the early 1920s through the literary explosion, the so-called "Boom," that began in the late 1960s. Two of the most notable of Latin America's Magic Realists are the Colombian novelist Gabriel Garcia Marquez (b. 1928) and the Chilean author Isabel Allende (b. 1943). Both are brilliant storytellers who interweave Latin America's legendary history with universal themes of language and love. Allende has credited the influence of film and television for her ability to "think in images."

---

[1] A paradox is a statement that seems contradictory or absurd, but may actually be true. An oxymoron is a combination of contradictory terms, such as "wise fool" or "cruel kindness."

|  | |
|------|---|
| 1957 | the first artificial satellite (*Sputnik 1*) is put in orbit by the Soviet Union |
| 1969 | an American astronaut is the first person to walk on the moon |
| 1981 | lasers are utilized for the study of matter |
| 1990 | the Hubble space telescope confirms the existence of extrasolar planets and fifty billion galaxies |
| 2004 | NASA scientists land rover probe on Mars |
| 2005 | International Space Station completed |
| 2007 | Computer imaging (CI) used to test spacecraft before production |

One of the earliest of the Latin American Magic Realists was the Argentinian Jorge Luis Borges (1899–1986). In his short stories and essays, Borges combined elements of Magic Realism—its unexpected shifts in time and place and its dreamlike, mythic settings—with a plurality of meanings and points of view common to Postmodernism. He cited among the basic devices of fantastic literature: the contamination of reality by dream, the voyage in time, and the "double." The fractured, reflexive self is both subject and object in "Borges and I," one of a group of parables and prose fragments that made up his most personal book, *The Maker* (1960).

### READING 37.3 Borges' "Borges and I" (1960)

It's Borges, the other one, that things happen to. I walk through Buenos Aires and I pause—mechanically now, perhaps—to gaze at the arch of an entryway and its inner door; news of Borges reaches me by mail, or I see his name on a list of academics or in some biographical dictionary. My taste runs to hourglasses, maps, eighteenth-century typefaces, etymologies, the taste of coffee, and the prose of Robert Louis Stevenson; Borges shares those preferences, but in a vain sort of way that turns them into the accoutrements of an actor. It would be an exaggeration to say that our relationship is hostile—I live, I allow myself live, so that Borges can spin out his literature, and that literature is my justification. I willingly admit that he has written a number of sound pages, but those pages will not save *me*, perhaps because the good in them no longer belongs to any individual, not even to that other men, but rather to language itself, or to tradition. Beyond that, I am doomed—utterly and inevitably—to oblivion, and fleeting moments will be all of me that survives in that other man. Little by little, I have been turning everything over to him, though I know the perverse way he has of distorting and magnifying everything. Spinoza believed that all things wish to go on being what they are—stone wishes eternally to be stone, and tiger, to be tiger. I shall endure in Borges, not in myself (if, indeed, I am anybody at all), but I recognize myself less in his books than in many others', or in the tedious strumming of a guitar. Years ago I tried to free myself from him, and I moved on from the mythologies of the slums and outskirts of the city to games

with time and infinity, but those games belong to Borges now, and I shall have to think up other things. So my life is a point-counterpoint, a kind of fugue, and a falling away—and everything winds up being lost to me, and everything falls into oblivion, or into the hands of the other man.

I am not sure which of us it is that's writing this page.

**Q** Based only on the evidence of this sketch, describe the setting, the age of the speaker(s), and his (their) main concerns. Borges considered this piece a parable; what might be the lesson of this parable?

## Science Fiction

Science fiction has come to be one of our most entertaining genres. At its best, it evokes a sense of awe and a spirit of intellectual curiosity in the face of the unknown. It also is a vehicle by which writers express their concern for the future of the planet. During the twentieth century—a virtual golden age of science fiction—Futurists contemplated the possibility of life in outer space, the interface between computers and human beings, the consequences of a nuclear disaster, and the potential for a bioengineered new species.

The beginnings of modern science fiction may be traced to the French novelist Jules Verne (1828–1905) and the British writer H. G. Wells (1866–1946). But the more recent flowering of the genre dates from the birth of space exploration—specifically the Soviet Union's historic launching of an artificial earth satellite (*Sputnik 1*) in 1957 and the American moon landing of 1969. These events triggered an outpouring of fiction related to space exploration. In 1950, Arthur C. Clarke (1917–2008), one of Britain's most successful writers, had produced the intriguing science fiction story "The Sentinel," which in turn became the basis for an extraordinary cinematic conceptualization of the space age—*2001: A Space Odyssey*.

In the last decades of the twentieth century, science fiction spawned a unique subgenre known as *cyberpunk*. Influenced by *Gravity's Rainbow* (1974), the dense masterpiece of Thomas Pynchon (b. 1937), cyberpunk deals with futuristic societies, dominated by computers, artificial intelligence, illicit drugs, and punk rock music. Pynchon's novel, an archetypal Postmodernist text, is packed with an encyclopedic array of references to (and puns on) world history, chemistry, mathematics, religion, film, and popular music.

## The Literature of Social Conscience

Urban violence, poverty, corporate greed, and the search for spiritual renewal in a commodity-driven world have inspired much of the literature of the late twentieth and early twenty-first centuries. Such writing is usually realistic and straightforward in its narrative style. One of the leading voices in this genre is the American writer Joyce Carol Oates (b. 1938). Oates deals with the violent underlayer of contemporary urban society. In the story "Ace," she makes use of a highly concentrated kind of prose fiction that she calls the "miniature narrative." Its tale of random

## Science Fiction Film

Directed by one of America's most brilliant filmmakers, Stanley Kubrick (1928–1999), *2001: A Space Odyssey* (1968) builds on the intriguing hypothesis of most science fiction: that intelligent life exists in outer space. The plot, which loosely follows Arthur C. Clarke's short story "The Sentinel," involves the quest to locate a mysterious four-million-year-old crystal monolith that appears to be emitting powerful radio waves in the direction of the planet Jupiter. Outfitted with a state-of-the-art spaceship called *Discovery*, which is engineered by a supercomputer named HAL-9000, the fictional heroes of the space odyssey set out for Jupiter. Their adventures include a contest of wills between the astronauts and the ruthless and deviant HAL, breathtaking encounters with the perils of outer space, and a shattering revelation of regeneration and rebirth. Kubrick's *2001* is the modern counterpart of ancient myth and legend. Like Homer's *Odyssey*, the film celebrates the adventures of a hero who, as part of a quest, challenges the unknown by force of wit and imagination. The vast, mysterious realm of outer space is the twentieth-century equivalent of Gilgamesh's untamed wilderness, Odysseus' wine-dark sea, and Dante's Christian cosmos. Just as the ancients looked across the lands beyond the sea to the earth's outermost reaches, so for moderns extraterrestrial space constitutes the unprobed celestial fringe of the universe. "On the deepest psychological level," explained Kubrick, "the film's plot symbolizes the search for God, and it postulates what is little less than a scientific definition of God."

More recently, the American movie industry produced a compelling science fiction trilogy in which digital wizardry plays a major role. *The Matrix* (1999), followed by *The Matrix Reloaded* (2003) and *The Matrix Revolutions* (2003), picture a world dominated by an artificial intelligence that uses human beings as sources of energy. The known world—the matrix—is actually a computer simulation, a virtual reality planted inside each human mind. Drawing elements from Classical mythology, the Bible, Lewis Carroll's *Alice in Wonderland*, Zen Buddhism, and the choreography of gravity-defying martial arts, the film introduced a unique photographic technique ("flow motion") that employs more than 100 meticulously coordinated still cameras to create extraordinary special effects. *The Matrix*, which explores ideas of time and space by way of both content and form, has become the single greatest influence on science fiction film of the twenty-first century.

---

violence—the familiar fare of the daily broadcast television news—unfolds with cinematic intensity, an effect embellished by powerful present-tense narrative and vivid characterization.

### READING 37.4 Oates' "Ace" (1988)

A gang of overgrown boys, aged eighteen to twenty-five, has taken over the northeast corner of our park again this summer. Early evenings they start arriving, hang out until the park closes at midnight. Nothing to do but get high on beer and dope, the police leave them alone as long as they mind their own business, don't hassle people too much. Now and then there's fighting but nothing serious—nobody shot or stabbed. 1

Of course no girl or woman in her right mind would go anywhere near them, if she didn't have a boyfriend there.

Ace is the leader, a big boy in his twenties with a mean baby-face, pouty mouth, and cheeks so red they look fresh-slapped, sly little steely eyes curling up at the corners like he's laughing or getting ready to laugh. He's six foot two weighing maybe two hundred twenty pounds—lifts weights at the gym—but there's some loose flabby flesh around his middle, straining against his belt. He goes bare-chested in the heat, likes to sweat in the open air, muscles bunched and gleaming, and he can show off his weird tattoos—ace of spades on his right bicep, inky-black octopus on his left. Long shaggy hair the color of dirty sand and he wears a red sweatband for looks. 10 ... 20

Nobody notices anything special about a car circling the park, lots of traffic on summer nights and nobody's watching then there's this popping noise like a firecracker and right away Ace screams and claps his hand to his eye and it's streaming blood—what the hell? Did somebody shoot him? His buddies just freeze not knowing what to do. There's a long terrible minute when everybody stands there staring at Ace not knowing what to do—then the boys run and duck for cover, scattering like pigeons. And Ace is left alone standing there, crouched, his hand to his left eye screaming, Help, Jesus, hey, help, my eye—Standing there crouched at the knee like he's waiting for a second shot to finish him off. 30

The bullet must have come at an angle, skimmed the side of Ace's face, otherwise he'd be flat-out dead lying in the scrubby grass. He's panicked though, breathing loud through his mouth saying, O Jesus, O Jesus, and after a minute people start yelling, word's out there's been a shooting and somebody's hurt. Ace wheels around like he's been hit again but it's only to get away, suddenly he's walking fast stooped over dripping blood, could be he's embarrassed, doesn't want people to see him, red headband and tattoos, and now he's dripping blood down his big beefy forearm, in a hurry to get home. 40

Some young girls have started screaming. Nobody knows what has happened for sure and where Ace is headed people clear out of his way. There's blood running down his chest, soaking into his jeans, splashing onto the sidewalk. His friends are scared following along after him asking where he's going, is he going to the hospital, but Ace glares up out of his one good eye like a crazy man, saying, Get the fuck away! Don't touch me! and nobody wants to come near. 50

On the street the cops stop him and there's a call put in for an ambulance. Ace stands there dazed and shamed and the cops ask him questions as if he's to blame for what happened, was he in a fight, where's he coming from, is that a bullet wound?—all the while a crowd's gathering, excitement in the air you can feel. It's an August night, late, eighty-nine degrees and no breeze. The crowd is all strangers, Ace's friends have disappeared. He'd beg the cops to let him go but his heart is beating so hard he can't get his breath. Starts swaying like a drunk man, his knees so weak the cops have to steady him. They can smell the panic sweat on him, running in rivulets down his sides. 60

In the ambulance he's held in place and a black orderly tells him he's O.K., he's going to be O.K., goin' to be at the hospital in two minutes flat. He talks to Ace the way you'd talk to a small child, or an animal. They give him some quick first aid trying to stop the bleeding but Ace can't control himself can't hold still, he's crazy with fear, his heart gives a half-dozen kicks then it's off and going—like a drum tattoo right in his chest. The ambulance is tearing along the street, siren going, Ace says **70** O God O God O God his terrible heartbeat carrying him away.

He's never been in a hospital in his life—knows he's going to die there.

Then he's being hauled out of the ambulance. Stumbling through automatic-eye doors not knowing where he is. Jaws so tight he could grind his teeth away and he can't get his breath and he's ashamed how people are looking at him, right there in the lights in the hallway people staring at his face like they'd never seen anything so terrible. He can't keep up with the attendants, knees buckling and his heart beating so hard **80** hard but they don't notice, trying to make him walk faster, Come on man they're saying, you ain't hurt that bad, Ace just can't keep up and he'd fall if they weren't gripping him under the arms then he's in the emergency room and lying on a table, filmy white curtains yanked closed around him and there's a doctor, two nurses, What seems to be the trouble here the doctor asks squinting at Ace through his glasses, takes away the bloody gauze and doesn't flinch at what he sees. He warns Ace to lie still, he sounds tired and annoyed as if Ace is to blame, how did this happen he asks but doesn't wait for any **90** answer and Ace lies there stiff and shivering with fear clutching at the underside of the table so hard his nails are digging through the tissue-paper covering into the vinyl, he can't see out of his left eye, nothing there but pain, pain throbbing and pounding everywhere in his head and the nurses—are there two? three?—look down at him with sympathy he thinks, with pity he thinks, they're attending to him, touching him, nobody has ever touched him so tenderly in all his life Ace thinks and how shamed he is hauled in here like this flat on his back like this bleeding like a stuck pig and **100** sweating bare-chested and his big gut exposed quivering there in the light for everybody to see—

The doctor puts eight stitches in Ace's forehead, tells him he's damned lucky he didn't lose his eye, the bullet missed it by about two inches and it's going to be swollen and blackened for a while, next time you might not be so lucky he says but Ace doesn't catch this, his heart's going so hard. They wrap gauze around his head tight then hook him up to a machine to monitor his heartbeat, the doctor's whistling under his breath like he's surprised, lays the flat of his hand against Ace's **110** chest to feel the weird loud rocking beat. Ace is broken out in sweat but it's cold clammy sick sweat, he knows he's going to die. The machine is going bleep-bleep-bleep high-pitched and fast and how fast can it go before his heart bursts?—he sees the nurses looking down at him, one of the nurses just staring at him, Don't let me die Ace wants to beg but he'd be too ashamed. The doctor is listening to Ace's heartbeat with his stethoscope, asks does he have any pain in his chest, has he ever had an attack like this before, Ace whispers no but too soft to be heard, all the blood has drained from his face and **120** his skin is dead-white, mouth gone slack like a fish's and toes like ice where Death is creeping up his feet: he can feel it.

The heart isn't Ace's heart but just something inside him

gone angry and mean pounding like a hammer pounding pounding pounding against his ribs making his body rock so he's panicked suddenly and wants to get loose, tries to push his way off the table—he isn't thinking but if he could think he'd say he wanted to leave behind what's happening to him here as if it was only happening in the emergency room, there on that table. But they don't let him go. There's an outcry in the place **130** and two orderlies hold him down and he gives up, all the strength drained out of him and he gives up, there's no need to strap him down the way they do, he's finished. They hook him up to the heart monitor again and the terrible high-pitched bleeping starts again and he lies there shamed knowing he's going to die he's forgotten about the gunshot, his eye, who did it and was it on purpose meant for him and how can he get revenge, he's forgotten all that covered in sick clammy sweat his nipples puckered and the kinky hairs on his chest wet, even his belly button showing exposed from the struggle and how silly and **140** sad his tattoos must look under these lights where they were never meant to be seen.

One of the nurses sinks a long needle in his arm, and there's another needle in the soft thin flesh of the back of his hand, takes him by surprise, they've got a tube in there, and something coming in hot and stinging dripping into his vein the doctor's telling him something he can't follow, This is to bring the heartbeat down the doctor says, just a tachycardia attack and it isn't fatal try to relax but Ace knows he's going to die, he can feel Death creeping up his feet up his legs like stepping **150** out into cold water and suddenly he's so tired he can't lift his head, couldn't get up from the table if they unstrapped him. And he dies—it's that easy. Like slipping off into the water, pushing out, letting the water take you. It's that easy.

They're asking Ace if he saw who shot him and Ace says, Naw, didn't see nobody. They ask does he have any enemies and he says, Naw, no more than anybody else. They ask can he think of anybody who might have wanted to shoot him and he says, embarrassed, looking down at the floor with his one good eye, Naw, can't think of nobody right now. So they let him go. **160**

Next night Ace is back in the park out of pride but there's a feeling to him he isn't real or isn't the same person he'd been. One eye bandaged shut and everything looks flat, people staring at him like he's a freak, wanting to know What about the eye and Ace shrugs and tells them he's O.K., the bullet just got his forehead. Everybody wants to speculate who fired the shot, whose car it was, but Ace stands sullen and quiet thinking his own thoughts. Say he'd been standing just a little to one side the bullet would have got him square in the forehead or plowed right into his eye, killed him dead, it's something to think about **170** and he tries to keep it in mind so he'll feel good. But he doesn't feel good. He doesn't feel like he'd ever felt before. His secret is something that happened to him in the hospital he can't remember except to know it happened and it happened to him. And he's in a mean mood his head half-bandaged like a mummy, weird-looking in the dark, picking up on how people look at him and say things behind his back calling him Ace which goes through him like a razor because it's a punk name and not really his.

Mostly it's O.K. He hides how he feels. He's got a sense of **180** humor. He doesn't mind them clowning around pretending they hear gunshots and got to duck for cover, nobody's going to remember it for long, except once Ace stops laughing and backhands this guy in the belly, low below the belt, says in his old jeering voice, What do you know?—you don't know shit.

- **Q** **How would you describe the character, Ace?**
- **Q** **What aspects of contemporary American culture does Oates treat?**

## The Visual Arts in the Information Age

In the last half-century the visual arts have been overwhelmingly diverse in styles and techniques. Collectively, they are characterized by an indebtedness to mass media and electronic technology, by an emphasis on process and medium, and by Postmodern parody and irony. High-tech materials—fiberglass, Plexiglas, stainless steel, neon, and polyester resin—have become as commonplace in the art world of the last fifty years as marble, clay, and oil paints were in the past 500. Performance and environmental art reach out of the studio and into daily life. The mixed-media experiments of early Modernism have expanded to include film, video, television, and the computer.

The electronic media have revolutionized the visual arts of our time: computer-manipulated photographs, virtual environments, and mixed-media installations are among the unique projects of the Information Age. The electronic synthesis of music, video, dance, and performance opens up new kinds of theatrical experience, some of which invite the participation of the audience. In the Information Age, the image, and especially the moving image, has assumed a position of power over the printed word. In fact, the visual image has come to compete—in value and in authority—with all other forms of cultural expression.

Artists of the Information Age have joined popular musicians and world-class athletes in becoming the superstars of contemporary society. The art of prominent living painters, sculptors, and performance artists may command fortunes comparable to those of former industrial barons. Critics and gallery owners compete with websites to influence the marketing and commercialization of art, so that (for better or for worse) artists have become celebrities and art has become "big business."

### Pop Art

Pop Art, the quintessential style of the Information Age, embraced the imagery of consumerism and celebrity culture as mediated by television, film, and magazines. As a style, it departed dramatically from postwar abstraction, giving new life to the Western representational tradition. Its subject matter, however, while rendered in an overtly realistic style, was filtered through the prism of commercial advertising.

The term "Pop Art" was coined in the 1950s by a group of British artists who began to paste advertisements clipped from American magazines into their artworks. The movement came to fruition in New York a decade later. In the 1960s, 60 percent of America's population owned television sets. Commercial products, stage and screen personalities, along with the newsworthy events of the day, came to life via an image-driven medium that—more compelling than any printed vehicle—took its viewers hostage in their own living rooms.

The pioneer American Pop Artist Andy Warhol (1931–1987) dryly explained the meaning of the new style: "Pop Art," he observed, "is about liking things." Trained as a commercial artist, Warhol took some of his earliest subject matter from the shelves of the supermarket. While he hand-painted his first Brillo boxes, Campbell's soup cans, and Coca-Cola bottles on canvas, he soon turned to the photo-silkscreen technique of commercial advertising to reproduce the images mechanically (thereafter employing studio assistants to replicate them). Warhol's media-documented silkscreens of social violence, such as the civil rights riots of the 1960s, share the deadpan objectivity of his Coca-Cola bottles (see Figure 37.2). Warhol worked to depersonalize a subject by enlarging it or reproducing it in monotonous, postage-stamp rows resembling supermarket displays. Rendered by way of impersonal advertising techniques, his iconic portraits of political figures and celebrities (Figure 37.3) challenged traditional distinctions between fine and applied art, even as they endorsed art as a saleable commodity.

**Figure 37.2 ANDY WARHOL**, *Green Coca-Cola Bottles*, 1962. Oil on canvas, 6 ft. 10½ in. × 4 ft. 9 in.

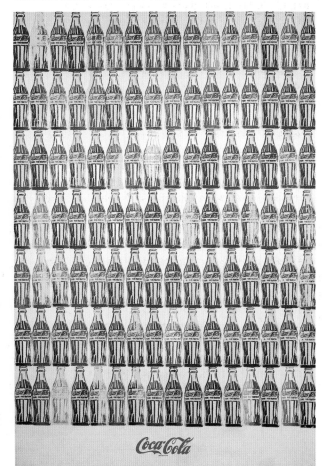

**Figure 37.3 ANDY WARHOL,** *Mint Marilyn Monroe,* 1962. Oil and silkscreen enamel on canvas, 20½ × 16½ in. Marilyn Monroe, a glamorous blonde film star of the 1950s, died in what was thought to be a drug overdose in 1962. A talented comic actor, she became an iconic figure in American entertainment history.

## Warhol and Experimental Film

Andy Warhol pioneered some of the most novel experiments in Postmodern film. Between 1963 and 1968 he produced sixty experimental films. He focused a fixed camera on a single object and let it "roll" until the film ran out—thus bringing to film the (uniquely cinematic) "dead time" between "events," as John Cage had brought to music the "silence" between moments of sound. In *Outer and Inner Space* (1965), Warhol experimented with double-screen formats to present multiple versions of his female "star" watching images of herself on televised videotape. Warhol also exploited the "long take": in the homoerotic film *My Hustler* (1967) a single thirty-minute shot documents the interaction between two gay men who groom themselves before the bathroom sink.

Jasper Johns (b. 1930), an artist whose career has spanned more than half a century, shared Warhol's interest in commonplace objects. When Willem de Kooning quipped that Johns' high-powered art dealer could sell anything—even two beer cans—Johns created *Painted Bronze* (1960), a set of bronze-cast, hand-painted cans of ale (Figure **37.4**). Johns' beer cans, like his early paintings of flags and targets, are Neodada tributes to Marcel Duchamp (see Figure 33.6), whom Johns knew personally. Some critics see them as Postmodern parodies of the cherished icons of contemporary culture. But they are also mock-heroic commentaries on the fact that art, like beer, is a marketable commodity.

Among the most witty vehicles of pop parody are the monumental soft vinyl sculptures of Claes Oldenburg (b. 1929)—gigantic versions of such everyday items as clothespins, hot dogs, table fans, typewriter erasers, and toilets. Often enlarged ten to twenty times their natural size, these objects assume a comic vulgarity that forces us to reconsider their presence in our daily lives (Figure **37.5**).

The oversized paintings of Roy Lichtenstein (1923–1997), modeled on comic-book cartoons, bring attention to familiar clichés and stereotypes of popular entertainment. Violence and romance are trivialized in the fictional lives of Lichtenstein's superheroes and helpless women (Figure **37.6**). Like other Pop Artists, Lichtenstein employed commercial techniques, including stencil and airbrush; he imitated the Benday dots used in advertising design to achieve tonal gradation. The resulting canvases, with their slickly finished surfaces and flat, bold shapes, are burlesque versions of mass-media advertisements. Ironically, the commercial world has now "reclaimed" Pop Art: just as Warhol and Lichtenstein appropriated the

**Figure 37.4 JASPER JOHNS,** *Painted Bronze (Beer Cans),* 1960. Painted bronze, 5½ × 8 × 4¼ in.

Figure 37.5 **CLAES OLDENBURG**, *Clothespin*, Central Square, Philadelphia, 1976. Cor-ten (steel) and stainless steel, 45 ft. × 12 ft. 3 in. × 4ft. 6in.

## Art Film

Traditional film usually obeys a narrative sequence or presents a story; experimental film, however, like Léger's *Ballet méchanique* (see chapter 34) and Warhol's *Outer and Inner Space,* explores the artistic potential of the medium itself. Narrative-free films, often called "art films," depend exclusively on the associational nuances evoked by sequences of imaginatively juxtaposed images. Like Rauschenberg's silkscreen collages, the experimental films of Bruce Conner (1930–2008) consist of footage assembled from old newsreels, pornographic movies, and Hollywood films. They may achieve additional effect by being "choreographed" to a specific musical score, such as with Conner's first film, *The Movie* (1958). As with music, Conner's films defy explicit meaning; the power to arouse emotions lies with an ingenious cinematic union of image and sound.

Ushering in the new millennium is *Cremaster 3* (2002), the final segment in a five-part, ten-hour-long film cycle conceived by Matthew Barney (b. 1967). A ritualistic, non-narrative behemoth that interweaves many disparate subjects, from the construction of the Chrysler Building to the differentiation of male and female sexuality, this complex work makes its impact by way of lush, disquieting, and (often) erotic images. The film is best compared to a fevered dream: powerful, perverse, haunting—and ultimately, inscrutable.

Figure 37.6 **ROY LICHTENSTEIN**, *Torpedo . . . Los!*, 1963. Oil on canvas, 5 ft. 8 in.× 6 ft. 8 in.

images of popular culture, so commercial advertising and fashion design freely "quote" from the works of these two artists.

## Assemblage

Art that combines two- and three-dimensional elements has a history that reaches back to the early twentieth century—recall Picasso's collages and Duchamp's modified ready-mades. Since the middle of that century, however, the American artist Robert Rauschenberg (1925–2008) monumentalized the art of *assemblage* in works that incorporate what he wryly referred to as "the excess of the world." Boldly assembling old car tires, street signs, broken furniture, and other debris, he produced artworks he called "combines." These creations attack the boundary between painting and sculpture. They work, as did the artist himself, "in the gap between art and life."

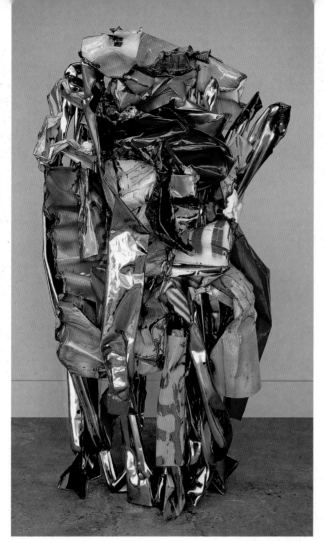

Rauschenberg was an extraordinary printmaker. For more than fifty years, he experimented with a wide variety of transfer techniques, lithograph, and silkscreen, to produce large-scale prints whose images are drawn from contemporary magazines and newspapers (see Figure 37.1). His disparate bits and pieces of cultural debris appear thrown together, as if all were equally valuable (or equally useless). But this bewildering array of visual information is assembled with an impeccable sensitivity to color, shape, and form. Rauschenberg's sly juxtaposition of familiar "found" images—like the visual scramble of Postmodern channel-grazing—invites viewers to create their own narratives.

Numerous artists have used assemblage to bring attention to the random and violent aspects of contemporary society. John Chamberlain (b. 1927) has created seductive sculptures out of junked automobiles, whose corroded sheet-metal bodies and twisted steel bumpers suggest the transience of high-tech products and the dangers inherent in their misuse (Figure 37.7). Louise Nevelson (1900–1988) collected wooden boxes, filled them with discarded fragments of found and machine-made objects, and painted them a uniform black, white, or gold. Like decaying altarpieces, these huge structures enshrine the vaguely familiar and haunting refuse of modern materialist culture (Figure 37.8).

## Geometric Abstraction

Not all contemporary artists have embraced the ironic stance of pop and assemblage art. Some remained loyal to the nonobjective style of *geometric abstraction*, first initiated

**Figure 37.7 JOHN CHAMBERLAIN**,
*Debonaire Apache*, 1991.
Painted and chromium plated steel,
7 ft. 10 in. × 4 ft. 6¾ in. × 4 ft. 2½ in.

**Figure 37.8 LOUISE NEVELSON**, *Royal Tide IV* 1960. Wood, with gold spray technique, 86 × 40 × 8 in. Nevelson, who came to the United States from Kiev, Ukraine, at the age of six, did not receive significant critical attention until she was sixty-eight years old. She selected wood as her creative medium to avoid, as she explained, the distraction of color.

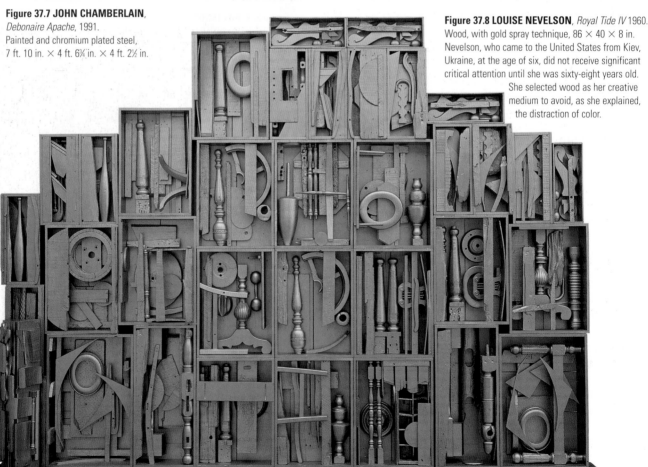

Figure 37.9 **FRANK STELLA**, *Tahkt-i-Sulayman I*, from the "Protractor" series, 1967. Polymer and fluorescent paint on canvas, 10 ft. ¼ in. × 20 ft. 2¼ in.

in painting by Malevich and Mondrian (see chapter 32). Obedient to the credo of the Bauhaus architect Mies van der Rohe that "less is more," these artists have pursued the machinelike purity of elemental forms, occasionally enlarging such forms to colossal sizes.

Early in his career, the American artist Frank Stella (b. 1936) painted huge canvases consisting of brightly colored, hard-edged geometric patterns that look as though they are made with a giant protractor (Figure **37.9**). The canvases in the "Protractor" series, which are named individually after the ancient circular cities of Asia Minor, depart from the standard square and rectangular format. Shaped like chevrons, circles, or triangles, they are fastened together to create unique geometric configurations. Stella's more recent artworks are flamboyant steel and aluminum pieces that capture in three dimensions the intensity of a Jackson Pollock painting. Nevertheless, the artist continues to reject value-oriented art in favor of a style that is neutral and impersonal. "All I want anyone to get out of my paintings, and all I ever get out of them, is the fact that you can see the whole thing without confusion," explains Stella: "What you see is what you see."

## Op Art

The idea that what one sees is determined by *how* one sees has been central to the work of Hungarian-born Victor Vasarely (1908–1997) and Britain's Bridget Riley (b. 1931). Both Vasarely and Riley explore the operation of conflicting visual cues and the elemental effects of colors and shapes on the faculties of the human retina—a style known as *Optical Art*, or *Op Art*. In Riley's *Current* (Figure **37.10**), a series of curved black lines painted on a white surface creates the illusion of vibrating movement and elusive color—look for yellow by staring at the painting for a few minutes.

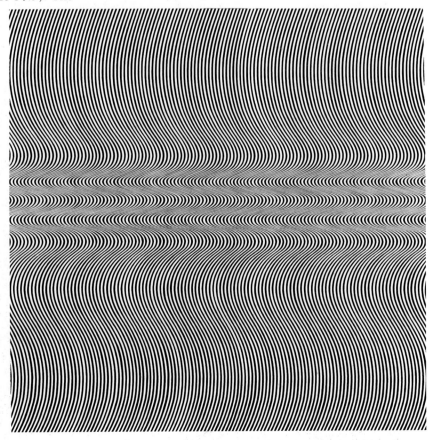

Figure 37.10 **BRIDGET RILEY**, *Current*, 1964. Synthetic polymer paint on composition board, 4 ft. 10⅞ in. × 4 ft. 10⅞ in.

## Minimal Art

While Europeans pioneered optical abstraction, Americans led the way in the development of *Minimalism*. Minimalist sculptors developed a refined industrial aesthetic that featured elemental forms made of high-tech materials. The geometric components of Minimalist artworks are usually factory-produced and assembled according to the artist's instructions.

The untitled stainless steel and Plexiglas boxes of Donald Judd (1928–1994) protrude from the wall with mathematical clarity and perfect regularity (Figure **37.11**). They resemble a stack of shelves, yet they neither contain nor support anything. The visual rhythms of Judd's serial

forms create a dialogue between space and volume, between flat, bright enamel colors and dull or reflective metal grays, and between subtly textured and smooth surfaces.

More monumental in scale are the primal forms of the Japanese-American sculptor Isamu Noguchi (1904–1988). Poised on one corner of its steel and aluminum frame, Noguchi's gigantic *Cube* (Figure **37.12**) shares the purity of form and the mysterious resonance of the Egyptian pyramids and the crystal monolith in the film *2001*.

## New Realism

During the 1970s, there emerged a new approach to figural realism that emphasized the stop-action stillness and sharp-focus immediacy of the photograph. *New Realism* (also called *Neorealism*, *Hyperrealism*, and *Photorealism*) differs from previous realist styles (including Social Realism and Pop Art) in its disavowal of narrative content and its indifference to moral, social, and political issues. Although decidedly representational, it is as impersonal as Minimal art.

Most New Realists do not seek to imitate natural phenomena; rather, they recreate an artificially processed view

**Figure 37.11 DONALD JUDD**, *Untitled*, 1967. Green lacquer on galvanized iron, each unit 9 in. × 3 ft. 4 in. × 31 in. The space between the elements in this series takes on visual significance. As Judd explained, "Actual space is intrinsically more powerful and specific than paint on a flat surface."

**Figure 37.12 ISAMU NOGUCHI**, *Cube*, 1968. Steel subframe with aluminum panels, height 28 ft. Minimal sculptures play an important role as public artworks. This monumental piece playfully relieves the monotonous uniformity of high-rise office buildings in Manhattan's financial district.

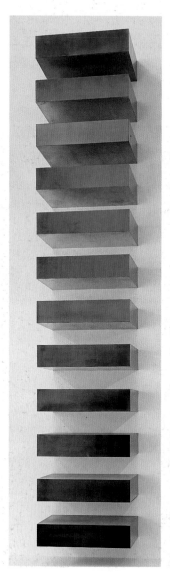

**Figure 37.13** (above) **RICHARD ESTES**, *Double Self Portrait*, 1976. Oil on canvas, 24 × 36 ft. Ostensibly a view of an urban restaurant, the plate glass façade takes in reflections of the buildings across the street, the sidewalk trees, and Estes himself (along with his photographic equipment).

**Figure 37.14** (below) **CHUCK CLOSE**, *Self-Portrait*, 1991. Oil on canvas, 100 × 84 in. After suffering a spinal blood clot in 1988, the partially paralyzed artist experimented with applying bits of colored paper and fingerprints to create the individual dots on the canvas.

of reality captured by the photographic image. Richard Estes (b. 1936), for instance, paints urban still lifes based on fragments of the photographs that he himself makes (Figure **37.13**). A virtuoso painter, Estes tantalizes the eye with details refracted by polished aluminum surfaces and plate-glass windows.

Chuck Close (b. 1940) transfers a photographic image to canvas after both photograph and canvas have been ruled to resemble graph paper; each square of the photo is numbered to correspond to an equivalent square on the canvas. He then fills each square with tiny gradations of color that resemble the pixels of a television screen (Figure **37.14**). While his early monochromatic works resemble impersonal "mug shots," his more recent portraits have the familiar look of televised "talking heads." They make use of new techniques involving multiple dots of color within each square.

High-tech materials and techniques have made possible the fabrication of New Realist sculptures that are shockingly lifelike. Duane Hanson (1925–1996) used fiberglass-reinforced polyester resin to recreate the appearance of ordinary and often working-class individuals in their everyday occupations (Figure **37.15**). He cast his polyester figures from live models, then added wigs, clothing, and accessories. Hanson's "living dead" are symbolic of modern life at its most prosaic.

**Figure 37.15 DUANE HANSON**, *Tourists*, 1970. Fiberglass and polyester polychromed, 5 ft. 4 in. × 5 ft. 5 in. × 3 ft. 11 in.

## Social Conscience Art

All art may be said to offer some perspective on the social scene; however, during the late twentieth century, many artists self-consciously assumed an activist, even missionary stance. Not overtly political nor even necessarily critical of the status quo, *social conscience art* seeks to transform

**Figure 37.16 LEON GOLUB**, *Interrogation II*, 1981. Acrylic on canvas, 10 ft. × 14 ft. Some of the imagery in Golub's two series, "Mercenaries" and "Interrogation," was based on newspaper photographs documenting specific incidents of political suppression, intimidation, and torture.

society by awakening its visionary potential. Such art works holistically to reclaim the spiritual authority that art once held in ancient societies. Issue-driven art, like social conscience literature, draws attention to ecological ruin and widespread drug use, to the threat of nuclear terrorism and the plight of marginalized populations, to decay in the quality of urban life and the erosion of moral values.

One of America's most outspoken social critics, Leon Golub (1922–2004), used figurative imagery based on Classical models to bring attention to state-sponsored aggression and political repression. Opposing both the Postmodern technology of war and the American presence in Vietnam, he painted large-sized canvases showing mercenary soldiers conducting acts of physical torture and gang violence (Figure **37.16**). Some of the assailants in these paintings stare blatantly at the viewer as they intimidate or mutilate their victims. Golub's oversized figures, whose national affiliations are left unidentified, appear against the indeterminate (usually red) background of his canvases, which he scraped and abraded to resemble ancient frescoes. Regarded during his lifetime as an "existential activist," Golub left visual statements that seem as relevant to former decades as to our own.

The Polish sculptor Magdalena Abakanowicz (b. 1930) draws on untraditional methods of modeling to cast hulking, life-sized figures that stage the drama of the human condition (Figure **37.17**). Sisal, jute, and resin-stiffened burlap make up the substance of these humanoids, whose scarred and patched surfaces call to mind earth, mud, and the dusty origins of primordial creatures. Abakanowicz installs her headless, sexless forms in groups that evoke a sense of collective anonymity and vulnerability. She brings to these works her experience as a survivor of World War II (and Poland's repressive communist regime).

## Total Art

The Information Age has generated creative strategies that reach beyond the studio and the art gallery and into the public domain. With *total art*, process (and conception) is generally more important than product—the work of art itself. Total art is a kind of communal ritual that involves planned (though usually not rehearsed) performance. The beginnings of total art are found in the aleatory enterprises of John Cage (see chapter 35) and in the wild experiments of the postwar Japanese Gutai Group (see chapter 35), whose artists/performers engaged their materials by pounding the canvas with

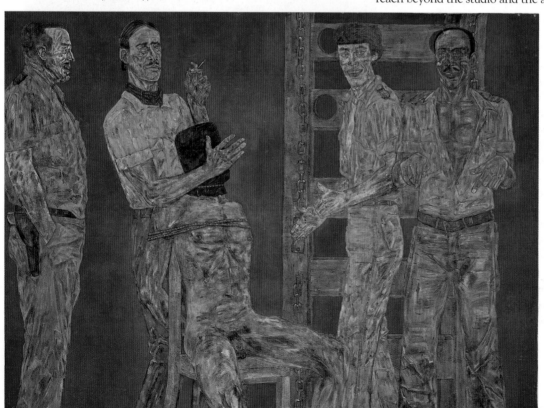

**Figure 37.17 MAGDALENA ABAKANOWICZ**, *Crowd 1* (detail), 1986–1987. Burlap and resin, 50 standing life-sized figures, each 5 ft. 6⅛ in. × 23⅜ in. × 11¾ in. In their denial of individuality and of human difference, these headless and sexless figures have been interpreted as a subtle criticism of Soviet ideology, that is, of communist collectivity; at the same time, they call to mind Ellul's "mass man."

paint-filled boxing gloves or hurling themselves against wet canvases. In one of the earliest examples of *performance art*, a work entitled *Anthropometry*, France's Yves Klein (1928–1962) employed nude women as "human brushes" (Figure **37.18**). Klein's contemporary Jean Tinguely (1925–1991) made a distinctive comment on twentieth-century technology with a series of machines he programmed to self-destruct amid a public spectacle of noise, fire, and smoke.

A classic kind of total art, the *Happening*, was pioneered by the American artist Allan Kaprow (1927–2006). Kaprow, who coined the name for this conceptual genre, called the Happening "a performance that occurs in a given time and space." Played out on a city street, a beach, or in a private home, the Happening involved a structured series of actions and scripted gestures. While conceived and directed by the artist, it welcomed chance and random elements. During the 1960s, Kaprow wrote and orchestrated more than fifty Happenings, most of which engaged dozens of ordinary people in the dual roles of spectator and performer. *Fluids* (1967), a Happening staged in Pasadena, California, called for participants to construct a house of ice blocks and then witness the melting process that followed. Like a ritual or theater piece, the performance was *itself* the artwork. The only record of its occurrence might be a photograph or videotape.

Obviously, performance art has limited value as a saleable commodity; yet, it has continued to attract artists

## Social Conscience Film

The late twentieth century was a golden age of cinematic creativity, an era in which the film medium (in alliance with television) reached a new level of social influence, its impact so great as to shape public opinion. The innovative films of the directors/artists who emerged in the 1970s and 1980s re-established the Hollywood film industry, which had faltered financially prior to the mid 1960s. The new directors, products of film schools rather than the Hollywood studio system, contributed to a reassessment of America's "master narratives" and dominant fictions: Arthur Penn's *Little Big Man* (1970), for example, exposed the myth of the Native American as "savage." Robert Altman, one of America's finest director/artists, launched a biting satire on the Korean War (and war in general) with the film *M*A*S*H* (1970). The image of the passive, male-dependent female was transformed in the film *Thelma and Louise* (1991), directed by Ridley Scott, and the plight of transgendered individuals was explored in Kimberly Peirce's *Boys Don't Cry* (1999). Filmmakers of the late twentieth century worked to develop signature styles, using cinematic and editing techniques (as sculptors use their media) to create effect and audience response. So, for instance, Altman favored the telephoto zoom lens to probe the faces of his (usually) socially troubled characters; fractured sounds and bits of dialogue overlap or intrude from off-camera. To achieve lifelike spontaneity, Altman often invited his actors to improvise as he filmed. In *Nashville* (1974), he traded the single cinematic

protagonist for some two dozen characters involved in a presidential election. Postmodern in style, Altman's films are vast kaleidoscopic scenarios, the products of judiciously assembled fragments. Issue-driven subjects were common fare in the history of late modern American film. But they have rarely been treated as powerfully as in Steven Spielberg's *Schindler's List* (1993), a story of the Holocaust adapted from Thomas Keneally's prize-winning 1982 novel. A virtuoso filmmaker, Spielberg made brilliant use of the techniques of documentary newscasting to create visually shattering effects.

Social conscience film is by no means confined to the United States. In *Salaam Bombay!* (1988), filmed in the brothel district of Bombay, one of India's leading filmmakers, Mira Nair, exposed the sordid lives of that country's illiterate street urchins. China's internationally celebrated filmmaker and cinematographer Zhang Yimou (b. 1951) lived among the peasants of Shaanxi Province prior to making films about China's disenfranchised rural population (*The Story of Qiu Ju*, 1992) and in particular its courageous women, many of whom remain hostage to feudal and patriarchal traditions (*Raise the Red Lantern*, 1991). An admirer of Ingmar Bergman and Akira Kurosawa (see chapter 35), Zhang rejected the socialist realism of the communist era in favor of purity of vision and fierce honesty. His films, at least three of which have been banned in China, are noted for their sensuous use of color and their troubling insights into moral and cultural issues.

Figure 37.18 **YVES KLEIN**, *Anthropometry ANT49*, 1960.

and participants. It has influenced the ways in which the Information Age processes many of its communal events: political demonstrations, rock concerts, and "raves" are "staged" like the rituals of total art.

A somewhat more permanent type of total art involves the remaking or transformation of a specific space. Room-sized installations, popular since the 1970s, invite the viewer into the work of art itself. One such piece, a "walk-in infinity chamber" consisted of mirrors studded with hundreds of miniature lights. Another was filled with menacing, fur-covered furniture, and yet another retooled the interior of an Airstream trailer with thousands of sparkling black and white beads. To such installations might be added recorded sound and even preconfigured odors.

The most ambitious of all total art genres is the *Earthwork*, a kind of installation that takes the natural landscape as both its medium and its subject. Also known as *Environmental* (or *site-specific*) *art*, earthworks are usually colossal, heroic, and temporary. Some, like Smithson's *Spiral Jetty* (see Figure 38.4), have ecological implications; others, however, are aesthetic transformations of large physical spaces or their landmarks.

The site-specific projects of the American husband-and-wife team Christo and Jeanne-Claude (both b. 1935), represent some of the most inventive examples of total art. The two artists have magically transformed rural and urban sites by embellishing or enveloping them with huge amounts of fabric. They have wrapped monumental public structures, such as the Pont Neuf in Paris and the Reichstag in Berlin, and they have reshaped nature, wrapping part of the coast of Australia, for instance, and surrounding eleven islands in Miami's Biscayne Bay with over six million square feet of pink woven polypropylene fabric. In 2005, they lined the 23-mile-long footpath of Manhattan's Central Park with 7500 saffron-colored fabric flags—a 16-day-long spectacle called "The Gates."

One of Christo and Jeanne-Claude's earliest projects, *Running Fence* (Figure **37.19**), involved the construction of a nylon "fence" 24½ miles long and 18 feet high. The nylon panels were hung on cables and steel poles and ran through Sonoma and Marin Counties, California, to the Pacific Ocean. The fence itself, meandering along the California hills like a modern-day version of the Great Wall of China, remained on site for only two weeks. Unlike Smithson, these artists do not seek to remake the natural landscape; rather they modify it temporarily in order to dramatize the difference between the natural world and the increasingly artificial domain of Postmodern society.

Figure 37.19 **CHRISTO AND JEANNE-CLAUDE**, *Running Fence*, Sonoma and Marin counties, California, 1972–1976. Nylon panels on cables and steel poles, height 18 ft., length 24½ miles. The installation of the "fence" mobilized the efforts of a large crew of workers and cost the artists over three million dollars. The fascinating history of this landmark piece is documented in films, photographs, and books.

**Figure 37.20 DAMIEN HIRST**, *The Physical Impossibility of Death in the Mind of Someone Living*, 1991. Tiger shark, glass, steel, 5% formaldehyde solution. Hirst, who considers himself a conceptual artist, commissioned the fisherman who caught the shark to find a specimen "big enough to eat you." The original shark was poorly preserved and had to be replaced in 2006.

Total art is generally conceptual, since it is driven by ideas rather than by purely visual or formal concerns. Perhaps the purest kind of *conceptual art*, then, is that which consists only of words. Since the 1960s, a variety of artists have created artworks that feature definitions, directions, or messages. Barbara Kruger's billboard-style posters (see Figure 36.15) combine photographic images and words that make cryptic comment on social and political issues.

The superstar of conceptual art is the American sculptor Jenny Holzer (b. 1950). Holzer carves paradoxical and often subversive messages in stone or broadcasts them electronically on public billboards. She often transmits her slogans by way of light-emitting diodes, a favorite medium of commercial advertising. In language that is at once banal and acerbic, Holzer informs us that "Lack of charisma can be fatal," "Myths make reality more intelligible," "Humanism is obsolete," "Decency is a relative thing," and "Ambivalence can ruin your life." Holzer's word-art tests the authority of public information, particularly as it is dispersed by contemporary digital media. Holzer's most recent work expands on the project *Truth Before Power* (2004), which displays large, silkscreened, declassified U. S. government documents, segments of which are obliterated by the censors' pen. By way of these cryptic images—official memos, records of interrogation, and accounts by military personnel that reflect recent U. S. foreign policy in the Middle East—the artist addresses issues of secrecy, censorship, and the manipulation of information associated with the politics of war.

### Art as Spectacle

The most recent trends in the art of the Information Age involve size and spectacle, that is, public performance or theatrical display. Such art, often technically complex, may be conceived by artists but fabricated by studio assistants or professional contractors. In the tradition of Duchamp's urinal (see Figure 33.6), the originality of much of today's art lies with the artist's *idea*, rather than with the physical creation of the artwork. The realization of the idea has become inseparable from art-world marketing and commercial display. When the bad boy of British art, Damien Hirst (b. 1965), exhibited his first dead animals (a shark, a sheep, and a cow) immersed in huge containers of formaldehyde, along with severed animal limbs and live maggots, the public found his work shocking (while collectors paid in the millions for each piece).

Hirst's *The Physical Impossibility of Death in the Mind of Someone Living* (1991), which consists of a shark preserved in a glass vitrine filled with formaldehyde, is one of a number of the artist's large-scale ruminations on death and decay (Figure **37.20**). This dangerous creature—familiar to us by way of the modern aquarium, as well as via television and film—is here hauntingly stilled, as remote and yet as palpable as the idea of death.

Public art, that is, art commissioned for outdoor sites, often assumes the nature of spectacle. One popular example of such is *Puppy* (1992), a 43-foot-high image of a West Highland Terrier conceived by the American artist-impresario Jeff Koons (b. 1955) as a topiary covered with colorful live flowers.

## Architecture in the Information Age

Some contemporary critics link the birth of Postmodernism to the architecture of the 1960s and, specifically, to the demise of the International Style. The American Robert Venturi (b. 1925), who first introduced architectural Postmodernism in his book *Complexity and Contradiction in Architecture* (1966), countered Mies van der Rohe's dictum "less is more" with the claim "less is a bore." Venturi rejected the anonymity and austerity of the glass and steel skyscraper (see Figure 35.14) and the concrete high rise (see Figure 32.26), along with the progressive utopianism of Modernists who hoped to transform society through functional form. Instead, he opted for an

**Figure 37.21 PEREZ ASSOCIATES WITH CHARLES MOORE, RON FILSON, URBAN INNOVATIONS, INC.**, Piazza d'Italia, New Orleans, 1976–1979.

architecture that emphasized visual complexity, individuality, and outright fun.

In contrast to the machinelike purity of the International Style structure, the Postmodern building is a playful assortment of fragments "quoted" from architectural traditions as ill-mated as a fast-food stand and a Hellenistic temple. Postmodern architecture, like Postmodern fiction, engages a colorful mix of fragments in a whimsical and often witty manner. It shares with *Deconstructivist* literary theorists the will to dismantle and reassemble "the text" in a search for its multiple meanings.

Just as there is (according to Deconstructivism) no single text for the whole of our experience, so there is no unifying pattern or defining style in the design of any single piece of architecture.

One example of this Postmodern aesthetic is the Piazza d'Italia in New Orleans, designed by Charles Moore (1925–1993). The plaza, which serves as an Italian cultural center, is a burlesque yet elegant combination of motifs borrowed from Pompeii, Palladio, and Italian Baroque architecture (Figure **37.21**). Its brightly colored colonnaded portico—looking every bit like a gaudy stage set—is adorned with fountains, neon lights, and polished aluminum balustrades. Moore's parodic grab-bag appropriation of the Italian heritage culminates in an apron shaped like a map of Italy that floats in the central pool of the piazza.

The Chinese-born American I. M. Pei (b. 1913) wedded Postmodern design to Minimalist principles in his inventive design for the courtyard of the Louvre Museum in Paris (Figure **37.22**). Three small steel and Plexiglas pyramids surround a central pyramid that covers the formal museum entrance. The large pyramid, which rises to a height of 70 feet, consists of 673 glass segments. Striking in its geometric simplicity, it looks back to Paxton's modular Crystal Palace (see Figure 30.26), to Buckminster Fuller's geodesic dome (see Figure 35.18), and to the steel-and-glass Minimalism of the International Style (Figure 32.25). The courtyard itself is a Postmodern triumph: it sets a twentieth-century version of the Great Pyramid at Giza amidst the wings of seventeenth-century Classical Baroque buildings. Futuristic in spirit, Pei's pyramid complex has become a kind of space station for the arts.

Since the beginning of the new millennium, many of the world's largest cities have been enjoying a "building boom." A great era of museum construction and expansion appears to be in process. Museums have become sacred spaces, visited by millions not only to see great art, but to

**Figure 37.22 I. M. PEI & ASSOCIATES**, Louvre Pyramid, Paris, 1988. The angle of the slope of the pyramid that marks the Louvre entrance is almost identical with that of ancient Egypt's Great Pyramid of Khufu at Giza.

enjoy an experience unlike that of other leisure activities. Some of the new art venues compete in their futuristic impact with Frank Lloyd Wright's Guggenheim Museum (see Figures 35.16 and 35.17). The expanded Milwaukee Museum of Art, designed by the Spanish-born Santiago Calatrava (b. 1951), is a case in point. Dominating the shore of Lake Michigan like the skeleton of a large bleach-boned dinosaur, its signature element is a 90-foot-high glass-enclosed reception hall covered by a movable wing-like sun screen (*brise-soleil*) made of 72 steel fins that control the temperature and light of the interior (Figure **37.23**). A 250-foot-long suspension bridge with angled cables links downtown Milwaukee to the lakefront and the museum. Calatrava, who has designed some extraordinary hotels and bridges throughout the world, brings a new bravura to steel-and-glass building construction.

The architectural giant of our time, Frank Gehry (b. 1930), was born in Toronto, Canada, but lives and works in California. His early buildings reflect an interest in humble construction materials, such as plywood, corrugated zinc, stainless steel, and chainlink fencing, which he assembled in serial units. Gehry's structures, in which façades tilt, columns lean, and interior spaces are skewed, reflect his deliberate rejection of the Classical design principles of symmetry and stability. More recently, in monumental projects that combine steel, titanium, glass, and limestone, he has developed a vocabulary of undulating forms and irregular shapes inspired by everyday objects: a fish, a guitar, a bouquet of flowers. Gehry's latest masterpiece is the Walt Disney Concert Hall in Los Angeles, California (see Figure 37.24). The 2265-seat hall engages glass curtain-walls and a majestic multileveled lobby; but it is in the breathtaking design of the exterior, with its billowing, light-reflecting stainless steel plates, that the building achieves its singular magnificence. His concert hall, like his highly acclaimed Guggenheim Museum in Bilbao, Spain (1997), combines the spontaneous vitality of action painting with the heroic stability of Minimalist sculpture.

Gehry's creative process is intuitive: he designs "in his head," develops the contours on paper and in models, and then makes use of five aerospace engineers and a sophisticated computer to direct the cutting of the actual building parts. In contrast to Gehry, younger architects are designing directly on computers, their virtual structures animated by curved, morphed forms. "Digital architecture" is still in its infancy, but it is likely that the buildings of the future will reflect the seductive morphing that Gehry has already anticipated in his sculptural designs.

**Figure 37.23 SANTIAGO CALATRAVA**, Milwaukee Art Museum, Milwaukee, Minnesota, 2003. Calatrava stated that in designing the museum, he "worked to infuse the building with a certain sensitivity to the culture of the lake—the boats, the sails, and the always changing landscape."

## Music in the Information Age

As with the visual arts and architecture, music since 1960 has been boldly experimental, stylistically diverse, and (with the exception of popular music) largely impersonal. Some late twentieth-century composers pursued the random style of John Cage, while others moved in the opposite direction, writing highly structured music that extends Schoenberg's serial techniques to pitch, counterpoint, and other aspects of composition. Two further developments are notable: First, in a discipline dominated for centuries by men, women composers and conductors have become increasingly visible—witness the Pulitzer Prize-winning American composer Ellen Taaffe Zwilich (b. 1938), and Sarah Caldwell (1924–2006), the Metropolitan Opera's first female conductor.

Second, electronic technology has affected all aspects of music, from composition and performance to distribution. Just as the electronic processes and media democratized the creation and distribution of images, so they have transformed the creation and reception of sound. The cheap and ready availability of digitally produced and reproduced music has worked to virtually eliminate the patronage system. It has also outmoded the avenues of commercial distribution that governed the music world of former decades.

### Electronic Music

In addition to its practical and commercial functions, electronic technology was responsible for the birth of entirely new types of sound. The history of electronic music began in the late 1950s, when John Cage and other avant-garde composers first employed magnetic tape to record and manipulate sound. By splicing and reversing the taped sounds of various kinds of environmental noise—thunder,

# MAKING CONNECTIONS

**Figure 37.24 FRANK GEHRY**, Walt Disney Concert Hall, Los Angeles, California, 2003.

As architecture has become more sculptural, so sculpture has become more architectural. The Postminimalist works of the American sculptor Richard Serra (b. 1939) share Gehry's (Figure **37.24**) affection for organic design and geometric regularity (Figure **37.25**). "There's an interconnection between the curvilinearity of Frank's building[s] and the obvious torquing of my pieces," says Serra. His monumental steel-rusted ellipses, which often measure more than 13 feet tall and 50 feet long (and can weigh well over 100 tons), reflect the direction in public art that invites the viewer to be a participant rather than simply an observer. Serra expects the spectator to walk through and around the piece in time, that is, to become part of the piece itself.

**Figure 37.25 RICHARD SERRA** (from front to back), *Torqued Ellipse I*, 1996; *Double Torqued Ellipse*, 1998–1999; *Double Torqued Ellipse II*; *Snake*, 1996. These torqued sculptures were inspired by Serra's visit to Borromini's Church of San Carlo in Rome (see Figures 20.19 and 20.20), whose elliptical spaces intrigued the artist.

bird calls, train whistles, and ticking clocks— they introduced a musical genre known as *musique concrète*. This type of music made use of electronic equipment to record and/or modify pre-existing sounds, either natural, instrumental, or mechanically contrived.

The second kind of electronic music involves the use of special equipment to generate sound itself. "Pure" electronic music differs from *musique concrète* in its reliance on oscillators, wave generators, and other electronic devices. The pioneer in this type of music was the German composer Karlheinz Stockhausen (1928–2007). As musical director of the Studio for Electronic Music in Cologne, Germany, Stockhausen employed electronic devices both by themselves and to manipulate and combine pretaped sounds, including music generated by traditional instruments and voices. His compositions—atonal patterns of sounds and silence that lack any controlling frame of reference—renounce all conventional rules of rhythm and harmony. Editing taped sounds as a filmmaker edits footage, Stockhausen dispensed with a written score and composed directly on tape, thus assuming simultaneously the roles of composer and performer. Like a Kaprow "happening" or a jazz improvisation, a Stockhausen composition is an artform in which process becomes identical with product.

The most revolutionary musical invention of the late 1960s was the computerized **synthesizer**, an electronic instrument capable of producing sounds by generating and combining signals of different frequencies. This artificial sound generator serves for both the production and manipulation of sound. Stockhausen's American contemporary Milton Babbitt (b. 1916) was the first composer to use the RCA Synthesizer to control the texture, timbre, and intensity of electronic sound. While traditional instruments produce only seventy to eighty pitches and a limited range of dynamic intensities, electronic devices like the synthesizer offer a range of frequencies from fifty to 15,000 cycles per second. This capacity provides the potential for almost unlimited variability of pitch. Further, electronic instruments can execute rhythms at speeds and in complex patterns that are beyond the capability of live performers. Because such features defy traditional notation, electronic music is often graphed in acoustical diagrams that serve as "scores."

Since the 1970s, portable digital synthesizers have been attached to individual instruments. These allow musicians to manipulate the pitch, duration, and dynamics of sound even as the music is being performed. The synthesizer has facilitated the typically Postmodern technique known as *sampling*. A sample is a short, "borrowed" segment of recorded sound, which may be stored digitally, manipulated at will (stretched out, played backwards, and so on), then reintroduced into another musical phrase or composition. As one critic points out, what one does with sounds has become more important than what the sounds are. Electronic sampling has generated sounds and strategies

See Music Listening Selections at end of chapter.

that, like the jump-cuts of Postmodern film, capture the fragmentation and tumultuousness of Postmodern life.

While musical instruments can be manipulated by computers, computers themselves have become "musical instruments." Equipped with a miniature keyboard, faders, and foot pedals, the digital computer is not only capable of producing a full range of sounds but is also able to produce and reproduce sounds more subtle and complex than any emitted by human voices or traditional musical instruments. For better or for worse, sound generators have now begun to replace musicians in the studio and in staged musical performances.

Two further developments may be mentioned. The hyperinstrument projects of Tod Machover (b. 1953) involve the use of electronically enhanced instruments, as well as "homemade" interactive instruments, that offer both musicians and nonmusicians a new range of performance possibilities. A second direction features the use of the computer itself to compose original music. The American composer Barton McLean (b. 1938), for instance, uses a Lightpen to draw the contours of sound waves on the video screen of a sophisticated computer that "emits" the composition.

## Microtonality and Minimal Music

The Hungarian composer György Ligeti (1923–2006) took an interest in electronic music after meeting Stockhausen and other avant-garde composers in Cologne. While inspired by its unique sounds, he composed few electronic pieces. Nevertheless, in his instrumental works, he recreated some of its unique aural effects. To achieve the textures of electronic music, he made use of **microtonality** (the use of musical intervals smaller than the semitones of traditional European and American music, but common to the music of India and the Near East). Almost completely lacking melody and harmony, Ligeti's technique, which he called "micropolyphony," produced dense clusters of sound: subtle, shimmering currents that murmur in a continuous, hypnotic flow. His instrumental *Atmospheres* (1961), and his choral work *Lux Eterna* (1966), both of which appear on the soundtrack of the film *2001*, achieved a new sonority that, as the composer explained, "is so dense that the individual interwoven instrumental voices are absorbed into the general texture and completely lose their individuality."

Ligeti's subtly shifting patterns of sound would become a hallmark of the musical style known as *Minimalism*. Minimal music, like Minimal art, reduces the vocabulary of expression to elemental or primary components that are repeated with only slight variations. In the "stripped down" compositions of Minimal music, tonality and melody are usually simple, while rhythms and textures, built through minute repetition, are dense and complex.

The most notable of Minimalist composers, Philip Glass (b. 1937) received his early training in the fundamentals of Western musical composition. In the 1970s, however, after touring Asia and studying with the Indian sitar master Ravi Shankar (b. 1920), Glass began writing music that embraced the rhythmic structures of Indian *ragas*, progressive jazz, and rock and roll. The musical drama *Einstein on the Beach* (1976), which Glass produced in collaboration with the designer/director Robert Wilson (b. 1941), was the first opera performed at the Metropolitan Opera House in New York City to feature electronically amplified instruments.

Like traditional opera, *Einstein on the Beach* combines instrumental and vocal music, as well as recitation, mime, and dance. But it departs radically from operatic tradition in its lack of a narrative story line and character development, as well as in its instrumentation. The opera, which is performed with no intermissions over a period of four and a half hours, is not the story of Albert Einstein's life or work; rather, it is an extended poetic statement honoring the twentieth century's greatest scientist. The score consists of simple melodic lines that are layered and repeated in seemingly endless permutations. Mesmerizing and seductive, Glass' music recalls the texture of Gregorian chant, the sequenced repetitions of electronic tape loops, and the subtle rhythms of the Indian *raga*. Harmonic changes occur so slowly that one must, as Glass explains, learn to listen at "a different speed," a feat that closely resembles an act of meditation.

Historical themes have continued to inspire much of the music of Glass. In 1980, he composed the opera *Satyagraha*, which celebrates the achievements of India's pacifist hero Mohandas Gandhi (see chapter 36). Sung in Sanskrit and English, the opera uses a text drawn from the *Bhagavad Gita*, the sacred book of the Hindu religion. For the quincentennial commemoration of the Columbian voyage to the Americas, the composer wrote an imaginative modern-day analogue (*The Voyage*, 1992) that links the idea of great exploration to the theme of interplanetary travel. Glass' most recent opera *Appomattox* (2007) deals with the role of racism in America.

## Postmodern Opera

In the late twentieth century, opera found inspiration in current events such as international hijacking (John Adams' *Death of Klinghofer*), black nationalism (Anthony Davis' *X*), gay rights (Stewart Wallace's *Harvey Milk*), and the cult of celebrity—witness Ezra Laderman's *Marilyn* (Monroe), John Adams' *Nixon*, and Robert Xavier Rodriguez's *Frida* (Kahlo). Other composers turned to the classics of literature and art as subject matter for full-length operas: Carlyle Floyd's *Of Mice and Men* (1970) is based on John Steinbeck's novel of the same name; William Bolcom's *A View from the Bridge* (1999) is an adaptation of the Arthur Miller play; John Harbison's *Gatsby* (1999) was inspired by F. Scott Fitzgerald's novel *The Great Gatsby*; and Tennessee Williams' classic play *A Streetcar Named Desire* (1998) received operatic treatment by the American composer Andre Previn.

Few of these operas attained the compositional sophistication of the century's first typically Postmodern opera: *The Ghosts of Versailles* (1992) composed by John

Corigliano (b. 1938). Scored for orchestra and synthesizer and cast in the style of a comic opera, *Ghosts of Versailles* takes place in three different (and interlayered) worlds: the eighteenth-century court of Versailles, the scenario of a Mozartean opera, and the realm of the afterlife—a place peopled by the ghosts of Marie Antoinette and her court. The score commingles traditional and contemporary musical styles, alternating pseudo-Mozartean lyricism with modern dissonance in a bold and inventive (although often astonishingly disjunctive) manner. In the spirit of Postmodernism, Corigliano made historical style itself the subject; his multivalent allegory tests the text against past texts by having one of his characters in the opera suddenly exclaim, "This is not opera; Wagner is opera."

The use of video technology is the most striking development in the staging of twenty-first century operas. Recent performances of John Adams' *Doctor Atomic* (2005), which examines the role of Robert Oppenheimer in the genesis of the atom bomb, made use of both electronically amplified instruments and electronic visual effects (see chapter 38). Computerized images, infrared cameras, digital projectors and scrims constitute some of the "spectacle-producing technology" now employed in staging the great operas of past and present.

## Rock Music

The origins of the musical style called *rock* lay in the popular culture of the mid 1950s. The words "rocking" and "rolling," originally used to describe sexual activity, came to identify an uninhibited musical style that drew on a broad combination of popular American and African-American music, including country, swing, gospel, and rhythm and blues. Although no one musician is responsible for the birth of rock, the style gained popularity with such performers as Bill Haley, Little Richard, and Elvis Presley. In the hands of these flamboyant musicians, it came to be characterized by a high dynamic level of sound, fast and hard rhythms, a strong beat, and earthy, colloquial lyrics.

From its inception, rock music was an expression of a youth culture: the rock sound, associated with dancing, sexual freedom, and rebellion against restrictive parental and cultural norms, also mirrored the new consumerism of the postwar era. While 1950s rock and roll often featured superficial, "bubble gum" lyrics, 1960s rock became more sophisticated—the aural counterpart of Western-style Pop Art.

With the success of the Beatles—a British group of the 1960s—rock became an international phenomenon, uniting young people across the globe. The Beatles absorbed the music of Little Richard and also the rhythms and instrumentation of Indian classical music. They made imaginative use of electronic effects, such as feedback and splicing. Their compositions, which reflected the spirit of the Western counterculture, reached a creative peak in the album *Sergeant Pepper's Lonely Hearts Club Band* (1967). Although the electric guitar was in use well before the Beatles emerged, it was with this group that the instrument became the hallmark of rock music, and it remains the principal instrument of the rock musician.

---

See Music Listening Selections at end of chapter.

During the 1960s, "establishment" America faced the protests of a youthful counterculture that was disenchanted with middle-class values, mindless consumerism, and bureaucratic authority. Counterculture "hippies"—the word derives from "hipster," an admirer of jazz and its subculture—exalted a neoromantic lifestyle that called for peaceful coexistence, a return to natural and communal habitation, more relaxed sexual standards, and experimentation with mind-altering drugs such as marijuana and lysergic acid diethylamide (LSD). The use of psychedelic drugs among members of the counterculture became associated with the emergence of a number of British and West Coast acid rock (or hard rock) groups, such as The Who and Jefferson Airplane. The music of these groups often featured earsplitting, electronically amplified sound and sexually provocative lyrics. The decade produced a few superb virtuoso performers, like the guitarist Jimi Hendrix (1942–1970). The 1960s also spawned the folk-rock hero Bob Dylan (b. 1941), whose songs gave voice to the anger and despair of the American counterculture. Dylan's lyrics, filled with scathing references to modern materialism, hypocrisy, greed, and warfare—specifically, the American involvement in Vietnam—attacked the moral detachment of contemporary authority figures.

While rock music of the 1970s was less concerned with social and political issues, the next two decades brought some changes, including an increase in the number of female performers and the use of rock concerts to benefit social causes. Fundraising concerts engaged an international cast of musicians. Between the 1980s and the present, world music—African and Asian—has come to influence rock. Among the best representatives of this trend is the folk-rock musician Paul Simon (b. 1964), who introduced to Western audiences the sounds of Ladysmith Black Mambazo, a South African vocal group. More recently, the influence of the genre in fueling youth-driven anti-communist movements in Eastern Europe found expression in the play *Rock 'n' Roll* (2006) by Britain's leading playwright, Tom Stoppard (b. 1937).

## Dance in the Information Age

Composed in conjunction with *Einstein on the Beach*, the choreography of Lucinda Childs (b. 1940)—who also danced in the original production—followed a Minimalist imperative. In line with the hypnotic rhythms of the piece, her choreography featured serial repetitions of ritualized gestures and robotlike motions. Childs reduced the credo of pure dance to a set of patterned movements that were geometric, recurrent, and—for some critics— unspeakably boring.

The role of improvisation in dance—the legacy of Merce Cunningham—has had a more successful recent history. Contemporary companies such as the Sydney (Australia) Dance Company, Pilobolus, and Momix have produced exceptionally inventive repertories that embrace acrobatics, aerobics, gymnastics, vaudeville, and streetdance. Contemporary dance projects combine playful action and vigorous explorations of body movement.

One of the most energetic figures in contemporary choreography is the African-American Rennie Harris (b. 1964). Brought up in a crime-ridden section of North Philadelphia—without the luxury of formal dance training—Harris resolved to bring hip-hop dance to the concert stage. To achieve that goal, he founded his own dance company (Rennie Dance Puremovement) in 1992. His explosive choreography has transformed the violence of street gangs into a multimedia collage that features breakdancing and electronically "souped up" sound. Music of a more traditional kind is essential to the choreography of Seattle-born Mark Morris (b. 1956). Since the establishment of his own company in 1980, Morris has choreographed more than 100 dance pieces, all of which take music—from Mozart and Vivaldi to dance hall tunes and rock—as the source of structural clarity. Morris studies the score of the music to devise corresponding action motifs. His music-driven dances, such as his "take-off" on Tchaikovsky's *The Nutcracker Suite*, entitled *The Hard Nut* (1999), bring humor and irony to contemporary dance.

# LOOKING BACK

### The Information Explosion

- The last decades of the twentieth century witnessed a transformation from an industrially based world-culture to one shaped by mass media, electronic technology, and space travel.
- Television and other electronic phenomena altered basic modes of communication and facilitated global homogeneity, while computer technology made possible the accumulation and transmission of huge amounts of information.

- The shift from book to screen has altered our way of perceiving reality and has had consequences in all of the arts.

### New Directions in Science and Philosophy

- Late twentieth-century advances in science have moved toward a greater understanding of both outer space and the inner workings of our bodies.
- Physicists continue to pursue a "theory of everything" that might

reconcile Einstein's theory of relativity with the principles of quantum physics. String theorists have proposed a universal model consisting of tiny loops of vibrating strings. Chaos theorists identify common denominators in nature: patterns that may seem random, but are actually self-similar.

- The mapping of the human genome by molecular biologists has led to major advances in medicine and experimentation in genetic engineering.
- Twentieth-century philosophers have generally abandoned the search for absolute truths, and instead, have given attention to the limits of language as a descriptive tool.

## Literature in the Information Age

- The "Postmodern turn" accompanied the shift away from the anxious subjectivity and high seriousness of Modernism toward a skeptical and bemused attention to the history of culture and its myriad texts.
- Postmodern writers examine language as verbal coding and as a vehicle for both parody and social reform. They draw on the vast resources of history in works that often fictionalize history. The voice of the author may interrupt the narrative to produce the clipped rhythms of a videofictional style.
- Some contemporary writers bring critical attention to the realities of urban violence and social inequity, while others explore the genres of Magic Realism and science fiction.

## The Visual Arts in the Information Age

- The visual arts of the Information Age have not assumed any single, unifying style. Rather, they are diverse and eclectic, reflecting the Postmodern preoccupation with the media-shaped image, with parody and play, and with the contradictory nature of contemporary life. Distinctions between high and low art have become increasingly blurred.
- Andy Warhol was among the pioneers of American Pop Art, which glorified the mass-produced, commercial image. In the "combines" of Robert Rauschenberg, found objects became part of an inventive art of assemblage. Minimalism, championed by Donald Judd, utilized commercial and industrial materials in works that redefined the early twentieth-century credo of absolute abstraction. At the other extreme, Hyperrealists provided a phenomenally detailed slice of life.
- Painters, photographers, and filmmakers addressed social conscience in works that brought attention to the plight of marginalized populations, criminal violence, and political unrest.
- The *process* of making art overtook the importance of the *product* with the birth of the Happening and the site-specific installation projects that followed. In the case of Earthworks, the artist moved out of the studio and into the environment.

## Architecture in the Information Age

- One of the earliest manifestations of Postmodernism was in architectural design, where architects united a playful assortment of historical styles within a single structure, such as the Piazza d'Italia in New Orleans.
- The new millennium has witnessed a trend toward sculptural architecture, most evident in the expansive (computer-aided) designs for museums and theaters conceived by Santiago Calatrava and Frank Gehry.

## Music in the Information Age

- The music of the Information Age often deviated from traditional European modes of harmony and meter to incorporate microtonality, improvisation, and a variety of non-Western forms and instruments.
- The Minimalist compositions of Philip Glass feature hypnotic patterns of repetition inspired by traditional forms of Indian music. Contemporary issues as well as historical themes dominate Postmodern operas, composed in a variety of musical idioms.
- Electronic technology has had a massive effect on all phases of musical culture, from composition to performance and distribution. Such technology facilitated the modification of pre-existing sound (as in "concrete music"), but also made possible the creation of Karlheinz Stockhausen's electronic music.
- Rock music came to popularity as an expression of the youth culture of the 1960s. With the availability of portable digital synthesizers, the techniques of mixing and sampling, and the continuing influence of African and Asian sounds, rock has endured as a popular genre.

## Dance in the Information Age

- The minimal choreography of Lucinda Childs and the ongoing work of Merce Cunningham have been complemented by new styles and dance companies that integrate acrobatics, gymnastics, vaudeville, and street-dance, including hip-hop.
- The choreography of Mark Morris, unlike that of Cunningham, is directly inspired by and written for specific works of music.

---

### Music Listening Selections

**CD Two Selection 24** Babbitt, *Ensembles for Synthesizer*, 1951, excerpt.

**CD Two Selection 25** Glass, *Einstein on the Beach*, "Knee Play 1," 1976.

---

# Glossary

**microtonality** the use of musical intervals smaller than the semitones of traditional European and American music

**musique concrète** (French, "concrete music") a type of electroacoustic music that uses real or "concrete" sounds, such as street noises, human voices, bird calls, and thunder, that are recorded, altered, and assembled on magnetic tape

**silkscreen** a printmaking technique employing the use of a stenciled image cut and attached to finely meshed silk, through which printing ink is forced so as to transfer the image to paper or cloth; also called "seriography"

**synthesizer** an integrated system of electronic components designed for the production and control of sound; it may be used in combination with a computer and with most musical instruments

# Chapter

# 38

## Globalism:
## The Contemporary World
### ca. 1960–present

*"To choose what is best for both the near and distant futures is a hard task, often seemingly contradictory and requiring knowledge and ethical codes which for the most part are still unwritten."*
E. O. Wilson

**Figure 38.1 CHERI SAMBA**, *Little Kadogo*, 2004. Acrylic on canvas, 78¾ × 106 in. Cheri Samba (b. 1956), a native of the Democratic Republic of Congo, depicts a *kadogo* (Swahili slang for "child soldier"), who raises his hands in surrender. The hand of an armed adult behind him warns, however, that the killing might very well continue.

# LOOKING AHEAD

In 1962, the Canadian communications theorist Marshall McLuhan predicted the electronic transformation of the planet earth into a "global village."* In the global village, communication between geographically remote parts of the world would be almost instantaneous, and every important new development—technological, ecological, political, economic, and intellectual—would affect every villager to some degree. Social and geographic mobility, receptivity to change, and a sense of collectivity would be the hallmarks of this new world community. Over the past four decades, McLuhan's futuristic vision has become a reality.

The roots of *globalism*—the promotion of interdependence of cultures and peoples in all parts of the world—may be found in the industrial and commercial technologies of the late nineteenth century. But the single factor that has been most significant in bringing together all parts of the world is twentieth-century electronic (and more recently digital) technology. The global community of the twenty-first century is challenged by some distinct problems: the effects of globalism on established religious, national, and ethnic traditions; the future health of the world ecosystem; and the continuing threat of terrorism. Globalism and its effects provide the main themes of this chapter. In the arts, the focus is on the transformative influence of electronic technology on traditional and untraditional genres. The multiple and often contradictory messages and styles in the arts of the global community make our own time one of the most exciting in the history of the humanistic tradition.

## The Global Perspective

Globalism has become the new model or paradigm for the contemporary world. While accelerated by electronic technology, it owes much to a broad array of late twentieth-century developments: the success of anticolonial movements (see chapter 36), the fall of the Berlin Wall (1989) and subsequent collapse of Soviet communism, and the end of the cold war (see chapter 36). With the elimination of these obstacles to freedom of communication among the populations of the earth, global cultural integration became a possibility, then a reality. Television was essential in providing immediate images of international events, and effective in promoting Western values and consumer goods. As Western consumer culture took hold across Asia and the Near East, it met a mixed reception

---

* The term was coined by the British Modernist Wyndham Lewis (1882–1957) in *America and Cosmic Man* (1948).

(with some critics objecting to the "McDonaldization" of the world). In India and China, its effects were transformative, while in some parts of the Muslim-occupied Near East, it was to produce virulent anti-Western antipathy (with enormous consequences for world peace).

Globalism itself, however, remains an inevitable contemporary paradigm. In an international best-selling book entitled *The World is Flat: A Brief History of the Twenty-First Century* (2005), the Pulitzer Prize-winning journalist Thomas L. Friedman describes a world that has become metaphorically "flat." With the collapse of most of the age-old barriers—physical, historical, and nationalistic—the global landscape offers a new, level playing field to all who choose to compete in the international marketplace. Interlinked networks of computer services, communication satellites, fiber-optic cables, and work-flow software provide an untrammeled exchange of data and the free flow of goods and ideas. These tools continue to transform the planet into a single world community.

### Globalism and Tradition

Many parts of continental Africa have had a difficult time meeting the challenge of globalism. Following the end of colonialism and the withdrawal of Western powers from Africa, a void developed between African traditions and the Modernist ways of life introduced by the European presence. Some African states, especially those crippled by poverty and epidemic disease, have faced serious problems arising from this void. Power struggles in some African countries have resulted in the emergence of totalitarian dictatorships, and age-old ethnic conflicts have been reignited, all too often resulting in bloody civil wars (Figure **38.1**). Vast parts of Africa are thus caught in the sometimes devastating struggle between the old ways and the new.

Africa's leading English-language writer, Chinua Achebe (b. 1930), has dealt sensitively with such problems. In the short story "Dead Men's Path," he examines the warp between premodern and modern traditions and the ongoing bicultural conflicts that plague many parts of Africa. At the same time, he probes the elusive, more universal tensions between tradition and innovation, between spiritual and secular allegiance, and between faith and reason—tensions that continue to test human values in our time.

## READING 38.1 Achebe's "Dead Men's Path" (1972)

Michael Obi's hopes were fulfilled much earlier than he had     1
expected. He was appointed headmaster of Ndume Central
School in January 1949. It had always been an unprogressive
school, so the Mission authorities decided to send a young and
energetic man to run it. Obi accepted this responsibility with
enthusiasm. He had many wonderful ideas and this was an
opportunity to put them into practice. He had had sound
secondary school education which designated him a "pivotal
teacher" in the official records and set him apart from the
other headmasters in the mission field. He was outspoken in     10

his condemnation of the narrow views of these older and often less-educated ones.

"We shall make a good job of it, shan't we?" he asked his young wife when they first heard the joyful news of his promotion.

"We shall do our best," she replied. "We shall have such beautiful gardens and everything will be just *modern* and delightful. . . ." In their two years of married life she had become completely infected by his passion for "modern methods" and his denigration of "these old and superannuated **20** people in the teaching field who would be better employed as traders in the Onitsha market." She began to see herself already as the admired wife of the young headmaster, the queen of the school.

The wives of the other teachers would envy her position. She would set the fashion in everything. . . . Then, suddenly, it occurred to her that there might not be other wives. Wavering between hope and fear, she asked her husband, looking anxiously at him.

"All our colleagues are young and unmarried," he said with **30** enthusiasm which for once she did not share.
"Which is a good thing," he continued.

"Why?"

"Why? They will give all their time and energy to the school."

Nancy was downcast. For a few minutes she became sceptical about the new school; but it was only for a few minutes. Her little personal misfortune could not blind her to her husband's happy prospects. She looked at him as he sat folded up in a chair. He was stoop-shouldered and looked frail. **40** But he sometimes surprised people with sudden bursts of physical energy. In his present posture, however, all his bodily strength seemed to have retired behind his deep-set eyes, giving them an extraordinary power of penetration. He was only twenty-six, but looked thirty or more. On the whole, he was not unhandsome.

"A penny for your thoughts, Mike," said Nancy after a while, imitating the woman's magazine she read.

"I was thinking what a grand opportunity we've got at last to show these people how a school should be run." **50** Ndume School was backward in every sense of the word. Mr. Obi put his whole life into the work, and his wife hers too. He had two aims. A high standard of teaching was insisted upon, and the school compound was to be turned into a place of beauty. Nancy's dream-gardens came to life with the coming of the rains, and blossomed. Beautiful hibiscus and allamanda hedges in brilliant red and yellow marked out the carefully tended school compound from the rank neighbourhood bushes.

One evening as Obi was admiring his work he was scandalized to see an old woman from the village hobble right **60** across the compound, through a marigold flowerbed and the hedges. On going up there he found faint signs of an almost disused path from the village across the school compound to the bush on the other side.

"It amazes me," said Obi to one of his teachers who had been three years in the school, "that you people allowed the villagers to make use of this footpath. It is simply incredible." He shook his head.

"The path," said the teacher apologetically, "appears to be very important to them. Although it is hardly used, it connects **70** the village shrine with their place of burial."

"And what has that got to do with the school?" asked the headmaster.

"Well, I don't know," replied the other with a shrug of the shoulders. "But I remember there was a big row some time ago when we attempted to close it."

"That was some time ago. But it will not be used now," said Obi as he walked away. "What will the Government Education Officer think of this when he comes to inspect the school next week? The villagers might, for all I know, decide to use the **80** schoolroom for a pagan ritual during the inspection."

Heavy sticks were planted closely across the path at the two places where it entered and left the school premises. These were further strengthened with barbed wire.

Three days later the village priest of Ani called on the headmaster. He was an old man and walked with a slight stoop. He carried a stout walking-stick which he usually tapped on the floor, by way of emphasis, each time he made a new point in his argument.

"I have heard," he said after the usual exchange of **90** cordialities, "that our ancestral footpath has recently been closed. . . ."

"Yes," replied Mr. Obi. "We cannot allow people to make a highway of our school compound."

"Look here, my son," said the priest bringing down his walking-stick, "this path was here before you were born and before your father was born. The whole life of this village depends on it. Our dead relatives depart by it and our ancestors visit us by it. But most important, it is the path of children coming in to be born. . . ." **100**

Mr. Obi listened with a satisfied smile on his face.

"The whole purpose of our school," he said finally, "is to eradicate just such beliefs as that. Dead men do not require footpaths. The whole idea is just fantastic. Our duty is to teach your children to laugh at such ideas."

"What you say may be true," replied the priest, "but we follow the practices of our fathers. If you re-open the path we shall have nothing to quarrel about. What I always say is: let the hawk perch and let the eagle perch." He rose to go.

"I am sorry," said the young headmaster. "But the school **110** compound cannot be a thoroughfare. It is against our regulations. I would suggest your constructing another path, skirting our premises. We can even get our boys to help in building it. I don't suppose the ancestors will find the little detour too burdensome."

"I have no more words to say," said the old priest, already outside.

Two days later a young woman in the village died in childbed. A diviner was immediately consulted and he prescribed heavy sacrifices to propitiate ancestors insulted by the fence. **120**

Obi woke up next morning among the ruins of his work. The beautiful hedges were torn up not just near the path but right round the school, the flowers trampled to death and one of the school buildings pulled down.

. . . That day, the white Supervisor came to inspect the school and wrote a nasty report on the state of the premises

**Figure 38.2 EL ANATSUI**, *Between Earth and Heaven*, 2006. Aluminum, copper wire, 91 × 126 in. Widely regarded as Africa's most significant sculptor, El Anatsui teaches at the university of Nigeria.

The sculptures of the Ghanaian artist El Anatsui (b. 1944) reveal the intersection of traditional and contemporary African themes. *Between Earth and Heaven* (2006) consists of thousands of aluminum seals and screw caps from bottles of wine and liquor (Figure **38.2**). The caps are flattened and woven with copper wire to create large, shimmering metal tapestries. El Anatsui recycles discarded objects into compelling artworks whose designs and colors (gold, red, and black) have much in common with the decorative cotton-cloth textiles known as *kente* (Figure **38.3**). The handwoven *kente*—the name derives from the designs of baskets traditionally woven in the kingdom of Asante (modern Ghana)—belong to a royal textile tradition that reaches back to the eleventh century. Vibrant in color and complex in their patterns, these textiles have come to be associated with a pan-African identity.

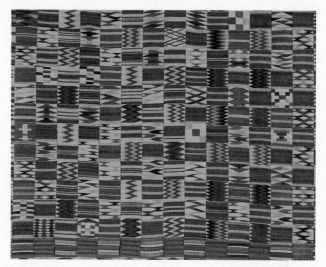

**Figure 38.3** Detail of a Sika Futura ("Gold Dust Aweaneasa") Asante *kente* textile, nineteenth to twentieth centuries. Whole textile 5 ft. 10½ in. × 5 ft. 11 in. The individual designs on the cloth are associated with seventeenth-century Asante kings who are said to have laid claim to specific signs and patterns.

but more seriously about the "tribal-war situation developing between the school and the village, arising in part from the misguided zeal of the new headmaster."

⌐ **Q** **How does this story illustrate the conflict between tradition and innovation?**

⌐ **Q** **What might the path in this story symbolize?**

# The Global Ecosystem

The future of the environment has become a major global concern. While modern industry brings vast benefits to humankind, it also works to threaten the global **ecosystem** (the ecological community and its physical environment). Sulphur dioxide emissions in one part of the world affects other parts of the world, causing acid rain that damages forests, lakes, and soil. Industrial pollution poisons the entire planet's oceans. Leaks in nuclear reactors endanger populations thousands of miles from their sites, and greenhouse gases (produced in part from the burning of the coal, oil, and natural gas that power the world's industries), contribute to global warming and other changes in the earth's climate. Although such realities have inspired increasing concern for the viability of the ecosystem, they have only recently attracted the serious attention of world leaders.

A landmark figure in the study of ecological systems is Edward Osborn Wilson (b. 1929). This distinguished sociobiologist is a leading defender of the natural environment. His early work in evolutionary biology examined parallels between ants and other animal societies, including those of human beings. More recently, he has proposed a new type of interdisciplinary research (which he calls "scientific humanism") that works to improve the human condition. In *The Diversity of Life*, Wilson makes a plea for the preservation of **biodiversity**, the variation of life forms within a given ecosystem. He seeks the development of a sound environmental ethic, shared by both "those who believe that life was put on earth in one divine stroke," and "those who perceive biodiversity to be the product of blind evolution." Wilson pleads for a practical ethic that will ensure the healthy future of the planet.

⌐ **READING 38.2** From Wilson's *The Diversity of Life* (1992)

Every country has three forms of wealth: material, cultural,    1
and biological. The first two we understand well because they are the substance of our everyday lives. The essence of the biodiversity problem is that biological wealth is taken much less seriously. This is a major strategic error, one that will be increasingly regretted as time passes. Diversity is a potential source for immense untapped material wealth in the form of food, medicine, and amenities. The fauna and flora are also part of a country's heritage, the product of millions of years of evolution centered on that time and place and hence as    10
much a reason for national concern as the particularities of language and culture.

The biological wealth of the world is passing through a bottleneck destined to last another fifty years or more. The human population has moved past 5.4 billion, is projected to reach 8.5 billion by 2025, and may level off at 10 to 15 billion by midcentury. With such a phenomenal increase in human biomass, with material and energy demands of the developing countries accelerating at an even faster pace, far less room will be left for most of the species of plants and    20
animals in a short period of time.

The human juggernaut creates a problem of epic dimensions: how to pass through the bottleneck and reach midcentury with the least possible loss of biodiversity and the least possible cost to humanity. In theory at least, the minimalization of extinction rates and the minimization of economic costs are compatible: the more that other forms of life are used and saved, the more productive and secure will our own species be. Future generations will reap the benefit of wise decisions taken on behalf of biological diversity by our generation.    30

What is urgently needed is knowledge and a practical ethic based on a time scale longer than we are accustomed to apply. An ideal ethic is a set of rules invented to address problems so complex or stretching so far into the future as to place their solution beyond ordinary discourse. Environmental problems are innately ethical. They require vision reaching simultaneously into the short and long reaches of time. What is good for individuals and societies at this moment might easily sour ten years hence, and what seems ideal over the next several decades could ruin future generations. To choose    40
what is best for both the near and distant futures is a hard task, often seemingly contradictory and requiring knowledge and ethical codes which for the most part are still unwritten.

If it is granted that biodiversity is at high risk, what is to be done? Even now, with the problem only beginning to come into focus, there is little doubt about what needs to be done. The solution will require cooperation among professions long separated by academic and practical tradition. Biology, anthropology, economics, agriculture, government, and law will have to find a common voice. Their conjunction has    50
already given rise to a new discipline, biodiversity studies, defined as the systematic study of the full array of organic diversity and the origin of that diversity, together with the methods by which it can be maintained and used for the benefit of humanity. The enterprise of biodiversity studies is thus both scientific, a branch of pure biology, and applied, a branch of biotechnology and the social sciences. It draws from biology at the level of whole organisms and populations in the same way that biomedical studies draw from biology at the level of the cell and molecule. . . .    60

The evidence of swift environmental change calls for an ethic uncoupled from other systems of belief. Those committed by religion to believe that life was put on earth in one divine stroke will recognize that we are destroying the Creation, and those who perceive biodiversity to be the product of blind evolution will agree. Across the other great philosophical divide, it does not matter whether species have independent rights or, conversely, that moral reasoning is uniquely a human    70 concern. Defenders of both premises seem destined to gravitate toward the same position on conservation.

The stewardship of the environment is a domain on the near side of metaphysics where all reflective persons can surely find common ground. For what, in the final analysis, is morality but the command of conscience seasoned by a rational examination of consequences? And what is a fundamental precept but one that serves all generations? An enduring environmental ethic will aim to preserve not only the health and freedom of our species, but access to the world in which      80
the human spirit was born.

— Q  **Why does Wilson contend that environmental problems are "innately ethical"?**

— Q  **Why does he regard "the stewardship of environment" as a global responsibility?**

The poets Gary Snyder (b. 1930) and Annie Dillard (b. 1943) share Wilson's concerns for the natural environment. To essays and poems inspired in part by her love for Virginia's Blue Ridge Mountains, Dillard brings a dimension of awe that has been called "ecospirituality." A Roman Catholic convert whose outlook is essentially pantheistic, Dillard tests the objective facts of nature against her mystical appreciation of its wonders. An excerpt from her Pulitzer Prize-winning book, *Pilgrim at Tinker Creek*, exemplifies the voice of the poet whose concerns are at once personal and global.

— **READING 38.3**  From Dillard's *Pilgrim at Tinker Creek* (1974)

. . . . Our life is a faint tracing on the surface of mystery. The      1
surface of mystery is not smooth, any more than the planet is smooth; not even a single hydrogen atom is smooth, let alone a pine. Nor does it fit together; not even the chlorophyll and hemoglobin molecules are a perfect match, for even after the atom of iron replaces the magnesium, long streamers of disparate atoms trail disjointedly from the rims of the molecules' loops. Freedom cuts both ways. Mystery itself is as fringed and intricate as the shape of the air in time. Forays into mystery cut bays and fine fiords, but the forested      10
mainland itself is implacable both in its bulk and in its most filigreed fringe of detail. "Every religion that does not affirm that God is hidden," said Pascal flatly, "is not true."

What is man, that thou are mindful of him? This is where the great modern religions are so unthinkably radical: the love of God! For we can see that we are as many as the leaves of trees. But it could be that our faithlessness is a cowering cowardice born of our very smallness, a massive failure of imagination. Certainly nature seems to exult in abounding radicality, extremism, anarchy. If we were to judge nature by its common sense or likelihood, we wouldn't believe the      20
world existed. In nature, improbabilities are the one stock-in-trade. The whole creation is one lunatic fringe. If creation had been left up to me, I'm sure I wouldn't have had the imagination

or courage to do more than shape a single, reasonably sized atom, smooth as a snowball, and let it go at that. No claims of any and all revelations could be so far-fetched as a single giraffe.

The question from agnosticism is, Who turned on the lights? The question from faith is, Whatever for? . . . .

Sir James Jeans, British astronomer and physicist,      30
suggested that the universe was beginning to look more like a great thought than a great machine. Humanists seized on the expression, but it was hardly news. We knew, looking around, that a thought branches and leafs, a tree comes to a conclusion. But the question of who is thinking the thought is more fruitful than the question of who made the machine, for a machinist can of course wipe his hands and leave, and his simple machine still hums; but if the thinker's attention strays for a minute, his simplest thought ceases altogether. And, as I have stressed, the place where we so incontrovertibly find      40
ourselves, whether thought or machine, is at least not in any way simple.

— Q  **How does Dillard picture humankind's place in the natural world?**

— Q  **To what does she attribute modern "faithlessness"?**

## Environmental Art

What Wilson calls "the stewardship of environment" has captured the imagination of some contemporary visual artists. Robert Smithson (1938–1973), for instance, pioneered one of the most important ecological landmarks of the late twentieth century, the piece known as *Spiral Jetty* (Figure **38.4**). Constructed on the edge of the Great Salt Lake in Utah, in waters polluted by abandoned oil mines, *Spiral Jetty* is a giant (1500 foot-long) coil consisting of 6650 tons of local black basalt, limestone, and earth. This snail-like symbol of eternity makes reference to ancient earthworks, such as those found in Neolithic cultures (see Figure 3.10), and to the origins of life in the salty waters of the primordial ocean; but it also calls attention to the way in which nature is constantly transforming the environment and its ecological balance.

When Smithson created *Spiral Jetty* in 1970, the lake was unusually shallow because of drought. Submerged twice by rising waters, the piece can now be seen again from ground level, its galactic coil partially encrusted with white salt crystals that float in the algae-filled rose-colored shallows. Earthworks like *Spiral Jetty* are often best appreciated from the air. Tragically, it was in the crash of a small airplane surveying a potential site that Smithson was killed.

## Green Architecture

Architects have always given practical consideration to the environment in which they build. Now, however, in the face of rising fuel prices, global warming, and the degradation of the ecosystem due to industrial growth, the job of designing structures that do the least possible damage to

**Figure 38.4 ROBERT SMITHSON**, *Spiral Jetty*, Great Salt Lake, Utah, 1970. Rock, salt crystals, earth algae; coil 1500 ft. The lake itself had been degraded by abandoned oil derricks. Documentary drawings, photographs, and films of *Spiral Jetty*, along with the recent rehabilitation of the earthwork itself, have heightened public awareness of the fragile balance between nature and culture.

the environment (a practice known as "green" or "sustainable" design), has become even more imperative. Green buildings—structures that are both friendly to the ecosystem and energy efficient—have been found to save money and preserve the environment. Although the United States launched the Green Building Council in 2000, fewer than 800 certified green buildings were constructed during the following seven years; however, the greening of architecture has become a global movement. It embraces architectural design that makes use of energy-efficient (and renewable) building materials, recycling systems that capture rainwater (for everyday use), solar panels that use sunlight to generate electricity, insulating glass, and other energy-saving devices and techniques.

Of the green buildings that have been constructed in the last ten years, one has already become a landmark: the Swiss Re office building (30 St. Mary Axe), designed in 2003 by the British architect Norman Foster (b. 1935), is London's first environmentally sustainable skyscraper (Figure **38.5**). Natural ventilation, provided by windows that open automatically, passive solar heating, and a double-glazed insulating glass skin (some 260,000 square feet of glass) are some of the features that work to reduce this forty-story building's energy costs by one-half of normal costs. While Foster's tower resembles a spaceship, its tall rounded picklelike shape has inspired Londoners to call it "the Gherkin."

**Figure 38.5 NORMAN FOSTER**, Swiss Re building (30 St. Mary Axe), London, 2003.

## Science and Technology

| | |
|---|---|
| **1962** | Rachel Carson's *Silent Spring* argues that man-made chemicals are damaging the earth's ecosystem |
| **1974** | American scientists demonstrate that chlorofluorocarbons (CFCs) are eroding the earth's ozone layer |
| **2006** | Al Gore publishes *An Inconvenient Truth: The Planetary Emergency of Global Warming and What We Can Do About It* |

**Figure 38.6 SHIRIN NESHAT**, *Rebellious Silence*, from "Women of Allah" series, 1994. Gelatin-silver print and ink.

# Globalism and Ethnic Identity

Ethnic identity—that is, one's bond to a group that shares the same cultural traditions, culture, and values—is a major theme in the global perspective. A "cluster" of traits (race, language, physical appearance, and religious values) that form one's self-image, ethnicity also differentiates the self from mass culture. The self-affirming significance of ethnic identity is apparent in the ancient Yoruba proverb: "I am because we are; what I am is what we are."

Ethnicity manifests itself in language, music, food, and ritual. Efforts to define and maintain ethnic identity have inspired many contemporary writers. In her poems, novels, and short stories, Leslie Marmon Silko (b. 1948) draws on the Pueblo folklore of her Native American ancestors; the Chinese-American writer Maxine Hong Kingston (b. 1940) blends fiction and nonfiction in novels that deal with family legends and native Chinese customs. The oral tradition—stories handed down from generation to generation, often by and through women—plays an important part in the works of these authors, even as it does in the formation of ethnic identity.

Ethnicity has also become a theme in the visual arts. We have seen earlier in this chapter evidence of one African artist's homage to his ethnic identity (see Figure 38.2). Other examples occur in the visual arts, especially photography and film. The latter are the favorite media of

Iranian-born Shirin Neshat (b. 1957), who now lives in New York City. Neshat's art deals with conflicting ethnic values and lifestyles: Islamic and Western, ancient and modern, male and female. Her photographic series, *Women of Allah* (1993–1997) explores the role of militant women who fought in the 1979 revolution that overthrew Iran's ruling dynasty. Neshat makes dramatic use of the *chador* (the large veil of black cloth that has become an ethnic symbol of Muslim women) to frame her face, which, intersected by a rifle, becomes the site of a poem (by the feminist writer Forough Farrokhzad, 1935–1967) transcribed in Farsi calligraphy (Figure **38.6**).

## Latino Culture

The process of globalization and the rise of ethnicity have accelerated yet another major phenomenon: immigration—the age-old process of people moving from *mother* country to *other* country—has increased dramatically in recent years. Every year, some 100 million people leave (or try to leave) their places of birth in search of political or economic advantage. This mass migration of peoples has resulted in the establishment of large ethnic communities throughout the world. The vast numbers of immigrants who have made the United States their home have had a dramatic impact: demographic changes, in the form of rising numbers of Asians and Latinos—persons from the various Latin American countries—have changed the face of the economy, the urban environment, and the culture. If current trends continue, by the year 2050 Latinos will constitute 30 percent of the population in the United States.

In all aspects of life, from literature and art to food and dance styles, there has been a flowering of Latino culture. With *The Mambo Kings Play Songs of Love* (1989), the first novel by a Hispanic to win the Pulitzer Prize, the Cuban-American Oscar Hijuelos (b. 1951) brought attention to the impact of Latin American music on American culture, and, more generally, to the role of memory in reclaiming one's ethnic roots. Younger writers have given voice to personal problems of adjustment in America's ethnic mosaic and to the ways in which language and customs provide a vital sense of ethnic identity. These are the themes pursued by one of today's leading *Chicana* (Mexican-American female) authors, Sandra Cisneros (b. 1954). Cisneros, who describes the struggle of Chicana women in an alien society, writes in the familiar voice of everyday speech. Of her writing style, she says:

> It's very much of an anti-academic voice—a child's voice, a girl's voice, a poor girl's voice, a spoken voice, the voice of an American Mexican. It's in this rebellious realm of antipoetics that I tried to create a poetic text with the most unofficial language I could find.

Cisneros dates the birth of her own political consciousness from the moment (in a graduate seminar on Western literature) she recognized her "otherness," that is, her separateness from the dominant culture. A vignette from *The House on Mango Street*, her classic novel, describes the experience of a young girl growing up in the Latino section of Chicago. It illustrates the shaping role of language and memory in matters of identity.

## READING 38.4 Cisneros' "No Speak English" from *The House on Mango Street* (1984)

*Mamacita*[1] is the big mama of the man across the street,-    1
third-floor front. Rachel says her name ought to be *Mamasota*,[2]
but I think that's mean.

The man saved his money to bring her here. He saved and
saved because she was alone with the baby boy in that
country. He worked two jobs. He came home late and he left
early. Every day.

Then one day *Mamacita* and the baby boy arrived in a yellow
taxi. The taxi door opened like a waiter's arm. Out stepped a
tiny pink shoe, a foot soft as a rabbit's ear, then    10
the thick ankle, a flutter of hips, fuchsia roses and green
perfume. The man had to pull her, the taxicab driver had to
push. Push, pull. Push, pull. Poof!

All at once she bloomed. Huge, enormous, beautiful to look
at, from the salmon-pink feather on the tip of her hat down to
the little rosebuds of her toes. I couldn't take my eyes off her
tiny shoes.

Up, up, up the stairs she went with the baby boy in a blue
blanket, the man carrying her suitcases, her lavender hatboxes,
a dozen boxes of satin high heels. Then we didn't    20
see her.

Somebody said because she's too fat, somebody because
of the three flights of stairs, but I believe she doesn't come
out because she is afraid to speak English, and maybe this is
so since she only knows eight words. She knows to say: *He not
here* for when the landlord comes, *No speak English* if
anybody else comes, and *Holy smokes*. I don't know where she
learned this, but I heard her say it one time and it surprised me.

My father says when he came to this country he ate    30
hamandeggs for three months. Breakfast, lunch and dinner.
Hamandeggs. That was the only word he knew. He doesn't eat
hamandeggs anymore.

Whatever her reasons, whether she is fat, or can't climb
the stairs, or is afraid of English, she won't come down. She
sits all day by the window and plays the Spanish radio show
and sings all the homesick songs about her country in a voice
that sounds like a seagull.

Home. Home. Home is a house in a photograph, a pink
house, pink as hollyhocks with lots of startled light. The man    40
paints the walls of the apartment pink, but it's not the same,
you know. She still sighs for her pink house, and then I think
she cries. I would.

Sometimes the man gets disgusted. He starts screaming
and you can hear it all the way down the street.

*Ay*, she says, she is sad.

---

[1] "Little Mama," also a term of endearment.
[2] "Big Mama."
[3] "When?"
[4] An exclamation, loosely: "Good grief."

Oh, he says. Not again.
*¿Cuándo, cuándo, cuándo?*[3] she asks.
*¡Ay, caray!*[4] We are home. This *is* home. Here I am and
here I stay. Speak English. Speak English. Christ!    50
*¡Ay, Mamacita*, who does not belong, every once in a while
lets out a cry, hysterical, high, as if he had torn the only skinny
thread that kept her alive, the only road out to that country.
And then to break her heart forever, the baby boy, who has
begun to talk, starts to sing the Pepsi commercial he heard on
T.V.

No speak English, she says to the child who is singing in
the language that sounds like tin. No speak English, no speak
English, and bubbles into tears. No, no, no, as if she can't
believe here ears.    60

## Q How does Cisneros bring Mamacita to life? What makes her a sympathetic figure?

No less than in literature, the visual arts document the Latino effort to preserve or exalt ethnic identity: Yolanda López (b. 1942) appropriates a popular Latin American icon of political resistance—the Virgin of Guadalupe (see Figure 20.2). She transforms the Mother of God into the autobiographical image of an exuberant marathon athlete outfitted in track shoes and star-studded cape (redolent of both Our Lady and Wonder Woman, Figure 38.7).

**Figure 38.7 YOLANDA M. LÓPEZ**, *Portrait of the Artist as the Virgin of Guadalupe*, part 3 from the "Guadalupe Triptych," 1978. Oil pastel on paper, 30 × 24 in.

The popular history of Latino culture also served as inspiration for Luis Jiménez (1940–2007). Born to Mexican parents in El Paso, Texas, Jiménez constructs life-sized, brightly colored fiberglass sculptures. These call attention to Mexican contributions to American culture and to the ongoing problems related to the migration of thousands of Mexicans across the United States/Mexican border. The 10-foot-high, totemlike sculpture called *Border Crossing (Cruzando El Rio Bravo)* evokes the heroic Mexican view of the crossing as a rite of passage heralding a transformation in status and lifestyle (Figure **38.8**).

## Ethnic Conflict

The exercise of ethnic identity has become a powerful social and political force in the global perspective. Having cast off the rule of foreign powers and totalitarian ideologies, ethnic peoples have sought to reaffirm their primary affiliations—to return to their spiritual roots. "Identity politics," the exercise of power by means of group solidarity, has—in its more malignant guise—pitted ethnic groups against each other in militant opposition. In Africa, the

**Figure 38.8 LUIS JIMÉNEZ**, *Border Crossing (Cruzando El Rio Bravo)*, 1989. Fiberglass with urethane finish, 10 ft. 7 in. × 4 ft. 6 in. × 4 ft. 6 in. The artist dedicated this piece to his father, who entered the United States legally in 1924.

Middle East, the Balkans, the Indian subcontinent, and the former Soviet Union, efforts to revive or maintain ethnic identity have coincided with the bitter and often militant quest for solidarity and political autonomy. Nowhere is this more evident than in the ongoing conflict between Palestinians and Israelis who lay claims to the same ancient territories of the Middle East. Hostilities between the Arab (and essentially Muslim) population of Palestine and the Jewish inhabitants of Israel preceded the establishment of an independent Jewish state in 1947. However, these have become more virulent in the past few decades, and the move toward peaceful compromise has only just begun.

The life of the Palestinian poet Mahmoud Darwish (1942–2008) was one of displacement and exile. Born to Sunni Muslim parents in a Palestinian village that was destroyed by Israel in 1948, Darwish lived in dozens of cities across the globe. Holding the bizarre status of a "present-absent alien," however, he remained a refugee from his homeland. Regarded by Palestinians as their poet laureate, this "poet in exile" published some twenty volumes of verse. His passion to redeem his lost homeland is expressed in a simple, yet eloquent, style illustrated in the poem "Earth Presses Against Us."

Darwish's Israeli counterpart, Yehuda Amichai (1924–2000) was born in Germany but moved to Palestine in 1936. Raised as an Orthodox Jew amidst Israel's turbulent struggle to become a state, Amichai began writing poetry in 1948. Israel's favorite poet takes as his themes the roles of memory, homeland, and religious faith. His poem, "The Resurrection of the Dead," looks beyond the immediacy of ethnic turmoil to consider both the weight of past history and the promise of the future.

## READING 38.5 The Poems of Darwish and Amichai

**Darwish's "Earth Presses Against Us" (2003)**

Earth is pressing against us, trapping us in the final passage.  1
To pass through, we pull off our limbs.
Earth is squeezing us. If only we were its wheat, we might die and yet live.
If only it were our mother so that she might temper us with mercy.
If only we were pictures of rocks held in our dreams like mirrors.
We glimpse faces in their final battle for the soul, of those who will be killed
by the last living among us. We mourn their children's feast.  10
We saw the faces of those who would throw our children out of the windows
of this last space. A star to burnish our mirrors.
Where should we go after the last border? Where should birds fly after the last sky?
Where should plants sleep after the last breath of air?
We write our names with crimson mist!
We end the hymn with our flesh.
Here we will die. Here, in the final passage.
Here or there, our blood will plant olive trees.  20

**Amichai's "The Resurrection of the Dead" (2004)**

We are buried below with everything we did,                    1
with our tears and our laughs.
We have made storerooms of history out of it all,
galleries of the past, and treasure houses,
buildings and walls and endless stairs of iron and marble
in the cellars of time.
We will not take anything with us.
Even plundering kings, they all left something here.
Lovers and conquerors, happy and sad,
they all left something here, a sign, a house,            10
like a man who seeks to return to a beloved place
and purposely forgets a book, a basket, a pair of glasses,
so that he will have an excuse to come back to the beloved place.
In the same way we leave things here.
In the same way the dead leave us.

(Translated, from the Hebrew, by Leon Wieseltier.)

**Q** How does each of these poets deal with history, memory, and hope?

**Q** Why do you think there is no mention of religion in either poem?

## The Challenge of Globalism

### Terrorism

Probably the greatest single threat to the global community is *terrorism*, the deliberate and systematic use of violence against civilians in order to achieve political, religious, or ideological goals. As a combat tactic, terrorism is not new; however, rapid forms of communication and transportation, and the availability of more virulent weaponry make contemporary terrorism both imminent and politically devastating. Terrorist attacks have taken place all over the world, from Madrid to Mumbai. One of the most ruthless involved a coordinated assault on New York's World Trade Center and the Pentagon in Washington, D.C. On September 11, 2001, Islamic militants representing the radical Muslim group known as al-Qaeda ("the base") hijacked four American airliners, flying two of them into the twin towers in Manhattan, and a third into the headquarters of the U. S. Department of Defense near the nation's capital. A fourth crashed before it could reach its target: the White House.

Masterminded by al-Qaeda's leader, Osama bin Laden (b. 1957), the attack, now called "9-11," killed more than 3000 civilians. Bin Laden justified the operation as retaliation for America's military presence and eco-political interference in the predominantly Muslim regions of the Middle East. Terrorist assaults on other primarily Western targets throughout the world underline the troubling rift between the ideology of radical Islamists defending strict Qur'anic theocracy and the (largely) Western ideology of democratic capitalism. Eighteen months after 9-11, on suspicions of an Iraqi stockpile of chemical and biological weapons, a multinational coalition force invaded Iraq; that military intervention, which led to armed conflict between Shiite and Sunni factions, has complicated the already tense situation in the Middle East. The war on terror currently continues in other regions, such as Afghanistan, where militant Sunni insurgents known as the Taliban threaten to create a new form of Islamic radicalism.

Initially, artists responded to the events of 9-11 by commemorating the destruction of the World Trade Center and those who died in the assault. One year after the attack, the American composer John Adams (whom we met in chapter 37) premiered his choral eulogy, *On the Transmigration of Souls*, which was awarded the 2003 Pulitzer Prize in music. Numerous photographs and films revisit the event, some of which (picturing those who jumped from the burning towers) are painful and powerful. Literary reflection on the atrocity and its aftermath inspired Don DeLillo's *Falling Man* (2006) and Laurence Wright's carefully researched study, *The Looming Tower: Al-Qaeda and the Road to 9-11* (2007). However, the realities of international terrorism are addressed more broadly in the poems of two contemporary writers: the Nobel Prize-winning poet Wislawa Szymborska (b. 1923) and the acclaimed Irish poet Seamus Heaney (b. 1939).

Szymborska has lived most of her life in communist-controlled Poland, a country that lost nearly one-fifth of its population during World War II. Her poems, while straightforward and conversational in tone, address personal and universal subjects and matters of moral urgency. "The Terrorist, He Watches," written in 1976, is a prescient anticipation of our current unease and insecurity.

Seamus Heaney shares with his countryman W. B. Yeats (see chapter 34) the gift of lyric brilliance. Heaney's ability to translate the small details of everyday experience into transcendent ideas is unsurpassed. While much of his poetry reflects his deep affection for the "bogs and barnyards" of rural life, his most recent volume of poetry, *District and Circle*, responds to the violence of our time, specifically the 2005 terrorist attacks on the District and Circle lines of London's subway system. Prompted by the Roman poet Horace, Heaney grapples with sobering, global uncertainties.

**READING 38.6** Szymborska's "The Terrorist, He Watches" (1976)

The bomb will explode in the bar at twenty past one.          1
Now it's only sixteen minutes past.
Some will still have time to enter,
some to leave.

The terrorist's already on the other side.                    5
That distance protects him from all harm
and, well, it's like the pictures:

A woman in a yellow jacket, she enters.
A man in dark glasses, he leaves.
Boys in jeans, they're talking.                               10
Sixteen minutes past and four seconds.

The smaller one, he's lucky, mounts his scooter,
but that taller chap, he walks in.

Seventeen minutes and forty seconds.
A girl, she walks by, a green ribbon in her hair.          15
But that bus suddenly hides her.
Eighteen minutes past.
The girl's disappeared.
Was she stupid enough to go in, or wasn't she.
We shall see when they bring out the bodies.                20

Nineteen minutes past.
No one else appears to be going in.
On the other hand, a fat bald man leaves.
But seems to search his pockets and
at ten seconds to twenty past one                            25
he returns to look for his wretched gloves.

It's twenty past one.
Time, how it drags.
Surely, it's now.
No, not quite.                                               30
Yes, now.
The bomb, it explodes.

**Q** **What does this poem suggest about the life of the individual in the global village?**

---

**READING 38.7** Heaney's "Anything Can Happen"

(2005)

**After Horace, Odes, I, 34**

Anything can happen. You know how Jupiter[1]
Will mostly wait for clouds to gather head
Before he hurls the lightning? Well just now
He galloped his thunder cart and his horses

Across a clear blue sky. It shook the earth
and the clogged underearth, the River Styx,[2]
the winding streams, the Atlantic shore itself.
Anything can happen, the tallest towers

Be overturned, those in high places daunted,
Those overlooked regarded. Stropped-beak Fortune
Swoops, making the air gasp, tearing the crest off one,
Setting it down bleeding on the next.

Ground gives. The heaven's weight
Lifts up off Atlas like a kettle lid.[3]
Capstones shift. Nothing resettles right.
Telluric[4] ash and fire-spores boil away.

**Q** **How does the poet's use of ancient mythology contribute to the poem?**

---

[1] Roman sky god.
[2] River in the underworld crossed by the souls of the dead.
[3] Mythic Titan condemned to support the heavens on his shoulders.
[4] Terrestrial.

## China: Global Ascendance

It is widely believed that the People's Republic of China will be the next great global power. In the last three decades, China has experienced a cultural transformation of enormous proportions. Once a country of rural villages, this vast nation now claims more than 150 cities with a population of one million or more people in each. Still governed by a communist regime, its rapid advances in industry, technology, and the arts have made it a formidable presence on the global stage.

China's ascendance has not been unmarred by internal strife. Following the death of Mao Zedong in 1976 (see chapter 34), communist officials tightened control over all forms of artistic expression. Nevertheless, young Chinese artists and writers continued to work, either in exile or at their own peril. In June 1989, at Tiananmen Square in Beijing, thousands of student activists demonstrated in support of democratic reform. With Beethoven's Ninth Symphony blaring from loudspeakers, demonstrators raised a plaster figure of the goddess of democracy modeled on the Statue of Liberty. The official response to this overt display of freedom resulted in the massacre of some protesters and the imprisonment of others. Since Tiananmen Square, literary publication has remained under the watchful eye of the state, but efforts to control music and the visual arts have been relaxed. A large body of Chinese literature, much of it written by women, has examined the traumatic years of Mao's Cultural Revolution (1966–1976). The enormous popularity of Western classical music in China has created a talent pool of highly trained performers. Outstanding filmmakers, such as Jia Zhang-ke and Zhang Yimou (see chapter 37) have received worldwide attention. Even more dramatic is the upsurge in painting and sculpture, where the Chinese have broken into the world art market with works that depart radically from Chinese tradition (and command huge prices in the Western art market).

In the past three decades, artists—most of them rigorously trained in China's Central Academy—have had the opportunity to explore the major styles and techniques of their Western contemporaries, a phenomenon made possible by international travel and mass electronic communication. In the early 1990s, there emerged two overlapping (and still flourishing) styles. The first, *political pop*, seizes on Western icons and images to glamorize or discredit various aspects of Chinese life. The second, *cynical realism*, engages commercial painting techniques to satirize social and political issues. Both of these styles are evident in the "Great Criticism" series by Wang Guangyi (b. 1956).

In one painting from the series (Figure **38.9**), bright colors and broad, simplified shapes, reminiscent of the communist-approved posters of the 1920s (see Figure 34.5), serve a sly and subversive end. Three Maoist workers, armed with the red flag of China, whose mast is an oversized pen, advance boldly into the arena of commercial combat, their mission approved by the official government stamps stenciled on the surface of the canvas. Here, collectivist socialism engages capitalist consumerism, represented

**Figure 38.9 WANG GUANGYI**, *Coca-Cola*, from the "Great Criticism" series, 1993. Enamel paint on canvas, 4 ft. 11 in. × 3 ft. 11 in.

by such populist commodities as Coca-Cola, McDonald's hamburgers, and Marlboro cigarettes.

More recently, the Chinese art scene has exploded with elaborately choreographed installations and mixed-media sculptures. The Chinese-born Cai Guo-Qiang (b. 1957) moved to Manhattan in 1995, bringing with him the age-old traditions of his homeland. Trained in stage design at the Shanghai Drama Institute, Cai creates public works that capture the disquieting nature of contemporary life. Many of his works explore the properties of gunpowder—an

explosive invented by the Chinese for firework displays.

Cai's most ambitious work is a four-part installation called *Inopportune*. The first stage of the piece features a brilliant array of colored lights pulsing from long transparent rods that burst from nine identical Ford sedans (Figure **38.10**). The cars, suspended in midair along a 300-foot gallery, call to mind a sequence of images unfurling in a Chinese scroll, or a series of frozen film frames. Stage Two, installed in an adjacent gallery, consists of nine prefabricated life-sized tigers pierced by hundreds of bamboo arrows—a reference to a popular thirteenth-century Chinese tale glorifying a hero who saves his village from a man-eating tiger. Stage Three is a startling ninety-second film loop (projected on a huge screen); here, a phantom car (filled with fireworks) bursts silently into flames, then floats in a dreamlike manner through Manhattan's bustling, nocturnal Times Square. The fourth and final part of the installation is a two-dimensional wall-hanging on which one sees nine exploding cars as "painted" by ignited gunpowder. In this project Cai has mixed an assortment of traditions, symbols, and images to capture the violence of contemporary urban life. He claims that he uses the tools and materials of destruction and terror for healing purposes—the Chinese character for "gunpowder" translates literally as "fire medicine," which was once thought to cure the ailing body.

The building boom that China has enjoyed in the last decade was markedly accelerated by Beijing's role as the site of the 2008 Olympics. Representative of the global perspective, the architectural projects for the Olympics involved multinational participation and cooperation: the extraordinary Beijing airport—now the largest in the world—was the brainchild of the British architect, Norman Foster (discussed earlier in this chapter); the National Stadium (nicknamed the "Bird's Nest" to describe its interwoven steel latticework) was designed by

**Figure 38.10 CAI GUO-QIANG**, *Inopportune*, Stage 1, 2005. Mixed media.

**Figure 38.11** The National Aquatics Center, Beijing.

the Swiss architects, Jacques Herzog and Pierre de Meuron; and the Aquatic Center (known as the "Water Cube") was designed and built by a consortium of Australian architects and Chinese engineers (Figure **38.11**). The Water Cube, a rectangular structure that covers almost 8 acres, consists of a steel frame and an exterior of blue-gray translucent plastic somewhat similar to Teflon. Its pillow-shaped modules, inspired by the bubbles in foam, weigh only one percent as much as glass and reduce energy costs by a third. Reviewing the buildings of China's Olympic Park on a visit to Beijing, America's leading architectural critic Paul Goldberger found them "unimpeachably brilliant," and "as innovative as any architecture on the planet, marvels of the imagination and engineering that few countries would have the nerve or the money to attempt."

## The Arts in the Global Village

The spirit of global collectivity is readily apparent in the arts. All forms of expression, from architecture to music and dance, reflect the abundance and exchange of electronically transmitted information, and the ease with which we (and our cultural baggage) travel. The migration of artists from one part of the world to another, and the media of television, film, and computers, link studio to stage and artist to artist. Megasurveys of the visual arts held regularly in Venice, Shanghai, Miami, and elsewhere attract large audiences, invite the exchange of ideas, and stimulate a vigorous commercial art market. Individual artworks are often hybrid projects incorporating a number of mediums and genres. Virtual environments and mixed-media installations have become more common than traditional painting and sculpture. While the arts of the global village are characterized by stylistic diversity and a plurality of ideas and techniques, they are nevertheless united by the wonders of digital technology.

### Video Art

In the 1950s, the Korean artist and musician Nam June Paik (1932–2007) predicted that the television cathode ray would replace the canvas as the medium of the future. The now acclaimed "father of video art" was not far from the mark, for art that employs one or another form of electronic technology has come to dominate the global art world. Video art had its beginnings in the 1960s. Influenced by the visionary work of John Cage, Paik initiated the genre with performance pieces and electronic installations. Some were among the first interactive experiments in sound and image. With the help of an electronic engineer, he designed and built one of the first videosynthesizers—a device that makes it possible to alter the shape and color of a video image.

In the 1990s, Paik assembled television sets, circuit boards, and other electronic apparatus to produce whimsical robots. More ambitious in size and conception, however, are the artist's multiscreen television installations. *Megatron* (1995), for instance, consists of 215 monitors programmed with a rapid-fire assortment of animated and live-video images drawn from East and West. The Seoul Olympic Games and Korean drummers, rock concert clips, girlie magazine nudes, and quick-cuts of Paik's favorite artists alternate with the national flags of various countries and other global logos (Figure **38.12**). The animated contour of a bird flying gracefully across a wall of screens brings magical unity to this ocular blitz, while a two-channel audio track adds booming syncopated sound to the visual rhythms. Paik's wall of video monitors dazzles viewers with a kaleidoscopic barrage of images whose fast-paced editing imitates mainstream television and film.

In contrast with the frenzied dazzle of Paik's video projects, the art of Bill Viola (b. 1951) is profoundly subtle. Viola uses rear-projected video screens to deliver personal narratives in the form of large, slow-moving, mesmerizing images. Mortality, identity, and consciousness, Viola's central themes, draw inspiration from Zen Buddhism, Christian mysticism, and Sufi poetry. In *Stations* (a reference to the Stations of the Cross, Christ's journey to Calvary), a computer-controlled, five-channel video/sound installation projects the image of a male body (immersed in water) onto three vertical slabs of granite; the image is reflected onto mirrored slabs placed on the floor (Figure **38.13**). Viola wants the viewer to experience the piece "insofar as possible, as a mental image" evoking the human journey from birth to death.

Viola's art is contemplative and deeply embedded in the exploration of conceptual reality. It makes reference to the current "crisis of representation and identity" in which new media technologies leave viewers unsure as to whether an optical image is real or fabricated. According to Viola, "representing information" will be the main issue in the arts of the future. Video and sound installations, which became a major form of late twentieth-century expression, are closely related to the film experience. Both immerse the viewer in the moving image; but, as with Viola's work, video art concentrates experience in a way that film—especially film as entertainment—does not usually achieve.

Since the 1970s, video installations have moved in the direction of political theater. More elaborate in their staging and often interactive, they make use of holograms, laser beams, digital images, and computer-generated special effects, all of which may be projected onto screens and walls to the accompaniment of electronically recorded sounds. Some, like Mary Lucier's (b. 1944) sound and video installation that recreates the disastrous effects of the 1997 flood in Grand Forks, North Dakota, are dramatic ruminations on personal and communal experience.

## Computers and the Visual Arts

Digital computers have put at our disposal the entire history of art. The Internet gives access to the contents of more than 5000 museums; and millions of photographic images are available on a variety of websites. In addition to its function in storing and distributing images, however, digital computers have transformed the manner in which art is made and experienced. Computer technology is now a standard part of architectural design and engineering (see chapter 37). It makes possible the execution of otherwise unachievable three-dimensional curves in fiberglass (and other media) sculpture and three-dimensional forms. More broadly, it is basic to all forms of *digital art*.

Digital art is art in which the computer is employed as a primary tool, medium, or creative partner. The vast array of digital artforms includes (to name only a few) two-dimensional imaging, virtual reality, performance, animation,

**Figure 38.12 NAM JUNE PAIK**, *Megatron*, 1995. 215 monitors, 8-channel color video and 2-channel sound, left side 11 ft. 10½ in. × 22 ft. 6 in. × 23½ in.; right side 10 ft. 8 in. × 10 ft. 8 in. × 23½ in. Images flow by on these monitors as if seen from a rapidly passing car. Paik was the first to use the phrase "electronic superhighway" to describe the fast-pace media resources that link different parts of the planet.

**Figure 38.13 BILL VIOLA**, *Stations* (detail), 1994. Video/sound installation with five granite slabs, five projections, and five projection screens.

game art, and Internet art. Digital imaging, the process by which computers manipulate old images or generate new ones, has revolutionized the world of film, television, video, holography, and photography. Such imaging is of two varieties: one involves the digital manipulation of photographic resources to create new images. The other makes use of purely digital means (a geometric model or mathematical formula) to create an entirely new image. In the latter method, the artist gives the computer a set of instructions by means of which the image is digitally produced.

Representative of the first type of computer imaging are the panoramic photographs of the German artist Andreas Gursky (b. 1957). Gursky's huge photographs (often more than 15 feet in width) are the products of his world travels. His tours through Europe, Brazil, Mexico, Japan, Vietnam, and the United States, have generated a global portrait of contemporary life: its rock concerts (Figure **38.14**), garbage dumps, stock exchanges, supermarkets, factories, prisons, and luxury hotels. Gursky's photographs are far from documentary, however; they are stitched together from transparencies of his own photographs, which undergo many rounds of editing, scanning, and proofing. By way of digital processes, Gursky creates realistically detailed images in which (ironically) individuality is lost. His works convey the anonymity of "mass man," or what the artist himself calls the "aggregate state" of nature and the world.

An example of the second type of digital imaging is found in the works of American artist Karl Sims (b. 1962). Sims has devised special computer-graphics techniques that generate abstract, three-dimensional simulations of genetic organisms (Figure **38.15**), and natural phenomena such as fog, smoke, and rain. According to Sims, a graduate of the MIT Media Lab and a student of biotechnology, his computer graphics "unite several concepts: chaos, complexity, evolution, self-propagating entities, and the nature of life itself."

The use of the computer in making art is no longer exclusive to artists, however. *Interactive art* programs, available both in the art gallery and on the home computer screen, invite the viewer to become a partner in the creative act. In *Piano* (1995) designed by the Japanese media

artist Toshio Iwai (b. 1962), the spectator creates a musical "score" by manipulating a trackball that triggers star-shaped points of light that travel along a scroll until they "strike" a piano keyboard; both visual and aural patterns are generated by the spectator—within limits predetermined by Iwai. With *Electronic Eve* (1997), an interactive project conceived by Jenny Marketou (b. 1944), "image consumers" create their own multimedia environment by selecting (through direct touch on the computer screen) from a database of video sequences, still images, computer graphics, texts, and sounds. Other electronic installations invite the audience to turn words (the sounds of speech) into colored shapes and images. The World Wide Web provides a virtual theater in which one may assume an on-line identity—or more than one identity—in cyberspace.

Perhaps the most intriguing computer-driven form of interactive art is **virtual reality**, a technology that allows the user to interact with a computer-simulated environment. By means of a series of special digital devices, artificial environments are flashed onto a huge screen or onto the inside of a helmet. Like a giant video game, virtual reality combines visual illusion, sound, and spoken texts. A synthesis of all retrievable informational forms, such interactive hypermedia genres offer an image-saturated playground for the mind.

## Computers and Performance

Performance art has been transformed by digital technology. The American experimental artist Laurie Anderson (b. 1947) began her career with theatrical performances that appropriated images from classic films, newsreels, and other video resources; these were "mixed" with recorded and live music. In the 1990s, Anderson began to use a 6-foot-long "talking-stick", a batonlike MIDI (Magnetic Instrument Digital Interface) controller that accesses and replicates sounds. For artists like Anderson, the computer is a "meta-medium" that transforms vocal and visual experience.

The age of digital communication finds a playful advocate in the work of the Japanese artist Noriko Yamaguchi (b. 1983). Wearing headphones and a body suit made of cell-phone ("*keitai*") keypads, the artist *becomes* a human mobile

**Figure 38.14 Andreas Gursky**, *Madonna I*, 2001. Cibachrome, edition 1 of 6, 9 ft. × 6 ft. 6 in. Gursky's photos, printed at colossal size, are digitally manipulated "records" of such public events as open-air raves and rock concerts. Some critics see in these images the loss of individuality in a globalized society. In this aerial view, Madonna appears at the lower left.

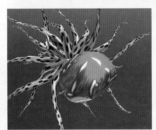

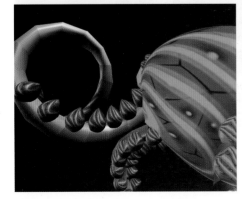

**Figure 38.15 Karl Sims**, Galapagos, 1997. Interactive media. This interactive artwork is part of a twelve-screen media installation that invites viewers to participate in the evolution of animated forms. Inspired by the theory of natural selection advanced by Darwin after he visited the Galapagos Islands in 1835, Sims invented a program whereby virtual "genetic" organisms appear to mutate and reproduce within the environment of the computer.

# MAKING CONNECTIONS

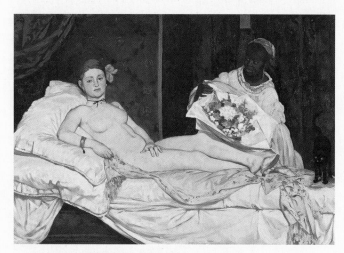

**Figure 38.16 EDOUARD MANET**, *Olympia*, 1863. Oil on canvas, 4 ft. 3¼ in. × 6 ft. 2¾ in.

**Figure 38.17 YASUMASA MORIMURA**, *Portrait (Futago)*, 1988. Color photograph, clear medium, 82½ × 118 in.

Contemporary Japanese artists have been particularly successful in using computer technology to generate photographic and video projects. Yasumasa Morimura (b. 1945) transforms Western masterpieces into camp spoofs in which he impersonates one or more of the central characters. In *Portrait (Futago)*, Morimura turns Manet's *Olympia* (Figure **38.16**) into a drag queen decked out in a blond wig and rhinestone-trimmed slippers (Figure **38.17**). Using himself as the model for both the nude courtesan and the maid, he revisualizes a landmark in the history of art. By "updating" Manet's *Olympia* (itself an "update" of a painting by Titian), Morimura also questions the authority of these historical icons, even as he makes sly reference to the postwar Japanese practice of copying Western culture. *Portrait* is a computer-manipulated color photograph produced from a studio setup—a combination of Postmodern techniques borrowed from fashion advertising. Here, and in his more recent photographs in which he impersonates contemporary icons and film divas (Madonna, Marilyn Monroe, and Liza Minnelli) Morimura pointedly tests classic stereotypes of identity and gender.

## Computers and Film

Digital technology has transformed the world of filmmaking. New technologies, such as high definition (HD) video, which gives visual images greater immediacy, have begun to replace film itself. The ease with which digital video can be produced, reproduced from film, and downloaded via computers has raised major issues concerning copyrights, but it has also made the archive of motion pictures readily available to a worldwide audience. In response to the new technology, new film centers are developing throughout the world. The website YouTube, which welcomes video postings, has become a forum for young and independent filmmakers, especially in the production of short and documentary films.

Computers have also revolutionized the way films are made: Computer-Generated Imaging (CGI) of realistic settings makes it unnecessary for filmmakers to use large-scale sets and locations. Special effects, achieved by way of computers, are used to juxtapose images in ways that distort reality. Like docufiction, films render believable what in actuality may be untrue. The 1994 film *Forrest Gump*, for instance, shows its antihero shaking hands with the long-dead president John F. Kennedy.

Digital technology also makes possible entirely new and hyperreal images, such as Steven Spielberg's dinosaurs (*Jurassic Park*, 1993), James Cameron's liquid-metal cyborgs (*Terminator 2*, 1991), and Larry and Andy Wachowski's science fiction trilogy *Matrix* (1999–2003). *Terminator* was the first film to feature the computer-generated shape-shifting technique called "morphing." *Matrix* introduced a unique photographic technique ("flow motion") that uses more than 100 meticulously coordinated still cameras to create extraordinary special effects. Just as CGI can create realistic settings, so it can replace human actors with computer-generated characters. The use of digital actors (as in the fantasy epic trilogy, *The Lord of the Rings*, 2001–2003) blurs the border between the traditional live action film and CGI animation. While digital artistry may not put live-action filmmaking in jeopardy, it provokes questions concerning differences between the original and the replica, the real and the virtual, truth and illusion.

Finally, film *animation* has undergone major changes since the early twentieth century, when still drawings and stop-motion techniques prevailed. The first feature-length, entirely computer-animated film, *Toy Story*, appeared in 1995. Since the turn of the twenty-first century, more sophisticated software for digital imaging, including three-dimensional graphics, has facilitated a greater range of color, movement, and special effects. In 2001, Hayao Miyazaki's award-winning *Spirited Away* brought Japanese *animé* to world attention. While animated films may be landmarks in cinematic technique, they generally provide little nourishment for the mind; however, the Disney/Pixar animated science fiction film *WALL-E* (2008), the story of a whimsical little robot who cleans up the garbage-ridden planet earth, may be a salutary exception.

phone—the telecommunications device that (in most parts of the world) also functions as a television, credit card, video player, portable music device, digital camera, and more (Figure **38.18**). Wires connect *Keitai Girl* to other receivers in cyberspace. Her futuristic armor is part of a performance involving interactive lasers, fast, upbeat music, and a popular Japanese dance style known as *Para-Para*—a type of line dancing.

## Music and the Global Perspective

The global perspective may be most apparent in contemporary music, in which Western traditions of harmony and form have been energized by the modes, rhythms, textures, and inflections of Asia, Africa, and the Caribbean. Inspired by ancient and non-Western oral and instrumental forms of improvisation, much of today's music relies less on the formal score and more on the ear. Some contemporary composers create musical tapestries that utilize conventional Western instruments along with ancient musical ones (such as the Chinese flute or the *balafon*, an African version of the xylophone), producing textures that may be manipulated by electronic means. These innovations are evident in the compositions of Tan Dun (b. 1957), a Chinese-born composer who has lived in the United States since 1986. Tan's works, ranging from string quartets and operas to multimedia pieces and film scores, represent a spirit of cultural pluralism that blends Chinese opera, folk songs, and instruments with traditional Western techniques and traditions ranging from medieval chant and romantic harmonies to audacious aural

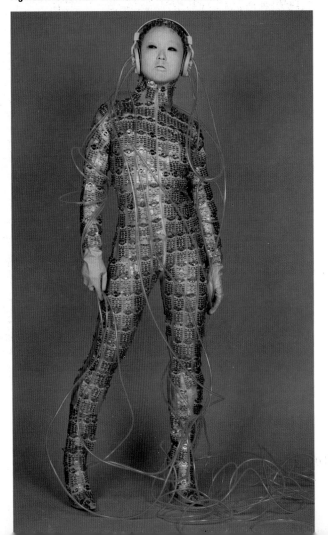

**Figure 38.18 NORIKO YAMAGUCHI**, *Keitai Girl*, 2003.

experiments (in the style of John Cage) using the sounds of water, torn paper, and bird calls.

Tan Dun's powerful opera, *The First Emperor* (2006), marries the singing style of Beijing opera and the use of Chinese instruments to Western performance style and a standard Western orchestra. Directed by the noted film-maker Zhang Yimou (see chapter 37), the opera tells the story of the visionary and brutal Qin Shi Huang Di, China's first imperial Son of Heaven. Filled with haunting, lyrical music, the work is more than a bridge between East and West; it portends a new direction. As Tan Dun predicts: "Opera will no longer be a Western form, as it is no longer an Italian form."

One of the most notable experiments in contemporary intercultural music is the Silk Road Project, which involves the exchange of Western musical traditions with those of the ancient Silk Road, the vast skein of trade routes that linked East Asia to Europe (see chapter 7). Begun in 1998, this extended effort to connect East and West was the brainchild of the renowned Japanese-American cellist Yo-Yo Ma (b. 1955). Ma aimed to revitalize the spirit of cultural exchange once facilitated by the Silk Road, which he has called "the Internet of Antiquity." In the current age of cultural pluralism, musicians from across Central Asia have joined with American virtuosos (selected by Ma) to produce works that integrate radically different compositional forms, instruments, and performance styles.

Cultural interdependence and the willful (and often electronically synthesized) fusion of different musical traditions have transformed contemporary music. The influence of Arabic chant, Indian *ragas*, and Latino rhythms is evident in jazz; rock and country blues give gospel music a new sound; Cuban brass punctuates contemporary rock; and shimmering Asian drones propel New Age music. The global character of contemporary music is also evident in popular genres that engage issue-driven lyrics. The Jamaican musician Bob Marley (1945–1981) brought to the international scene the socially conscious music known as *reggae*—an eclectic style that draws on a wide variety of black Jamaican musical forms, including African religious music and Christian revival songs. *Hip-hop*, which combines loud, percussive music (often electronically mixed and manipulated by disc jockeys), jarring lyrics, and break-dancing (an acrobatic dance style) has moved from its inner-city origins to assume an international scope. This "mutating hybrid" makes use of various musical traditions: modern (disco, salsa, reggae, rock) and ancient (African call and response). *Rap*—the vocal dimension of hip-hop—launches a fusillade of raw and socially provocative words chanted in rhymed couplets over an intense rhythmic beat.

While some critics lament that Western music has bifurcated into two cultures—art music and popular music—the fact is that these two traditions are becoming more alike, or, more precisely, they share various features of a global musical menu. One example of this phenomenon is the orchestral suite *Portraits in Blue* (1995) by the American jazz pianist Marcus Roberts (b. 1963). Composed in what Roberts calls "semi-classical form," the composition is a "personal listening mix" that conflates Beethoven, John Coltrane, Chopin, Little Richard, Billie Holiday, and George Gershwin. In the genre of free jazz, such musicians as John Zorn (b. 1953) borrow harmonic and rhythmic devices from the domains of bluegrass, klezmer (Jewish folk music), and punk rock. The new-music group known as Bang on a Can offers an eclectic mix of sounds that blur the boundary between classical and popular music. Part rock band and part amplified chamber group, its classically trained performers work in close collaboration with leading composers, jazz musicians, and pop artists. Such fusions of East and West, urban and folk, popular and classical styles, constitute the musical mosaic of the new millennium.

## Dance and the Global Perspective

Contemporary choreographers have been drawn increasingly to social issues and historical events: witness Charles Atlas' *Delusional* (1994), a meditation on death and decay in Bosnia, and Paul Taylor's 1999 spoof of the Ku Klux Klan (*Oh, You Kid*). The company known as Urban Bush Women, founded in 1984, uses dance to bring to light the histories of disenfranchised people. In their fiercely energetic performances, this Brooklyn-based ensemble of African, Caribbean, and black American women call on the spiritual traditions of the African diaspora.

The choreographer Ea Sola (b. 1970) fled her homeland at the height of the Vietnam War. Returning to Vietnam after fifteen years, she studied its traditional dance and music, both of which are present in her choreographed recollection of war, *Sécheresse et Pluie* (*Drought and Rain*, 1995). This work, as well as others by contemporary choreographers, reflects the influence of *butoh*, a Japanese dance form that features simple, symbolic movements performed in a mesmerizingly slow and hypnotic manner. *Ankoko butoh*, meaning "dance of utter darkness," grew out of ancient forms of Asian theater. Two other traditions have influenced contemporary choreography: Indian classical dance and German *Tanztheater* ("dance theater"), an expressionistic style that features everyday actions, speech, and theatrical props (including, occasionally, live animals).

## Chronology

| | |
|---|---|
| 1947 | Israel becomes an independent state |
| 1954–1975 | Vietnam War |
| 1966–1976 | Mao's Cultural Revolution |
| 1989 | Berlin Wall falls |
| 1989 | Massacre in Tiananmen Square |
| 2001 | al-Qaeda terrorists attack the United States |
| 2003 | United States and coalition forces invade Iraq |
| 2005 | Terrorists attack London's subway system |

See Music Listening Selections at end of chapter.

# LOOKING BACK

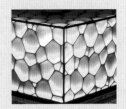

## The Global Perspective

- Globalism—the interdependence of cultures and peoples in all parts of the world—is the new model for contemporary society.
- Digital technology links all parts of the world, and electronic networks facilitate the dissemination of values and goods. The sense of collectivity in the integrated landscape of the global village has become a hallmark of a new world community.
- In this post-colonial era, efforts to reconcile Modernist modes of life with waning ancient traditions have challenged many regions, none more dramatically than Africa.
- The novels and short stories of Chinua Achebe deal with the warp between premodern and modern conditions in parts of Africa. Similarly, Africa's visual artists draw on past traditions in creative projects that often involve modern media.

## The Global Ecosystem

- While environmental issues are not new, it is only recently that world leaders have begun to come together to address the ailing health of the global ecosystem.
- E. O. Wilson, an early advocate for the preservation of the environment, has advanced "scientific humanism," an interdisciplinary discipline that values biodiversity and a sound environmental ethic.
- Annie Dillard is one of many writers whose works express concern for the natural environment. In the visual arts, earthworks and "green" architectural designs bring attention to the importance of a healthy ecosystem. The energy-efficient buildings of Norman Foster are models of environmentally sustainable projects that are both beautiful and practical.

## Globalism and Ethnic Identity

- Ethnic identity has become a dominant theme in the global community.
- While immigration contributes to the blending of different ethnic populations, it has inspired efforts to maintain distinctive ethnic values and traditions. In the United States, large numbers of Latin Americans have introduced into American culture a unique array of culinary, musical, and dance styles. The growing number of female writers and artists who deal with ethnic identity is represented by the Mexican-American novelist, Sandra Cisneros.
- Matters related to one's homeland and ethnic roots have provoked strife in many parts of the world, as illustrated by the ongoing conflict between Palestine and Israel. The role of memory in the painful progress toward peaceful coexistence is voiced in the poems of Yehuda Amichai and Mahmoud Darwish.

## The Challenge of Globalism

- Challenging the future of the global village, terrorism reflects an extremist response to ideological and political differences. The devastating attack of the radical Muslim group al-Qaeda on the United States on September 11, 2001, provoked a variety of creative and commemorative responses in literature, the visual arts, and music.
- The poets Wislawa Szymborska and Seamus Heaney have both addressed the threat of terrorism in the global community.
- In the last three decades, China has emerged as a major world power. As state officials have loosened controls over artistic expression, China's academically trained painters and sculptors have taken the world by storm with a variety of original projects.

## The Arts in the Global Village

- The visual arts of contemporary times are no longer limited to one medium or genre; they are often hybridized and are increasingly dependent on digital technology.
- Video plays a key role in the performance pieces and installation art of Nam June Paik and Bill Viola, which make use of images in ways that "represent information."
- Computers and digital innovations have allowed us to access all areas of the world without having to travel. They have become essential to creative projects in film, photography, and performance art, to the development of new techniques, such as animation and virtual reality, and to the emergence of new kinds of visual simulation.
- Western music and dance have responded to the influence of the cultures of Asia, Africa, and the Caribbean. Sharing the features of a global musical menu, distinctions between popular and art (classical) music are becoming less pronounced. The compositions of the Chinese composer Tan Dun and the efforts of the Silk Road Project are representative of the successful integration of widely diverse musical traditions.

## Music Listening Selection

**CD Two Selection 26** Kalhor, *Gallop of a Thousand Horses*, The Silk Road Project, 2005

## Glossary

**biodiversity** the preservation of all life forms in the ecosystem
**ecosystem** the ecological community and its physical environment
**virtual reality** the digital simulation of artificial environments

# Picture Credits

The author and publishers wish to thank the following for permission to use copyright material. Every effort has been made to trace or contact copyright holders, but if notified of any omissions, Laurence King Publishing would be pleased to insert the appropriate acknowledgement in any subsequent edition of this publication.

## Chapter 32

**32.1** © RMN/Musée D'Orsay/Gerard Blot/Herve Lewandowski. © ADAGP, Paris and DACS, London, 2010.

**32.2** The Museum of Modern Art, New York. Acquired through the Lillie P. Bliss Bequest. © 2010, Digital Image, the Museum of Modern Art, New York/Scala, Florence. © Succession Picasso/DACS, London 2010.

**32.3** Philadelphia Museum of Art. Purchased with the W. P. Wilstach Fund. Photo: Graydon Wood, 1988 (W'37–1–1).

**32.4** University Ethnographic Museum, Zürich.

**32.5** Philadelphia Museum of Art. Louise and Walter Arensberg Collection. © Succession Picasso/DACS 2010.

**32.6** Musée de l'Homme, Paris. Photo: © R.M.N., Paris.

**32.7** The Museum of Modern Art, New York. Gift of the Artist. © 2003 Digital Image MoMA, New York/Scala, Florence. © Succession Picasso/DACS, London 2010.

**32.8** The Museum of Modern Art, New York. Acquired through the Lillie P. Bliss Bequest. Photograph © 2000 The Museum of Modern Art, New York. © ARS, NY and DACS, London 2000.

**32.9** The Museum of Modern Art, New York. Acquired through the Lillie P. Bliss Bequest. © 2004 Digital Image MoMA, New York/Scala, Florence.

**32.10** Museum of Modern Art, New York. © 2004 Digital Image MoMA, New York/Scala, Florence. © ADAGP, Paris and DACS, London 2010.

**32.11** Philadelphia Museum of Art. Louise and Walter Arensberg Collection. © Succession Marcel Duchamp/ADAGP, Paris and DACS, London, 2010.

**32.12** Statens Museum for Kunst. Photo: Hans Peterson. © Succession H Matisse and DACS, London, 2010.

**32.13** The Museum of Modern Art, New York. Gift of Nelson A. Rockefeller in honor of Alfred H. Barr, Jr. © 2004 Digital Image MoMA, New York/Scala, Florence. © Succession H Matisse and DACS, London, 2010.

**32.14** The Museum of Modern Art, New York. Given anonymously. © 2004 Digital Image MoMA, New York/Scala, Florence. © ADAGP, Paris and DACS, London, 2010.

**32.15** Reproduced by permission of the Center for Creative Photography, University of Tucson Arizona.

**32.16** The Museum of Modern Art, New York. Mrs Simon Guggenheim Fund. © 2003 Digital Image MoMA, New York/Scala, Florence. © ADAGP, Paris and DACs, London 2010.

**32.17** The Museum of Modern Art, New York. © 2004 Digital Image MoMA, New York/Scala, Florence.

**32.18** Munson-Williams-Proctor Institute, Utica, New York. © 2010 Mondrian/Holtzman Trust c/o HCR International Warrenton, Virginia, USA.

**32.19** Collection Haags Gemeentemuseum, The Hague. © 2010 Mondrian/Holtzman Trust c/o HCR International Warrenton, Virginia, USA.

**32.20** The Museum of Modern Art, New York. Gift of Philip Johnson. © 2004 Digital Image MoMA, New York/Scala, Florence. © DACS, London 2010.

**32.21** State Trekiov Gallery, Moscow. Gift of George Custakis.

**32.22** Hedrich Belssing, Chicago.

**32.23** Photo: Hedrich-Blessing, courtesy Chicago Historical Society.

**32.24** Photograph courtesy The Museum of Modern Art, New York.

**32.26** London, Anderson and Low.

**32.27** Private collection. © Succession Picasso/DACS, London, 2010.

## Chapter 33

**33.1** Philadelphia Museum of Art. The Louise and Walter Arensberg collection, 1950. Photo: Graydon Wood. © DACS 2010.

**33.2** National Gallery Oslo. © The Munch Museum/The Munch-Ellingsen Group. BONO, Oslo/DACS, London 2010.

**33.3** The Museum of Modern Art, New York. Purchase. © 2003 Digital Image MoMA, New York/Scala, Florence.

**33.4** The Museum of Modern Art, New York. Purchase. © 2004 Digital Image MoMA, New York/Scala, Florence. © DACS, London, 2010.

**33.5** The Museum of Modern Art, New York. Mrs Simon Guggenheim Fund. © 2004 Digital Image MoMA, New York/Scala, Florence. © ADAGP, Paris and DACs, London 2010.

**33.6** Photo courtesy of Sidney Janis Gallery, New York. © Succession Marcel Duchamp/ADAGP, Paris/DACS, London, 2010.

**33.7** Collection of Mrs Mary Sisler. © Succession Marcel Duchamp/ADAGP, Paris/DACS, London, 2010.

**33.8** The Museum of Modern Art, New York. Gift of James Thrall Soby. © 2004 Digital Image MoMA, New York/Scala, London. © Successsion Picasso/DACS, London 2010.

**33.9** Albright-Knox Art Gallery, Buffalo, New York. Room of Contemporary Art Fund, 1940.

**33.10** Los Angeles County Museum of Art, Purchased with funds provided by the Mr and Mrs. William Preston Harrison Collection. Photograph © 2010 Museum Associates/LACMA, © ADAGP, Paris and DACS, London 2010.

**33.11** The Museum of Modern Art, New York. Given anonymously. © 2004 Digital Image MoMA, New York/Scala, Florence. © Kingdom of Spain, Universal heir of Salvador Dali/DACS, London, 2010.

**33.12** Museo Frida Kahlo, Mexico City. Collection Lola Olmedo. © 2010, Banco de Mexico Diego Rivera & Frida Kahlo Museums Trust, Mexico D.F. / DACS.

**33.13** Art Institute of Chicago. Gift of Georgia O'Keeffe. © ARS, New York and DACS, London, 2010.

**33.14** The Museum of Modern Art, New York. Purchase. © 2004 Digital Image MoMA, New York/Scala, Florence. © DACS, London, 2010.

**33.15** Nationalgalerie, Staatliche Museen Preussischer Kulturbesitz, Berlin. Photo © BPK, Berlin. © DACS, London, 2010.

## Chapter 34

**34.1** The Kobal Collection, London.

**34.2** © ADAGP, Paris and DACS, London, 2010.

**34.3** The Museum of Modern Art, New York. A. Conger Goodyear Fund. © 2003 Digital Image MoMA, New York/Scala, Florence. © DACS, London, 2010.

**34.4** The Museum of Modern Art, New York. Mrs Simon Guggenheim Fund. © ADAGP, Paris and DACS, London 2000.

**34.6** Collection, A3A Financial Inc. through its subsidiary The Equitable Life Assurance Society of the U.S., New York. Photo: Dorothy Zeidman 2000. © T. H. Benton and R. P. Benton Testamentary Trusts/VAGA, New York/DACS, London 2000.

**34.7** Philadelphia Museum of Art. Given by Mr. and Mrs. Herbert Cameron Morris ('43–46–1).

**34.8** Library of Congress, Washington, D.C.

**34.9** © Lee Miller Archives, England 2010. All rights reserved www.leemiller.co.uk.

**34.10** Museo Nacional de Arte Reina Sofia, Madrid. © Succession Picasso/DACS, London, 2010.

**34.11** Prado, Madrid.

**34.12** The Kobal Collection, London.

**34.13** Courtesy, The Museum of Modern Art/Film Stills Library.

**34.14** Lu Xun Memorial, Shanghai.

## Chapter 35

**35.1** University of California, Art Museum. Gift of an anonymous donor.

**35.2** Arts Council Collection, Southbank Centre, London, © Estate of Francis Bacon. All rights reserved, DACS 2010.

**35.3** Whitney Museum of American Art, New York. Purchase 55.35.Photograph: Geoffrey Clements © 1998 Whitney Museum of American Art, New York. © Willem de Kooning Revocable Trust/ARS, New York and DACS, London 2010.

**35.4** Whitney Museum of American Art, New York. Purchase with funds from the Friends of the Whitney Museum of American Art. © ARS, NY and DACs, London, 2010.

**35.5** Gitter-Yelen Collection, New Orleans.

**35.6** Photo: © Hans Namuth, New York, 1983.

**35.7** Richard Carafelli, Image courtesy of the Board of Trustees, National Gallery of Art, Washington, © The Pollock-Krasner Foundation ARS, NY and DACS, London 2010.

**35.8** San Francisco Museum of Modern Art. Acquired through a gift of Peggy Guggenheim. © Kate Rothko Prizel and Christopher Rothko/DACS, London, 2010.

**35.9** Art Institute of Chicago. Chicago Friends of American Art Collection, 1942.51.

**35.10** The Museum of Modern Art, New York. Purchase. Photograph © 2000 The Museum of Modern Art, New York. © ADAGP, Paris and DACS, London 2000.

**35.11** Hirshhorn Museum and Sculpture Garden. Smithsonian Institution, Washington, D.C. Gift of Joseph H. Hirshhorn, 1966. Photo: Lee Stalsworth. © George Segal/DACS, London/VAGA, New York, 2010.

**35.12** Photograph by David Smith, © Estate of David Smith/DACS, London/VAGA, New York 20

**35.13** Collection of Whitney Museum of American Art, New York. Purchase with funds from the Friends of the Whitney Museum of American Art, and exchange. Photograph by Geoffrey Clements.

© ADAGP, Paris and DACS, London, 2010 © Calder Foundation, New York/DACS London 2009.

**35.14** Photo: Ezra Stoller/© Esto. Courtesy Joseph E. Seagram & Sons, Inc.

**35.15** Photo: Balthazar Korab, Troy, Michigan.

**35.16** Photo: Robert E. Mates/Courtesy of the Solomon R. Guggenheim Museum. © ARS, New York and DACS, London 2010.

**35.17** Photo: David Heald/Courtesy of the Solomon R. Guggenheim Museum.

**35.18** © Michael Harding/Arcaid.

**35.19** © Robert Rauschenberg/DACS, London and VAGA, New York 2010.

## Chapter 36

**36.1** Courtesy the artist © Jeff Wall.

**36.2** The Museum of Modern Art, New York. Gift of Mrs. David M. Levy. © 2004 Digital Image MoMA, New York/Scala, Florence. © ARS, New York and DACS, London, 2010.

**36.3** Smithsonian American Art Museum, Washington, D.C., 1996.71. © Smithsonian American Art Museum/Art Resource, New York/Scala, Florence.

**36.4** University Art Museum, University of California at Berkeley. Purchased with the aid of funds from the National Endowment for the Arts. Selected by the Committee for the Acquisition of African-American Art.

**36.5** Collection of Hanford Yang, New York. Photo courtesy Phyllis Kind Gallery, New York.

**36.6** Photo by Dave Sweeney. Courtesy of Sikkema Jenkins & Co.

**36.7** Courtesy Hogan Jazz Archive, Tulane University.

**36.8** The Broad Art Foundation, Santa Monica. Photograph © Douglas M. Parker Studio, Los Angeles. © ADAGP, Paris and DACs, London 2010.

**36.9** The Dance Collection, The New York Public Library for the Performing Arts. Astor, Lenox, and Tilden Foundations.

**36.10** Whitney Museum of American Art, New York. Gift of the Howard and Jean Lipman Foundation, Inc. Photograph © 2000 Whitney Museum of American Art. Photography by Sandak, Inc/A Division of Macmillan Publishing. © 2009 Niki Charitable Art Foundation/ADAGP/DACS 2010.

**36.11** Museum of Natural History, Vienna.

**36.12** Collection of the Brooklyn Museum of Art © Judy Chicago, 1979. Photo: Donald Woodman. © ARS, NY and DACS, London, 2010.

**36.13** Courtesy Galerie Lelong, New York. © The Estate of Ana Mendieta.

**36.14** Courtesy of the artist and Metro Pictures, New York.

**36.15** Courtesy Mary Boone Gallery, New York. Photo: Zindman/Freemont, New York.

**36.16** © 2010 Estate of Robert Mapplethorpe. Courtesy Art + Commerce.

## Chapter 37

**37.1** The Robert B. Mayer Family Collection, Chicago, Illinois. © Robert Rauschenberg/VAGA, New York/DACS, London, 2010.

**37.2** Whitney Museum of American Art, New York. Purchased with funds from the Friends of the Whitney Museum of American Art. Photograph © 2000 Whitney Museum of American Art. © The

Andy Warhol Foundation for the Visual Arts, Inc./ARS, New York and DACS, London, 2010.

**37.3** Jasper Johns Collection © The Andy Warhol Foundation for the Visual Arts,/ARS, New York and DACS, London 2010.

**37.4** Private collection. © Jasper Johns/VAGA, New York/DACS, New York 2010.

**37.5** © Claes Oldenburg and © Coosje van Bruggen.

**37.6** Courtesy the artist, © The Estate of Roy Lichtenstein/DACS, London, 2010.

**37.7** Photo: Peter Foe/Fotoworks. Photograph courtesy of the Pace Gallery, New York. © ARS, New York and DACS, London 2010.

**37.8** © Rheinisches Bildarchiv Köln.

**37.9** Menil Collection Houston, Texas.

**37.10** The Museum of Modern Art, New York. Philip Johnson Fund. © 2004 Digital Image MoMA, New York/Scala, Florence.

**37.11** The Museum of Modern Art, New York. Helen Achen Bequest and Gift of Joseph A. Helman. © 2004 Digital Image MoMA, New York/DACS, London/Art © Judd Foundation. Licensed by VAGA, New York and DACS, London, 2010.

**37.12** Marine Midland Building, New York. Photo: Gloria Fiero.

**37.13** Copyright 2009. Digital image, The Museum of Modern Art, New York/Scala, Florence.

**37.14** Courtesy of The Pace Gallery, NY.

**37.15** Scottish National Gallery of Modern Art, Edinburgh. © Estate of Duane Hanson/VAGA, New York/DACS, London, 2010.

**37.16** Gift of The Society for Contemporary Art, 1983.264 Reproduction, The Art Institute of Chicago.

**37.17** Courtesy Malborough Gallery, New York. 1997 © Magdalena Abakanowicz. Photography © Artur Starewicz.

**37.18** Photo: © Harry Shunk, New York. © ADAGP, Paris and DACS, London 2010.

**37.19** © Christo 1976. Photo: Jeanne-Claude, New York.

**37.20** Courtesy DACS, © Damien Hirst. All rights reserved, DACS 2010.

**37.21** © Norman McGrath, New York.

**37.22** Photo: © R.M.N., Paris.

**37.23** © Joseph Sohm; Visions of America/CORBIS.

**37.24** © Kurt Krieger/Corbis.

**37.25** Guggenheim Museum, Bilbao. Photograph © FMGB Guggenheim Bilbao. Photographer: Erika Barahona Ede.

## Chapter 38

**38.1** © Chéri Samba. Courtesy C.A.A.C. - The Pigozzi Collection, Geneva. Photo: Christian Poite.

**38.2** The Metropolitan Museum of Art. Purchase, Fred M. and Rita Richman, Noah-Sadie K. Wachtel Foundation Inc., David and Holly Ross, Doreen and Gilbert Bassin Family Foundation and William B. Goldstein Gifts, 2007 (2007.96).

**38.3** Fowler Museum of Natural History,Universoty of California, Los Angeles.

**38.4** © Estate of Robert Smithson/VAGA, New York/DACS, London 2010.

**38.5** © Grant Smith/View Pictures.

**38.6** Courtesy of the Barbara Gladstone Gallery, New York.

**38.7** Collection of the artist.

**38.8** Courtesy the artist. Photo: Kirk Gittings, NM. © ARS, NY and DACS, London 2010.

**38.9** Collection of the artist.

**38.10** Location: Massachusetts Museum of Contemporary Art Photo: Courtesy Cai Guo Qiang Studio. Photo Hiro Ihara.

**38.11** © Marcel Lam/Arcaid/Corbis.

**38.12** Guggenheim Soho. Courtesy the artist and Holly Solomon Gallery, New York.

**38.13** The Museum of Modern Art, New York. Gift to the Bohen Foundation in honour of Richard F. Oldenburg. Photo: Kira Perov.

**38.14** © Andreas Gursky / Artist Rights Society (ARS), New York, Courtesy Matthew Marks Gallery, New York.

**38.15** Courtesy Karl Sims.

**38.16** NW House, Tokyo. Courtesy Luhring Augustine, New York.

**38.17** Musée d'Orsay, Paris. Photo R.M.N.— Hervé Lewandowski.

**38.18** © Noriko Yamaguchi, courtesy MEM, Inc

# Literary Credits

The author and publishers wish to thank the following for permission to use copyright material. Every effort has been made to trace or contact copyright holders, but if notified of any omissions or errors, Laurence King Publishing would be pleased to insert the appropriate acknowledgement in any subsequent edition of this publication.

## Chapter 32

### READING

**32.1** (p. 3): Ezra Pound, "In a Station of the Metro" and "The Bath Tub" from *Personae*, copyright © 1926 by Ezra Pound. Reprinted by permission of New Directions Publishing Corp.

**32.2** (p. 4): T.S. Eliot, "The Love Song of J. Alfred Prufrock" from *Collected Poems* 1909-1962 (Faber & Faber, 1963), © this edition by T. S. Eliot 1963.

**32.3** (p. 6): Robert Frost, "The Road Not Taken" from *The Poetry of Robert Frost*, edited by Edward Connery Lathem (Jonathan Cape, 1969), copyright 1944 by Robert Frost, © 1916, 1969 by Henry Holt & Company, LLC.

**(p.23)** Le Corbusier, *Towards a New Architecture*, translated by Frederick Etchells. New York: Praeger, 1970, 12–13.

## Chapter 33

**33.1** (p. 30): Sigmund Freud, from *Civilization and Its Discontents*, translated by James Strachey (W.W. Norton, 1989), © 1961 by James Strachey, renewed 1989 by Alix Strachey.

**33.2** (p. 33): Marcel Proust, "Swann's Way" from *Remembrance of Things Past*, translated by C.K. Scott Moncrieff (Chatto & Windus, 1981), translation © 1981 by Random House Inc. and Chatto & Windus. Reprinted by permission of The Random House Group Ltd.

**(p. 36):** James Joyce, from *Ulysses* (Vintage Books, 1966).

**33.4** (p. 37): E. E. Cummings, "she being Brand" from *Complete Poems*, 1904-1962, edited by George J. Firmage (Liveright Publishing, 1994), copyright 1926, 1954, © 1991 by the Trustees for the E. E. Cummings Trust, 1985 by George James Firmage. Reprinted by permission of W.W.Norton & Company.

## Chapter 34

**34.2** (p. 55): T. S. Eliot, from "The Waste Land" from *Collected Poems* 1909-1962 (Faber & Faber, 1974), © this edition by T.S. Eliot 1963.

**34.3** (p. 56): W. B. Yeats, "The Second Coming" from *Collected Poems* (Picador, 1990).

**34.4** (p. 56): Erich Maria Remarque, from *All Quiet on the Western Front* (Little, Brown & Company, 1929), © 1929, 1930 by Little, Brown and Company: © renewed 1957, 1958 by Erich Maria Remarque.

**(p. 64):** Adolf Hitler, from *Mein Kampf*, translated by Ralph Manheim (Houghton Mifflin, 1943).

**34.5** (p. 66): Randall Jarrell, "The Death of the Ball Turret Gunner" from *The Complete Poems* (Faber & Faber, 1971).

**34.6** (p. 66): Kato Shuson, three haiku from *Modern Japanese Literature: An Anthology*, edited by Donald Keene (Grove Atlantic, 1956), © 1956 by Grove Press Inc.

**34.7** (p. 67): Elie Wiesel, from *Night*, translated by Stella Rodway (MacGibbon & Kee, 1960), © 1960 by MacGibbon & Kee; © renewed 1988 by The Collins Publishing Group.

## Chapter 35

**35.1** (p. 78): Jean Paul Sartre, from *Existentialism is a Humanism*, translated by Bernard Frechtman (Philosophical Library, 1947), © Edition Gallimard, 1996. Reprinted by permission of Georges Borchardt, Inc. for Editions Gallimard.

**35.2** (p. 82): Samuel Beckett, from *Waiting for Godot* (Grove Press, 1954), © 1954 by Grove Press; © renewed 1982 by Samuel Beckett.

**35.3** (p. 83): Dylan Thomas, "Do Not Go Gentle Into That Good Night" from *Collected Poems*, 1934-1952 (Dent, 1989), copyright © 1952 by Dylan Thomas. Reprinted by permission of New Directions Publishing Corp.

**(p. 90):** Candida Smith et al, from T*he Fields of David Smith* (Thames & Hudson, 1999).

## Chapter 36

**36.1** (p. 99): Mohammad Iqbal, "Revolution" and "Europe and Syria" from *Poems from Iqbal*, translated by V. Kiernan (John Murray, 1955).

**36.2** (p. 99): Pablo Neruda, "United Fruit Co" from *Five Decades: Poems 1925-1970*, translated by Ben Belitt (Grove Press, 1974), © 1974 by Ben Belitt.

**36.3** (p. 101): Langston Hughes, "Theme for English B" and "Harlem" from *Collected Poems of Langston Hughes* (Alfred A Knopf, 1994), © 1994 by the Estate of Langston Hughes.

**36.4** (p. 101): Gwendolyn Brooks, "The Mother" and "We Real Cool" from *Blacks* (Third World Press, 1991).

**36.5** (p. 102): Richard Wright, from *Uncle Tom's Children* (Harper and Row, 1937), © 1937 by Richard Wright, © renewed 1965 by Ellen Wright.

**36.6** (p. 104): Martin Luther King, "Letter from Birmingham Jail" from *Why We Can't Wait* (1963), © 1963 Martin Luther King Jr., renewed 1991 by Coretta Scott King.

**36.7** (p. 106): Malcolm X, from *Malcolm X Speaks* (Pathfinder Press, 1965), © 1965, 1989 by Betty Shabazz and Pathfinder Press.

**(p. 107):** Bloke Modisane, "it gets awful lonely" from *Poems from Black Africa*, edited by Langston Hughes (Indiana University Press, 1963).

**36.8** (p. 108): Ralph Ellison, from *Invisible Man* (Random House, 1952), © 1952 by Ralph Ellison.

**36.9** (p. 108): Alice Walker, "Elethia" from *You Can't Keep a Good Woman Down: Short Stories* (Harcourt Brace Jovanovich, 1981), copyright © 1979 by Alice Walker.

**(p. 110):** Lowery S. Sims and M.D. Kahan, from *Robert Colescott, A Retrospective*, 1975-1986 (San Jose Museum of Art, 1987).

**36.10** (p. 116): Virginia Woolf, from *A Room of One's Own* (Harcourt Brace Jovanovich, 1929), © 1929 by Harcourt Brace Jovanovich Inc., renewed 1957 by Leonard Woolf.

**36.11** (p. 117): Simone de Beauvoir, from *The Second Sex*, translated by H. M. Parshley (Random House, 1989), © 1952 and renewed 1980 by Alfred A. Knopf Inc.

**36.12** (p. 119): Anne Sexton, "Self in 1958" from *Live or Die* (Houghton Mifflin, 1966), copyright © 1966 by Anne Sexton, renewed 1994 by Linda G Sexton. Reprinted by permission of Houghton Mifflin Harcourt Publishing Company. All rights reserved; Sonia Sanchez, "Woman" from *I've Been a Woman: New and Selected Poems* (Black Scholar Press, 1978); Adrienne Rich, "Translations" from *Diving Into The Wreck: Poems 1971-1972* (W.W. Norton & Company, 1973), copyright © 1973 by W. W. Norton & Company, Inc.; (p. 924): Rita Dove, "Rosa" from *On The Bus With Rosa Parks* (W.W. Norton & Company, 1999), copyright © 1999 by Rita Dove.

## Chapter 37

**(p. 128):** Jacques Ellul, from *The Technological Society* (Alfred A. Knopf, 1964).

**(p. 128):** Brian Greene, from *The Elegant Universe: Superstrings, Hidden Dimension and the Quest for the Ultimate Theory* (W.W.Norton, 1999).

**(p. 129):** Candace Pert, from *Molecules of Emotion* (Scribner's, 1997).

**37.1** (p. 131): Octavio Paz, "To Talk" from *Collected Poems 1957-1987*, translated by Eliot Weinberger (1986), copyright © 1986 by Octavio Paz and Eliot Weinberger. Reprinted by permission of New Directions Publishing Corp.

**37.2** (p. 131): John Ashbery, "Paradoxes and Oxymorons" from *Collected Poems, 1956-1987* (The Library of America, 2008).

**37.3** (p. 132): Jorge Luis Borges, "Borges and I" from *Collected Fictions*, translated by Andrew Hurley (Penguin Books, 1999).

**37.4** (p. 133): Joyce Carol Oates, "Ace" from *The Assignation: Stories* (Ecco Press, 1988), © 1988 by Ontario Review Inc.

## Chapter 38

**38.1** (p. 154): Chinua Achebe, "Dead Men's Path" from *Girls at War and Other Stories* (Doubleday, 1973), © 1972, 1973 by Chinua Achebe.

**38.2** (p. 157): Edward O. Wilson, from *The Diversity of Life* (Harvard University Press, 1992), © 1992 by Edward O. Wilson.

**38.3** (p. 158): Annie Dillard, "Pilgrim at Tinker Creek" from *The Annie Dillard Reader* (HarperCollins, 1994), © 1994 by Annie Dillard.

**38.4** (p. 160): Sandra Cisneros, "No Speak English" from *The House on Mango Street* (Vintage Books, 2004), © 2004 by Sandra Cisneros.

**38.5** (p. 162): Mahmoud Darwish, "Earth Presses Against Us" from *Unfortunately, It was Paradise: Selected Poems*, trans/ed Munir Akash and Carolyne Forche, with Sinan Antoon and Amira El Zein (University of California Press, 2003), © 2003 Regents of the University of California Press. Reprinted by permission of the publisher; Yehuda Amichai, "The Resurrection of the Dead", translated by Leon Wieseltier (2004).

**38.6** (p. 163): Wislawa Szymborska, "The Terrorist, He Watches" from People on a Bridge, translated by Adam Czerniawski (Forest Books, 1990).

**38.7** (p. 164): Seamus Heaney, "Anything Can Happen" from *Anything Can Happen: A Poem and Essay* (TownHouse Dublin, 2004).

# Index